A SURVEY OF
METAPHYSICS

E. J. Lowe

OXFORD
UNIVERSITY PRESS

OXFORD

UNIVERSITY PRESS

Great Clarendon Street, Oxford OX2 6DP

Oxford University Press is a department of the University of Oxford.
It furthers the University's objective of excellence in research, scholarship,
and education by publishing worldwide in

Oxford New York

Auckland Bangkok Buenos Aires Cape Town Chennai
Dar es Salaam Delhi Hong Kong Istanbul Karachi Kolkata
Kuala Lumpur Madrid Melbourne Mexico City Mumbai Nairobi
São Paulo Shanghai Singapore Taipei Tokyo Toronto
with associated companies in Berlin

Oxford is a registered trade mark of Oxford University Press
in the UK and in certain other countries

Published in the United States
by Oxford University Press Inc., New York

British Library Cataloguing in Publication Data
Data available

Library of Congress Cataloging in Publication Data
Data available
ISBN 0–19–875253–9

1 3 5 7 9 10 8 6 4 2

Typeset in Adobe Minion
by RefineCatch Limited, Bungay, Suffolk
Printed in Great Britain by
T.J. International Ltd,
Padstow, Cornwall

PREFACE

As its title indicates, the scope of this book is broad, my intention being that it should be capable of serving as a core text for students of modern metaphysics, covering all of the most important topics that they are likely to encounter in a typical metaphysics course. It is aimed primarily at intermediate and advanced undergraduate students of philosophy, that is, at students who have already been introduced to some basic metaphysical concepts and doctrines and who have acquired some familiarity with the techniques of philosophical analysis and argumentation. At the same time, I hope that the book will be reasonably accessible to a wider range of readers with philosophical interests, including those with backgrounds in other disciplines, who want a general overview of modern metaphysics. Although the book aims to provide a systematic treatment of all the main areas of modern metaphysics, most of the chapters are relatively self-contained, so that it should be possible for teachers of the subject to select those chapters which best meet the requirements of their courses.

It must be acknowledged that no two teachers of metaphysics are likely to agree as to what exactly should be included in a course on the subject and that such disagreements can sometimes reflect different conceptions of what metaphysics is or ought to be. The conception of metaphysics that informs *A Survey of Metaphysics* is, however, a fairly traditional and still very widely shared one—namely, that metaphysics deals with the most profound questions that can be raised concerning the fundamental structure of reality. According to this conception, metaphysics goes deeper than any merely empirical science, even physics, because it provides the very framework within which such sciences are conceived and related to one another. A core text in metaphysics written from this point of view must aim, first and foremost, to elucidate certain universally applicable concepts—for example, those of *identity, necessity, causation, space*, and *time*—and then go on to examine some important doctrines which involve these concepts, such as the thesis that truths of identity are necessary and the claim that temporally backward causation is impossible. In addition, it must endeavour to provide a systematic account of the ways in which entities belonging to different ontological categories—for example, *things, events*, and *properties*—are interrelated. These, accordingly, are the main objectives of *A Survey of Metaphysics*. A subsidiary objective is to explain and defend the conception of metaphysics which informs the book: for students need to be aware of the many and varied opponents of metaphysics and how they may be countered.

I should emphasize that my aim in this book is to provide a survey of major themes and problems in modern metaphysics, *not* a comprehensive survey and critique of the views of major contemporary metaphysicians, much less a systematic history of the subject. Consequently, I tend not to engage in direct debate with the published work of other philosophers, past or present—although I do refer to it very frequently and have included an extensive bibliography of mostly recent publications. Such direct engagement would have made the book considerably longer and more complex than it already is and, I think, less useful to its intended audience, who need to understand the issues before engaging in current debate or historical investigation for themselves. It should also be stressed, however, that the book is by no means narrowly partisan, in the sense of promoting my own opinions on particular issues whilst excluding mention of others. At the same time, I try to avoid bland neutrality in matters of controversy.

I should like to express my gratitude to Peter Momtchiloff of Oxford University Press for encouraging me to write this book, to the Press's anonymous readers for some very helpful advice on how to improve it, and, especially, to John Heil and Trenton Merricks for their detailed comments on the penultimate version of the manuscript.

Chapter 4 draws on material contained in my paper 'Substantial Change and Spatiotemporal Coincidence', *Ratio* 16 (forthcoming 2003) and Chapter 11 draws on material contained in my paper 'Event Causation and Agent Causation', *Grazer Philosophische Studien* 61 (2001), pp. 1–20. I am grateful to the editors and publishers concerned for permission to use this material.

CONTENTS

PART III: CAUSATION AND CONDITIONALS

PART IV: AGENTS, ACTIONS, AND EVENTS

PART VI: UNIVERSALS AND PARTICULARS

1

INTRODUCTION: THE NATURE OF METAPHYSICS

What is metaphysics?

People who are not familiar with metaphysics are apt to have a false, or at least a somewhat distorted, conception of what it involves. Sometimes they think it has something to do with mysticism and magic, which is completely mistaken. Sometimes they think that it has something to do with *physics*, which is true enough in a way. But it would be wrong to think that metaphysics is to physics as metalogic is to logic, or as metaethics is to ethics—that is, a kind of second-order inquiry into the conceptual foundations and methods of a first-order discipline. Metaphysics does include some features of such an inquiry, but even in that respect its focus is not exclusively upon the concerns of physics. Indeed, it is largely just an historical accident that metaphysics is called what it is. Aristotle wrote a treatise (or, more exactly, some of his lecture notes were collected to form a treatise) which much later came to be called the *Metaphysics*, simply because it was placed in the canonical order of Aristotle's works *after* another treatise of his, the *Physics* (the Greek prefix *meta* signifying this relation).[1] Even so, this was a happy accident, inasmuch as physics and metaphysics do overlap in many of their fundamental concerns. In fact, perhaps it wasn't so much of an accident after all, since it was natural, in the light of that overlap, to place the *Metaphysics* after the *Physics*. (Though we should acknowledge here that there are some significant differences between Aristotle's conception of the subject-matter of physics and that of modern physicists. I shall return, briefly, to Aristotle's view of metaphysics later in the chapter.)

---

[1] See J. L. Ackrill, *Aristotle the Philosopher* (Oxford: Oxford University Press, 1981), ch. 9. For an English translation of Aristotle's *Metaphysics*, see W. D. Ross (ed.), *The Works of Aristotle Translated into English. Volume VIII: Metaphysica*, 2nd edn. (Oxford: Clarendon Press, 1928).

What is it, then, that metaphysics and physics have in common? Well, physics—and here I speak of modern physics—is an empirical science concerned to explain certain basic and ubiquitous phenomena in the natural world, that is, in the realm of things existing in space and time. Physics appeals to putative causal laws to explain such phenomena—for example, the laws of electromagnetism and of gravitation, which causally explain the motions of electrically charged and massive objects respectively. Metaphysics is also concerned, though not exclusively, with the nature of things existing in space and time, with the nature of space and time themselves, and with the nature of causation. But metaphysics is not at heart an empirical science—it does not typically appeal to experimental or observational data in support of its claims. Nor are metaphysicians *solely* concerned with the nature of the physical world—unless they happen to espouse the doctrine of physicalism, which maintains that the only things that exist are physical entities in space and time. They are also concerned with the nature of abstract entities, such as the objects of mathematics and logic—numbers, sets, propositions, and so forth. Such entities plausibly do not exist in space and time, but need not be deemed any less part of reality on that account. Moreover, there are, very arguably, entities which do exist in space and time but which are, even so, not the proper subject-matter of the empirical science of physics—entities such as persons and their mental states of thought and feeling, and entities such as social and political groups. According to many philosophers and scientists, the behaviour of these entities can never be explained solely by appeal to the laws of physics, not least because their behaviour is, in large measure, subject to *rational* rather than merely to *causal* explanation. Of course, physicalist philosophers may want to challenge this view: but then they are engaging precisely in a *metaphysical* debate, not one which belongs to the province of physics itself.

What begins to emerge from these observations is that one of the roles of metaphysics, as an intellectual discipline, is to provide a forum in which boundary disputes between other disciplines can be conducted—for instance, the dispute as to whether the subject-matter of a special science, such as biology or psychology or economics, can properly be said to be subsumed under that of another, allegedly more 'fundamental' science, such as physics. According to one traditional and still widespread conception of metaphysics—which is basically the conception of metaphysics which informs the present book—metaphysics can occupy the interdisciplinary role just described because its central concern is with *the fundamental structure of reality as a whole.* No special science—not even physics—can have that concern, because the subject-matter of every special science is identified more narrowly than this: for instance, biology is the science of living things, psychology is the science of mental states, and physics—as I have already indicated—is the science of those states and processes (energetic states and dynamic processes, for example) which are apparently common to all things existing in space and time. Even if it can be successfully argued, as the physicalist maintains it can, that the whole of reality is confined to things existing in space and time, it wouldn't follow that metaphysics reduces to physics—because the very argument that reality *is* thus confined, which is a metaphysical argument, is not an argument that physics can provide.

Metaphysics, as traditionally conceived, is very arguably ineliminable and conceptually necessary as the intellectual backdrop for every other discipline. Why? Ultimately, because truth is single and indivisible or, to put it another way, the world or reality as a whole is unitary and necessarily self-consistent. The various special sciences, and other intellectual disciplines whose practitioners would probably not care to call themselves 'scientists'—such as historians and literary theorists—are all concerned, at least in part, with the pursuit of truth, but pursue it according to their own methods of inquiry and within their own prescribed domain. None the less, the indivisibility of truth means that all of these forms of inquiry must, if they are to succeed in their aim, acknowledge the need to be consistent with each other. Nor can any one of them presume to adjudicate such questions of mutual consistency, because none of them has a jurisdiction beyond its own limited domain. Such adjudication can only be provided by the practitioners of an intellectual discipline which aspires to complete universality in its subject-matter and aims—and that discipline is metaphysics, as traditionally conceived.

The foregoing argument may be looked upon suspiciously as special pleading on the part of self-styled metaphysicians seeking to guarantee themselves an intellectual role. And, to be fair, it would be wrong to advance that argument in a purely dogmatic spirit, as though its conclusion was beyond debating. But, in a way, this point merely serves to strengthen the claims of metaphysics to be an autonomous and indispensable form of rational inquiry: because the point is that absolutely *everything*, including even the status and credentials of metaphysics itself, comes within the purview of the universal discipline which metaphysics claims to be. None of this means that metaphysicians have to be seen as a caste apart, loftily making their pronouncements from intellectual heights above the common crowd. Precisely because metaphysics is a universal intellectual discipline, it is one which no rational being can avoid engaging in at least some of the time. We are all metaphysicians whether we like it or not, and whether we know it or not. But this isn't to say that anyone's opinion on a question of metaphysics is just as good, or as bad, as anyone else's. There is no reason to deny that there can be such a thing as expertise in metaphysical thinking, which takes some pains to acquire. If I had had any doubts about this, I would not have bothered to write this book!

The threat of relativism

Of course, the argument that we have just been examining in defence of metaphysics as traditionally conceived—the argument from the indivisibility of truth, or from the unity of the world—may seem vulnerable to attack from those who question this conception of truth and its associated 'universalist' conceptions of reason and rationality. I am thinking of those philosophers, and practitioners of some other intellectual disciplines, who espouse some form of cultural or historical relativism. Such people may deny that truth is single and indivisible, maintaining that what is true for one culture or historical epoch may not be true for another, and that different cultures and epochs have different and incommensurable conceptions of reason and rationality. But, of course, such a doctrine is itself a metaphysical thesis, in the sense of 'metaphysics' that I have been expounding and trying to defend: for it is nothing less than a claim about the fundamental nature of reality, which could not be substantiated solely by the methods of any special science or intellectual discipline, such as anthropology or history or sociology. To the extent that the practitioners of any such discipline are tempted to espouse such a doctrine, they must acknowledge that what they are advocating is precisely a metaphysical thesis, because it is one which transcends the boundaries of any more limited form of rational inquiry. So, once again, we see that the attempt to undermine or eliminate the metaphysical dimension of our thinking is self-defeating, because the very attempt necessarily constitutes a piece of metaphysical thinking itself.

This shows that the argument from the indivisibility of truth is not absolutely essential to the defence of metaphysics, in the sense that metaphysics would be left completely without justification in its absence: which, once again, should not surprise us, because *everything*, including even the question of whether truth is indivisible, is potentially open to metaphysical inquiry. On the other hand, this isn't to say that the argument from the indivisibility of truth is idle or superfluous: for I think that the doctrine of the indivisibility of truth can survive critical inquiry, whereas the denial of that doctrine cannot. That being so, metaphysics may be said to contain within itself, in the form of this argument, the grounds of its own justification. That is to say, metaphysical reasoning may be used to defend the doctrine of the indivisibility of truth, and that doctrine can in turn be used to argue for the indispensability of metaphysics. There need be nothing viciously circular or question-begging about such a procedure.

The objection from naturalized epistemology

There are, however, other people besides cultural and historical relativists who seek to undermine the credentials of metaphysics, traditionally conceived as a universal discipline, of a non-empirical character, concerned with the fundamental structure of reality. For instance, there are those philosophers who adhere to what is often known as the programme of 'naturalized epistemology'.[2] The thought here is that any kind of knowledge attainable by human beings, including anything that might deserve to be called 'metaphysical' knowledge, must be compatible with our status as a kind of natural creature—in fact, a species of animal—that has arisen through wholly natural processes of biological evolution. Moreover, any inquiry into the nature of such knowledge must, it may be alleged, be part of a more general scientific inquiry into the cognitive capacities of creatures of our kind. Thus, epistemology—the theory of knowledge—is properly to be conceived of as being a part of the natural science of human psychology, which must in turn have a biological and ultimately a purely physical foundation. But what scope does such a conception of human knowledge and its sources have for acknowledging the existence of metaphysical knowledge, as traditionally conceived? Very little if any, it may be thought. For how could a naturally evolved life-form, with cognitive capacities 'designed' by nature solely to equip it to survive in a hostile

---

[2] Much of the inspiration for this programme stems from the work of W. V. Quine: see especially 'Epistemology Naturalized', in his *Ontological Relativity and Other Essays* (New York: Columbia University Press, 1969). For discussion, see Hilary Kornblith (ed.), *Naturalizing Epistemology* (Cambridge, Mass.: MIT Press, 1985).

environment, attain non-empirical knowledge of the fundamental structure of reality? On this view, the only kind of 'metaphysics' deserving of recognition would be, if there can be such a thing, *naturalized* metaphysics—that is, a metaphysics knowledge of whose truths could plausibly be seen as knowable by and practically advantageous to animals with our particular biological capacities and needs. Any such 'metaphysics', it may be alleged, must be at least continuous with natural science itself, or more likely just a part of it. So, on this view, there is no question that metaphysics is equipped to answer which isn't properly in the domain of some natural science—either the fundamental science, physics, or one of the special sciences, if these are not ultimately reducible to physics.

The trouble with this line of thinking is, once more, that it is liable to undermine itself and in the course of doing so demonstrate yet again the indispensability or ineliminability of metaphysics as traditionally conceived. In the first place, to the extent that a wholly naturalistic and evolutionary conception of human beings seems to threaten the very possibility of metaphysical knowledge, it equally threatens the very possibility of *scientific* knowledge—for it is equally mysterious how a naturally evolved creature should have any capacity to acquire knowledge of such arcane matters as the formation of stars or the structure of DNA. No other animal species with which we are acquainted is or ever has been capable of such scientific knowledge. It is debatable whether the possession of such knowledge is advantageous to our species: indeed, it may well turn out to be the cause of our untimely extinction. More to the point, though, no one has the slightest idea as to how or why early humans acquired this capacity within the constraints imposed by the theory of evolution by natural selection. Natural science itself cannot presently explain, then, how natural scientific knowledge is possible in creatures like ourselves. So the fact that it cannot explain how metaphysical knowledge, as traditionally conceived, is possible in creatures like ourselves gives us no very good reason to suppose that such knowledge is *not* possible. For if it did, we would equally have good reason to suppose that natural scientific knowledge is not possible in creatures like ourselves—and this would mean that we would no longer have any grounds to believe in the scientific theories to which naturalized epistemology appeals, such as the theory of evolution itself.

Furthermore, it has to be recognized that the very debate that I am now conducting with the advocate of naturalized epistemology is one which itself necessarily rests upon certain metaphysical assumptions—some of which are shared and some of which are disputed. In short, the very doctrine of naturalized epistemology, and the kinds of arguments that are invoked in its support, have a metaphysical dimension to them which is at odds with the central claims of that doctrine—so that the naturalized epistemologist is apparently guilty of a curious failure of self-awareness, casting all humankind in a severely naturalistic mould but not recognizing that this very act betrays a style of thinking on his own part which cannot easily be accommodated by such naturalism.

Kant and the possibility of metaphysics

But we should not allow these defensive moves on the part of metaphysics to lull us into thinking that there is, after all, no need to explain the possibility of metaphysical knowledge. It may well be that this possibility cannot be explained entirely naturalistically, and we may be entitled to conclude from this *not* that there is no such possibility but rather that naturalism is inadequate. However, this still leaves us looking for a positive explanation of the possibility. Here we may be reminded that it was Immanuel Kant who first posed the momentous question 'How is metaphysics possible?'[3] Kant's answer, however, was inimical to metaphysics as traditionally conceived, that is, conceived as a form of rational inquiry into the fundamental structure of reality. For Kant held that metaphysical claims in fact concern not the fundamental structure of a mind-independent reality, even if such a reality exists, but rather the fundamental structure of rational *thought* about reality. Kant believed that only by construing metaphysical claims as having this concern could our non-empirical knowledge of their truth be explained and certified—the assumption here being that the structure of our own thought is something unproblematically accessible to us in a way in which the structure of mind-independent reality is not. That assumption may itself be questioned. More fundamentally, however, it may be objected to the Kantian conception of metaphysics that if nothing about the structure of mind-independent reality is accessible to us then, by the same token, nothing about the structure of our own thought is accessible to us either—for, in the relevant sense of 'mind-independent', our thought itself is nothing if

[3] See Immanuel Kant, *Critique of Pure Reason*, B22 in Kemp Smith (London: Macmillan, 1929), pp. 56–7.

not part of mind-independent reality. By 'mind-independent reality', I mean the sum total of things whose existence is not dependent upon our thinking of them. But our own thoughts have an existence which is not dependent upon our thinking of them and so constitute part of mind-independent reality in this sense. It is true that our thoughts would not exist if we were not *thinking* them, but that is not to say that we must think *of* them for them to exist. Some metaphysicians have held that the only things that exist are thoughts and their thinkers, that is, the things having those thoughts. This is not, however, a position according to which there is no mind-independent reality, in the relevant sense of that expression.

It may be objected to the foregoing argument that it misconstrues the nature of the Kantian view of metaphysical claims. In maintaining that metaphysical claims concern the structure of our thought about reality as opposed to the structure of mind-independent reality itself, it is saying that such claims concern structural features of the *contents* of our thoughts, not any features of the thoughts themselves conceived as real psychological processes going on in our minds or heads. But how can it coherently be said that structural features of the contents of our thoughts are *not* features of our thoughts themselves? The content of a thought—what it is a thought *about*—is an *essential* feature of that thought, partly serving to determine the very identity of that thought. A thought of mine that two plus two equals four, or that lemons are bitter, would not be that very thought but for its having that very content. Consequently, it seems there is no possibility of our circumscribing the supposed subject-matter of metaphysics in such a way that it can be held to concern the *contents* of thoughts without having any concern for the nature of thoughts themselves. And, I repeat, thoughts themselves are nothing if not part of mind-independent reality.

Perhaps the Kantian will try to counter this latest line of objection in some way. But, ironically enough, any such attempt would undermine the very position that he is trying to defend: for in order to make any such attempt, the Kantian will have to engage in genuine metaphysical argument as traditionally conceived. He will have to deny, for instance, that the content of a thought is an essential feature of that thought: and this is to deny a certain thesis concerning the nature of a certain category of entities—thoughts—conceived as being elements of a mind-independent reality. Once again we see how metaphysics, as traditionally conceived, is inescapable for any rational thinker. The Kantian attempt to avoid metaphysics in this sense by restricting our critical concerns purely to the contents of our thoughts appears doomed to failure. Questions to do with content themselves have, inescapably, a genuinely metaphysical dimension, that is, a dimension which does not have solely to do with the content of thoughts about content.

The reason why Kant sought to redefine the nature of metaphysical claims as being claims about the structure of our thought about reality rather than the structure of reality itself is that he believed that only in this way could the absolutely certain and non-empirical character of metaphysical knowledge be explained. If metaphysical claims concerned mind-independent reality, he reasoned, we could not possibly have certain knowledge of their truth—and yet, he considered, we do know some metaphysical truths with absolute certainty. Notice here, first of all, that the very assertion that it would not be *possible* to have certain knowledge of metaphysical truths if metaphysical truths concerned mind-independent reality is itself a *metaphysical* claim, in the traditional sense of 'metaphysics', rather than in Kant's own redefined sense of the term. This in itself shows, once more, the self-defeating nature of Kant's attempted redefinition. Secondly, however, even granting the truth of this metaphysical assertion, why shouldn't we respond to it by saying *not* that metaphysical knowledge as traditionally conceived is impossible (itself a self-defeating claim, inasmuch as it is precisely a metaphysical claim as traditionally conceived), but rather that metaphysical knowledge is almost never *certain* knowledge—that is, that metaphysical knowledge-claims can almost never be absolutely invulnerable to falsification or disproof? Why should we imagine that metaphysics affords us a method of rational inquiry which *guarantees* the truth of its conclusions, beyond any possibility of their subsequent reversal in the light of further inquiry? Not even in mathematics do we think that we have such incontrovertible methods of discovery. It is true, of course, that a mathematical 'proof' relinquishes the title of 'proof' once it has been 'proved' to be invalid, so that any genuine 'proof' cannot but be successful. But that is like saying that all knowledge is, by definition, knowledge of what is *true*, and consequently that what we 'know' cannot but be true.

Metaphysics and empirical knowledge

Of course, it may be considered that the greater problem about metaphysical knowledge-claims, as traditionally conceived, is not so much how they could attain to certainty as how they could be *non-empirical*. Now in this respect, too, metaphysical knowledge-claims are akin to mathematical knowledge-claims, which are likewise held to be non-empirical, in the sense that they are not answerable to empirical evidence for their support or confirmation. And then the worry might be this. If metaphysical knowledge-claims concern the fundamental structure of mind-independent reality then, if that structure is, at least in some respects, *contingent* rather than *necessary*, it is hard to see how we can have knowledge of it which does not rely upon empirical evidence, for it seems that only such evidence could reveal to us that the world we inhabit has one contingent structure rather than another which it is equally possible for the world to have had. In this respect, metaphysics differs from mathematics, it may be said, where there is no element of contingency since the objects and structures investigated by mathematics are purely abstract. (Of course, it may be urged that the supposedly abstract nature of mathematical objects—numbers, sets, functions and the like—also makes our putative knowledge of them problematic, but for a quite different reason, namely, because it is hard to understand how our minds, which belong to the concrete world of things in space and time, can grasp relationships between purely abstract objects.)

This kind of consideration, then, may seem to drive us in the direction of regarding metaphysical knowledge, to the extent that it is possible at all, as being a species of *empirical* knowledge. But then it is not clear, after all, that metaphysics can legitimately claim to be distinct from, and in any sense prior to, natural science: we seem to be compelled, after all, to accept the view of naturalized epistemology that the only kind of metaphysics available to us is one that is continuous with, or indeed just a part of, empirical scientific inquiry into the nature of the world.

The proper response to this apparent difficulty is, I think, the following. We should concede that, where a metaphysician asserts the existence of some fundamental structural feature of reality which he deems to be *contingent* in character, then, indeed, he should acknowledge that this claim is answerable to empirical evidence, at least in part. But it is important to see that such a claim is not answerable *solely* to empirical evidence. For where a metaphysician makes such a claim, it is incumbent upon him to establish—though not necessarily with absolute certainty, for reasons given earlier—that the existence of that feature is at least *possible*. The key point here is that empirical evidence cannot be evidence for the existence of anything which is not a *possible* feature of reality. But establishing that the existence of a certain feature of reality is *possible* is not something that can, in general, be achieved by merely empirical means of inquiry, precisely because empirical evidence can only be evidence for states of affairs that can independently be shown to be possible. Thus metaphysics, like mathematics, does have a non-empirical subject-matter, to the extent that it is the intellectual discipline whose concern it is to chart the *possibilities* of real existence. Metaphysics is concerned to discover what the totality of existence *could* embrace: that is to say, what categories of entities could exist and which of them could co-exist. Having charted the possibilities, the question will remain as to which of many mutually incompatible possibilities for the fundamental structure of reality *actually* obtains—and this question can only be answered, if at all, with the aid of empirical evidence, and then only tentatively and provisionally.

Possibility, concepts, and semantics

We see, then, how, on this conception of the task of metaphysics, metaphysics can genuinely be concerned with the fundamental structure of reality itself, rather than just with the structure of our *thought* about reality, and at the same time can have a non-empirical character which distinguishes it from natural science. But a problem may still remain. For how, it may be asked, is non-empirical knowledge of what is possible itself possible? How is it possible for creatures like ourselves to chart the realm of possibilities? Of course, this is a curious question, to the extent that it is, itself, a question—addressed to ourselves—about the very realm of possibilities whose accessibility is being called into question. Suppose we were to come up with an argument whose conclusion was that it is *not* possible for us to chart the realm of possibilities. That conclusion would seem to undermine itself, because the conclusion itself concerns the realm of possibilities, maintaining that that realm does not include the possibility of our charting it. We could only have reason to believe the conclusion if the conclusion were false: so we can have no reason to believe it. Is this just a debater's trick? I don't think so: rather, it is yet another example of the unavoidability of metaphysics. As rational beings, we cannot but consider ourselves capable of knowing at least something about the realm of possibilities. This should not be surprising. Reasoning itself depends upon a grasp of possibilities, because a valid argument is one in which it is not *possible* for the conclusion to be false if the premises are true—and a rational being is a creature which can discern the validity of at least some arguments.

Some philosophers maintain that questions of what is possible are, ultimately, just questions about what concepts we deploy or the meanings of our words. For example, it may be said that the only reason why it is not possible for a bachelor to be married is that 'bachelor' *means* 'unmarried man'. If all possibility is grounded in the meaning of words, which is purely conventional in nature, perhaps there is, after all, no 'realm of possibilities' for metaphysics to chart in any ontologically serious sense. Indeed, the task we have been assigning to the metaphysician might, on this view, more appropriately be assigned to the lexicographer. But, in fact, it doesn't make sense to suppose that all possibility is grounded in the meaning of words, not least because there are possibilities and impossibilities concerning the meanings of words themselves which cannot without absurdity be taken to be grounded in the meanings of words. In any case, returning to our bachelor example, it is clear that there is in fact a perfectly good sense in which it *is* possible for a bachelor to be married: what is not possible is for a bachelor to be married and still correctly be described as a 'bachelor', given the meaning of this English word. This is an impossibility concerning the meaning of a word. But the sense in which it *is* possible for a bachelor to be married has nothing whatever to do with the meanings of words. Similarly, the sense in which it is possible for a human being to run a mile in four minutes, or the sense in which it is possible for a pint of water to be contained in a two-pint jug, has nothing whatever to do with the meanings of words. These are *real* possibilities, which are grounded in the natures of things, not in the meanings of the words we use to describe things.

There may be an innocuous sense in which at least some possibilities have a 'conceptual' basis. Reflection on the concepts of a pint of water and of a two-pint jug suffices to persuade us that it is possible for the latter to contain the former, just as reflection on the concept of an isosceles triangle suffices to persuade us that it is possible to divide it into two equal right-angled triangles. But this isn't to deny that the possibilities in question are grounded in the natures of the things concerned, nor is it to imply that these possibilities are grounded merely in the meanings of the words we use to describe those things. For an adequate concept of a thing of a certain kind should embody a correct grasp of that thing's nature. Someone cannot, for instance, be in possession of an adequate concept of an isosceles triangle if he conceives of this as a three-sided geometrical figure none of whose sides are the same in length—because an isosceles triangle is not a figure of that nature. No harm is necessarily done, then, in saying that a knowledge of real possibilities may be arrived at by reflection on concepts: properly understood, this needn't be seen as implying that possibilities don't exist independently of our ways of thinking about or 'conceptualizing' the world.

I make these points about meanings and concepts because there are some philosophers who would seek a basis in language, or more precisely in the theory of meaning, for any legitimate claims that they would be prepared to characterize as 'metaphysical'.[4] In many ways, such a view of the status of metaphysical claims is a modern-dress version of Kant's view of metaphysical claims as being concerned with the structure of thought. Indeed, for those philosophers who consider that the structure of thought just is, at bottom, the structure of the language in which thought is expressed, the two views are very close indeed, if not identical. In any case, objections similar to those against Kantianism may be raised against what we may call the *semantic* conception of metaphysics. It is quite possibly true that different languages reflect in their vocabulary and grammatical structures the different metaphysical preconceptions of the speech communities whose languages they are. But even if this is true, it wouldn't serve to show that metaphysical claims are grounded purely in language. Moreover, it is important to recognize that human beings are not incapable of challenging and rejecting the metaphysical preconceptions of the speech community in which they happen to have been born and educated. To be persuaded of this fact, one has only to reflect on the enormous variety of metaphysical systems that have been proposed and defended over the centuries by philosophers belonging to the same or closely related speech communities. So there really is no evidence that metaphysical thinking is invariably or unavoidably subject to a strong degree of linguistic or cultural relativity. However, I have already said enough in rebuttal of the relativist critics of metaphysics as traditionally conceived.

Ontology and ontological categories

At the outset of this chapter, I mentioned Aristotle, whose view was that metaphysics is the science of being qua being, and for that reason

[4] See, for example, Michael Dummett, *The Logical Basis of Metaphysics* (London: Duckworth, 1991), introd.

conceptually prior to any special science with a more limited subject-matter. This view places *ontology*—the study of what categories of entities there are and how they are related to one another—at the heart of metaphysics. Clearly, it is a view which accords well with the conception of metaphysics that I have been defending in this chapter—the view that metaphysics is concerned with the fundamental structure of reality as a whole. Aristotle does not commit what I have characterized as the Kantian error of supposing that metaphysics concerns the structure of our *thought* about being rather than being itself. It is true, of course, that we can only discourse rationally about the nature of being inasmuch as we are capable of entertaining thoughts about what there is or could be in the world. But this doesn't mean that we must substitute a study of our thought about things for a study of things themselves. Our thoughts do not constitute a veil or curtain interposed between us and the things we are endeavouring to think of, somehow making them inaccessible or inscrutable to us. On the contrary, things are accessible to us precisely because we are able to think of them. The things we think of do not thereby collapse into the thoughts we have of them, as idealist philosophers are apt to suppose. In the remainder of this book, then, I shall be following Aristotle's lead rather than Kant's concerning the nature of metaphysics as an intellectual discipline though I should stress that it is no part of my aim to promote Aristotle's views on other matters to do with metaphysics. For reasons given earlier, my stance on this issue does not imply that it is inappropriate, in metaphysics, to attempt to justify certain judgements by reflecting on concepts. In what follows, I shall frequently adopt this procedure when I examine, amongst others, the concepts of *identity, persistence, change, necessity, possibility, causation, agency, space, time,* and *motion*. For it is only if we can achieve a clear understanding of such fundamental metaphysical concepts and their interrelationships that we can hope to deploy them successfully in our attempts to articulate the fundamental structure of reality.[5]

I have not included in this book a separate chapter on ontological

[5] For a fuller account of the conception of metaphysics defended here and assumed throughout the book, see my *The Possibility of Metaphysics: Substance, Identity, and Time* (Oxford: Clarendon Press, 1998), ch. 1. For other recent accounts of the nature of metaphysics, all of which I sympathize with to some degree if not entirely, see Peter van Inwagen, *Metaphysics* (Oxford: Oxford University Press, 1993), ch. 1; Michael Jubien, *Contemporary Metaphysics* (Oxford: Blackwell, 1997), ch. 1; Michael J. Loux, *Metaphysics: A Contemporary Introduction* (London: Routledge, 1998), introd.; and Frank Jackson, *From Metaphysics to Ethics: A Defence of Conceptual Analysis* (Oxford: Clarendon Press, 1998). For a rather older but still very influential statement of the character of metaphysics, see P. F. Strawson, *Individuals: An Essay in Descriptive Metaphysics* (London: Methuen, 1959), pp. 9 ff., where he distinguishes between 'revisionary' and 'descriptive' metaphysics.

categories, because it is difficult to motivate a discussion of categorization in abstraction from a detailed treatment of the metaphysical questions that arise as to whether this or that category of entities should or should not be embraced by our ontology, or theory of what there is. (The nearest I come to providing such a discussion is in Chapter 13, although even there my focus is only on selected issues of categorization; certain questions of categorization also figure importantly in Chapters 19 and 20.) But it may be worth while saying a little here about the general shape that a system of categories may be expected to have. Traditionally, most such systems are hierarchical in structure, having the form of an inverted tree, the topmost category being that of *entity* or *being* in general. Anything that does or could exist is, it would seem, uncontroversially describable as an 'entity' of some sort. The next highest level of categorization is, however, a matter of some controversy. Some metaphysicians, for instance, think that all entities are fundamentally divisible at this level into *universals* and *particulars*, while others see the most fundamental division as being between *abstract* entities (for example, numbers, sets, and propositions) and *concrete* entities.[6] (I shall say more about both of these divisions in Part VI of this book.) These high-level categories may then be further subdivided into a range of subordinate categories at a third level of categorization— although, again, there is no consensus amongst metaphysicians as to how exactly these divisions should be made. For example, one might want to divide the category of universals into the two sub-categories of *properties* and *relations*. Again, one might want to divide the category of concrete entities into *things* (or persisting objects) and *events*—a division I discuss in some detail in Chapter 13. 'Things' might then be further subdivided into *substances* and *non-substances*—examples of the latter being such things as a heap of sand or a bundle of sticks, which lack any internal principle of unity and depend for their existence and identity upon things which do possess such a principle (things like plants, animals, molecules, and stars, which are consequently classifiable as 'substances').

But there will inevitably be some types of entity whose place in any hierarchy of categories is difficult to settle. How, for instance, should we categorize such putative entities as *holes*, *gaps*, and *shadows*? Are they

---

[6] For a third view, which sees the most fundamental division as being between *contingent* entities and *necessary* entities, see Roderick M. Chisholm, *A Realistic Theory of Categories: An Essay on Ontology* (Cambridge: Cambridge University Press, 1996), especially p. 3. I discuss ontological categorization more fully in *The Possibility of Metaphysics*, ch. 8. See also Joshua Hoffman and Gary S. Rosenkrantz, *Substance among Other Categories* (Cambridge: Cambridge University Press, 1994), ch. 1.

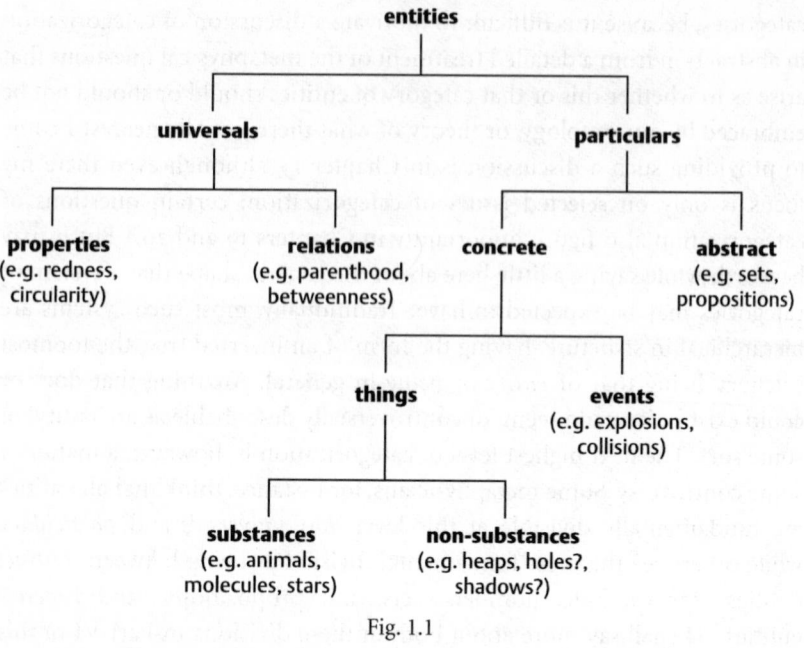

Fig. 1.1

concrete or abstract entities? Are they properly describable as 'immaterial objects', or are they mere 'privations' or 'absences' and as such not really *beings* at all, but 'non-beings'? (Of course, if we really want to include 'non-beings' in our ontology, then we had better not treat the terms 'entity' and 'being' as synonymous after all, at least so long as 'entity' is taken to denote our topmost ontological category.) Space and time themselves, together with their various parts (individual regions of space and moments of time, for example), are equally difficult to categorize, as will emerge from some of the discussions in Part V of this book. With these caveats in mind, it may none the less be helpful if, purely for purposes of illustration, I indicate by means of a simple tree diagram how a system of categories might in part be organized, along the lines just suggested (see Fig. 1.1). But I must stress that this diagram is merely illustrative and has no claim to being either complete or uncontroversial.

A short outline of this book

It may also be helpful to readers if I now conclude this introductory chapter by providing a brief synopsis of the topics that will be covered in the remainder of the book. As befits a survey of the subject, the book's contents are as comprehensive as I could practically make them. But many readers will have a narrower range of concerns, which I hope they may be helped to locate with the aid of the following overview.[7]

Chapters 2, 3, and 4 concern problems of identity, persistence, and change. Some of these problems involve cases of fission and fusion, in which one thing 'becomes two' or two 'become one'—as in the notorious puzzle of the ship of Theseus. In Chapter 2, I look at such cases with a view to determining whether, and if so how, a composite thing can retain its identity over time while undergoing a change of its component parts. I also raise the question of whether identity could be vague, or a matter of degree. In Chapter 3, I turn to the rather different question of whether, and if so how, a thing can retain its identity over time while undergoing a change of its intrinsic qualities—the so-called problem of intrinsic change. Here I explain and evaluate the doctrine of temporal parts, which offers one solution to this problem. Then, in Chapter 4, I look at the question of whether our concept of identity should be a relative or an absolute one, in the course of discussing how we can best conceptualize cases of so-called substantial change—for example, the case of a statue being formed from a lump of bronze. Should we allow that two different things, such as the statue and its constituent bronze, can exist in exactly the same place at the same time? How indeed, if at all, does the relation of constitution differ from the relation of identity?

The next three chapters concern the metaphysics of modality, that is, metaphysical issues to do with possibility and necessity. In Chapter 5, after considering some analogies between time and modality, I look at a well-known attempt to prove that true identity statements are necessarily true and raise some possible objections to this alleged proof. I also examine some of its supposed metaphysical implications, in particular its bearing upon the mind–body problem. In Chapter 6, I introduce the distinction between essential and accidental properties and raise the question of whether this distinction is founded in convention or has a more objective basis. I also examine two important essentialist theses concerning the

---

[7] This is also a convenient place for me to draw the attention of readers to the following very useful reference works and collections of readings on contemporary metaphysics: Hans Burkhardt and Barry Smith (eds.), *Handbook of Metaphysics and Ontology* (Munich: Philosophia Verlag, 1991); Jaegwon Kim and Ernest Sosa (eds.), *A Companion to Metaphysics* (Oxford: Blackwell, 1995); Stephen Laurence and Cynthia Macdonald (eds.), *Contemporary Readings in the Foundations of Metaphysics* (Oxford: Blackwell, 1998); and Steven D. Hales (ed.), *Metaphysics: Contemporary Readings* (Belmont, Calif.: Wadsworth, 1999).

necessity of origin and the necessity of constitution. In this connection, I describe certain modal paradoxes and the threats they pose for essentialism. Next, in Chapter 7, I discuss the ways in which so-called possible worlds have been invoked to interpret modal statements and raise some questions concerning the ontological status of possible worlds and their inhabitants. I also discuss the so-called problem of transworld identity and examine some arguments for and against the doctrine of actualism, that is, the view that only actual entities, not merely possible ones, exist.

The following group of three chapters focuses on the nature of causality and the interpretation of counterfactual conditional statements. Many currently popular accounts of such statements invoke possible worlds for their interpretation, and such statements are in turn commonly invoked for the purpose of analysing causal relations. In Chapter 8, I explain and discuss some of the leading possible-worlds analyses of counterfactual conditionals, looking in particular at problems raised by the context-dependency of counterfactuals and by the difficulty of making judgements of similarity between possible worlds. In Chapter 9, I look at the so-called 'Humean' or 'regularity' theory of causation and contrast it with counterfactual analyses of causal statements and probabilistic theories of causation. I raise questions concerning the relata of causal relations—whether, for example, we should take causes and effects to be *events* or *facts*—and concerning the objectivity of the concept of cause. Finally, in Chapter 10, I examine various counterfactual analyses of causation, giving special attention to the question of whether such analyses can adequately accommodate the possibility of certain forms of causal overdetermination. I also raise some questions concerning conceptual priority, and the issue of whether counterfactual analyses of causation are compatible with the view that causal relations are purely objective.

Chapters 11, 12, and 13 follow on naturally from the preceding three, being concerned with actions and events. In Chapter 11, I raise the question of whether the senses in which events and agents are causes are distinct and independent. Is one of these senses more fundamental than the other, and if so, which? Can agent causation be 'reduced' to event causation, or vice versa? ('Agent', here may be understood in a broad sense, to include inanimate objects—indeed, to include any object possessing causal powers.) In Chapter 12, I inquire whether the class of actions can simply be identified with a subclass of events, or whether actions and events belong to quite distinct ontological categories. I explore this issue by discussing how actions and events are to be individuated, focusing on problem cases which raise difficulties concerning the location or time of occurrence of an action or an event. I examine both spatiotemporal and causal criteria of identity for actions and events. The initial focus in Chapter 13 is on the question of whether persisting things (and more especially substances) are ontologically prior to events, or vice versa. Should we be reductivists, eliminativists, or non-reductive pluralists in such matters? A further issue I examine is how places and times are related to the things and events which occupy or occur at them: could there, for instance, be a stretch of time during which nothing happens?

The topics of Chapter 13 lead us smoothly into those of the next five chapters, which concern the nature of space and time in general. In Chapter 14, I examine the distinction between absolute and relational conceptions of space and evaluate Sir Isaac Newton's celebrated dynamical arguments in favour of absolute motion. I also look at the implications for the nature of time of Albert Einstein's thesis of the relativity of simultaneity. In Chapter 15, I look at Kant's famous problem concerning incongruent counterparts (objects such as a right hand and its mirror-image left hand) and ask what implications, if any, it has for the nature of space. Is space a system of relations, a substance in its own right, or, as Kant himself thought, 'transcendentally ideal'? Chapter 16 concerns the notorious paradoxes of motion attributed to the ancient Greek philosopher Zeno of Elea. Here I ask whether any of these paradoxes establishes that continuous motion is impossible, or whether modern mathematics can resolve the apparent difficulties raised by them. I also examine the issue of whether space, time, and motion could be discontinuous. In Chapter 17, I discuss a well-known argument for the unreality of time developed by the Cambridge philosopher J. M. E. McTaggart. In doing so, I look at the relation between time and tense and raise the question of whether or not there are tensed facts. I discuss the notion of temporal 'becoming' and the rivalry between 'static' and 'dynamic' conceptions of the nature of time. I also consider the question of whether the future is as 'real' as the present and past and examine its bearing on the truth or falsehood of determinism. In the last chapter of this group of five, Chapter 18, I raise the question of how the direction of time is related to the direction of causation. Is backward causation possible? I explore this issue by examining, amongst other things, the possibility of time travel into the past. The discussion includes a consideration of whether the 'arrow of time' can be explained by reference to physical laws.

The last two chapters of the book are concerned with two very fundamental but closely related metaphysical distinctions, the distinction between universals and particulars and the distinction between abstract and concrete entities. In Chapter 19, I examine various accounts of the first of these distinctions and raise the question of whether we really need to include both universals and particulars in our ontology. Can particulars be regarded, in effect, as bundles of universals, or, conversely, can classes of particulars serve the purposes for which universals are usually invoked? In this context I discuss the merits and difficulties of theories which invoke the existence of so-called 'tropes', sometimes also called 'particularized qualities'. Finally, in Chapter 20, I look at the question of how we should draw the distinction between abstract and concrete objects, and ask what reason we can have, if any, to believe in the existence of abstract objects, such as numbers, sets, and propositions. There is also some discussion of how we should categorize 'facts' or 'states of affairs' and what place, if any, we should grant such items in our ontology.

PART I

IDENTITY AND CHANGE

2

IDENTITY OVER TIME AND CHANGE OF COMPOSITION

Numerical and qualitative identity

The concept of identity is a puzzling one, seeming at once perfectly simple and yet enormously complex. On the side of simplicity, there is the indisputable fact that everything is identical with itself and with no other thing. And whatever is true of a thing is true of anything identical with that thing, since anything identical with that thing is that very thing itself. This latter principle is sometimes known as 'Leibniz's Law', in deference to its most famous advocate, Gottfried Wilhelm Leibniz. From what has been said so far, identity seems to be an utterly trivial relation which can have no metaphysical significance—trivial because everything whatever stands in this relation to itself and to nothing else. Indeed, one may even wonder with what propriety identity can be called a *relation* at all, since we normally think of relations as holding between *different* things. However, we are happy to say that a relation which holds between different things may also sometimes hold between a thing and itself: for example, a person may hit another person, but we also say that a person may hit himself. The odd thing about identity, thought of as a relation, is that it can *only* ever hold between a thing and itself. But perhaps that just makes it an unusual relation, rather than not a genuine relation at all.

The more puzzling aspects of identity begin to emerge when we consider it in combination with the phenomenon of *change*. We regularly say that things can change over time, meaning thereby that one and the same thing can be different at different times. But it may seem to be nothing short of a contradiction to say that a thing can be both the same and different, that is, both the same and not the same. Here philosophers are usually quick to draw a distinction between what they call *numerical* and *qualitative* identity. At least in many cases, they say, when a thing changes, it remains numerically one and the same thing but becomes qualitatively different—for example, it is one and the same banana that is first green in colour and later yellow, or one and the same tree that is first small in size and later large. Are there, then, two different kinds of identity, or two different senses of the word 'same'? Most philosophers and logicians would answer 'No' to this question. They would say that when we speak of a thing becoming qualitatively different over time, we simply mean that this thing has numerically different qualities at numerically different times—for instance, that the banana has one quality, greenness, at one time and another quality, yellowness, at another time. On this view, all identity is really numerical identity, but we have to distinguish between the identity of a thing and the identity of its qualities.

Composite objects and change of parts

We shall be looking more closely at the nature of qualitative change in the next chapter. In this chapter, I want to focus on another kind of change which may seem at least as puzzling—change of composition. Many of the objects that we refer to in everyday conversation are *composite* objects—that is to say, they are composed of various other objects, which are therefore *parts* of them. For instance, a typical table is composed of four wooden legs attached to the four corners of a rectangular wooden surface. Human beings and other living organisms are, of course, composite objects, with a very complex compositional structure. A tree is composed of trunk, branches, leaves, roots, and so forth—and these in turn are composed of other things, such as cells, which are composed of yet smaller organic bodies and, ultimately, of subatomic particles. Thus we find in nature various *hierarchies of composition.* We find such hierarchies also in the realm of artefacts of our own making, such as cars and computers. In fact, examples drawn from the realm of artefacts are popular in philosophical discussions of change of composition, because we tend to be more familiar with the ways in which such objects are composed, they being products of deliberate human design.

Just as we find it perfectly natural to say that one and the same thing can change its qualities over time, we find it perfectly natural to say that one and the same thing can change its *parts* over time. Indeed, we seem compelled to say this in the case of living organisms, in whose very nature it is to undergo processes of growth and metabolism which involve an exchange of matter between an organism and its environment. But even in the case of artefacts, we find it natural to speak of such change. When I take my watch or car to be repaired, I do not complain that it is not the same watch or car if it is returned to me with some of its worn parts replaced by new ones. Of course, there *is* a sense in which the watch is not 'the same' after it has been repaired: it is not the same in respect of its component parts—it now has different ones. But it is still, we want to say, one and the same *watch*—it is 'numerically' the same. It is not the case that the watch which I took to be repaired has ceased to exist and a new and numerically different watch has replaced it. That, at least, is what we naturally want to say. But the question is: can we say this, without falling into absurdity or even contradiction? It is relatively easy to construct certain puzzle cases which seem to threaten the intelligibility of our ordinary ways of talking about such matters. By the far the best known of these puzzle cases is the problem of the ship of Theseus. The version we shall examine was first stated by Thomas Hobbes, based on a passage from a work of the ancient Greek biographer Plutarch.[1]

The puzzle of the ship of Theseus

According to legend, when the hero Theseus died, his famous ship was preserved in the harbour at Athens for many years. In the course of time, parts of it began to decay and these were replaced by new parts of the same form and materials as the originals. Eventually, none of the original parts remained, posing the question of whether the ship in the harbour was still the same ship as the ship that Theseus had sailed in—that is, whether it was numerically identical with the original ship of Theseus. Since we customarily allow that an artefact can undergo replacement of its parts, at least if the replacement occurs in a gradual and piecemeal fashion, the obvious answer to this question would seem to be that the renovated ship, as we may call it, is indeed identical with the original ship. The only alternative would be to impose some limit on the proportion of a ship's parts that could be replaced without loss of its identity—that is, without its ceasing to exist. But it is easy to see that this will compel us to say that a

---

[1] See Thomas Hobbes, *De Corpore*, ch. 11, in *The English Works of Thomas Hobbes*, ed. William Molesworth (London: John Bohn, 1839–45).

ship cannot survive the replacement of *any* of its parts, which seems absurd, or at least strongly in conflict with common sense.

The reason for this consequence is that identity is a *transitive* relation: that is to say, if a is identical with b and b is identical with c, then, of necessity, a is identical with c. Suppose, then, that we impose some limit on the proportion of a ship's parts that can be replaced without loss of identity: for instance, suppose we stipulate that up to 5 per cent of a ship's parts, but no more, can be replaced without that ship ceasing to exist. According to this criterion, it would be possible to replace 4 per cent of ship a's parts in such a way that the resulting ship, ship b, is still identical with ship a. But then it would likewise be possible to replace 4 per cent of ship b's parts in such a way that the resulting ship, ship c, is still identical with ship b—in which case, the transitivity of identity implies that ship a is identical with ship c. However, in such a case it could well be that ship a and ship c differ in their parts by *more* than the 5 per cent limit (in fact, by up to 8 per cent), implying that, according to the proposed criterion, they could *not* be the same ship. Thus we have a contradiction, the criterion implying, in such a case, both that ship a *is* identical with ship c (because of the transitivity of identity) and that ship a is *not* identical with ship c (because the proposed limit is exceeded). Consequently, the only consistent limit to impose is one of 0 per cent, allowing no change of parts at all.[2] If we want to allow change of parts at all, it seems that we must allow a *complete* change of parts. (A rather different proposal would be to say that a ship cannot have more than a certain proportion of its *original* parts replaced, but this, too, runs into difficulties: first, because any limit that might be set would appear to be arbitrary, and second, because the *original* parts of a thing are, by definition, the parts which that thing had when it first came into existence, yet part of our problem is to distinguish between a case of a new ship coming into existence and one of an existing ship undergoing a change of parts.)

So far, we have seen that it is plausible to allow that something like a ship can, in time, undergo even a complete replacement of its parts—provided, of course, that this is done little by little. But now we come to the real puzzle of the ship of Theseus. Suppose that, as the original parts of Theseus' ship are gradually replaced by new ones, those original parts are carefully removed to a warehouse and stored there, until the warehouse

---

[2] The view that a composite object cannot, strictly speaking, ever undergo a change of parts is known as 'mereological essentialism' and is espoused by Roderick M. Chisholm: see his *Person and Object: A Metaphysical Study* (London: George Allen and Unwin, 1976), ch. 3 and app. B.

eventually contains all of the original parts, while all the replacement parts belong to the ship in the harbour (the renovated ship, as we have decided to call it). And then suppose that someone puts all of the original parts together again to form a ship which is exactly like the original ship of Theseus: call this ship the reconstructed ship. Now we have *two* very similar ships, the renovated ship and the reconstructed ship, each of which might seem to have some claim to be identical with the original ship of Theseus. The claim of the renovated ship we have already examined: it rests upon the apparent fact that a ship can undergo, in time, a complete replacement of its parts. But the reconstructed ship also seems to have a good claim, for not only is it exactly like the original ship in respect of its appearance (as is the renovated ship), but also it is composed of exactly the same parts. A further consideration apparently in support of this claim is that we commonly allow that an artefact can be disassembled at one time and later reassembled, the implication being that the reassembled artefact is numerically identical with the one that was earlier disassembled—think, for example, of a tent or a bicycle that is designed to be treated in this way, or of a watch that is taken to pieces for cleaning and later put back together again. If the original ship of Theseus had simply been gradually dismantled, without replacement of any of its parts, and the parts had been successively removed to the warehouse, there eventually to be reassembled to form a ship of exactly the same structure, the natural thing to say in this case would be that the original ship had been moved, piece by piece, to the warehouse. But isn't this also exactly what happens in the case in which the original parts are replaced by new ones as they are removed from the ship in the harbour?

Our problem, then, is this. In the case in which both renovation and reconstruction occur, we have, at a later time, *two* ships, the renovated ship in the harbour and the reconstructed ship in the warehouse, *both* of which seem to have a good claim to be identical with the original ship of Theseus. If there had been renovation without reconstruction, we would happily have identified the renovated ship with the original ship; and if there had been reconstruction without renovation, we would happily have identified the reconstructed ship with the original ship. But we can't say, in the case where both renovation and reconstruction occur, that *both* the renovated ship *and* the reconstructed ship are identical with the original ship, because this again falls foul of the fact that identity is a transitive relation. If the renovated ship is identical with the original ship and the original ship is also identical with the reconstructed ship, then it follows, by the transitivity of identity, that the renovated ship is identical with the reconstructed ship—and yet this surely cannot be the case, because the renovated ship and the reconstructed ship are two quite distinct ships, each having a quite distinct location. On the other hand, it may seem arbitrary to say that one rather than the other of the two later ships is identical with the original ship—for how can we choose, in a principled way, one rather than the other for this distinction? Moreover, if we do choose one of them for this distinction—say, the renovated ship—then we may seem to have the following absurd consequence on our hands. It seems that we shall have to say, concerning the reconstructed ship, that although it is not in fact identical with the original ship and, indeed, only came into existence for the first time when its parts were assembled in the warehouse, neverthe-less it *would* have been identical with the original ship if renovation had never occurred, that is, if the original parts had not been replaced but had simply been removed from the harbour to the warehouse. In *that* case, it seems, the reconstructed ship *would* have been identical with the original ship, in which case it would have come into existence much earlier, namely, when the ship of Theseus was first built. But how can it make sense to say that a certain thing *a*, which is *not* in fact identical with a certain other thing *b*, *would* have been identical with *b* if a certain thing *c* (in this case, the renovated ship) had not existed? Surely, whether or not *a* is identical with *b* is a matter which concerns only *a* and *b*, quite independently of what other things do or do not exist.

Two radical solutions to the puzzle

In the light of this conundrum, we may be tempted to conclude that *neither* of the later ships is identical with the original ship, though that is scarcely more palatable than any of our other alternatives. We may even be tempted to conclude that our common-sense conception of composite objects as things which can persist over time is ultimately incoherent. However, before we resort to such desperate measures, let us be sure that we have properly understood the options that confront us. It may be that we shall have to surrender some aspects of our common-sense conception of objects and their persistence on account of the puzzle, or it may even be that we can defend that conception in its entirety by noticing some dis-tinctions that may so far have escaped us. One aspect of our common-sense conception of objects is that we deem it impossible for the same object to be in two different places at once, or for different objects (or, at least, different objects of the same kind) to be in the same place at the same time. If we were to give up this assumption, then one or other of the following solutions to the puzzle of the ship of Theseus would theoretically be available to us. One solution would be to say that *both* the renovated ship *and* the reconstructed ship are identical with the original ship, accepting that this implies that, at the later time, one and the same ship is in two different places at once, that is, both in the harbour and in the warehouse. Another solution would be to say, while accepting that the renovated ship and the reconstructed ship are two quite distinct ships, that *both* of these ships were originally in the harbour, so that, in fact, it was misleading to speak of *the* ship of Theseus: according to this solution, the two later ships exactly coincided with one another until the process of renovation and removal began, whereupon they gradually became separated.

It must be admitted that both of these solutions seem to be logically unimpeachable, in that they apparently transgress no law of logic and respect the transitivity of identity. But they require us to make such extensive revisions to our common-sense conception of objects and their persistence that we may doubt whether they make good sense, metaphysically speaking. As I remarked in the previous chapter, the answers to questions of what is *possible* are not, in general, determined purely by linguistic conventions or the meanings of words, but rather by the natures of things themselves, quite independently of the language which we use to describe those things. Thus, we are in no position simply to *stipulate* that one and the same thing 'can' exist in two places at once, or that two different things 'can' exist in the same place at the same time: if we want to say that either possibility obtains, then we must earn the right to do so by advancing cogent arguments—and that may not prove to be at all easy. Moreover, both of these proposed solutions to the puzzle suffer from the difficulty that they make it impossible for us to say how many things of a certain kind, such as ships, exist in a certain number of places at a certain time without reference to events occurring earlier or later than that time. For instance, according to the first solution, we cannot tell whether, at a certain time, we are confronted by two distinct ships in two different places or just one and the same ship, without knowing about the prior history of the ship or ships concerned. And according to the second solution, we cannot tell whether, at a certain time, we are confronted by just one ship in a certain place or two distinct ships, without knowing about the future history of the ship or ships concerned. These consequences seem to render the proposed solutions absurd and intolerable.

A better solution?

Maybe, however, our common-sense conception of objects and persistence can escape altogether unscathed from the puzzle of the ship of Theseus, if we handle it with due care. This is my own opinion, as I shall now try to explain.[3] First of all, we need to distinguish, in a way in which we have not done so far, between ordinary cases in which a composite artefact, such as a ship, is gradually disassembled and later reassembled and what happens in the puzzle case to the original parts of the ship of Theseus. In the ordinary cases, the various parts concerned are, at all times throughout the process, either incorporated into a single, partially dismantled ship, or else not incorporated into any ship at all. For example, there will be a time when half of the parts are still connected together in a half-dismantled ship, while the remaining half are loose and separate in a warehouse. At such a time, it seems proper to say that the ship in question has a full complement of parts, but that half of them are in the warehouse and half of them are still in the partially dismantled ship. But what are we to say at the corresponding time during the process involved in the puzzle case, that is, when half of the original parts of the ship of Theseus have been removed to the warehouse and have been replaced by new ones in the harbour? It seems indisputable that, at that time, we have in the harbour one entire ship, in fully working order, with a full complement of parts. But do we *also* have, at that time, a ship with a full complement of parts, half of which are in the warehouse and half of which are in the harbour? If we answer 'Yes', then we must say, it seems, that half of these parts are *shared* by two distinct ships, namely, the half which are in the harbour. The ships in question must be *distinct* ships, because they do not have exactly the same parts— one of them has parts all of which are in the harbour, while the other has half of its parts in the harbour and half in the warehouse. However, it is very doubtful that it makes sense to say that two distinct ships can, at the same time, share half of their parts. Certainly, our common-sense conception of objects and their persistence does not license us to say this. I

[3] The following view was first defended in my 'On the Identity of Artifacts', *Journal of Philosophy* 80 (1983), 222–32.

suggest, then, that we should *not* say this. But then we must decide to which ship the various parts concerned belong at the time in question. Clearly, all of the parts in the harbour belong to the ship that is in the harbour. But if, as we have decided, none of those parts simultaneously belongs to any other ship, it follows that, at the time in question, there is *no* ship which has a full complement of parts half of which are in the harbour and half of which are in the warehouse. I conclude, indeed, that the parts in the warehouse belong to *no ship at all* at that time. This is quite different from what we say about the parts in the warehouse in an ordinary case of disassembly and reassembly.

What I am contending is that there is a relevant difference between how the original ship is related to the reconstructed ship in the puzzle case and how the original ship is related to the reconstructed ship in an ordinary case of disassembly and reassembly. The difference turns on the fact that, in the latter sort of case, none of the original parts of the original ship is ever *appropriated* by another, distinct ship. Once the original parts of a ship have been appropriated by another, distinct ship, I suggest, they cease to be parts of that original ship: and even if those parts are later reassembled to compose a ship, the ship that they then compose is a new ship, numerically different from the original one. In the puzzle case, however, as we have just seen, if we suppose that the original ship is identical with the reconstructed ship, then we must say that there are times at which many of its parts have been appropriated by another, distinct ship—namely, the renovated ship—but that these parts later become, once again, parts of the original ship. And this contravenes the principle that I have just proposed.

In defence of a generalized version of this principle, consider what we might be committed to saying once we allow, without restriction, that a thing's parts may be appropriated by other things but later become, once again, parts of that thing. Suppose, for instance, that all of the atoms composing a certain tree were to be dispersed throughout the universe for many years, becoming parts of various other objects during that time, but that at some much later time they were to come together again by chance to form a tree, exactly similar to the original tree. Would this original tree be numerically identical with the much later tree? Surely not. A generalized version of the principle that I have proposed explains why that is so—and this fact may be adduced in support of the principle. Of course, we must not state the principle in such strong terms that it prevents us from saying that I may temporarily borrow a wheel from your car to replace my missing one and later return it to you for reincorporation into your car. In such a case, two distinct cars clearly exist throughout the period in question, yours and mine, though first mine and then yours lacks a full complement of parts. However, in the puzzle case of the ship of Theseus, it seems that we can identify the reconstructed ship with the original ship only if we are prepared to say that there is a time at which *most* of the ship of Theseus' parts have been appropriated by another, distinct ship, the renovated ship—namely, the time at which only the first few parts have been removed to the warehouse and replaced by new ones. It seems perfectly proper to insist that we should not be prepared to say this.

My proposed solution to the puzzle of the ship of Theseus implies that it is the *renovated* ship that is identical with the original ship. But how, then, can I escape the difficulty which, as I remarked earlier, seems to attend the choice of *either* of the two later ships as being identical with the original ship? This difficulty, as it applies to my solution, is that it seems that we shall have to say, concerning the reconstructed ship, that although it is not in fact identical with the original ship, nevertheless it *would* have been identical with the original ship if renovation had never occurred, that is, if the original parts had not been replaced but had simply been removed from the harbour to the warehouse. My answer to this apparent difficulty is that it is a mistake to suppose that the expression 'the reconstructed ship' refers to the same ship in the two different possible situations—the situation in which renovation does occur and the situation in which renovation does not occur. In both situations, there is *a* reconstructed ship, that is, a ship which, at the later time, is put together from all the original parts of the ship of Theseus that are stored in the warehouse. But the reconstructed ship that *would* have been composed of those parts if renovation had not occurred is not to be identified with the reconstructed ship that *is* composed of those parts in the puzzle situation, in which renovation does occur. For the former ship would simply have been the ship of Theseus itself, having undergone a process of disassembly and reassembly, whereas the latter ship is a quite different ship which first comes into existence at the later time. Thus, far from it being the case that the expression 'the reconstructed ship' refers to the same ship in the two possible situations, this expression, as it is used in the no-renovation situation, refers to the same ship as the expression 'the renovated ship' does in the renovation situation—namely, the original ship of Theseus. So, in answer to the apparent difficulty for my proposed solution, we can see that I certainly do *not* have to say that the reconstructed ship in the renovation situation would have been identical with the ship of Theseus if renovation had not occurred, because the reconstructed ship of the renovation situation would not even have existed if renovation had not occurred—rather, a quite different reconstructed ship would then have existed and *this* would have been identical with the original ship of Theseus.

It may be felt that this still leaves us with a puzzle. For the implication of my proposed solution is that, in two different possible situations, the very same ship parts can undergo exactly the same individual histories and yet end up composing two quite different ships—the ship of Theseus in one situation and a newly composed ship in the other. The only difference between the two situations concerns not what happens to those individual ship parts, but rather what happens, or fails to happen, to certain *other* ship parts: in one of the situations, certain new ship parts are created and put in place in the harbour, whereas this fails to happen in the other situation. However, it is unclear to me why this should be deemed in any way para-doxical, since it is a straightforward consequence of the intuitively plaus-ible principle that I advanced earlier, namely, that if sufficiently many of a thing's parts are incorporated into *another* thing, then those parts are appropriated by that other thing and cease to be parts of the first thing. In the renovation situation, the original parts of the ship of Theseus cannot all go on being parts of a ship that is steadily being dismantled, because sufficiently many of them belong instead to a fully functioning ship which contains new parts. By the time all of the original parts are in the ware-house, none of them belongs to any pre-existing ship and so any ship which is put together from them is a newly existing ship, not a previously dismantled ship.

Intermittent existence

A further question which this discussion provokes is whether it is possible for a composite thing, such as a ship, to enjoy an *intermittent* or *interrupted* existence. So far, I have tried to avoid this issue, which is itself an extremely vexed one. In an ordinary case of disassembly and later reassembly—as when a tent is taken down and later erected again, or a watch is taken to pieces for cleaning and later put back together again—it seems that we have two options when asked what happens to the composite object con-cerned. We could say that it goes on existing in a disassembled state, or we could say that it temporarily ceases to exist until it is reassembled. If we say the latter, then we have to recognize a certain ambiguity implicit in talk of a thing's 'beginning to exist': for if a thing can cease to exist and later 'begin to exist' again, then 'begin to exist' in this latter sense does not mean the same as 'come into existence for the first time'. Of logical necessity, nothing can come into existence *for the first time* more than once, but we should not allow the implicit ambiguity in talk of a thing's 'beginning to exist' to beguile us into supposing that it is *logically* impossible—a contradiction in terms—for a thing to enjoy an intermittent existence. Even so, this still leaves us with the question of whether it is *metaphysically* possible for a thing to enjoy an intermittent existence.

I consider that the answer to this question depends, as we might expect, upon the nature of the thing concerned—that is, upon what kind of thing it is. In the case of an artefact, such as a tent or a watch, which is designed to be capable of disassembly and reassembly, I think that it is proper to say that it continues to exist when it has been taken apart, provided that its parts have not been incorporated into other, fully assembled things of the same kind. Thus, if all the parts of my watch are used to replace parts in various other fully functioning watches, my watch ceases to exist, for reasons explained earlier. But if my watch is simply taken to pieces for cleaning, it goes on existing in a disassembled state. However, other kinds of composite objects are of such a nature that they cannot survive disassembly—for example, a living organism, such as an animal, cannot survive disassembly of its body parts. But I should also point out that, even in the case of something like a watch, which can survive disassembly, we have to be careful to specify into what *kinds* of parts the thing can be disassembled without its ceasing to exist. Clearly, my watch cannot survive 'disassembly' into its constituent *atoms*: to atomize my watch is to destroy it for ever. Into what kinds of parts, if any, a composite thing can be disassembled without its ceasing to exist will again be determined by the nature of the thing in question. This simply reflects the fact, emphasized in the previous chapter, that metaphysical possibility is grounded in the natures of things. Now, given that even in the case of things like tents and watches, which are designed to be disassembled and reassembled, we need never speak of a composite thing's having an intermittent existence, I think it improbable that we should, in fact, ever have need to speak in this way. So my tentative verdict is that no composite object whatever enjoys a merely intermittent existence—but I concede that my opinion in this matter is controversial.

Fission and fusion

The problem of the ship of Theseus is just one of a large class of problems involving the *fission* or *fusion* of persisting objects. In a case of fission, one object becomes two or more, whereas in a case of fusion, two or more objects become one. (I shall not discuss fusion cases separately in what follows, because it appears that they are merely the inverses of fission cases and present no distinct problems of their own.) Now, we must be careful here as to what we understand by the verb 'become'. When it is said, for example, that one object *becomes* two, this cannot unproblematically be taken to mean that one object existing at an earlier time is at a later time identical with two distinct objects—for this, as we saw earlier, conflicts with the principle of the transitivity of identity, at least as that principle is standardly understood. A few philosophers, it is true, would like to inter-pret that principle in a non-standard way, so that it only applies to things at a single moment of time, not at different moments of time.[4] Whether this proposal is really intelligible is a difficult question, though my own conviction is that it is not. That being so, to say that one object 'becomes' two can, it seems, only mean either that one object ceases to exist and two new objects are created from its parts, or else that one object continues to exist but another new object is created from some of the old object's former parts. The latter, I have suggested, is what happens in the case of the ship of Theseus, which may therefore be classified as a case of fission.

Fission cases may be either symmetrical or asymmetrical. (In what fol-lows, for the sake of simplicity I shall restrict consideration to cases of one object becoming two.) In asymmetrical cases, such as the case of the ship of Theseus, the 'fission products'—the two objects existing at the later time—are differently related to the original object. In symmetrical cases, they are related in the same way. An example of a symmetrical fission case would be that of a single amoeba dividing into two distinct amoebas, or that of a single water drop dividing into two distinct water drops. In such a case, there is quite a compelling reason to say that the original object ceases to exist and gives rise to two new objects—the reason being that if we say, instead, that the original object continues to exist as one of the fission products, symmetry considerations make it impossible for us to decide, in

---

[4] See, for example, André Gallois, *Occasions of Identity: The Metaphysics of Persistence, Change, and Sameness* (Oxford: Clarendon Press, 1998).

a non-arbitrary way, which of the two fission products is identical with the original object. Here it may be asked why we shouldn't say, in such a case, that one of the fission products is indeed identical with the original object, but that it is simply *indeterminate* which of the fission products this is. The answer is that this suggestion seems to fall foul of a quite compelling argument that identity cannot be vague or indeterminate. Since that argument has been very influential, we should spend a little time looking at it.

Is vague identity possible?

The argument against the possibility of vague or indeterminate identity runs as follows.[5] Suppose, for the sake of argument, that it is indeterminate whether a certain object *a* is identical with a certain object *b*. Now, Leibniz's Law—which we met at the beginning of this chapter—implies that if something is true of an object *a* which is not true of an object *b*, then *a* and *b* cannot be identical. But, given that it is indeterminate whether *a* is identical with *b*, it seems to follow that it is true of *a* that it is indeterminate whether it is identical with *b*. However, it is plausibly *not* true of *b* that it is indeterminate whether it is identical with *b*, since every object is surely determinately identical with itself. Hence, it seems, something is true of *a* which is not true of *b*, whence we can conclude, by Leibniz's Law, that *a* is not identical with *b*. This reduces to absurdity our original supposition that it is indeterminate whether *a* is identical with *b*, so we may conclude that identity cannot be indeterminate.

It must be confessed that there is an air of sophistry about this argument—and I certainly have doubts about its cogency.[6] In particular, it may be questioned whether we are in fact entitled to assume that it is *not* true of *b* that it is indeterminate whether it is identical with *b*. Notice, however, that it will not do to challenge the argument simply on the grounds that, in many cases, there is a degree of indeterminacy in the language which we use to refer to things. Consider a name such as 'Mount Everest', which refers to a certain mountain. This mountain, as is well

[5] One well-known version of this argument is due to Gareth Evans: see his 'Can There Be Vague Objects?', *Analysis* 38 (1978), 208. See also Nathan U. Salmon, *Reference and Essence* (Oxford: Blackwell, 1982), 243 ff.

[6] See further my 'Vague Identity and Quantum Indeterminacy', *Analysis* 54 (1994), 110–14, or my *The Possibility of Metaphysics: Substance, Identity, and Time* (Oxford: Clarendon Press, 1998), 63 ff.

known, is located in the Himalayas, along with many other tall mountains, which are separated from one another by valleys. But it is to a degree arbitrary where we say that the foot of one mountain ends and the foot of another begins. Consequently, there is no single, precisely delimited piece of terrain which indisputably deserves to be referred to as 'Mount Everest'—many different, but very largely overlapping, pieces of terrain are equally good candidates for this title. Call one of these pieces of terrain T. Then, it seems, it is to a degree vague or indeterminate whether Mount Everest is identical with T, simply because our use of the term 'Mount Everest' does not fix its reference sufficiently determinately to decide the matter one way or the other. However, what we have here is not indeterminacy in the relation of *identity*, but merely indeterminacy of linguistic reference. Moreover, it does not seem that we can treat a case of symmetrical fission as involving indeterminacy of this merely linguistic sort. For the latter sort of indeterminacy typically arises when there is a degree of 'fuzziness' in spatiotemporal boundaries—as there is, for instance, in the spatial boundary of Mount Everest. But in a case of symmetrical fission, as when one amoeba divides into two, there is no such fuzziness: the moment of separation is precise and the fission products are spatially disconnected from one another.

The paradox of the thousand and one cats

Problems of vagueness afflict our talk about composite objects quite generally. One notorious problem of this kind is the so-called paradox of the thousand and one cats.[7] Suppose that Tibbles the cat is sitting on the mat. Tibbles has, naturally, many hairs, but perhaps he is moulting, so that some of these hairs are loose and about to drop from his coat. Once a hair has definitely become separated from Tibbles, it is no longer a part of him. But some of the hairs, maybe at least a thousand of them, are neither definitely separated from Tibbles nor definitely not separated from Tibbles. One conceivable way to describe the situation is to say that there are on the mat many different, but largely overlapping, candidates for the name of 'Tibbles', which differ from one another in respect of the number and identity

---

[7] The problem was first posed by Peter Geach: see his *Reference and Generality*, 3rd edn. (Ithaca, NY: Cornell University Press, 1980), 215. In its original form, the problem was not specifically one of vagueness: I discuss it in that form in my *Kinds of Being: A Study of Individuation, Identity and the Logic of Sortal Terms* (Oxford: Blackwell, 1989), 68 ff.

of the hairs which may be said to belong to them. According to this conception, there are in fact many different *cats* on the mat—at least 1,001 of them—rather than just one cat. That may seem an absurd thing to say, but defenders of this conception may urge that it involves less of a departure from common sense than we might imagine. First of all, they may point out that, while there are, strictly speaking, many different cats on the mat, all of these cats may be *counted* as one and the same cat for everyday purposes. It is not as though we have 1,001 *quite separate* cats on the mat, since the many different cats overlap one another almost entirely—that is to say, they share the vast majority of their parts, differing from one another by no more than a few hairs. Secondly, it may be urged that nothing in our use of the name 'Tibbles' fixes its reference decisively to just one of the many cats rather than any other, and consequently nothing that we are ordinarily inclined to say about Tibbles will be at all compromised by the multiplicity of cats present on the mat. Where we are sure that something is definitely true of Tibbles, such as that Tibbles is sitting on the mat, this will be true because it is true of *every* cat in question. Where something is *not* true of every cat in question but only of some of them, however—such as that it possesses a certain hair—we shall correspondingly not be sure that that thing is definitely true of Tibbles.[8]

It may have been noticed already that the foregoing conception of Tibbles's situation is not one that I can endorse, given principles that I have already advocated earlier in this chapter. For I have expressly denied that two distinct things of the same kind, such as two ships or two cats, can share the majority of their parts at the same time. I cannot allow, then, that things like cats can *overlap* one another to a very high degree. This may seem to create a problem for me, for how can I decide, in a non-arbitrary way, which of the many slightly different collections of cat parts present on the mat composes the *one* cat that, according to my principles, is sitting on the mat? The answer is that I do not have to decide. I can say that, in many cases, the relation of part to whole is to a degree vague or indeterminate.[9]

[8] See further David Lewis, 'Many, but Almost One', in John Bacon, Keith Campbell, and Lloyd Reinhardt (eds.), *Ontology, Causality and Mind: Essays in Honour of D. M. Armstrong* (Cambridge: Cambridge University Press, 1993), 23–38, reprinted in David Lewis, *Papers in Metaphysics and Epistemology* (Cambridge: Cambridge University Press, 1999). For more on problems of vagueness in general and different approaches to solving them, see Rosanna Keefe, *Theories of Vagueness* (Cambridge: Cambridge University Press, 2000) and also Rosanna Keefe and Peter Smith (eds.), *Vagueness: A Reader* (Cambridge, Mass: MIT Press, 1997).

[9] See further my 'The Problem of the Many and the Vagueness of Constitution', *Analysis* 55 (1995), 179–82.

This does not commit me to saying that there is any vagueness in the relation of *identity* (even if it should be thought that the latter relation cannot be vague), since the relation of part to whole and the relation of identity are quite different relations. According to my conception of Tibbles's situation, there is only one *cat* sitting on the mat—Tibbles—but many slightly different collections of cat parts are present there: and it is indeterminate which of these collections composes Tibbles. Of course, this conception of the situation requires me to say that a collection of cat parts is not a *cat*, even though it may *compose* a cat. But that contention is not difficult to defend, because cats and collections of cat parts have different persistence conditions. That is to say, there are different kinds of changes that cats and collections of cat parts can and cannot survive. For instance, a collection of cat parts can survive the mutual separation of all of its members, but a cat cannot likewise survive if all of its parts are separated from one another.

As will be gathered from my treatment of earlier problems in this chapter, my inclination is to find a common-sense solution to a metaphysical problem if such a solution is available. My solution to the problem of Tibbles is, I think, more in line with common sense than is the alternative solution, which concedes that there are, strictly speaking, many different cats sitting on the mat. It can hardly be objected that my solution is ontologically more extravagant than its rival in that it invokes the existence of collections of cat parts in addition to that of cats, for the existence of such collections can scarcely be denied by advocates of the alternative conception of Tibbles's situation.

However, perhaps it will instead be objected that my solution does not, after all, relieve me of the obligation to recognize the simultaneous existence of many different cats on the mat. For if any one of the collections of cat parts present on the mat is capable of composing a cat, why don't they *all* compose cats?—in which case, they will have to compose *different* cats, since they are different collections. My answer, once again, is that it is in the nature of cats that they cannot overlap one another to any significant extent: it is this fact—that cats largely exclude one another from occupying the same place at the same time— that prevents there from being more than one of the many largely overlapping collections of cat parts that can compose a cat at one and the same time. (To insist that *cats* largely exclude one another from occupying the same place at the same time is quite consistent with allowing that *collections of cat parts* can largely overlap one another, because cats and collections of cat parts are things of very different kinds.)

As is the case with most difficult metaphysical problems, however, it would be foolish to suppose that one person's solution will necessarily convince everyone else. I have presented my own proposed solutions to two such problems in this chapter—the puzzle of the ship of Theseus and the paradox of the thousand and one cats—not so much in order to persuade readers that these solutions are correct, as to try to motivate them to pursue their own solutions.

3

QUALITATIVE CHANGE AND THE
DOCTRINE OF TEMPORAL PARTS

Leibniz's Law and the problem of qualitative change

At the outset of the preceding chapter, I briefly mentioned the phenomenon of qualitative change—the sort of change which occurs when a banana changes in colour from being green to being yellow, or when a tree changes in size from being small to being large. In such a case, I said, one and the same object possesses numerically different qualities at numerically different times. I also mentioned Leibniz's Law, characterizing this as the principle that whatever is true of a thing is true of anything identical with that thing. But some philosophers feel that there is a tension between Leibniz's Law and the notion of qualitative change.[1] Consider, for instance, a piece of wire which is thought to change from being straight to being bent, so that at first it possesses the quality of being straight and later the quality of being bent. Now, something which is bent is, for that very reason, not straight: the quality of being bent is incompatible with the quality of being straight. How, then, can it be true of one and the same object that it is both straight and bent? For if it is true of the object that it is straight, then, by Leibniz's Law, it is *not* true of that same object that it is *not* straight, and so not true of it that it is bent.

The obvious answer to this apparent problem is to say that what is true

---

[1] For more on the background to the problem about to be discussed see, especially, David Lewis, *On the Plurality of Worlds* (Oxford: Blackwell, 1986), 202 ff. See also D. M. Armstrong, 'Identity Through Time', in Peter van Inwagen (ed.), *Time and Cause: Essays Presented to Richard Taylor* (Dordrecht: D. Reidel, 1980).

of the object in our example is not simply that it is both straight and bent, but rather that it is straight at one time and bent at another, later time. Although one and the same object cannot be both straight and bent at the same time, because straightness and bentness are mutually incompatible qualities, nothing prevents it from being straight at one time and bent at another. However, it may be felt that this answer does not go to the heart of the problem. Given that straightness and bentness are mutually incompatible qualities, as they certainly appear to be, how is it that one and the same object can possess both of them, even at different times? How does reference to the times at which the object allegedly possesses the mutually incompatible qualities render those qualities any the less mutually incompatible and hence make such an alleged case of qualitative change any the more intelligible? In fact, doesn't the present answer to our apparent problem simply assume the very thing that needs to be explained—namely, the possibility of qualitative change?

Presentism

A number of very different metaphysical positions have been developed in response to the problem of qualitative change. We can characterize these different positions in terms of the different analyses they offer of a simple statement ascribing a quality to an object at a time—that is, a statement of the form 'a is F at t'. Examples of such statements, in everyday English, would be: 'The banana is yellow today', 'The tree will be tall twenty years from now', and 'The wire was straight a moment ago'. Of course, these statements, being expressed in everyday English, use the grammatical device of *tense* to convey reference to different times, but perhaps this is unnecessary: perhaps the same information could be conveyed by *tenseless* statements making use of dates to refer to different times. The question of how tense (that is, talk of past, present, and future) is related to the nature of time is a deep and difficult one, which we shall examine much more fully in Chapter 17. However, for current purposes I should mention that according to one philosophical view of the nature of time, only those things which exist at the present moment—*now*—really exist at all; and the only qualities which these things really possess are the qualities that they possess now. According to this view—*presentism*, as it is often called—the only statements ascribing qualities to objects that can strictly be true are those that ascribe those qualities now to objects that exist now.[2] On this view, then, the only strictly true statements of the form 'a is F at t' are ones of the form 'a is F now'. That being so, the word 'now' in such a statement is really redundant and can be dropped without loss of informative content. This seems to solve the problem of qualitative change without more ado, for then it follows that it is simply never strictly true to say that one and the same object possesses mutually incompatible qualities at different times, since the only real time is the present.

Of course, this leaves advocates of presentism with the problem of how to make sense of our everyday talk about past and future times. But they may say, for instance, that talk of what is allegedly the case at past and future times can be construed as talk of what would be the case if a certain past or future time were present. There is a parallel between this proposed way of construing talk about past and future times and certain ways of construing talk about possibilities. As we shall see more fully in Chapter 7, talk about what is *possibly* the case is often interpreted, at least by many philosophers, as talk about what *is* the case 'in' or 'at' possible worlds that are different from this, the actual world. However, if we do not wish to be realists about other possible worlds—that is, do not wish to grant them the same ontological status as we grant to the actual world—we may seek to construe talk about what is the case 'in' another possible world as talk about what would be the case if that other world were actual. (Proponents of such a view are, naturally, called 'actualists'.) In this way, we may be able to license talk about other possible worlds but hold that, in reality, only the actual world exists. In a similar way, then, the presentist, by adopting the proposal suggested earlier, may be able to license talk about other times, past or future, while holding that, in reality, only the present time exists.

Three temporal realist solutions to the problem

Most modern philosophers of time, it must be said, are not in favour of presentism, so that the presentist's somewhat drastic 'solution' to the problem of qualitative change is not one that is likely to have a very wide appeal. To many, indeed, it may appear more like an evasion of the problem than a

[2] In modern times, the doctrine of presentism owes much to the work of A. N. Prior: see, for example, his *Papers on Time and Tense* (Oxford: Clarendon Press, 1968). For a recent application of the doctrine, see Trenton Merricks, 'On the Incompatibility of Enduring and Perduring Entities', *Mind* 104 (1995), 523–31.

solution to it—and, certainly, it seems to me to require a very considerable departure from common-sense ways of thinking. If we are realists about times other than the present moment, we must take seriously the reference to time that appears in a statement of the form 'a is F at t' and find some other solution to the problem of qualitative change. There are three realist solutions that we need to consider, each of which corresponds to a different way of analysing or parsing a statement of this form. The first solution builds the time referred to, t, into what is predicated of the object a, which is regarded as the genuine subject of the statement. On this view, then, what is predicated of, or ascribed to, the object a is not the simple quality of Fness, but rather the relational property of being F-at-t—so that the statement as a whole is more perspicuously expressed in the hyphenated form 'a is F-at-t'.

There is nothing strange about relational properties as such: they are properties which things possess in virtue of being related in various ways to other things. Thus, for example, the property of being a brother is a relational property, because someone has this property just in case he is the son of parents who have other children. However, it is natural (and perhaps even necessary) to assume that, in addition to relational properties, there are *non*-relational or *intrinsic* properties—and natural to assume that these are exemplified by qualities of colour and shape, such as yellowness and straightness. But the solution to the problem of qualitative change which is now under consideration holds, in effect, that it is an error to suppose that objects undergoing such change possess such intrinsic qualities: rather, they stand in certain relations to times, in virtue of which they possess such relational properties as that of being yellow-today or that of being straight-yesterday. On this view, qualitative change is possible because, for example, straightness-yesterday and bentness-today are compatible relational properties, even though straightness-now and bentness-now are incompatible.

However, the obvious objection to this proposal is that, rather than explaining how qualitative change is possible, it denies that such change ever really occurs, because it denies that the objects concerned possess the intrinsic qualities that such change is supposed to involve. Moreover, to the extent that the proposal threatens to deprive these objects of all intrinsic properties whatever, permitting them to possess only relational properties, it is of doubtful coherence. For an object can only possess relational properties if it can stand in various relations to other objects—and yet, it seems, unless both it and those other objects possess at least some intrinsic properties which serve to characterize them independently of their relations to anything else, it is hard to see how any of these objects could exist at all, and consequently hard to understand how there could be anything to stand in the relations in question. Of course, it might be suggested that changeable objects always possess *some* permanent characteristics, which could therefore consistently be regarded as intrinsic properties of them. But it seems that we have no a priori guarantee that this is so.

The second of the three temporal realist solutions to the problem of qualitative change analyses or parses a statement of the form '*a* is *F* at *t*' as follows. It builds the time referred to, *t*, into the subject of this statement, which is now regarded as being not the object *a* itself, but rather the *temporal part* of *a* that exists at time *t*, that is to say, *a*-at-*t*. Consequently, the whole statement is, on this view, more perspicuously expressed in the form '*a*-at-*t* is *F*'. Thus construed, the statement ascribes the intrinsic quality of *F*ness to a certain temporal part of *a*, rather than to *a* as a whole. And then it is easy to see why, for instance, it can be perfectly consistent to say that a piece of wire is bent now but was straight a moment ago, despite the mutual incompatibility of the qualities of straightness and bentness—because, according to the current proposal, these qualities are not in fact being ascribed to one and the same object, but to two numerically distinct objects, albeit ones which are both temporal parts of the same object.

But there are several questions which this supposed solution to the problem immediately provokes, some of which I can discuss now but some of which I shall have to postpone. The most pressing question, perhaps, is this: what exactly *is* a 'temporal part' of a persisting object, such as a piece of wire or a banana? It is not as though talk of such parts is a familiar feature of everyday language. However, since this is a very big issue, I shall discuss it later in this chapter, after we have looked at the third temporal realist solution to the problem of qualitative change. For the time being, then, let us just pretend that we understand what sort of thing a temporal part of a persisting object is supposed to be—perhaps by loose analogy with the *spatial* parts of extended objects, such as the top inch of an upright wooden pole.

One question which we should obviously ask about the temporal-parts solution to the problem of qualitative change is whether it really does solve the problem or whether, like the previous 'solutions', it effectively denies that qualitative change ever really occurs. Certainly, the temporal-parts solution respects our common-sense idea that properties of colour and shape are *intrinsic qualities* of the things that have them, rather than relational properties of a special sort, involving relations to times. But it implies that the things which have such intrinsic qualities are always the *temporal parts* of persisting objects, rather than the persisting objects themselves (except, perhaps, in the unlikely event of there being at least some persisting objects which never change in respect of their properties of colour and shape). And these temporal parts, it would seem, cannot *themselves* be supposed capable of undergoing qualitative change—for if we did suppose this, it is not clear how such entities could help us with the problem of qualitative change, since they would then be subject to exactly the same difficulty as besets the changeable, persisting objects of which they are supposedly parts. So it emerges that, according to the temporal-parts solution, nothing which really has intrinsic qualities, such as yellowness and straightness, ever *changes* in respect of its qualities. Is this not simply to deny, in effect, that qualitative change ever really occurs? Of course, the temporal-parts theorist can say that a persisting, 'changeable' object, such as a banana, can 'possess' intrinsic qualities, such as greenness and yellowness, in a derivative sense—that is, in the sense that such an object can have temporal parts which possess those intrinsic qualities. But what such a persisting object really possesses, when it 'possesses' such an intrinsic quality in this derivative sense, is in fact a certain sort of *relational* property—one which it has in virtue of standing in the whole-to-part relation to a certain thing which literally possesses the intrinsic quality in question. And the persisting object never *changes* in respect of its relational properties of this sort. So it never really changes at all. Indeed, nothing ever really changes: change is just an illusion. If this is a 'solution' to the problem of qualitative change, then it seems to be like the presentist's 'solution' in denying the existence of the very phenomenon whose possibility we seek to understand. I have no doubt that most temporal-parts theorists (and, likewise, most presentists) would object to this characterization of their position, but it is not at all clear to me what grounds they could have for doing so.

Let me then turn to the third temporal realist solution to the problem of qualitative change. According to this solution, when we analyse or parse a statement of the form 'a is F at t', the reference to the time, t, should be built *neither* into the subject of the statement *nor* into what is predicated of, or ascribed to, the object in question. That is to say, we should take the property ascribed to be the intrinsic quality of Fness, rather than the relational property of being F-at-t; and we should take the object to which this property is ascribed to be a itself, not the supposed temporal part of a

existing at *t*, *a*-at-*t*. But where else can the temporal reference go? The answer, quite simply, is that it can go into the predicative or ascriptive link itself, which is expressed in the original statement by the verb 'is'. So, according to this view, the most perspicuous way to express that statement is in the form '*a* is-at-*tF*'. From a logico-grammatical point of view, what this means is that the expression 'at *t*' has the status of a *predicate modifier*, or *adverb*.[3] It is understandable, perhaps, why such a solution should have been overlooked, at least by philosophers trained to think in terms of the categories of modern quantificational or predicate logic, as it is called. For such logic simply has no place for adverbs.

A clarification of the adverbial solution

However, it may still seem rather obscure what this third solution is really proposing, so some clarification is required at this point. The idea is that, at least in the case of objects which exist *in* time, a quality can only be ascribed to an object in some temporal mode, whether past, present, or future: and this is the primary function of the basic tenses of verbs in everyday language. The qualities of objects that exist in time are genuinely intrinsic properties of them, not relational properties which those objects have in virtue of their relations to certain times: but the *possessing* of a quality by such an object is itself a temporally relative affair and so involves, if you like, a relation to a time. Qualitative change then consists in the fact that, relative to different times, one and the same object possesses different qualities. If that sounds like a statement of the obvious, so much the better.

Some people object that this proposal is no different, really, from the first temporal realist solution that we examined, which turns qualities into relational properties. But I think that that is unfair: there is a very great difference between ascribing a non-relational property in a temporally relativized way and ascribing a temporally relational property in an abso-lute or unrelativized way. It may also be objected that the proposal does not so much solve the problem of qualitative change, in the sense of explaining how such change is possible, as simply assume that such change

[3] See further my 'The Problems of Intrinsic Change: Rejoinder to Lewis', *Analysis* 48 (1988), 72–7, or my *The Possibility of Metaphysics: Substance, Identity, and Time* (Oxford: Clarendon Press, 1998), 129 ff. See also Sally Haslanger, 'Endurance and Temporary Intrinsics', *Analysis* 49 (1989), 119–25.

does, and therefore can, occur. I accept that the proposal assumes that time itself, and existence in time, are of such a nature that possession of a quality by an object existing in time is a temporally relative affair. But, according to this approach, that is what we must assume if we are to suppose that qualitative change is possible. And the assumption appears to be a perfectly coherent one. Since we are strongly inclined to believe, as a fundamental article of common sense, that qualitative change is indeed possible, it follows that we ought to adopt that assumption, at least until someone can show us what is wrong with it. What I am suggesting, in fact, is that we ought to adapt our conception of time, if need be, to accommodate the possibility of qualitative change, so strong is our conviction that such change really occurs. We shouldn't assume that we have a sufficiently firm grasp of the nature of time that we should be prepared to deny the possibility of qualitative change rather than abandon any preconceptions we might have about the nature of time.

It may help us to comprehend the current proposal better if we contrast what it claims about the possession of qualities by objects which exist *in* time with what may be said about the possession of properties by *timeless* objects, if indeed there are such objects. Abstract objects, such as the objects of mathematics—numbers, sets, functions, and so forth—are commonly thought not to exist in time, nor indeed in space. That is why the language of mathematics is characteristically *tenseless*. We say 'Two plus three are five', not 'Two plus three *were* five' or 'Two plus three *will be* five': and in saying 'Two plus three *are* five', it is implausible to think that we mean 'Two plus three are *now* five'—that is, the 'are' is a tenseless 'are', not the 'are' of the present tense. For it seems plausible that five does not possess the property of being the sum of two and three *at* any time— neither at some time nor even at every time. Where mathematical objects and their properties are concerned, reference to time simply does not appear to enter into the picture. But modern logic was designed with the language of mathematics largely in mind, so it would not be surprising if the conception of predication, or property ascription, which it encourages is a fundamentally tenseless one. Philosophers trained in modern logic may accordingly feel that there is something either obscure or else superficial in the notion of irreducibly tensed predication. They may tend, even if not deliberately, to model the possession of properties by time-bound objects on the possession of properties by abstract, timeless objects. It is this tendency, perhaps, that motivates the first two temporal realist solutions to the problem of qualitative change, for in both cases property possession is treated as timeless and all reference to time is placed either in the nature of the properties or in the nature of the objects concerned.

Perdurance versus endurance

Theories of persistence over time are commonly divided into two species: *perdurance* theories and *endurance* theories.[4] A perdurance theorist holds that objects persist through time in virtue of possessing successive temporal parts, so that, on this view, only *part* of a persisting object, its current temporal part, is present at any one time during its existence. By contrast, an endurance theorist holds that an object persists through time in virtue of being *wholly present* at every time at which it exists. In effect, this just means that an endurance theorist denies that persisting objects have any temporal parts. Of the four theories that we have examined so far in connection with the problem of qualitative change, one is obviously a perdurance theory; the remaining three all qualify as endurance theories. Presentism automatically qualifies as an endurance theory: quite trivially, it holds that every object is wholly present at every time at which it exists, because, according to presentism, the only time at which anything at all exists is the present moment—*now*—and so every part of anything that exists exists now. But, clearly, the division between perdurance theories and endurance theories is somewhat unnatural, because 'endurance' theories differ so radically amongst themselves. Indeed, the division between perdurance theories and endurance theories is potentially misleading, inasmuch as it may tempt us to imagine that the most important issue concerning the persistence of objects over time is whether or not such objects have temporal parts. The prominence given to this question may suit the temporal-parts theorist, of course, but it may also distort philosophical debate by obscuring other important issues.

Temporal-parts theories are undeniably popular at present, which may seem a little puzzling in view of the strangeness of the notion of a temporal part of a persisting object. Some temporal-parts theorists tend to attribute this sense of strangeness to an ignorance on the part of ordinary folk about scientific conceptions of time and space-time. They suggest that in mathematical physics, especially since the advent of Einstein's theories of

---

[4] See again Lewis, *On the Plurality of Worlds*, 202. Lewis himself favours a perdurance theory, partly because he thinks that it provides the best solution to the problem of qualitative change.

relativity, time is treated as a dimension akin to and inseparable from the three dimensions of space, so that we should feel no more uncomfortable about the notion of temporal parts than we do about the notion of spatial parts. If an object is extended along any dimension, be it spatial or temporal, it must surely make sense to think of that object as having parts which take up less of that dimension than the object does as a whole. If only we can bring ourselves to think of persisting objects as four-dimensional entities, 'spread out', as it were, in four wholly different directions, then it would be only natural to think of them as having four-dimensional parts, extended in one 'direction' along the time axis. But, it is suggested, because we only ever perceive objects as they are at a moment of time and so only ever encounter in experience the momentary three-dimensional 'cross-sections' of objects, we get the false impression that the objects themselves are only three-dimensional, being extended solely in space.

I do not want to suggest that I have a great deal of sympathy for the foregoing 'explanation' of our supposedly mistaken conception of persisting objects and the strangeness that the notion of temporal parts has for us. The purported explanation itself rests on some very contentious assumptions about the nature of time, which do not receive as much support from physical science as temporal-parts theorists may be apt to suppose. However, these are matters which we must postpone for later discussion, in Part V of this book. In any case, it may be that temporal-parts theories need not be strongly committed to any particular theory of time—though they are apparently committed to temporal realism—and if so, that will make them more, rather than less, difficult to discredit. So let us see what sense, if any, we can make of the notion of temporal parts, without presuming too much about the nature of time, other than its reality.[5]

The notion of temporal parts

So far, the only real grip that we have been given on the notion of a temporal part of a persisting object is through the construction of a special

[5] David Lewis, one of the best-known advocates of temporal parts, says rather little about their nature: see, however, his second postscript to 'Survival and Identity', in his *Philosophical Papers*, vol. 1 (New York: Oxford University Press, 1983), 76–7. See also my *The Possibility of Metaphysics*, 98 ff. and 114 ff., where some of the criticisms that follow can be found in more detail.

way of referring to such an entity—an expression of the form 'a-at-t', where a is a persisting object and t is a time at which that object exists. It doesn't appear that expressions of this form ever really occur in ordinary language. It is true that we sometimes say things such as 'Tom at six years of age was a promising child'. But it doesn't seem that in making such a statement we are using the expression 'Tom at six years of age' to refer to a certain entity which existed when Tom was six years of age but not at any later time. In fact, it doesn't seem that, in such a statement, the words 'Tom at six years of age' constitute any sort of referring expression, or indeed any sort of semantic unit at all. Rather, the statement is just a stylistic variant of the statement 'At six years of age, Tom was a promising child', in which the only object referred to is *Tom*, and the words 'at six years of age' constitute an adverbial phrase modifying the predicate 'was a promising child'. The same sort of thing may be said of the words 'Tom as a child', as they appear in the statement 'Tom as a child was promising'.

It seems, then, that we cannot expect to get much help from ordinary language in trying to understand what sort of entities temporal parts of persisting objects might be. Ordinary language simply does not provide ready-made ways of referring to such entities. However, another strategy might be to exploit parallels with our everyday ways of talking about *events* and *processes*. For many philosophers consider that entities of these kinds quite obviously and unproblematically have temporal parts. Consider, for instance, an event or process of some duration, such as a certain perform-ance of a play. We happily say that such a performance has early, middle, and late *parts*. For instance, the performance of Scene 1 of Act 1 is an early part of the performance as a whole. However, we cannot unproblematically transfer this way of talking to persisting *objects*—things such as bananas, trees, and pieces of wire. For these things are not, or at least are not at all obviously, *processes* of any kind, even if certain processes are intimately associated with them. We may speak, for instance, of the *life* of a tree, or the *career* of a person, thinking of this as a process which the object in question undergoes over time—and a life or career may have its early, middle, and late parts. But the life of a tree is not identical with the tree of which it is the life: to suppose so would be to make a simple category mistake. Indeed, some opponents of temporal-parts theories contend that the theory rests on just such a category mistake—the mistake of treating persisting objects as if they were processes. A process has a *duration*—it 'goes on' for a certain period of time. But an object, although it 'endures' or 'lasts' for a certain period of time, does not 'go on' in the sense in which a process does. Of course, temporal-parts theorists may urge that this categorial distinction between objects and processes is a superficial and philosophically unjustifiable one, rooted in the idiosyncracies of everyday grammatical forms. But it is not at all obvious that this is so; and the burden of proof lies with the temporal-parts theorist to demonstrate that it is so, rather than with their opponents to demonstrate that it is not.

Another suggestion, which I have touched on already, is to try to model the notion of a temporal part of a persisting object on some already well-understood notion of a *spatial* part of a spatially extended object. The most uncontroversial examples of persisting objects are, of course, spatially extended—things such as bananas, trees, and pieces of wire—and thus would appear to possess, quite unproblematically, spatial parts. But we should be aware of a potential ambiguity implicit in talk of the 'spatial parts' of persisting objects. Recall the discussions of the previous chapter, where we were concerned with issues to do with the *composition* of objects. Things such as trees are composite objects, possessing other such objects as parts, thus giving rise to hierarchies of composition. Ultimately, we are led to suppose, all material objects are composed of subatomic particles. The trunk, branches, and roots of a tree are parts of which it is composed; and these parts are in turn composed of other objects. But the trunk, branches, and roots of a tree are, like the tree itself, spatially extended objects—so there is a clear sense in which such objects are *spatial parts* of the tree. But it seems most unlikely that the supposed temporal parts of persisting objects can fruitfully be modelled on their 'spatial parts' in *this* sense of the term. For, in this sense of the term, the 'spatial parts' of persisting objects—their *component* parts—are themselves just other persisting objects. And, clearly, there is not much prospect of modelling the supposed temporal parts of persisting objects on persisting objects themselves—not, at least, if we seek to do so with a view to gaining some insight into the nature of *persistence*.

There is, however, a second possible sense of the term 'spatial part' in which we might suppose persisting objects to possess such parts. We might think of such a part as an entity whose spatial boundaries are defined in relation to the object of which it is a part. Earlier I gave a putative example of an entity of this sort: the top inch of an upright wooden pole. This, it seems, is an object whose spatial boundaries are defined by the surface of the pole and a horizontal plane intersecting the pole one inch from its top. This object contains all the matter of the pole that is confined within these boundaries. That persisting objects really do have spatial parts of this kind is not incontestable, however. It is far from clear, on the basis of the description so far given, what the identity conditions of something like the top inch of a wooden pole are supposed to be. Are we to suppose, for instance, that if a cut were made through the pole one inch from its top, the object that we have designated 'the top inch of the pole' would become separated from the pole—and if so, would it then have ceased to be the top inch of the pole? If we answer 'Yes' to both questions, the implication is that the top inch of the pole is not *essentially* the top inch of the pole, but is something which could in principle be identified in a quite different way, without reference to the pole of which it is supposedly a part. In that case, however, it is not clear that we are dealing with something which is really any different from what we earlier called a *component* part of a persisting object. A key feature of an object's component parts is that they can exist, and be identified, independently of the whole object which they help to compose. Thus, a branch of a tree can be preserved while the rest of the tree is destroyed; indeed, perhaps it can even be grafted on to another, quite different tree. We do not need to know to which tree, if any, it belongs in order to identify the branch as the particular object that it is.

It emerges, then, that if we are to think of something like the top inch of the wooden pole as being a spatial part of it, but not merely in the sense in which a component part of the pole is such a part, we must take the spatially defined characteristics of that entity to be *essential* properties of it—that is, to be properties of it which *it* could not lack, because they help to determine its very identity. According to this conception, it makes no sense to talk of *separating* a spatial part of an object from the whole of which it is a part. Whether we must allow spatially extended persisting objects to have spatial parts in this sense is debatable. Certainly, even if such parts exist, they should not be thought of as entities which literally *compose* the whole of which they are parts. It might be better, indeed, not to call them 'parts' at all, but to describe them instead as spatial 'sections' or 'regions' of spatially extended objects. But whatever we call them, if we are indeed prepared to acknowledge their existence at all, we must accept that they are entities whose very identities are dependent upon the persisting objects to which they supposedly belong. This fact has important implications for any attempt to model the supposed temporal parts of persisting objects on their spatial parts thus conceived. For the temporal parts of persisting objects, thought of according to this model, will likewise have to be entities whose very identities are dependent upon those persisting objects. And this threatens to compromise their intended role in a theory of persistence, as I shall now try to explain.

A problem for perdurance theories

Clearly, a theory of persistence should explain what it is for a persisting object to persist through time—that is to say, what it is for one and the same object to exist continuously throughout a certain period of time, perhaps undergoing qualitative change as it does so. Theories of persistence which invoke temporal parts for this purpose—so-called perdurance theories—maintain, as noted earlier, that an object persists through time in virtue of possessing, or indeed consisting of, a succession of different temporal parts, each part existing at a different time in the life of the object. However, if temporal parts are thought of on the model of spatial parts which we have just been looking at, the different temporal parts of a persisting object cannot be identified independently of the persisting object of which they are supposedly parts. According to this model, if a persisting object, O, has a temporal part that exists at a certain time t, then that temporal part is an entity which can only be identified in terms of its relations to O and t. Hence, on pain of circularity, it can only be identified if O itself can be identified independently of that temporal part—and the same applies to all the rest of O's supposed temporal parts. But now we can see that this presents a serious problem for any perdurance theory of O's persistence. For if the only way in which we can identify the different temporal parts of O is in terms of their being the temporal parts that one and the same object, O, possesses at various different times, this presupposes that we already grasp what it is for that very object, O, to exist at different times and hence to persist through time. A perdurance theory cannot, it seems, convey to us, in non-circular terms, what it is for O to persist through time, because the successively existing entities which it invokes for this purpose—O's supposed temporal parts—are entities which we are only able to conceive of in terms of their relations to O, itself already conceived of as something persisting through time. Nor can it make sense to suppose that O literally *consists* of a succession of temporal parts thus conceived—any more than it makes sense to think of a persisting object as being *composed* of its spatial parts, in the sense of 'spatial part' currently being entertained.

Temporal parts as theoretical entities

These considerations may persuade us that a perdurance theorist would be ill-advised to adopt the foregoing model of temporal parts. Temporal parts will have to be thought of as entities which are ontologically more fundamental than the persisting objects to which they supposedly belong. The problem is that we have not, so far, managed to find a way of thinking of them that seems to meet this requirement. But perhaps the temporal-parts theorist could urge that we are putting the cart before the horse. Maybe we shouldn't even attempt to understand what temporal parts might be independently of the theoretical framework which invokes them. Perhaps we should regard them as *theoretical entities*, by analogy with the theoretical entities invoked by explanatory scientific hypotheses—entities such as electrons and genes—belief in the existence of which is justified by the explanatory success or utility of the theories which postulate them. The temporal-parts theorist may urge that perdurance theories solve so many metaphysical problems, so economically, that we are justified in believing in the existence of temporal parts—and that all we need to understand about their nature is that they possess the characteristics which perdurance theories require them to possess in order to serve the explanatory purposes for which they are invoked. In order to assess this line of argument, we first need to evaluate the alleged explanatory successes of perdurance theory.

It is generally considered a virtue in an explanatory scientific theory if it manages to unify, within a single explanatory structure, phenomena which were previously thought to be quite independent. Thus, one of the notable successes of Newton's theory of gravitation was that it provided a unifying framework of explanation for both celestial mechanics (which deals with planetary and lunar motions) and terrestrial mechanics (which deals with the motions of projectiles near the surface of the earth). In a similar way, it may be urged on behalf of perdurance theories that they provide a unitary framework of explanation for both qualitative change and change of composition—the two kinds of change discussed in this and the preceding chapter. We have already seen, in this chapter, how perdurance theories deal with the problem of qualitative change—and, although I have questioned how successful they really are in this respect, it must be acknowledged that they are widely thought to offer the best solution to this problem. To this we may now add that temporal-parts theories offer seemingly simple and economical solutions to the problems of fission and fusion described in the previous chapter. For example, in the case of the ship of Theseus, the temporal-parts theorist can maintain that the renovated ship and the reconstructed ship, although different persisting objects, share their earlier temporal parts with each other. That is to say, each of these ships consists of a different succession of temporal parts, but not of *wholly distinct* successions, for the two successions overlap in their earlier stages, until the process of renovation and removal begins. In a way, this is to say that, prior to the beginning of that process, the two ships exactly coincide with one another in the harbour at Athens. But, it may be said, there is nothing mysterious or objectionable about the notion of such coincidence, because we never have two different *temporal parts* of a ship in the same place at the same time: in the earlier stages of their existence, the two ships have exactly the same—that is to say, numerically identical—temporal parts.

How does this answer the question as to which ship—the renovated ship or the reconstructed ship—is identical with the original ship of Theseus? The answer provided is that, in fact, there was no such thing as *the* ship of Theseus, because there never was *just one ship* in the harbour at Athens, even though there was, at every time until the process of renovation began, just one *temporal part* of ship there. In the previous chapter, a similar solution was briefly entertained, but without appeal being made to the theory of temporal parts. The question is, then, whether the temporal-parts version of this solution escapes the objections raised against the original version. My own feeling is that it does not. In particular, there is the important objection that, according to this solution, unless we know the future course of events, we cannot tell how many ships we may be confronted with in a single place at any given moment of time. If it should turn out that one or more processes of fission are due to occur, then we are confronted with two or more ships in the same place at the same time, prior to the occurrence of those processes. But how can the number of ships existing here and now depend upon what may or may not happen in the future—unless, perhaps, determinism is true and there is, whether we now know it or not, only one possible course of future events consistent with present facts and the laws of nature? The fact that, according to the temporal-parts theorist, there need never be more than one *temporal part* of a ship in the same place at the same time, while a commendable consequence of the theory, does nothing, as I see it, to mitigate the difficulty just raised.

I should not give the impression that temporal-parts theorists are obliged to offer the foregoing solution to the problem of the ship of Theseus. They could urge, instead, that this case is one in which either one or both of the fission products is a newly created persisting object—for instance, that the renovated ship is identical with the original ship, but that the reconstructed ship is a new ship coming into existence for the first time when the original parts are put together again in the warehouse. This was my own solution, of course. However, it may be wondered what could really motivate this solution when advanced in the context of a temporal-parts theory. I was able to advance it by appealing to the common-sense principle that distinct ships cannot overlap to any significant degree. But, as we have just seen, there is nothing in temporal-parts theory to support that principle, since the theory can quite consistently allow that distinct ships may share some of their temporal parts. So, altogether, it is not perhaps so clear as some temporal-parts theorists would like us to think that their approach provides the simplest and most economical solutions to problems of fission and fusion.

Another range of problems for which temporal-parts theorists may claim to have the best solutions are problems involving vagueness, such as the paradox of the thousand and one cats discussed in the previous chapter. But here, too, the superiority of their approach is not incontestable. And even if we accept that temporal-parts theories provide a unitary explanatory framework in which problems of qualitative change, fission, and vagueness can conveniently be dealt with, we have to wonder whether this is enough to justify our acceptance of an idea so apparently obscure and contrary to common sense as that of temporal parts. Metaphysics is quite a different enterprise from the construction of explanatory scientific theories, as we saw in Chapter 1. When a scientific theory postulates a new species of theoretical entity, it is a prerequisite of the intelligibility of the theory that the entities in question be introduced to us as belonging to some intelligible ontological category. Ontological categories themselves cannot be regarded as theoretical posits, our grasp of which can be seen to derive from our grasp of the theories in which they are embedded—for we can have no real grasp of those theories without first understanding the categories in question. But the notion of a temporal part of a persisting object is precisely the notion of a putative ontological category—one of a supposedly very fundamental kind. Thus, it is after all illegitimate, I think, to assimilate the perdurance theorist's invocation of temporal parts to the physicist's postulation of a new species of subatomic particle. Perdurance theorists owe us an explicit and perspicuous account of the nature of temporal parts. So far, it may well seem, they have failed to provide one.

What should we say about persistence, if we reject the perdurance approach to it? Clearly, several alternatives are possible which may be described, however misleadingly, as 'endurance' approaches. What such views have in common is the conviction that the notion of something's persisting through time is ultimately primitive and irreducible. This is not to deny that particular cases of persistence may have *causal* explanations, as when we explain why the members of one species of animal or plant are longer-lived than those of another. It is just to say that the fact of persistence through time as such—one and the same thing's being continuously in existence for a period of time—is not something that is reducible to any fact or set of facts of a kind which does not involve persistence. That this should be so is certainly conceivable, even if we may not yet be convinced that it must be so.[6]

[6] There is a very extensive literature on each side of the debate between perdurance and endurance approaches to the nature of persistence. For a classic statement of the perdurance position, see W. V. Quine, 'Identity, Ostension, and Hypostasis', in his *From a Logical Point of View*, 2nd edn. (Cambridge, Mass.: Harvard University Press, 1961). For a more recent defence, see Mark Heller, *The Ontology of Physical Objects: Four-Dimensional Hunks of Matter* (Cambridge: Cambridge University Press, 1990). For a recent defence of an endurance approach, see Trenton Merricks, 'Endurance and Indiscernibility', *Journal of Philosophy* 91 (1994), 165–84.

4

SUBSTANTIAL CHANGE AND SPATIOTEMPORAL COINCIDENCE

Beginning and ceasing to exist

In the previous two chapters, we have looked at two different kinds of change that persisting objects can undergo: change of composition and qualitative change. The first sort of change occurs when a composite object undergoes a change of its component parts. The second sort occurs when one and the same object has numerically different qualities at numerically different times. Of course, these two kinds of change are not entirely independent of one another. Sometimes, a change of the one kind brings about a change of the other kind. For example, if a composite object acquires new parts possessing qualities that are different from those of its old parts, the composite object itself may undergo a change of its qualities—as when a house changes in colour because new bricks of a different colour are used to replace its old bricks. But a composite object can also undergo qualitative change without undergoing any change of composition—for instance, when its component parts are simply rearranged, with the result that the shape of the composite object as a whole changes. But there is also a third kind of change that we need to consider, which is traditionally called *substantial change*. This is the kind of change which occurs when a persisting object either begins or ceases to exist. It is thus not exactly a kind of change which happens *in* or *to* an object, in the way that qualitative and compositional changes are, but rather it is a change *of* objects—a change with respect to what objects there are in the world. This is called 'substantial change' because persisting objects—things such as houses, apples, and planks of wood—are traditionally called 'individual substances', or 'substantial individuals'. Of course, this was a kind of change which I did discuss to some extent in

Chapter 2, but in the present chapter it will be the main focus of our attention.

Most of the substantial individuals that we are familiar with—indeed, perhaps all of them—are composite objects. It is natural to assume that there must exist *some* non-composite substantial individuals, because it is natural to assume that hierarchies of composition cannot be infinitely descending: that is to say, it is natural to assume that although an object's component parts may themselves be composite objects, and the parts of these parts may again be composite, there must eventually be an end to such a series of whole–part relations, the terminus being provided by objects which are by their very nature simple or non-composite. The 'atoms' of the ancient Greek philosopher Democritus played precisely this role in his ontology—'atom' meaning, originally, that which cannot be cut or divided into any lesser parts. In modern physics, the so-called 'elementary particles', such as electrons and quarks, play a similar role—though in many other ways they are quite unlike Democritean atoms, since they are not conceived of as being perfectly hard and rigid bodies with precise geometrical shapes. Whether it is really metaphysically impossible for hierarchies of composition to be infinitely descending is a difficult question, which I shall not attempt to answer here. Perhaps the most that we can safely say is that empirical evidence currently suggests that all material objects do in fact have ultimate component parts of a simple or non-composite nature. However, since no macroscopic material object is non-composite as far as we know and macroscopic objects will be our main concern in this chapter, we can effectively confine our attention in what follows to composite objects.

One way for a substantial individual to come into existence is for certain other objects to be united together so as to form its component parts. This is what happens when a house is built from bricks or a ship is constructed from planks and spars. Another way, however, is for certain objects, which are already united together to form a composite whole, to be rearranged in such a way that a composite whole of a new kind comes into existence. This is what happens when a mass of bronze is moulded into the form of a statue: a statue, we say, is *created* out of the bronze. Perhaps this is also what happens when a living organism, such as a plant or animal, is created out of a mass of organic matter. Substantial change of this kind raises some difficult metaphysical problems, however. Consider the case of the bronze and the statue. We seem compelled to say that the mass or lump of bronze is a numerically distinct object from the statue, because the lump and the statue will ordinarily have come into existence at different times—the lump first and later the statue. Moreover, the lump and the statue plausibly have different *persistence conditions*—that is to say, there are different kinds of changes that can and cannot be survived by the lump and the statue respectively. For example, the lump can survive a change in which it is flattened into the shape of a disc, but the statue cannot survive such a change. Conversely, the statue can survive the loss or replacement of some of the bronze particles that compose it, but the lump of bronze cannot: removing or replacing some of the bronze particles leaves us with a numerically distinct lump of bronze. However, if the lump and the statue are numerically distinct substantial individuals, then they are individuals bearing a seemingly strange relationship to one another—for during at least part of their existences they exactly coincide with one another, occupying precisely the same place at the same time. Moreover, while this is the case, exactly the same bronze particles compose these two numerically distinct individuals, the lump and the bronze—and we may wonder how this is possible.

Can there be coinciding objects?

Many philosophers think that it is fundamentally absurd to suppose that the lump and the statue are two numerically distinct objects which exactly coincide with one another for a period of time and are composed of exactly the same particles. They complain that they cannot understand what would *make* these objects distinct at such a time.[1] How could either object have any property which the other object lacked? Of course, it may be replied that the objects could have different *historical* and *modal* properties—where an historical property of an object is one which it has in respect of what *has* happened to it in the past and a modal property of an object is one which it has in respect of what *could* happen to it. We have already said, for instance, that the lump and the statue may have come into existence at different times and that there are different kinds of change that they can and cannot survive. However, it may be wondered how two objects which are, at a certain moment in time, exactly alike in their non-historical and non-modal properties could, none the less, differ in respect

---

[1] See, for example, Michael B. Burke, 'Copper Statues and Pieces of Copper', *Analysis* 52 (1992), 12–17, and Eric T. Olson, 'Material Coincidence and the Indiscernibility Problem', *Philosophical Quarterly* 51 (2001), 337–55.

of their historical and modal properties. And the lump and the statue do appear to be exactly alike in their non-historical and non-modal properties when they exactly coincide with one another. That being so, if this implies that they cannot, after all, differ from one another in their historical and modal properties, then the principle of the *identity of indiscernibles*—if we are prepared to accept it—would apparently compel us to judge that they are in fact one and the same object, not two numerically distinct objects. (Note that the principle of the identity of indiscernibles, which maintains that no two objects can possess exactly the same properties, should not be confused with what is commonly known as 'Leibniz's Law'—the principle that whatever is true of a thing is true of anything identical with that thing: see Chapter 3. Confusion is sometimes encouraged by the fact that Leibniz himself endorsed both principles and made them famous; but it is generally agreed that Leibniz's Law is the less contentious of the two principles.)

Relative versus absolute identity

Faced with this apparent conundrum, philosophers have responded in a number of different ways, most if not all of which seem to require some departure from everyday ways of thinking. One possibility is to question certain standard assumptions about the nature of identity itself. Identity is normally thought of as being an *absolute* relation, in the following sense. Let 'F' and 'G' be certain *sortal* terms, that is to say, general terms denoting certain sorts or kinds of substantial individual. Examples would be the terms 'tree', 'planet', 'tiger', and, indeed, 'statue' and 'lump of bronze'. Then it is standardly assumed that if a and b are numerically the same F and are also both Gs, then a and b are also numerically the same G. Indeed, it is easy to see that Leibniz's Law implies this, if we take the law to assert, in effect, that if, for some sortal term 'X', a is the same X as b, then whatever is true of a is also true of b. For then it follows that if a and b are the same F, then whatever is true of a is also true of b; but if a is a G, then it is surely true of a that it is the same G as a, whence it is also true of b that it is the same G as a.[2] But perhaps this standard assumption—and with it the standard version of Leibniz's Law—should be questioned. Perhaps it makes sense, after all, to suppose that a and b may be the same F and yet not the same G. This is what a proponent of a *relative* conception of

---

[2] See further David Wiggins, *Sameness and Substance* (Oxford: Blackwell, 1980), 19–20.

identity maintains.[3] According to this view, we cannot say of certain individuals *a* and *b* that they are, or are not, identical *simpliciter*—that is, without further qualification. They may be identical relative to one sortal characterization of them, but distinct relative to another.

How might this help us with the case of the statue and the lump of bronze? Simply as follows. We felt pressed to say, on the one hand, that the statue and the lump are two numerically distinct objects, because they differ in their historical and modal properties. On the other hand, at least while the statue and the lump exactly coincide with one another, we feel pressed to say that they cannot, after all, be two numerically distinct objects. The relative identity theorist may, however, diagnose our difficulties as arising from a misconception that identity and distinctness are absolute relations, when in fact they are sortally relative. According to the relativist, we cannot intelligibly speak of the statue and the lump being, or failing to be, numerically identical *objects*, because this is to attempt to speak of identity and distinctness without relativizing them to appropriate sortal characterizations of the objects that we are referring to. Perhaps what we should say—and what, according to the relativist, we can consistently say—is that the statue and the lump of bronze are one and the same *lump of bronze*, but *not* one and the same *statue*.

In order to make this proposal a little more intuitively appealing, consider what we might say if the lump of bronze were to be melted down again and formed into a *different* statue (perhaps the first statue was a statue of Napoleon and the second a statue of Wellington). According to the relativist, we might say of the first and second statues that they are different *statues* but the same *lump of bronze*. But then, it seems, if the lump of bronze is a statue at the time at which the first statue exists, it is not the *same* statue as the first statue. For, if it were, then, by the same token, the lump of bronze would have to be the same statue as the second statue when that exists. But if the first statue were the same statue as the lump of bronze and the lump of bronze were also the same statue as the second statue, then it seems that the transitivity of identity implies that the first statue would be the same statue as the second statue—which, we have agreed, it is not. So we must conclude that the first statue and the lump of bronze are not one and the same *statue*, even if they are one and the same *lump of bronze*. The attraction of this account is that it explains

---

[3] The best-known proponent is Peter Geach: see his *Reference and Generality*, 3rd edn. (Ithaca, NY: Cornell University Press, 1980), 181.

why we are pulled in two different directions concerning the statue and the lump of bronze, wanting to say both that they are distinct and that they are identical. Moreover, it even reconciles, in a way, the two judgements that we feel inclined to make, so that we are not compelled to surrender either in favour of the other: we can retain both judgements, provided that we qualify each in the way that the relativist recommends.

I have tried to represent the relativist solution to our problem in as favourable a light as possible, but it is not without difficulties of its own. For one thing, in abandoning the standard version of Leibniz's Law, it abandons what many philosophers and logicians would see as the most fundamental principle of identity, without which we effectively lose all real grip on the notion of identity. The 'relativized identity relations' of the relativist, it may be objected, are not really relations of *identity* at all, but something else—relations of similarity, perhaps. Another problem is that questions of identity are intimately bound up with questions of *existence*, so that if one wants to relativize identity to sortal characterizations, one must be prepared to relativize existence to sortal characterizations also. This seems to have very strange implications.[4] Suppose that the (first) statue is destroyed by melting down the bronze, but the bronze remains intact and so continues to exist. Now, according to the relativist, the statue is the same *lump of bronze* as the lump of bronze—and, as we have just said, the lump of bronze continues to exist. So, even after the process of melting has occurred, there still exists something which is the same thing of *some* sort as the statue, according to the relativist. This seems to imply that the statue *does* still exist, albeit only 'as' the lump of bronze rather than 'as' the statue. But it would also seem that the relativist is not entitled to any 'absolute' or 'unrelativized' conception of existence. So the relativist must judge that is wrong to say that the statue ceases to exist *simpliciter* when it is melted down—it only ceases to exist 'as' a statue. Perhaps this is not an absurd thing to say, but it certainly seems to require a very big departure from common-sense ways of thinking about existence and substantial change. We may have to give up saying, for instance, that a piece of paper is simply *destroyed* when it is burnt to ashes, or even that a human being simply ceases to exist upon undergoing a fatal accident.

---

[4] See further my *Kinds of Being: A Study of Individuation, Identity and the Logic of Sortal Terms* (Oxford: Blackwell, 1989), 56 ff.

Temporal parts and coinciding objects

Suppose we decide that the absolute conception of identity is too fundamental to be given up. How else might we handle the case of the statue and the lump of bronze? Temporal-parts theories, of the sort we discussed in the previous chapter, provide what may seem to be an attractive solution to our problem. The temporal-parts theorist can say that, so long as the statue and the lump of bronze exactly coincide, they have exactly the same temporal parts, even though they may have different temporal parts before or after that period. This allows us to say that, considered as 'four-dimensional' wholes, the statue and the lump of bronze are indeed numerically distinct objects—and yet that, at any given time during their coincidence, just *one* temporal part of an object exists in the place they occupy, because the temporal part of the statue which exists at that time is numerically identical with the temporal part of the lump of bronze which exists at that time. This account, like the relativist one, both explains and to some extent justifies our inclination to say that the statue and the lump of bronze both are and are not identical with one another during the time of coincidence. As temporally extended wholes they are not identical, but they are 'partly' identical during the period of coincidence, inasmuch as they have exactly the same temporal parts during that time.

Naturally, this solution will only appeal to those who do not consider temporal-parts theories subject to insuperable objections. But even for someone who accepts a theory of temporal parts, coinciding objects can still present a problem. Consider a case in which a bronze statue is made from bronze which only comes together into a lump at the time when the statue is formed and which is dispersed or destroyed when the statue itself is destroyed. In that case, the statue and the lump of bronze coincide throughout their entire existence, so that, according to the temporal-parts theory, they have exactly the same temporal parts at all times and consequently are one and the same 'four-dimensional' whole. The trouble now is that we still want to say that there are changes which the statue could have survived but which the lump of bronze could not have survived and vice versa—in short, that they have different *modal* properties. But this difference in their properties is enough, by Leibniz's Law, to imply that the statue and the lump of bronze are numerically distinct objects, even granting that they possess the same non-modal properties throughout their respective existences and consequently do not differ in respect of any of their historical properties.

One possible response that the temporal-parts theorist can give to this apparent difficulty is to say that, when we ascribe a modal property to an object, our ascription must be in a certain sense *relativized* to some appropriate sortal characterization of the object—and that one and the same object may possess a certain modal property relative to one sortal characterization of that object and yet lack it relative to another such characterization.[5] We shall have to say, for instance, that 'as' a *lump of bronze* a certain 'four-dimensional' whole could survive flattening, but that 'as' a *statue* it could not. This suggestion is, of course, reminiscent of what the relative identity theorist was envisaged as saying about the existence of objects—the difference being that, whereas the temporal-parts theorist need only relativize judgements of what changes an object *could* survive to how that object is characterized sortally, the relative identity theorist has to relativize judgements of what changes an object actually *does* survive to how that object is characterized sortally. One may well wonder, however, whether, if one is going to have to admit such relativization in any case, it is not preferable to adopt the relative identity theorist's position, since that does not require us to include in our ontology such seemingly strange and obscure entities as the supposed temporal parts of persisting objects. It is true that the temporal-parts theory allows us to retain the standard, absolutist notion of identity and the standard version of Leibniz's Law, but perhaps a commitment to the existence of temporal parts is too heavy a price to pay for this advantage.

Some radical solutions to the problem of coincidence

Can we solve the problem of the statue and the lump of bronze without either relativizing identity or adopting the doctrine of temporal parts? In particular, can we do so without having to say that two numerically distinct persisting objects can exist in exactly the same place at the same time? Yes, we can, but only if we are prepared to give up some other

---

[5] See, for instance, Harold W. Noonan, 'Indeterminate Identity, Contingent Identity and Abelardian Predicates', *Philosophical Quarterly* 41 (1991), 183–93, and 'Constitution is Identity', *Mind* 102 (1993), 133–46.

common-sense assumptions. For instance, we could deny that there are really any such things as 'statues', conceived as constituting a distinctive kind of persisting object. We could hold instead that, although a lump of bronze may become 'statue-shaped' for a certain period of time, this does not amount to the creation of any new substantial individual distinct from the lump itself. Alternatively, we could deny that there are really any such things as 'lumps of bronze', holding instead that, although a number of bronze particles may become united together for a certain period of time, this does not ordinarily amount to the creation of any new substantial individual in addition to the many bronze particles themselves—but that when an intelligent agent deliberately imposes a specific form upon the particles, they then begin to compose a new substantial particular, such as a statue. If we adopt either of these positions, we may have to admit that a plurality of different objects (the bronze particles) can together occupy exactly the same place as some *one* object of a certain sort—either a lump of bronze or a statue, as the case may be. But this is obviously quite different from saying that some one object of a certain sort can exactly coincide with some one object of another sort.

However, if we are prepared to entertain either of these positions, it is not clear why we should not be prepared to combine them, denying the existence of *both* statues *and* lumps of bronze and accepting only the existence of bronze particles. But it is easy to see where this train of thought is likely to lead, namely, to the view that, in reality, the only persisting objects that exist are simple or non-composite ones, the most likely candidates being the so-called elementary particles of physics. The implication would be that none of the assumed objects of common-sense ways of thinking really exist, including not only artefacts, plants, and animals, but even we human beings ourselves (on the assumption that if we are anything, we are composite beings). Perhaps a case can be made out for saying that living organisms are special in some way and so really do exist, despite being composite objects.[6] But that will certainly not be easy. It seems, then, that the position we are now contemplating is potentially a paradoxical one, in which we have to deny even our own existence in favour of the existence of certain theoretical entities—the elementary particles of modern physics—whose status as 'persisting objects' is in any case

---

[6] See, for example, Peter van Inwagen, *Material Beings* (Ithaca, NY: Cornell University Press, 1990), 81 ff. For a sustained argument in favour of the view that *conscious* beings, including ourselves, are the only composite macroscopic objects, see Trenton Merricks, *Objects and Persons* (Oxford: Clarendon Press, 2001).

questionable, in view of the notorious 'wave–particle duality' of quantum-mechanical phenomena. The danger is that we shall have to end up concluding that there are no persisting objects in the world at all.

Is there any way in which we can, without adopting either the theory of relative identity or the doctrine of temporal parts, acknowledge the real existence of macroscopic composite objects such as statues and lumps of bronze and still deny that two numerically distinct objects can exactly coincide? The answer is that yes, we can, provided that we are prepared to abandon yet another feature of common-sense ways of thinking about objects and their persistence. What we could say in the case of the statue and the lump of bronze is that when the lump of bronze is formed into the statue, bringing the latter into existence, the lump of bronze itself ceases to exist. We may still want to say that *a* lump of bronze exists after the statue has been created, but it is open to us to deny that this lump of bronze is identical with the lump of bronze from which the statue was formed. We can say instead that this new lump of bronze is simply identical with the statue itself and thus came into existence when the statue did.[7] There is nothing logically inconsistent about this combination of judgements. But it can hardly be said to respect our common-sense ways of thinking about the persistence of objects. For its implication is that merely by imposing a certain shape upon a lump of bronze—the kind of shape that is necessary to form it into a statue of a certain sort—we bring it about that that lump of bronze ceases to exist. Why should that be so? How *could* a lump of bronze cease to exist merely for this reason? Our common-sense notion of a lump of bronze is precisely the notion of something which *can* undergo any manner of change in its overall shape, provided that it continues to be composed of the same bronze particles united together into a mass. I conclude that there is very little prospect for an acceptable solution to our problem along these lines.

In defence of coinciding objects

Having considered every other alternative that seems even remotely plausible, let us now consider again the view that the statue and the lump of bronze are numerically distinct persisting objects which exactly coincide

---

[7] See, for example, Michael B. Burke, 'Preserving the Principle of One Object to a Place: A Novel Account of the Relations among Objects, Sorts, Sortals, and Persistence Conditions', *Philosophy and Phenomenological Research* 54 (1994), 591–624.

with one another for a certain period of time. As I have already indicated, an apparent difficulty with this view is that the statue and the lump of bronze seem to be *indistinguishable* from one another at such a time: we cannot tell them apart by the minutest scrutiny, or so it seems. However, much depends on what precisely is understood by 'indistinguishability' in this context. It certainly seems to be true that the statue and the lump of bronze are *empirically* indistinguishable during the period of their coincidence, at least in the sense that during that time they do not differ from one another in respect of any *perceptible* property—say, of shape, colour, or weight. But persisting objects may—and, in fact, must—possess many other properties in addition to their perceptible ones, if by a 'perceptible property' one means a property whose possession by an object at a time can in principle be discovered by observation of that object at that time. We have already mentioned certain kinds of property which are clearly not perceptible in this sense—the historical and modal properties of objects. Of course, many of the historical properties of objects can be detected empirically, although not simply by observing the objects at the time at which they possess them. A man may possess the historical property of having had a beard ten years ago, but no observation of him now can be expected to reveal this fact about him. As for modal properties, consider such so-called dispositional properties as elasticity and solubility. Elasticity is a modal property, because it is the property an object has of being *able* to return to its original shape upon being stretched. An empirical test can certainly reveal whether or not an object has this property: one can simply attempt to stretch the object and see whether it returns to its original shape. But such a test takes time to perform, so it does not provide an empirical means of detecting, at a certain time, that an object is elastic *at that time*. This is why elasticity is not, strictly speaking, a perceptible property of an object, in the sense I have just defined. By contrast, we can very often detect an object's colour or shape at a certain time simply by observing at it at that time, which is why colour and shape are, in this sense, perceptible properties. These considerations suggest that although it may be the case that the statue and the lump of bronze are empirically indistinguishable during the time of their coincidence, this still leaves scope for them to possess different properties from one another during that time and hence to be 'distinguishable' in a broader sense. However, it remains to be seen whether, and if so how, this possibility can be exploited by the advocate of spatiotemporal coincidence.

Earlier, I suggested that some philosophers find it difficult to understand how two numerically distinct objects could be exactly alike in respect of their non-historical and non-modal properties at a certain time and yet differ from one another in respect of their historical and modal properties—particularly if, as is supposedly the case with the statue and the lump of bronze, the two objects in question are composed of exactly the same material particles. Now, it is certainly true that the statue and the lump of bronze cannot be expected to differ from one another in respect of their physical dispositional properties during the time of coincidence. If the bronze is electrically conductive and soluble in sulphuric acid, so too will be the statue. This is because such dispositional properties are grounded in, or 'supervene upon', the properties and relations of the material particles composing the statue and the lump of bronze. However, not all modal properties are like such dispositional properties in this respect. Some of an object's modal properties arise not from its material constitution but from its *persistence conditions*, which determine what sorts of changes the object can and cannot survive—and this is a matter of what *kind* of object the object is. A statue, for instance, is a kind of object which, unlike a lump of bronze, cannot survive much change to its shape. Conversely, a lump of bronze is a kind of object which, unlike a statue, cannot survive any change to its material composition.

These modal properties of the objects in question are evidently not to be explained by reference to the properties and relations of the material particles which compose statues and lumps of bronze respectively. Such modal properties are not really empirical properties at all, but rather a priori ones that are grounded in categorial distinctions of a metaphysical nature. It is an a priori truth that what is required for a lump of bronze to persist over time is for certain bronze particles to be united together for a period of time, without any of them being separated from the rest or being replaced by any new particles. Equally, it is an a priori truth that what is required for a statue to persist over time is for sufficiently many material particles—but not necessarily the *same* material particles—to be united together for a period of time while constantly exhibiting a certain overall shape. The concepts of a lump of bronze and of a statue are precisely the concepts of persisting objects of kinds governed by the foregoing persistence conditions. The consequence is that one cannot in principle tell, simply by examining an object empirically at a certain moment of time, that it is a statue or a lump of bronze. For whether or not something qualifies as an object of one of these kinds at a certain moment of time is partly a matter of what is the case at earlier and later moments of time. If, by chance, a large number of bronze particles were to come together for just a moment in the shape of a statue, immediately to be dispersed again a moment later, that would not imply that either a lump of bronze or a bronze statue had existed for that moment—for no persisting object composed of those particles would have been created. In this respect, the properties of being a lump of bronze and being a statue are similar, it seems, to the property of being in motion. Whether or not an object is in motion at a certain moment of time cannot be established simply by an empirical examination of the object at that time, because it is partly a matter of what is the case at earlier and later moments of time—namely, whether the object is in a different position at earlier and later moments of time. (Or so it seems: but we shall see in Chapter 16 that the metaphysics of motion is a controversial topic.)

We now have to hand the materials with which to answer the objections that have been raised against the notion of the spatiotemporal coincidence of persisting objects, such as the statue and the lump of bronze. It is true that, at any given moment of their coincidence, the statue and the lump of bronze do not differ in respect of any property whose possession by them is determined solely by what is the case at that moment of time, without any reference to what is the case at earlier or later moments of time. This is why the statue and the lump of bronze are indistinguishable in respect of their perceptible properties at any moment of their coincidence. It is also true that the statue and the lump of bronze do not differ, at any moment of their coincidence, in respect of any of their *physical* dispositional properties—understanding these to be dispositional properties that are grounded in the properties and relations of the material particles composing them. However, it can still be true that the statue and the lump of bronze differ, at any moment of their coincidence, in respect of many of their modal and historical properties: for their possession of these properties is not determined solely by what is the case at the times at which they possess them, nor are these properties grounded in the properties and relations of the material particles composing the statue and the lump of bronze.

Here it is important to appreciate that modal and historical properties, quite generally, are only ascribable to objects in virtue of the fact that certain appropriate persistence conditions are assignable to those objects. Clearly, we cannot properly say of a certain presently existing object that something befell *it* in the past, or that *it* would behave in such-and-such a way in the future if it were to be acted on in a certain fashion, unless we can say, in principle, what is required for *that very object* to exist both now and in the past, or both now and in the (actual or possible) future. One consequence of this is that the statue and the lump of bronze can in fact differ from one another, during the time of their coincidence, even in respect of certain of their *dispositional* properties—the implication being that not *all* of their dispositional properties are simply grounded in the properties and relations of the material particles which compose them. For example, we may say of the statue that it is disposed to cast a shadow of a certain shape, implying that if it were to be set on the ground and exposed to sunlight, a shadow of that shape would be cast on the ground at its foot. But we cannot say of the lump of bronze, without qualification, that it is disposed to cast a shadow of any particular shape. For, whereas the statue, so long as it exists, must retain a certain constant shape, this is not true of the lump of bronze—these facts being consequences of the respective persistence conditions of the statue and the lump of bronze.

I have taken considerable pains to defend the view that two numerically distinct persisting objects can coincide, because, although it may superficially seem peculiar, any alternative view seems to have still more peculiar consequences. Perhaps the view seems peculiar, in part, because it is confused with another, much less easily defensible view—namely, that two numerically distinct persisting objects *of exactly the same kind* can coincide. The idea that two *statues*, or two *lumps of bronze*, could exist in exactly the same place at the same time seems very strange indeed—although, as we have seen, some accounts of objects and their persistence require us to say precisely this.[8] The view that I have defended restricts cases of spatiotemporal coincidence between persisting objects to ones in which the objects in question possess different persistence conditions and are consequently objects of quite different kinds. If one were to ask an ordinary member of the public whether or not two different objects could exist in the same place at the same time, one might well receive an emphatic 'No' for an answer—but that, I think, is only because the respondent would not have in mind the kind of case that we have been discussing.

---

[8] See, for example, Christopher Hughes, 'Same-Kind Coincidence and the Ship of Theseus', *Mind* 106 (1997), 53–67. For an opposing view, see David S. Oderberg, 'Coincidence Under a Sortal', *Philosophical Review* 105 (1996), 145–71.

Identity and constitution

If we accept that the statue and the lump of bronze are two numerically distinct objects even when they coincide, a question still remains concerning their relationship to one another when they do: if that relationship is not one of identity, what then is it? A standard answer would be to say that the relationship is one of 'constitution': the lump of bronze *constitutes* the statue during the period of their coincidence.[9] Constitution is understood to be an asymmetrical relation: that is, if *a* constitutes *b*, then *b* does *not* constitute *a*. The statue, for instance, does not constitute the lump of bronze. But how do we decide which object constitutes which? That question can perhaps only be answered satisfactorily by providing an analysis or definition of the constitution relation, which is no easy matter. I shall not attempt to present a definitive analysis here, though I do want to mention one quite promising proposal. The proposal assumes, as seems reasonable, that the relation of constitution only ever obtains between persisting objects which are *composite*, as are the statue and the lump of bronze. And the proposal is this: that one composite object, *a*, constitutes another composite object, *b*, at a time *t* just in case *a* and *b* exactly coincide at *t* and every component part of *a* at *t* is a component part of *b* at *t*, but not every component part of *b* at *t* is a component part of *a* at *t*. This definition has the desirable feature of implying that constitution is an asymmetrical relation. But it may be wondered how it is satisfied in the case, say, of the statue and the lump of bronze. The answer is that while it is plausible to say that every component part of the lump of bronze is a component part of the statue—for example, each particle of bronze is—it is also plausible to say that there are certain parts of the statue which are *not* component parts of the lump of bronze. I am thinking of such parts of the statue as its head, arms, legs, and so forth. Each of these parts of the statue, it seems right to say, is *constituted* by a part of the lump of bronze, but is not *identical* with that part of the lump of bronze, for the same reason that the statue itself is not identical with the lump of bronze as a whole—namely, because a part of the statue such as its head has different persistence conditions from those of the part of the lump of bronze which exactly coincides with that part of the statue. This helps to explain why it definitely seems wrong to say that the head of the statue is a *part* of the

---

[9] See Wiggins, *Sameness and Substance*, 30 ff.

lump of bronze as a whole. But a full defence of this proposal would require much more discussion, so I offer it here merely as an illustration of how one might attempt to analyse the relation of constitution.

The problem of Tibbles and Tib

Our discussion of spatiotemporal coincidence would not be complete without consideration of another kind of case which threatens to be, in some ways, even more troubling than that of the statue and the lump of bronze. Let us recall from Chapter 2 our friend Tibbles the cat. Tibbles, like any normal cat, has a tail, which we can call, quite simply, 'Tail'. Tail is clearly a component part of Tibbles. But now consider the rest of Tibbles—the whole of Tibbles apart from Tail—and let us call this 'Tib'. Whether there really is any such object as Tib is a debatable matter, as we shall see, but for the time being let us assume that there is.[10] Then Tib would also appear to be a component part of Tibbles. Clearly, Tibbles and Tib are not identical with one another, for Tibbles has Tail as a part whereas Tib does not. However, cats can survive the loss of their tails. So suppose that Tibbles loses Tail, perhaps in an accident. Since Tail was no part of Tib, the loss of Tail can apparently have no bearing on the existence or non-existence of Tib.[11] So when Tibbles loses Tail, it seems that Tib must still exist. If so, however, then it is now the case that Tibbles and Tib exactly coincide with one another. And the question is: how is it possible for them exactly to coincide and yet to remain numerically distinct from one another?

One's initial thought might be that this is not really any different from the case of the statue and the lump of bronze: we can say that, after the loss of Tail, Tib *constitutes* Tibbles—and constitution is not identity. But it is not clear that such an answer is in fact available to us in this case, because it is not clear that Tib and Tibbles are objects of different kinds, in the sense of possessing different persistence conditions from one another. Tib is not like the lump of bronze in being something which cannot undergo a change of its material composition. Nor does it appear that we can

---

[10] For doubts about the existence of such objects as Tib, see Peter van Inwagen, 'The Doctrine of Arbitrary Undetached Parts', *Pacific Philosophical Quarterly* 62 (1981), 123–37, reprinted in his *Ontology, Identity, and Modality: Essays in Metaphysics* (Cambridge: Cambridge University Press, 2001).

[11] But this might be questioned: see Michael B. Burke, 'Dion and Theon: An Essentialist Solution to an Ancient Puzzle', *Journal of Philosophy* 91 (1994), 129–39.

plausibly say, after the loss of Tail, that Tibbles has any component part which is not also a component part of Tib, as well as vice versa. So the definition of the constitution relation that I offered a moment ago would not seem to permit us to say that Tib constitutes Tibbles after the loss of Tail.

As usual, several other solutions to this problem, of varying plausibility, can be suggested. A proponent of the doctrine of temporal parts can say that, after the loss of Tail, Tibbles and Tib have all their temporal parts in common, so that they are 'four-dimensional' objects which exactly coincide with one another after, but not before, a certain moment of time. Another possibility is to say that Tib does, after all, cease to exist when Tail is lost. Yet another possibility is to say that no such object as Tib ever existed—and perhaps no such object as Tail, either. But any putative solution to the problem should take into account its full ramifications. If a solution defends the view that, after the loss of Tail, Tib and Tibbles are two numerically distinct objects which exactly coincide with one another, then it must also defend the possibility of there being *any number* of such exactly coinciding objects. This is because we can easily imagine a *succession* of losses of parts of a cat, each one of which would generate an addition to the number of exactly coinciding objects. For instance, after the loss of Tail, Tibbles and Tib might suffer the loss of Ear, so that now *three* objects exactly coincide—Tibbles, Tib, and the part of Tib and Tibbles that did not include Ear.

I think there may be something to be said for the suggestion that Tib does exist prior to the loss of Tail, but ceases to exist thereafter. But this will require us to say that Tib does not, after all, have the same sort of persistence conditions as Tibbles the cat does. However, once we do say that, then it perhaps becomes more questionable whether we should admit the existence of Tib at all. Tib's existence would be awkward to deny if that committed us to denying also the existence of Tail, because it is an article of common sense that cats have tails amongst their component parts. However, it may well be possible to deny that the existence of Tib and that of Tail stand or fall together. Tail certainly has a claim to being a genuine component part of Tibbles—that is, to being something which helps to compose Tibbles because it is identifiable independently of Tibbles and, indeed, could continue to exist even if Tibbles were to cease to exist. (Recall here my characterization in the previous chapter of 'component parts' in these terms.) But it is very doubtful that the same can be said for the putative object Tib. For Tib was only introduced to us as 'the rest of

Tibbles apart from Tail'—that is, as the 'difference' between two other objects, Tibbles and Tail. It is not clear, then, that we are provided with any way of identifying the putative object Tib independently of Tibbles and Tail—and so it is not clear that Tib, even if it exists, could qualify as a genuine component part of Tibbles. (Certainly, it is hard to see how Tib could continue to exist even if Tibbles were to cease to exist, in the way that Tail plainly could.) But once we deny Tib this role, it becomes questionable why we should acknowledge Tib's existence at all. And if we deny Tib's existence, then of course there is no question of Tib exactly coinciding with Tibbles after the loss of Tail: the problem is dissolved.

PART II

NECESSITY, ESSENCE, AND POSSIBLE WORLDS

5

NECESSITY AND IDENTITY

Two kinds of possibility

In the preceding three chapters, my central theme has been the identity over time of persisting objects capable of undergoing various kinds of change in time. In the course of my discussions, I sometimes had occasion to talk about the *modal* properties of persisting objects, such as the modal property that a lump of bronze has of being able to survive a change of shape. Closely related to this modal property of the lump of bronze is another kind of modal property: the property it has, at any given moment of time, of being such that it *could have had* a different shape from the shape it *actually* has at that time. Clearly, to say that it has this property at a given moment of time is different from saying that it has, at that time, the property of being such that it *could change* its shape and thus actually acquire a different shape from the shape it has at that time. In the latter case, we are talking about a possibility of change over time. Not so in the former case: there we are talking about what might have been the case at a given time, in contrast with what is actually the case *at that same time*. This latter kind of possibility we may call 'counterfactual possibility'. The former kind of possibility—a possibility of change over time—we could perhaps call 'temporal possibility'. (There is, however, one respect in which the term 'counterfactual possibility' is potentially misleading: it may suggest that only what is *not* actually the case can be 'possible' in this sense, whereas in fact we want to say that what is actually the case is, for that very reason, something which *could have been* the case and so is 'counterfactually possible' in the sense intended.)

How are the two kinds of possibility related to each other? Does a possibility of either kind imply a corresponding possibility of the other kind? It does not seem so. Consider first the question of whether a counterfactual possibility implies a corresponding temporal possibility. Given that something could have had a different shape now from the shape that it actually has now, does it follow that that thing can acquire that different shape in the future? I don't think so. For example, a sculptor could perhaps have given a somewhat different shape to a statue that he has just made—but it doesn't follow that the statue can now be made to take on that different shape. Equally, it seems clear that a temporal possibility does not imply a corresponding counterfactual possibility. Just because a thing can acquire a different shape in the future from the shape that it actually has now, it doesn't follow that it could have had a different shape now. For example, it might be that a plant of a certain kind *must* possess a certain shape at a certain stage of its existence—for instance, when it is a seed—even though it is possible for it to change its shape thereafter. In the case of such a plant, it is true to say of it, when it is a seed, that it could not have had a different shape from the shape that it actually has at that moment. Yet it is also true to say of it that it can acquire a new shape in the future.

Possibility as a dimension of variation

In this and the next two chapters, we shall be mostly concerned with what I have just called 'counterfactual' possibilities. Although I have just contrasted such possibilities with 'temporal' possibilities, there are certain tempting analogies between the notion of counterfactual possibility and the notion of time itself. Because of the pervasive phenomena of temporal change, time is often thought of as being a certain kind of *dimension of variation*. The three dimensions of space are even more obviously dimensions of variation in this generic sense: spatially extended things can vary in certain ways along their width, breadth, or height. For example, a river gets broader as it approaches the sea and a poker whose tip is stuck in a fire gets hotter along its length. Whether time really *is* a dimension of variation is a contentious issue, discussion of which must be postponed until we reach Part V of this book. But let us accept the suggestion for present purposes. In that case, some of the parallels that we may be tempted to draw between time and counterfactual possibility—or just plain *possibility*, as I shall call it from now on—rest upon our being able to see possibility, too, as a kind of dimension of variation. Just as we think of a persisting object as existing 'at' different times, which are ordered in a linear sequence from earlier to later, so we may think of an object as existing 'in' different possible situations, which are also ordered in some way: we may, for instance, think of some of these possible situations as being more 'remote' ('less close') than others. But we must be careful not to press such an analogy too far, even if we deem it to be basically sound: for there is really no reason to suppose that 'possible situations'—whatever exactly we make of this notion—can be ordered into a linear sequence in the way that times can. Nor, plausibly, is this because possibility is not just one-dimensional, as time is, but more like space in having several different dimensions. Rather, it is because the only tenable notion of 'closeness' between possible situations appears to be based on considerations of *similarity*—and entities of any given kind can normally be deemed similar to or dissimilar from one another in indefinitely many different ways, depending on which features of them we choose to focus upon.

I have been speaking of 'possible situations', as though these are items that can be likened in certain ways to *times* and *places*, the latter being spatiotemporal 'locations' and the former being, as we might put it, *modal* 'locations'. Again, the analogy can at best be only a loose one. Apart from anything else, a modal 'location', or possible situation, will normally include its own spatiotemporal features. When we speak of a possible situation 'in' which a certain object exists, that situation will certainly have to be one in which the object exists *at* a certain time and *in* a certain place, at least if that object is something concrete such as a tree or an animal or a mountain: for there is no possible situation in which a tree, say, exists, but has no spatiotemporal location. A further fact to notice is that possible situations, as we have been speaking of them so far, are not necessarily mutually incompatible: very often, both of two different possible situations could obtain together—for instance, a possible situation in which I am rich and a possible situation in which you are poor. This is just to say that, in addition to there being two such possible situations, there is a possible situation in which I am rich and you are poor. By contrast, although there is both a possible situation in which I am rich and a possible situation in which I am not rich, there is no possible situation in which I am both rich and not rich.

Possible worlds

Modern modal metaphysics lays great emphasis upon a certain special class of possible situations, designating these *possible worlds*. Possible worlds, unlike possible situations in general, are—by definition, in effect—

mutually incompatible. This is because they are conceived of as being 'maximal' possible situations. A possible situation is 'maximal' just in case it satisfies the following condition: for any proposition, p, either it is the case that p is true in the situation in question, or else it is the case that p is not true (and hence that not-p is true) in the situation in question. It should be obvious why any one maximal possible situation is mutually incompatible with, or excludes, any other maximal possible situation. For two maximal possible situations will be numerically distinct only if there is some proposition, p, which is true in one of them but not true in the other. But then there cannot be a possible situation which includes *both* of these maximal possible situations, because it would have to be one in which p was both true and not true—and there is no such possible situation. It is important not to confuse the condition that I have just stated for the maximality of a possible situation with another condition which *every* possible situation must satisfy, namely, this: for any proposition, p, it is the case that *either p or not-p* is true in the situation in question. The earlier condition implies that, if we were to list all the propositions that are true in a given maximal possible situation, then, for any proposition, p, we would always find in the list either the proposition p itself or else the proposition not-p (but not, of course, both of them). The other condition merely implies that, if we were to list all the propositions that are true in any possible situation whatever (whether or not it is maximal), we shall always find in the list the proposition *either p or not-p*. This second condition is simply a condition which any situation must satisfy if it is to be a *possible* situation, whereas the former condition is the condition which any possible situation must satisfy if it is to be *maximal*.

Necessary truths and necessary beings

Because possible worlds are maximal possible situations, each possible world is, as it were, a *complete* way that everything could be. In Chapter 7, we shall look more closely into the ontological implications of talk about possible worlds and examine several different theories concerning their nature and the role they should play in the metaphysics of modality. For the time being, however, we shall adopt talk of such worlds relatively uncritically, accepting that it is at least a convenient means of rendering perspicuous certain kinds of modal claim. In this connection, the first thing to notice is that there are some propositions that are true in *every* possible world. These propositions are *necessary* truths. A relatively uncontroversial example would be any proposition of the form *either p or not-p*, such as the proposition that either grass is green or it is not the case that grass is green. That this proposition is a necessary truth is guaranteed by the laws of logic, which hold in every possible world. (I am assuming here that the so-called *law of excluded middle*—of which the proposition just cited is an instance—is correct. This has been disputed by some logicians; but although logicians may dispute what exactly the laws of logic are, that there are some such laws is much less open to dispute.) Rather more interesting examples of necessary truths are supplied by mathematics: for instance, any proposition of elementary arithmetic, such as the proposition that two plus three equals five. (Some philosophers of mathematics maintain that mathematics is not in fact a body of truths; however, most who do accept that it is a body of truths would also accept that it is a body of *necessary* truths—and this is the view that I am assuming for present purposes. I shall return to the issue of mathematical truth in Chapter 20.) A much more controversial example of a putative necessary truth would be the proposition that God exists, though many philosophers and theologians have maintained that it is a genuine example. Just as there are necessary truths—propositions that are true in *every* possible world—so there are *possible* truths, these being propositions that are true in *some* possible world. Any proposition which is *actually* true is for that very reason a possible truth, because the actual world is itself a possible world. But many propositions that are actually false are, none the less, possible truths, being true in some possible world other than the actual world. A plausible example would be the proposition that I am rich—for, although I am not in fact rich, I surely could have been. Notice that any necessary truth is, *ipso facto*, a possible truth, because if a proposition is true in every possible world, then it is, a fortiori, true in some possible world. Finally, we can use possible-worlds talk to characterize the class of *contingent* propositions: these are propositions that are true in some possible worlds but not true in others.

As well as using the language of possible worlds to characterize the modal status of propositions, we can use it to characterize the modal status of *beings*. For example, a *necessary* being is something which exists in every possible world, a *possible* being is something which exists in some possible world, and a *contingent* being is something which exists in some possible worlds but not in others. Traditionally, God has been taken to be a paradigm example of a necessary being, but less contentious examples are some of the abstract objects of mathematics—things such as the natural numbers. Many metaphysicians also regard *propositions* as being abstract objects that are necessary beings. However, we must be careful to avoid a confusion which may arise. I earlier characterized a necessary *truth* as being a proposition that is true in every possible world and a possible *truth* as being a proposition that is true in some possible world. The question of a proposition's modal status in this sense is quite different from the question of whether propositions are necessary beings. If a proposition is a necessary being, then it *exists* in every possible world—but that is quite a different matter from that proposition being *true* in every possible world. Some propositions, indeed—such as the contradictory proposition *p and not-p*—are not true in any possible world: and yet, if propositions are necessary beings, these propositions *exist* in every possible world.

An argument for the necessity of identity

We are now in a position to proceed to the main business of this chapter, which is to examine the modal status of a special class of propositions—*identity* propositions. An identity proposition is any proposition that an object *a* is identical with an object *b*, where *a* and *b* are any objects whatever. For example, the proposition that George Orwell is identical with Eric Blair is an identity proposition—one that is actually true. Some identity propositions are, of course, actually false, such as the proposition that George Orwell is identical with D. H. Lawrence. And some are quite plainly *necessarily* true, such as the arithmetical identity proposition that five is identical with five. An interesting question, however, is whether there are any *contingent* identity propositions, that is, any identity propositions that are true in some possible worlds but not true in others. Many modal metaphysicians consider that there are no contingent identity propositions, basing this judgement on a famous argument or proof which seems to have been developed independently by Ruth Barcan Marcus and Saul Kripke.[1]

---

[1] For Kripke's version of the proof, see his 'Identity and Necessity', in Milton K. Munitz (ed.), *Identity and Individuation* (New York: New York University Press, 1971), reprinted in the very useful collection edited by Stephen P. Schwartz, *Naming, Necessity, and Natural Kinds* (Ithaca, NY: Cornell University Press, 1977). See also Saul A. Kripke, *Naming and Necessity* (Oxford: Blackwell, 1980), which first appeared in Donald Davidson and Gilbert Harman (eds.), *Semantics of Natural Language* (Dordrecht: D. Reidel, 1972). For the work of Ruth Barcan Marcus, see her *Modalities: Philosophical Essays* (New York: Oxford University Press, 1993).

The argument has two premises, both of which are taken to be necessary truths. The first premise is that everything is necessarily identical with itself—the principle of the necessity of self-identity. The second premise is Leibniz's Law—the principle that whatever is true of something is true of anything identical with that thing. Suppose, then, that a certain identity proposition is true: say, the proposition that *a* is identical with *b*, where *a* and *b* are any objects whatever. Now, by the principle of the necessity of self-identity, we can say that *a* is necessarily identical with *a*. From this it follows that it is true of *a* that it is necessarily identical with *a*. But from this and the assumption that *a* is identical with *b* it follows, by Leibniz's Law, that it is also true of *b* that it is necessarily identical with *a*—from which it follows that *a* is necessarily identical with *b*. What we seem to have proved, then, is that if it is *true* that *a* is identical with *b*, then it is *necessarily true* that *a* is identical with *b*—and consequently that there cannot be an identity proposition that is merely *contingently* true (true in some possible worlds but not in others).

It may be helpful to set out the foregoing argument in a rather more formal fashion, as follows, each numbered line constituting a step in the proof. Lines (1) and (2) are the two premises of the argument, each assumed to be a necessary truth. Line (3) has the status of an assumption or hypothesis.

(1) For any object *x*, it is necessarily the case that *x* is identical with *x*. [the necessity of self-identity]

(2) For any objects *x* and *y*, if *x* is identical with *y*, then whatever is true of *x* is also true of *y*. [Leibniz's Law]

(3) *a* is identical with *b*. [assumption]

(4) It is necessarily the case that *a* is identical with *a*. [from (1)]

(5) It is true of *a* that it is necessarily identical with *a*. [from (4)]

(6) If *a* is identical with *b*, then whatever is true of *a* is also true of *b*. [from (2)]

(7) Whatever is true of *a* is also true of *b*. [from (3) and (6)]

(8) It is true of *b* that it is necessarily identical with *a*. [from (5) and (7)]

(9) It is necessarily the case that *a* is identical with *b*. [from (8)]

Therefore,

(10) If *a* is identical with *b*, then it is necessarily the case that *a* is identical with *b*.

The conclusion, (10), rests on the fact that from the assumption made in line (3) we can derive the claim made in line (9).

There are many reasons why the conclusion of this argument is interesting and perhaps even surprising. One is that, if the argument is correct, it shows us that there can be necessary truths that are not knowable a priori, that is, not knowable independently of empirical evidence. Take the proposition that Hesperus is identical with Phosphorus, these being the ancient Greek names for the morning star and the evening star respectively. Astronomers now know, of course, that the morning star and the evening star are one and the same heavenly body, namely, the planet Venus. If the Barcan–Kripke proof is correct, it is a necessary truth that Hesperus is identical with Phosphorus: but if so, it is plainly one whose truth was, and had to be, discovered empirically, by means of astronomical observation. The epistemological status of this identity proposition is thus quite different from that of the identity proposition that Hesperus is identical with Hesperus, which is an a priori truth of logic. This implication of the Barcan–Kripke proof renders it suspicious in the eyes of some philosophers, especially those who think that necessity cannot reside in the nature of things themselves, independently of the ways in which we conceptualize things or describe them in language. However, I am not at all sympathetic to the latter view of the nature of necessity, as I hope I made clear in Chapter 1, so I shall raise no objection to the Barcan–Kripke proof from this direction.

Some objections to the argument

Is the Barcan–Kripke proof valid? Most modal logicians would agree that it is. Yet it may be possible to object that it is subtly question-begging, that is, that it implicitly assumes precisely what it is supposed to prove.[2] The objection that I have in mind focuses on the step from line (4) of the proof to line (5), that is, from the proposition that it is necessarily the case that a is identical with a to the proposition that it is true of a that it is necessarily identical with a. It might be objected that all that really follows from the former proposition is the much weaker consequence that it is true of a that it is necessarily identical with *itself*. After all, line (4) is derived directly

<hr />

[2] For further details, see my 'On the Alleged Necessity of True Identity Statements', *Mind* 91 (1982), 579–84.

from the principle of the necessity of self-identity, (1), which is simply the principle that *everything* is necessarily identical with itself. From this we surely can conclude that it is true of *a*, in particular, that it is necessarily identical with itself—but it is not perhaps so clear that we can conclude that it is true of *a* that it is necessarily identical with *a*. To assume that we can conclude the latter is, it may be said, effectively just to assume that any truth of identity concerning *a* is a necessary truth, which is the very thing to be proved. If this objection is correct, line (5) of the proof should be replaced by the following line:

(5*) It is true of *a* that it is necessarily identical with itself. [from (4)]

This means that line (8) of the proof must be changed to:

(8*) It is true of *b* that it is necessarily identical with itself. [from (5*) and (7)]

This in turn means that line (9) of the proof will be replaced by:

(9*) It is necessarily the case that *b* is identical with *b*. [from (8*)]

And (9*), of course, is a wholly uninteresting and unsurprising a priori truth.

Even if the Barcan–Kripke proof is subtly question-begging, that does not mean, of course, that its conclusion is false, just that it does not provide us with a good reason for thinking that its conclusion is true. That conclusion, recall, is that any true identity proposition is necessarily true. The implication is, for instance, that if Hesperus is identical with Phosphorus—if they are in fact one and the same object—then Hesperus and Phosphorus *could not have been* distinct. In the language of possible worlds: if Hesperus and Phosphorus are one and the same object in the actual world, then there is no possible world in which Hesperus and Phosphorus are two distinct objects. (Of course, there are worlds in which Hesperus and Phosphorus do not exist at all, since Hesperus and Phosphorus are not necessary beings: but the claim is that any world in which either of them exists is a world in which both of them exist and they are identical with each other.) Against this claim, it may be urged that one can perfectly well *imagine* a possible world in which astronomers discover that Hesperus and Phosphorus are two distinct planets. However, that one can imagine a situation does not necessarily imply that it is a genuinely possible situation. We can perhaps imagine a time traveller going back to the past and changing the course of history: but it is not genuinely possible to change the course of history, that is, to make it the case that something which has happened has not happened, for this involves a contradiction. (As we shall see in Chapter 18, it is important to distinguish between *changing* the past, which is not possible, and *affecting* the past, which may be.) Furthermore, when it is urged that one can imagine a possible world in which astronomers discover that Hesperus and Phosphorus are two distinct planets, it may be questioned whether this really does characterize the content of a possible act of imagination: perhaps all that we can really imagine is a possible world in which there exist two planets *very similar* to Hesperus and Phosphorus, which the astronomers of that world discover to be two distinct planets.

It is also unsatisfactory to object to the thesis that any true identity proposition is necessarily true that it has 'counterexamples' such as the following: it is true, but not *necessarily* true, that the largest planet in the solar system is identical with the planet which is fifth nearest to the sun. The proposition in question is certainly true, since Jupiter is both the largest planet in the solar system and the planet which is fifth nearest to the sun. And the proposition is not *necessarily* true, both because the solar system could have had a larger planet than Jupiter and because Jupiter could have had a different orbit around the sun. However, such a proposition is not a genuine 'identity proposition', in the sense that we have been discussing. Earlier, I said that an identity proposition is any proposition that an object *a* is identical with an object *b*, where *a* and *b* are any objects whatever. It should be understood that the terms '*a*' and '*b*' in such a context serve purely to refer to the object(s) in question and therefore contribute nothing else to the proposition expressed with their aid. So-called 'definite descriptions'—noun phrases such as 'the largest planet in the solar system' and 'the planet which is fifth nearest to the sun'—do not have a purely referential function: they make a further contribution to propositions that are expressed with their aid, in virtue of their descriptive content. In everyday language, it seems, so-called *proper names*—such as 'Jupiter', 'Hesperus', and 'Eric Blair'—serve purely to refer to certain objects and make no descriptive contribution to the propositions that are expressed with their aid. Hence, propositions such as the proposition that Hesperus is Phosphorus and the proposition that George Orwell is Eric Blair are genuine identity propositions in the intended sense. It is propositions such as these that are alleged to be necessarily true if true at all. (Some philosophers of language, it must be acknowledged, have claimed that everyday proper names, such as

'Jupiter', are in fact 'disguised' definite descriptions, or are 'abbreviations' for such descriptions. This is implausible, though the issue is too large to go into here. Suffice it to say that, if this view of everyday proper names were correct, then propositions expressed with their aid would not be identity propositions in the intended sense—but this would certainly not imply that there are no such propositions and would have no direct bearing on the claim that true identity propositions in this sense are necessarily true. For present purposes, then, I shall assume that this view of everyday proper names is false and continue to use them in order to express identity propositions.)

Rigid designators

In this connection, it is often claimed, by proponents of the thesis that any true identity proposition is necessarily true, that everyday proper names are 'rigid designators'.[3] Using the language of possible worlds, a *rigid designator* is standardly defined to be a term which designates the same object in every possible world in which it designates anything at all. However, if it is now stipulated that an 'identity proposition', in the intended sense, is any proposition that is expressible by means of a sentence of the form '*a* is identical with *b*', where '*a*' and '*b*' are rigid designators, then the thesis that any true identity proposition is necessarily true is in danger of being trivialized. For if '*a* is identical with *b*' is true and hence '*a*' and '*b*' designate the same object in the actual world, but we also stipulate that both '*a*' and '*b*' designate this same object in any other possible world, then we appear to have no option but to say that there is no possible world in which '*a*' and '*b*' designate different objects and hence that '*a* is identical with *b*' is necessarily true. However, a victory secured by these means would be a hollow one. The thesis of the necessity of identity is only of metaphysical interest if it is a substantive one that needs to be argued for, rather than just a consequence of a linguistic stipulation. That is why I have not stipulated that the terms used to express an identity proposition must be rigid designators, in the sense just defined, but only that these terms must serve purely to refer to certain objects and contribute nothing else to the propositions expressed with their aid. If it turns out that the thesis of the necessity of identity is correct, then it will turn out that such terms may be

---

[3] This is Kripke's terminology: see *Naming and Necessity*, 48 ff.

described as 'rigid designators': but to define them as such in advance would appear to beg the very question at issue.

A minor complication here, which I have so far glossed over, is that if two rigid designators, '*a*' and '*b*', are co-designative—that is designate the same object—in every possible world in which either of them designates anything at all, this still leaves open the possibility that there are worlds in which neither of them designates anything, namely, all those worlds in which neither *a* nor *b* exists. Unless *a* and *b* are necessary beings, there must be some such worlds. But then it might be questioned whether it can, after all, be a *necessary* truth that *a* is identical with *b*, because it may be questioned whether the proposition that *a* is identical with *b* is true in *every* possible world, including those worlds in which *a* and *b* do not exist. However, we should not too lightly assume that the proposition that *a* is identical with *b* is *not* true in such worlds, merely because *a* and *b* do not exist in them. It may be better to say that this proposition is trivially or 'vacuously' true in such worlds. We should bear in mind here that if propositions are themselves necessary beings, as was suggested earlier, then this proposition certainly *exists* in any world in which neither *a* nor *b* exists—and hence is either true or else not true in any such world. Alternatively, however, we could weaken our characterization of necessary truth, saying that the proposition that *a* is identical with *b* is a necessary truth, in the weak sense, just in case it is true in every possible world in which either *a* or *b* exists. Either way, it seems that the complication just mentioned does not threaten to raise a major issue, so I shall ignore it for present purposes.

Transworld identity

The question of whether one object could have been two distinct objects is reminiscent of the question, touched on in Chapter 2, of whether one object could *become* two distinct objects—that is, whether one object existing at an earlier time could at a later time be identical with two distinct objects. I remarked that the latter possibility conflicts with the principle of the transitivity of identity, at least as this is ordinarily interpreted. If *transtemporal* (or 'diachronic') identity—that is, identity over time—is transitive, it follows that one object could not become two in the sense just explained. By the same token, it would seem, if *transworld* identity— identity across possible worlds—is transitive, it follows that one object could not have been two. For to say that one object could have been two, in the language of possible worlds, is to say that an object a in a world w_1 is identical with both of two distinct objects, b and c, in another world w_2. But if object b in world w_2 is identical with object a in world w_1 and yet object a in world w_1 is also identical with object c in world w_2, then, by transitivity, object b in world w_2 is identical with object c in world w_2. However, I have already warned that we should be cautious about drawing parallels between time and modality, despite certain superficial resemblances between them.[4] There is a strong case for saying that when we talk about identity over time, we are genuinely talking about *identity*, that is, about the relation which, of necessity, every object bears to itself and only to itself. It is less clear that this can literally be what we are talking about when we talk about identity 'across possible worlds'—because it is much less clear what is meant by saying that an object exists 'in' a number of different possible worlds than what is meant by saying that an object exists 'at' a number of different times. We shall have to postpone further discussion of this question until Chapter 7, when we shall look more closely into the nature of possible worlds as they are characterized by various theories. Until we have done that, I suspect, the language of possible worlds is likely to render more, rather than less, obscure the question of whether one thing could have been two.

Could two objects have been one?

It is, admittedly, difficult to think of prima facie examples of one object which could have been two. As well as asking whether one object could have been two, however, we can ask whether two objects could have been one. Just as the first question is about the necessity of *identity*, the second is about the necessity of *diversity*. It is natural to assume that the answers to the two questions must be the same, but this assumption may be coherently challenged. Indeed, prima facie examples of two objects which could have been one are perhaps not so hard to come by. Consider, for instance, the case of a pair of monozygotic twin boys, Tom and Jack. One might be tempted to say that, if their common zygote had not split, Tom and Jack would literally have been identical—not just 'identical twins', as they are in actuality, but *numerically* identical with one another. The only alternative,

---

[4] See further my 'On a Supposed Temporal/Modal Parallel', *Analysis* 46 (1986), 195–7.

it seems, would be to say that, if their common zygote had not split, Tom and Jack would not have existed at all. It is not, I think, simply obvious that this alternative is preferable. However, it is not so easy to adapt this sort of example to the converse question of whether one object could have been two. Suppose that Harry is *not* a monozygotic twin, because his zygote did not split. Is it then plausible to say that, if his zygote *had* split, Harry would have been two different people? If so, who would those two people have been? The trouble is that we don't have two different names for them, or, indeed, *any* means of designating them differently. If we say that one of them would have been Harry, then we have to say that the 'other' one would also have been Harry—but this seems to imply that Harry would have been in two different places at once, which is absurd. In this case, it seems preferable to say either that, if Harry's zygote had split, then Harry would not have existed at all, or else that, if Harry's zygote had split, then Harry would have had a monozygotic twin brother. I am inclined to think that, of these two alternatives, the second is the more plausible. What it implies is that, if Harry's zygote had split, then both Harry *and someone else* would have existed—which is quite different from saying that Harry would have been two different people. The other person who would have existed is someone whom we *do* now have a means of designating, even though we may not yet possess a name for him. We can say, quite simply, that this other person would have been *Harry's monozygotic twin brother*. I don't mean to claim that the argument that I have just been advancing is perfectly compelling, however. In fact, I think that the broader lesson is that questions to do with the necessity of identity and diversity are rather less cut-and-dried than some philosophers tend to suppose.[5]

The necessity of identity and the mind–body problem

The thesis of the necessity of identity has important metaphysical implications, so we should not regard the question of its truth too lightly. To illustrate its metaphysical importance, I shall now consider its bearing on one of the central questions of philosophy, the mind–body problem.

---

[5] For two interesting challenges to the thesis of the necessity of identity, see Hugh S. Chandler, 'Rigid Designation', *Journal of Philosophy* 72 (1975), 363–9, and Allan Gibbard, 'Contingent Identity', *Journal of Philosophical Logic* 4 (1975), 187–222. For discussion of Chandler's paper, see Nathan U. Salmon, *Reference and Essence* (Oxford: Blackwell, 1982), 219 ff.

According to one currently prevalent view, a person is identical with his or her body. On this view, then, I just *am* my body. Suppose we call my body '*B*'. Then the claim is that I am identical with *B*. However, it seems plausible to claim also that I could have existed without *B* existing—either because I could have had a different body or else, more radically, because I could have existed without having any body at all. These possibilities certainly seem to be imaginable. Of course, as I have already emphasized, we shouldn't suppose that everything which is imaginable is therefore genuinely possible. But that something is imaginable is at least prima facie evidence that it is genuinely possible—and if we can find no good reason to deny that it is possible, perhaps we should accept, even if only provisionally, that it really is possible. Suppose, then, that it is indeed possible that I should have existed without *B* existing. In the language of possible worlds, this is to say that there is a possible world in which I exist but *B* does not. In such a world, clearly, the proposition that I am identical with *B* is not true. So there is some possible world in which I exist and the proposition that I am identical with *B* is not true. But, according to the thesis of the necessity of identity, if the proposition that I am identical with *B* is true in this, the actual world, then it is true in *every* possible world (or, at least, in every possible world in which either I or *B* exists). Hence we must conclude that the proposition that I am identical with *B* in this, the actual world is *not* true. The reasoning here is perfectly straightforward and doesn't even need to be expressed in the language of possible worlds to be made clear. Avoiding that language, the reasoning effectively reduces to this. According to the thesis of the necessity of identity, if it is true that I am identical with *B*, then it is necessarily true that I am identical with *B*. But I could have existed without *B* existing, so it is *not* necessarily true that I am identical with *B*. Therefore, it is not true that I am identical with *B*.[6]

If this argument is correct, one thing that it shows is that the claim that a person is identical with his or her body is in fact an extremely strong claim, because it has implications not only for what is the case in this, the actual world, but also for what is the case in *every* possible world (or, at least, in every possible world in which either the person or his or her body exists). Indeed, for this reason, one may doubt whether *empirical* evidence— which can only make reference to what is the case in this, the actual world, since that is the only world we can observe—could ever suffice to establish

---

[6] For some recent doubts about this sort of argument, see Trenton Merricks, 'A New Objection to A Priori Arguments for Dualism', *American Philosophical Quarterly* 31 (1994), 80–5.

the truth of such an identity claim. This may not be at all congenial to those philosophers who are apt to make such identity claims, because in support of those claims they tend to appeal to scientific evidence of correlations between the psychological states of persons and physiological states of their bodies. It would be much more convenient for these philosophers if they could simply concede that a person *could have* failed to be identical with his or her body, while insisting none the less that a person *is* identical with his or her body, as a matter of contingent fact. However, if the thesis of the necessity of identity is correct, such a position is simply not available to these philosophers.

Here it may be objected that earlier I raised no such problem for the empirically based claim that Hesperus is identical with Phosphorus, which I represented as having been established by astronomical observation. Yet, if the thesis of the necessity of identity is correct, this identity claim equally has implications for what is the case in every possible world. However, there is a significant difference between the two cases, I think. In the case of Hesperus and Phosphorus, we are already satisfied, quite independently of the identity claim concerning them, that they are objects of the same kind, governed by the same identity conditions. We are satisfied that each of them is a planet—a persisting mass of matter which orbits the sun in a certain clearly definable path. It is easy to see how careful astronomical observations could establish that the orbits of Hesperus and Phosphorus coincide, so that they can be predicted to be in the same place at the same time. Given that they are masses of matter and that numerically distinct masses of matter cannot exist in the same place at the same time, it follows that Hesperus and Phosphorus are identical. The reasoning here does clearly appeal to more than merely empirical evidence: it appeals also to certain metaphysical principles, albeit ones that are relatively uncontentious. However, in the case of a person and his or her body, what are fundamentally in contention are the relevant metaphysical principles themselves. If it could be agreed that persons and their bodies are objects of the same kind, with the same identity conditions, it would be no more problematic to appeal to empirical evidence to establish an identity between a particular person and a particular body than it is to do so in the case of Hesperus and Phosphorus. The question would not be whether a particular person was identical with any body at all, but merely *which* particular body a person was identical with. But that is *not* how matters stand with regard to persons and bodies: here the dispute is precisely as to the nature of entities of these kinds and whether, indeed, they are entities of the *same* kind or not. That is why it is facile to suppose that the question of whether or not a person is identical with his or her body could be settled straightforwardly by appeal to empirical evidence, such as evidence of correlations between a person's psychological states and physiological states of that person's body.

I think that the point I have just been making is one which to some extent holds good whether or not the thesis of the necessity of identity is correct, though to say this is not in any way to belittle the metaphysical significance of that thesis. The thesis undoubtedly has important implications for the nature of identity claims and for the kinds of evidence and argument that are needed to confirm their truth. For what it is worth, I am inclined to think that the thesis is correct, even though I have raised some doubts concerning some purported ways of establishing it and even though I am less convinced that its counterpart, the thesis of the necessity of diversity, is also correct.

6

ESSENTIALISM

Essential and accidental properties

It is customary, both in everyday speech and in philosophical discussion, to distinguish between the *essential* and the *accidental* properties of objects. Commonplace though this distinction is, it gives rise to certain puzzles and paradoxes which threaten its tenability, at least if it is conceived as a distinction which obtains independently of language and human convention. Yet, abandoning the distinction, or representing it as having a merely conventional basis, threatens to undermine so much of our common-sense ontology as to leave us, perhaps, with no coherent conception of the world at all. Hence, much of importance hinges on the question of whether the distinction can be justified and defended—and it is with this question that the present chapter will chiefly be concerned.

At the outset of the previous chapter, I distinguished between two different kinds of possibility—'temporal' possibility and 'counterfactual' possibility—the first being the possibility of something's changing in some respect over time and the second being the possibility of something's having been different in some respect from how it actually is. Corresponding to the two different kinds of possibility, there are two different notions of an *essential property*. According to the first notion, an essential property of an object is a property which that object has always possessed and which it cannot cease to possess without thereby ceasing to exist.[1] According to the second notion, an essential property of an object is a property which that object always possesses and which it could not have failed to possess— in other words, in the language of possible worlds, it is a property which that object possesses at all times in every possible world in which it exists.

---

[1] Compare Baruch A. Brody, *Identity and Essence* (Princeton, NJ: Princeton University Press, 1980), 81 ff. and 116 ff.

The second of these senses in which a property may be said to be 'essential' is stronger than the first. That is to say, if a property P is an essential property of an object O in the second sense, then P is also an essential property of O in the first sense; but the converse is not true—P may be an essential property of O in the first sense without being an essential property of O in the second sense. Thus, many of an object's *historical* properties are plainly essential properties of it in the first sense, but are plausibly not essential properties of it in the second sense. For example, if a certain object, O, first came into existence at a certain time, t, then that object has always had the property of having first come into existence at t and cannot cease to possess it, unless it ceases to exist and thereby ceases to possess any properties whatever. But it does not follow that O could not have first come into existence at a different time—and if it had, then it plainly would not have possessed the property of having first come into existence at t. Plausibly, this property is not an essential property of O in our second sense—it is not a property which O possesses at all times in every possible world in which O exists.

The second notion of an essential property—the counterfactual notion—is not only the stronger notion but also the more interesting and contentious one. It is this notion that we shall be focusing on in the present chapter, along with the corresponding notion of an *accidental property*. An accidental property of an object, in this sense, is a property which an object possesses at some time but which it could have failed to possess—in other words, it is a property which that object possesses at some time in the actual world but which it does not possess at any time in some other possible worlds in which it exists. However, it is one thing to define what we mean by speaking of 'essential' and 'accidental' properties in this fashion and quite another to demonstrate that certain properties of an object really are essential or accidental in the defined senses. If it should turn out that we cannot maintain at all convincingly that any property of any object is essential, then the very distinction between essential and accidental properties will serve no useful purpose and might as well be abandoned.

But before we inquire into this issue, I want to divide the essential properties that an object might possess into two different sorts. If an object has any essential properties, some of them may be properties which can be possessed by more than one object, while others may be properties which only that object can possess. A plausible example of an essential property of the first sort would be any particular dog's property of being a dog: for many different objects possess this property, and yet, plausibly, any object which does possess it could not have failed to possess it—in other words, any such object possesses the property of being a dog in every possible world in which that object exists. However, in different possible worlds, different objects possess the property of being a dog: it is not the case that the *same* dogs exist in every possible world, even if we restrict ourselves to worlds in which some dogs do exist. I shall say a little more later about essential properties like this. But now let us turn to the other and rather more contentious sort of essential property—one which only one object can possess.

There is nothing especially problematic about the notion of a property which only one object can possess. For instance, only one dog can possess the property of being the first dog to reach the North Pole. It may be that no dog possesses this property, either because no dog has ever reached the North Pole or else because, before any other dog reached the North Pole, two or more dogs simultaneously reached it. But it plainly cannot be the case that two different dogs both possess the property of being the first dog to reach the North Pole. However, this property is plausibly not an *essential* property of whichever dog it is that possesses it, assuming that some dog does: because, plausibly, there is another possible world in which this dog exists but does not possess the property—either because no dog possesses the property in that world or because some other dog possesses it in that world. So, although it is the case that, in every possible world in which something possesses this property, it is possessed by just one object, it is not the case that in every possible world in which something possesses this property, it is the *same* object that possesses it. Clearly, however, if there is a property which only one object can possess which is an *essential* property of whichever object it is that possesses it, it cannot be possessed by different objects in different possible worlds. For if a certain object, O, possesses the property in one world and it is an essential property of O, then it is either O alone or else nothing that possesses the property in any other world: it is O alone that possesses it in any other world in which O exists, while nothing possesses it in any other world in which O does not exist. (Here it may be asked why the property should not be an essential property of O that is possessed by O alone in all the worlds in which O exists and yet also be an essential property of some other object that is possessed by that other object alone in other worlds in which O does not exist. The answer is that there is some possible world in which O and this other object *both* exist and in this world it is O alone that possesses the property, given that it is an essential property of O and that only one object can possess it in that world: but that means that the property cannot be possessed by the other object in every possible world in which *that* object exists and hence it cannot be an essential property of that other object.)

Essential properties and the necessity of identity

So, we may ask, are there in fact any such essential properties—essential properties which only one object can possess? If the thesis of the necessity of identity is correct—as I tentatively concluded at the end of the previous chapter—then it would seem that there certainly are some essential properties of this sort. I have in mind a property such as the property of being identical with O, where O is any particular object. For if the thesis of the necessity of identity is correct, then anything which is identical with O in this, the actual world is identical with O in every possible world in which O exists. And, it would seem, only whatever is identical with O in any given possible world possesses the property of being identical with O in that world. Hence, whatever is identical with O in this, the actual world possesses the property of being identical with O in every possible world in which anything possesses that property—so that the *same* thing, O, alone possesses that property in any world in which anything does. But this is precisely to imply that the property of being identical with O is an essential property which only O can possess. So there is at least one essential property which only one object can possess, which is what we set out to show.

It may seem that I have made rather heavy weather of this argument. But it is advisable to spell it out in some detail, because it is not incontestable. The thesis of the necessity of identity is clearly a crucial, but contestable, premise of the argument. Suppose, contrary to that thesis, that there is something, X, which is identical with O in this, the actual world, but which is not identical with O in some other possible world in which O exists. Then, it seems, the property of being identical with O is possessed by X in this, the actual world, but is possessed by something different from X in some other possible world. Hence, the property of being identical with O is not possessed by the same object in every possible world in which something possesses it. It follows that the property of being identical with O is not an essential property which only one object can possess, for we concluded earlier that such a property cannot be possessed by different objects in different possible worlds.

As well as depending on the thesis of the necessity of identity, the argument we are examining makes another important and contestable assumption. This is that, in any possible world in which O exists, the property of being identical with O exists and is possessed by something—in particular, by O. But why should we suppose that there is any such property as the property of being identical with O, even in a world in which O exists? We may accept that the proposition that O is identical with O is a necessary, a priori truth, which is therefore true in every possible world, or at least in every possible world in which O exists. We may even accept that the proposition that O is identical with O is itself a necessary being, which therefore exists in every possible world. But none of this suffices to guarantee the existence of the *property* of being identical with O in any world whatever. Here we have hit upon a difficult question which we cannot really hope to resolve in the present chapter: the question of what properties *are* and, if there are indeed such entities, what their existence conditions and identity conditions are. These are matters whose fuller treatment will have to be postponed until we reach Part VI of this book. But one point is worth emphasizing already: it cannot be the case, on pain of contradiction, that *every* meaningful predicate expresses an existing property. We know this as a matter of logic, because the predicate 'is non-self-exemplifying' is meaningful and yet cannot be taken to denote the property of being non-self-exemplifying: for such a property, if it existed, would exemplify itself if and only if it did *not* exemplify itself, thereby giving rise to a contradiction.[2] Hence, it cannot be the case that, if we have a meaningful sentence of the form '*a* is *F*', there must therefore exist the property of being *F*. And so, in particular, we cannot assume that, just because 'O is identical with O' is a meaningful and indeed true sentence, the property of being identical with O therefore exists and is possessed by O. It is very plausible to suppose that *some* meaningful predicates express existing properties, but how to ascertain which of them do is a very difficult and contentious matter.

Essential properties and the problem of transworld identity

Why should it matter whether or not there are any essential properties which only one object can possess? For the following reason: if there are,

---

[2] See further Michael J. Loux, *Metaphysics: A Contemporary Introduction* (London: Routledge, 1998), 34–5. See also Ch. 19 of the present book.

they may help us to solve the problem of *transworld identity*.[3] We have been speaking quite freely of one and the same object existing in different possible worlds, as though there were no difficulty in principle about identifying an object existing in one possible world with an object existing in another possible world. As we shall see in the next chapter, some theorists of possible worlds maintain that there really is no such difficulty and that questions of transworld identity are trivial, because we can and must simply *stipulate* the answers to such questions. Others consider, quite to the contrary, that there is *never* identity between objects existing in different possible worlds, because no object can exist in more than one possible world. And yet others hold that, although it makes perfect sense to speak of identity between objects in different possible worlds, it is not a trivial business to determine which such identities obtain. It is the latter theorists, who are probably in the majority, for whom it especially matters whether there are any essential properties which only one object can possess: for they may hope to appeal to such properties for the purpose of determining the answers to questions of transworld identity. Clearly, if, as I have just explained, such a property is one which, of necessity, is possessed by the *same* object in every possible world in which it is possessed by anything at all, we may hope to appeal to such a property to answer a question of transworld identity as follows. Suppose that P is a property which only one object can possess and that it is an essential property of whichever object it is that possesses it. And suppose that O possesses P in this, the actual world. Then, faced with the question of *which* object, if any, in another possible world is identical with O, we may say, quite simply, that the object in question is that object, if any, which possesses P in the other world. There will either be one such object, or else none. If there is one, then that is the object, in that world, which is identical with O; if there is none, then nothing in that world is identical with O and so O does not exist in that world.

Individual essences and haecceities

It may be, of course, that for any object O, there is more than one such property P. Let us call the set of all such properties of O, in deference to

---

[3] See further Roderick M. Chisholm, 'Identity Through Possible Worlds: Some Questions', *Noûs* 1 (1967), 1–8, reprinted in Michael J. Loux (ed.), *The Possible and the Actual: Readings in the Metaphysics of Modality* (Ithaca, NY: Cornell University Press, 1979).

tradition, *O*'s *individual essence*. *O*'s individual essence, then, comprises all those essential properties of *O* which are properties which only one object can possess. So far, we have encountered only one candidate for such a property of an object *O*: the property of being identical with *O*, if indeed such a property exists. However, if *O*'s individual essence were to consist solely of the property of being identical with *O*, it might seem that it would be useless, because circular, to appeal to *O*'s individual essence in order to identify *O* in any other possible world. For if we say that the object that is identical with *O* in any other possible world is the object which, in that world, possesses the property of being identical with *O*, it seems that this already presupposes an answer to the question of which object is *O* in that world.

But it is in fact open to question whether this complaint is justified. First of all, it should be emphasized that the problem of transworld identity, if there really is such a problem, is not primarily an epistemological problem: it is not a problem about how we *know*, or can *tell*, which object in another possible world, if any, is identical with a given object *O* which exists in this, the actual world. Rather, it is an ontological problem: the problem of what *makes it the case* that one rather than another of the objects existing in some other possible world is identical with a given object *O* which exists in this world. In short, it is a problem about what *grounds* transworld identity. Secondly, just because the property of being identical with *O*, assuming that it exists, is standardly expressed by means of the predicate 'is identical with *O*', we should not assume that this property is simply a relational one—the property of standing in the relation of identity to the object *O*. It may be more appropriate to think of this property as being a special kind of *intrinsic* property. (For more on the distinction between intrinsic and relational properties, see Chapter 3 of this book.) We might think of each object as having a special and necessarily unshareable intrinsic property of being the very thing that it is—the property of being *that* thing—and hold that it is just such a property that is expressed by the predicate 'is identical with *O*'. For historical reasons, such a property is called a *haecceity*—literally, a 'thisness'—and so we may say that the property of being identical with *O* is *O*'s haecceity.[4] According to this way of thinking, there need be no vicious circularity in saying that the object, if any, that is identical with *O* in another possible world is the object, if any, that possesses the property of being identical with *O* in that world, for this property is now

---

[4] See further Gary S. Rosenkrantz, *Haecceity: An Ontological Essay* (Dordrecht: Kluwer, 1993).

conceived to be an intrinsic one whose possession by an object is not constituted by its standing in a certain relation to an already identifiable object O.

The necessity of origin

It must be acknowledged that many metaphysicians are not happy with the notion of a haecceity, finding it intolerably obscure and mysterious. But if we abandon that notion, it seems that individual essences will only be of any use in solving the problem of transworld identity if they comprise other properties besides ones like the property of being identical with O. What other suitable properties might there be? Here we may turn to two further essentialist theses, which have been advanced in addition to the thesis of the necessity of identity: the thesis of the necessity of *origin* and the thesis of the necessity of *constitution*.[5] According to the thesis of the necessity of origin, if an object, O, originated from a certain source in this, the actual world, then O also originates from that same source in any other possible world in which O exists. According to the thesis of the necessity of constitution, if an object, O, had a certain original constitution in this, the actual world, then it also has the same original constitution in any other possible world in which O exists. It must be conceded that the notions of 'originating from a certain source' and 'having a certain original constitution' require some clarification, which I shall now try to provide. The best way to do this will be by means of illustrative examples.

Let us consider first the thesis of the necessity of origin. Suppose that T is a certain oak tree existing in this, the actual world, and that T originated from a certain acorn, A. The claim then is that, in any other world in which T exists, T originates from A. In other ways, it may be supposed, T is very different in these other worlds from the way it is in the actual world: it may be taller or shorter, for instance, and it may be growing in a different place. The implication is that, if an acorn different from A had been planted exactly where A was planted and had grown into a tree exactly like T in respect of its size, location, and so forth, then that tree would none the less not have been T. By contrast, if A had been planted elsewhere and had grown into a tree very unlike T in respect of its size, location, and so forth,

[5] Much of the inspiration for these theses comes from the work of Saul Kripke: see especially his *Naming and Necessity* (Oxford: Blackwell, 1980). See also Colin McGinn, 'On the Necessity of Origin', *Journal of Philosophy* 73 (1976), 127–34.

then that tree would none the less still have been *T*. That being so, it seems that we can identify *T* in any possible world in which it exists as the tree which originates from *A* in that world, if any tree does; if no tree does, then *T* does not exist in that world. Hence, the property of originating from acorn *A* belongs to the individual essence of *T* and can be invoked to answer questions of transworld identity concerning *T*. (I am assuming here, of course, that only *one* tree can originate from a single acorn. This may be queried as a matter of biological fact, but let us ignore that complication, since we are only concerned with the example for purposes of illustration.)

A four-worlds argument for the necessity of origin

Why, however, should we think that the thesis of the necessity of origin is correct? We might attempt to argue for it, in the case just described, by employing what may be called a *four-worlds argument*, which goes as follows.[6] We are given that *T* originates from acorn *A* in this, the actual world, which we may call world w_0. Suppose, then, that there is another possible world, w_1, in which *A* does not exist and a tree, T_1, originates from a different acorn, *B*. And suppose that we maintain, contrary to the thesis of the necessity of origin, that T_1 is identical with *T*. Then the following problem seems to arise. There is, it seems, yet another possible world, w_2, in which *both* acorn *A* *and* acorn *B* exist and grow into exactly similar trees—let us call them T_{2a} and T_{2b} respectively. If we ask which of these two trees is identical with *T*, it seems that we should say that it is T_{2a}, rather than T_{2b}, that is identical with *T*—because T_{2a} and T_{2b} being otherwise exactly similar to one another, T_{2a} more closely resembles *T* in virtue of having grown from the same acorn, *A*. So far, then, we have claimed that T_1 is identical with *T* and that *T* is identical with T_{2a}, from which it follows by the transitivity of identity that T_1 is identical with T_{2a}. But now consider a fourth possible world, w_3, which is just like w_2 except that acorn *A* does not exist and so does not grow into a tree. Since w_3 is just like w_2 except that

---

[6] A somewhat similar line of argument is developed by Graeme Forbes in his *The Metaphysics of Modality* (Oxford: Clarendon Press, 1985), 138 ff., but my own discussion is not directed at his argument, the merits of which I leave readers to judge for themselves. See also the discussion in Nathan U. Salmon, *Reference and Essence* (Oxford: Blackwell, 1982), 197 ff., which critically examines another, closely related argument by Kripke for the necessity of origin.

acorn A does not exist, the tree which originates from acorn B in w_3, which we may call T_3, is identical with T_{2b}—and T_{2b}, we know, is not identical with T_{2a}. So it follows that T_3 is not identical with T_{2a}. But if T_3 is not identical with T_{2a} and yet, as we have just concluded, T_{2a} is identical with T_1, it follows that T_3 is not identical with T_1. However, for all that we have said so far, world w_1 and world w_3 are indistinguishable from one another, both being worlds in which acorn A does not exist and a certain tree grows from acorn B. Yet we have been compelled to conclude that those worlds do differ, in that numerically different trees grow from B in the two worlds. That seems absurd, for two worlds surely cannot differ *merely* in respect of the identity of a certain object. The only way to avoid this absurdity, it seems, is to reject the supposition that T is identical with T_1 and so uphold the thesis of the necessity of origin.

However, this argument may certainly be challenged. In the first place, why should *either* of the two trees in w_2, T_{2a} and T_{2b}, be identical with T? If we say that neither of these trees is identical with T, as it seems we may quite coherently do, we can quite consistently reject the thesis of the necessity of origin. Secondly and more importantly, even if we suppose that one of these trees is indeed identical with T, it is questionable whether it is T_{2a} that has the stronger claim to be identified with T. After all, T_{2a} and T_{2b}, being numerically distinct trees existing at the same time in the same possible world, *must* differ from one another in various ways in addition to their difference of origin—for instance, they must occupy different locations in space, since no two trees can occupy exactly the same place at the same time. Even if T_{2a} and T_{2b} are exactly similar in respect of their *intrinsic* properties at any given time, they must differ in respect of many of their *relational* properties, as well as having the different *historical* properties of having grown from acorn A and acorn B respectively. So, in judging which of T_{2a} and T_{2b} more closely resembles T, why should we assign special weight to the fact that T_{2a} resembles T more closely than T_{2b} does in respect of its origin and ignore other respects in which T_{2b} might resemble T more closely than T_{2a} does? Of course, if we already had reason to believe that T's property of having originated from A was included in its individual essence, this preferential treatment would be justified: but whether it is reasonable to believe this is the very question at issue. In short, it may be objected that the four-worlds argument implicitly assumes precisely what it sets out to prove.

Here it may be retorted that we can and should choose world w_2 in such a way as to ensure that T_{2a} and T_{2b} both resemble T to exactly the same degree in respect of *all* their properties except those which concern their origins—so that it really is the case that T_{2a}'s having originated from A rather than B is the *only* respect in which one of the two trees in w_2 resembles T more closely than the other does. For example, we can specify that T_{2a} and T_{2b} are located equidistant from the location of T and in exactly similar environments. However, if we are to do this completely rigorously, we must specify that T_{2a} and T_{2b} inhabit a perfectly symmetrical universe, the two symmetrical halves of which differ from one another solely in respect of the identities of the objects contained in them. And then we are faced with the difficult metaphysical question of whether such a universe is really possible. If it is not, then w_2 is not a possible world at all, in which case it should not be invoked in any argument for the necessity of origin. Moreover, we can see that the difficulty which has now been raised is, in fact, precisely the same sort of difficulty as was raised, in the four-worlds argument itself, against the suggestion that T_3 is not identical with T_1. Recall that it was said to be absurd to suppose that two worlds could differ from one another merely in respect of the identity of a certain object. But if this is absurd, then it is surely equally absurd to suppose that the two halves of one world could differ from one another merely in respect of the identities of the objects contained in them. In each case, the claim of absurdity is based upon the principle that there cannot be a numerical difference where there is exact similarity in respect of all properties which do not involve mere numerical difference. We could call this *the principle of no bare numerical differences*. (It is in fact one interpretation of the principle of the identity of indiscernibles.) And then the point is that since this principle had to be invoked in the four-worlds argument itself, a proponent of that argument should not violate the principle in the course of defending the argument against the objection that I raised earlier. We seem to have created a dilemma for proponents of the four-worlds argument: if they abandon the principle of no bare numerical differences, they cannot get the four-worlds argument to deliver their desired conclusion, but if they adhere to the principle they cannot respond satisfactorily to the objection that the argument implicitly assumes what it sets out to prove.

The necessity of constitution

If the four-worlds argument, or something like it, is the best argument that can be mustered in favour of the thesis of the necessity of origin, then it seems that that thesis has no adequate proof. This is not to deny that the thesis may, for all that, be correct. Moreover, it would seem that, quite generally, essentialist theses are not capable of being deduced from premises which do not already include, even if only implicitly, an essentialist thesis—in which case at least some such theses must be incapable of demonstration. Perhaps, then, in the end, it is enough that we should find the thesis of the necessity of origin intuitively compelling, if indeed we do so find it. But it may be that we can do a little better than this in the case of the other essentialist thesis mentioned previously, the thesis of the necessity of constitution, to which I now turn. As I stated it earlier, this is the thesis that if an object, O, has a certain original constitution in this, the actual world, then it also has the same original constitution in any other possible world in which O exists. Again, the best way to understand the thesis is with the aid of an illustrative example. Recalling the case of the ship of Theseus that we discussed in Chapter 2, suppose that a certain ship, S, which exists in this, the actual world, first came into existence when a certain number of ship parts (planks, spars, ropes, and so on) were put together at a certain time. Suppose, for simplicity, that there were one hundred such parts and call them $P_1, P_2, P_3, \ldots P_{100}$. It is these parts, then, that originally constituted ship S in this, the actual world. Now, in our discussion of the case of the ship of Theseus, we agreed that a ship can persist through a change in its parts over time, so that it is perfectly conceivable that, following a sequence of such changes, S should come to be composed of a wholly different set of parts. However, what we are now concerned with is not the question of whether S can undergo a change in its parts over time, but the question of whether S could have been composed of a different set of parts when it first came into existence. According to the thesis of the necessity of constitution, strictly interpreted, the answer to this question is 'No'. If this answer is correct, then any ship which had been composed of a different set of parts when it first came into existence would have been, for that very reason, a numerically different ship from S. And by a 'different set of parts', I mean a set of parts differing even minimally from the set of parts of which S was originally composed. Thus, for example, if a ship had been originally composed of ship parts $P_1, P_2, P_3,$ $\ldots P_{99}$ and one other, different part, P_{101}, then that ship would not have been S, no matter how similiar in appearance to S it might have been.

It seems natural to protest that this thesis is too strong and that it should be replaced by another, weaker one. Perhaps it will readily be conceded that any ship which had been originally composed of a *completely* different set of parts from those which originally composed S would therefore have been a numerically different ship from S, but at the same time it may be urged that S could surely have come into existence for the first time composed of a *slightly* different set of parts. However, the problem is that it appears to be impossible to set a threshold for how different a ship's original set of parts could have been without running into contradiction. If we say, for instance, that S could have had an original set of parts differing by 3 per cent, but no more, from the set of parts which actually composed it when it first came into existence, then the following absurdity seems to arise. We must allow that a ship S_1, existing in a possible world w_1, which is originally composed of the one hundred parts $P_1, P_2, P_3, \ldots P_{98}, P_{101}, P_{102}$, is identical with ship S existing in the actual world, w_0, because these ships have 98 per cent of their parts in common, which is less than the 3 per cent threshold. By the same token, we must allow that a ship S_2, existing in a possible world w_2, which is originally composed of the one hundred parts $P_1, P_2, P_3, \ldots P_{96}, P_{101}, P_{102}, P_{103}, P_{104}$, is identical with ship S_1 existing in world w_1, again because these ships have 98 per cent of their parts in common. However, we seem compelled to deny that S is identical with S_2, because they have only 96 per cent of their parts in common, which is more than the 3 per cent threshold allows. But these judgements collectively conflict with the principle of the transitivity of identity, which implies that if S is identical with S_1 and S_1 is identical with S_2, then S is indeed identical with S_2. And, clearly, the same problem would arise whatever percentage we were to choose for the threshold, other than 0 per cent or 100 per cent. It transpires, then, that no weaker version of the thesis of the necessity of constitution is available to us: we must either allow that an object could have come into existence for the first time with a completely different set of component parts, or else insist that it could not have come into existence for the first time while differing in respect of any one of its component parts. However, since the first of these two alternatives seems unreasonably liberal, it seems that we must adopt the thesis of the necessity of constitution in its strong form. (Notice that this argument for the thesis of the necessity of constitution relies upon an essentialist premise, namely, that it is not possible for one and the same ship to have been composed of a completely different set of parts when it first came into existence; but I have already remarked that one cannot expect to be able to prove an essentialist thesis from premises which do not themselves contain any essentialist thesis.)

A temporal comparison and accessibility relations

It will be recalled that an argument very similar to this one was deployed in Chapter 2, in order to rule out the proposal that there is some threshold to the proportion of an object's original parts which it can *change* over time. In that case, rather than concluding that an object cannot change *any* of its parts over time, I concluded that it can change *all* of them, provided that the process of change takes place in a gradual and piecemeal fashion. So it may be wondered why I chose the liberal option in the case of identity over time but the illiberal option in the case of identity across possible worlds, judging in the latter case that an object could not have differed in respect of *any* of its orginal parts rather than that it could have differed in respect of *all* of them. Is there any relevant difference between identity over time and identity across possible worlds which justifies this difference of judgement? I think there is—namely, the fact that the *times* at which an object exists may be ordered into a unique linear sequence, whereas there seems to be no principled way to order the *possible worlds* in which an object exists into such a sequence.[7] We may be tempted to overlook this fact when, as in the example I have just been discussing, worlds are characterized only in a very partial and incomplete fashion—for instance, when we describe world w_1 as a world in which a ship S_1 is originally composed of parts $P_1, P_2, P_3, \ldots P_{98}, P_{101}, P_{102}$. The point is that there is not just *one* such possible world, but infinitely many, which differ from each other in infinitely many other respects. And just because ship S is very similar to ship S_1, which is in turn very similar to ship S_2 and indeed more similar to S_2 than S is, it doesn't follow that any three *worlds* in which these ships exist can be ordered into a unique linear sequence on account of those similarities: for there will be other similarities and differences between any three such worlds in virtue of which they can be ordered in other ways. Nor does it appear that there is any other basis on which possible worlds can be ordered into a unique linear sequence analogous to the sequence of times in the temporal domain. The consequence is that there seems to be nothing, in the modal case of identity across possible worlds, which corresponds to the notion of a *gradual and piecemeal change* in the temporal case of identity over time.

[7] See further my 'On a Supposed Temporal/Modal Parallel', *Analysis* 46 (1986), 195–7. See also W. V. Quine, 'Worlds Away', *Journal of Philosophy* 73 (1976), 859–64, reprinted in his *Theories and Things* (Cambridge, Mass.: Harvard University Press, 1981).

There is, however, a possible response to the foregoing argument, as follows.[8] Remember that talk of what is the case in a possible world other than the actual world is a way of talking about what *could have been*—but actually is not—the case. Thus, when it is maintained that there is a ship S_1, existing in a world w_1, which is originally composed of the ship parts P_1, P_2, P_3, ... P_{98}, P_{101}, P_{102} and is identical with ship S, existing in world w_0, this is tantamount to saying that S could have been originally composed of parts P_1, P_2, P_3, ... P_{98}, P_{101}, P_{102}, even though S was actually originally composed of a different set of parts, P_1, P_2, P_3, ... P_{100}. Our proposed justification for this modal judgement is that the sets of parts in question do not differ by more than 3 per cent. But now let us ask the following question. Suppose that S *had* been originally composed of the set of parts P_1, P_2, P_3, ... P_{98}, P_{101}, P_{102}—which we have just conceded it could have been. Would it *then* have been possible for S to have been originally composed of the still more different set of parts P_1, P_2, P_3, ... P_{96}, P_{101}, P_{102}, P_{103}, P_{104}? We may be tempted to answer 'Yes', on the grounds that that set of parts would not have differed by more than 3 per cent from a set of parts of which, we have just agreed, S could have been originally composed. The objection to this answer, developed earlier, is that this compels us to say, by virtue of the transitivity of identity, that S could have been originally composed of the set of parts P_1, P_2, P_3, ... P_{96}, P_{101}, P_{102}, P_{103}, P_{104}, but that this judgement conflicts with the proposed 3 per cent threshold for any possible variation in the set of S's original component parts. However, for this objection to be valid we must assume, quite generally, that the following principle of modal logic is correct:

(1) If it is possible that it is possible that p is the case, then it is possible that p is the case.

In our example, the relevant instance of (1) is this: if it is possible that it is possible that S should have been originally composed of the parts P_1, P_2, P_3, ... P_{96}, P_{101}, P_{102}, P_{103}, P_{104}, then it is possible that S should have been originally composed of those parts. But perhaps (1) can be challenged. Just because there is a possible world, different from the actual world, in which a certain proposition is possibly true, why should it follow that that proposition is also possibly true in the *actual* world? In the technical terminology of modal logic, what is at issue here is a question concerning the

[8] See further Hugh S. Chandler, 'Plantinga and the Contingently Possible', *Analysis* 36 (1976), 106–9, and Salmon, *Reference and Essence*, 238 ff.

accessibility relation between possible worlds. If we suppose, as we coherently may, that not every possible world is 'accessible' to every other possible world, then we may consistently deny (1). More particularly, what we need to deny, in order to deny (1), is that the accessibility relation between possible worlds is *transitive*: that is, we need to deny the claim that if world w_1 is accessible to world w_0 and world w_2 is accessible to world w_1, then it follows that world w_2 is accessible to world w_0.

As for the question of what exactly may be meant by 'accessibility' in this sense, perhaps we can simply say, for present purposes, that one possible world is accessible to another just in case a proposition which is true in the former world is, for that very reason, *possibly* true in the latter world. And then the point is that, by denying that accessibility is a transitive relation, we can consistently say that there is a possible world in which a certain proposition concerning ship *S* is true, even though that proposition is not possibly true in the actual world. This, in turn, means that we shall have to refine the way in which we characterize the possible truths of any world: instead of saying, without qualification, that a possible truth is any proposition which is true in some possible world, we shall have to say that a proposition is possibly true in any given world just in case that proposition is true in some possible world which is accessible to the given world. If every possible world is accessible to every other possible world, these two characterizations of possible truth collapse into one another, but they do not if, for example, the accessibility relation between possible worlds is non-transitive. The condition which must be satisfied if every possible world is to be accessible to every other possible world is that the accessibility relation between possible worlds be an *equivalence* relation—that is, a relation which is not only transitive but also reflexive (every world is accessible to itself) and symmetrical (if one world is accessible to another, then the latter world is also accessible to the former world).

The upshot of this discussion is that there does, after all, appear to be a way in which, technically at least, one can allow that a ship could have been originally composed of a slightly, but not a completely, different set of parts, without falling into contradiction. However, one may doubt whether such a strategy can be provided with any very convincing metaphysical motivation. When we are using the language of possible worlds to talk about *metaphysical* possibility, why should we suppose that the accessibility relation between possible worlds should be regarded as anything other than an equivalence relation? It may be urged that talk of metaphysical possibility is talk of what is *absolutely* possible, without qualification—not talk of what is *relatively* possible, or possible given some further assumption. If there *is* a possible world in which S is originally composed of a completely different set of parts, then, surely, it just *is* metaphysically possible, without qualification, that S should have been originally composed of those parts.

A brief stock-taking

Let us now briefly take stock of our discussion of the theses of the necessity of origin and of constitution. We saw that it is not easy to provide an independent argument for the correctness of the first of these theses, but that the second thesis may perhaps be more amenable to demonstration (albeit only from premises which themselves contain an essentialist thesis). Both theses have some intuitive plausibility, which may be enough to convince some metaphysicians of their correctness—though we have also seen that there is plenty of scope to resist either thesis in various ways, even if it may be questioned how well motivated such resistance may be. I confess that I also left rather vague the question of what, in general, might be meant by talking of the 'origin' or 'source' of an object in articulating the content of the thesis of the necessity of origin. In the example I used, that of an oak tree, I took the source to be a certain acorn—and, more generally, in the case of plants and animals the source will typically be a certain fertilized seed or egg. But in the case of an artefact, such as a ship, it is perhaps less clear what we should describe as being its 'source', in the relevant sense: it might perhaps be a plan drawn up for the ship's construction, or maybe just an intention in the mind of its designer.

Despite a number of uncertainties surrounding the issue, we have seen that some sense can be made of the idea that objects have individual essences which may, in principle, help us to identify those objects across possible worlds (assuming that such help is needed). But such help will at best be rather limited, for both the thesis of the necessity of origin and the thesis of the necessity of constitution can only serve to identify an object across possible worlds given that the transworld identities of certain other objects are already assured—namely, those objects which constitute the sources or original component parts of the objects whose transworld identity is in question. For example, it may help us to identify a certain tree across possible worlds to know that that tree originates from the same acorn in every possible world in which it exists, but this still leaves open the question of how to identify that acorn across possible worlds. Clearly, a regress looms here, whose terminus, if it has one, is problematic.

Essence and conventionalism

I should not conclude this chapter without recalling that objects may possess other essential properties beside those, if any, which comprise their individual essences—namely, certain essential properties which can be possessed by more than one object. In the case of an oak tree, for example, such a property is, very plausibly, its property of being an oak tree: for although there are many objects which possess this property, it is plausible to maintain that any object which does possess it in this, the actual world, also possesses it, at all times, in any other possible world in which that object exists. In short, it is true of any particular oak tree that it could not have failed to be an oak tree—it could not have been, say, a horse or a rubber ball. Why not? That is a surprisingly difficult question to answer in a completely non-question-begging way. It won't do to point out that an oak tree cannot *change* into a horse or a rubber ball, even granting that that is true: for our concern now is with counterfactual rather than with temporal possibility. However, I am strongly tempted to say that I simply don't understand what it could really mean to say that a certain oak tree—*that very object*—could have been a horse or a rubber ball. Conventionalists who reject talk of 'essence' altogether or who regard it at best as reflecting malleable human interests and prejudices will be unimpressed by such an attitude. They will say that to describe a certain physical object as being 'essentially' an oak tree but only 'accidentally' situated in a certain place is just to betray a greater practical concern for this object's biological character than for its geographical position. Another culture, with different interests, might well reverse our judgements, describing the object as being 'essentially' situated in a certain place but only 'accidentally' an oak tree. But what *is* this 'object' which is supposedly so freely redescribable without its identity, apparently, ever coming into question? What, indeed, do the conventionalists themselves understand in speaking of the world as containing identifiable 'objects' at all? How could there *be* something—some identifiable particular thing—which was not by its very nature, and thus essentially, an object of some quite specific kind? The whole world, for the conventionalist, seems doomed to merge into an amorphous lump in which there is no real individuality or distinctness, no genuine differentiation into a multiplicity of particulars, apart from the divisions which we or people of other cultures impose or project upon the world through the filter of our thought and language. And then we must ask: what place can we ourselves have in such a world, seemingly so much of our own making? For we can hardly be supposed to make ourselves, in the sense in which, for the conventionalist, it seems we have to make the other objects of which we speak. If the only way to avoid the 'amorphous lump' conception of the world is to embrace essentialism, then at least essentialism has common sense on its side, for what that is worth.[9]

[9] For a conventionalist approach, see Alan Sidelle, *Necessity, Essence, and Individuation: A Defense of Conventionalism* (Ithaca, NY: Cornell University Press, 1989).

7

POSSIBLE WORLDS

The language of possible worlds

In the preceding two chapters, I have made extensive use of the language of possible worlds in order to state and evaluate various modal claims, including certain important essentialist theses, such as the theses of the necessity of identity, the necessity of origin, and the necessity of constitution. Much of the time, however, I have resorted to more familiar and everyday ways of expressing modal claims, using modal auxiliary verbs such as 'must', 'can', and 'could', modal adverbs such as 'necessarily' and 'possibly', and modal sentence-modifiers such as 'it is necessary that' and 'it is possible that'. But now we need to look more closely into how these two different ways of expressing modal claims are related to one another and whether the differences between them have any metaphysical significance. In particular, what are the ontological implications, if any, of resorting to the language of possible worlds to express modal claims? Can we, and if so should we, regard that language as no more than a convenient *façon de parler*, or as merely a useful heuristic device?

There is one context in which the language of possible worlds is undoubtedly useful and even illuminating, namely, in the study of formal axiomatic systems of modal logic.[1] Systems of modal logic make use of *modal operators* to represent statements of possibility and necessity. For example, a statement of the form 'It is necessary that p' may be represented by the formula '$\Box\, p$', where the box symbol, '$\Box$', is the necessity operator. Correspondingly, a statement of the form 'It is possible that p' may be represented by the formula '$\Diamond p$', where the diamond symbol, '$\Diamond$', is the possibility operator. These operators may be *iterated* so that, for example,

---

[1] See, for example, Brian F. Chellas, *Modal Logic: An Introduction* (Cambridge: Cambridge University Press, 1980), or G. E. Hughes and M. J. Cresswell, *A New Introduction to Modal Logic* (London: Routledge, 1996).

the statement 'It is necessary that it is necessary that p' may be represented by the formula '$\Box\Box\,p$' and the statement 'It is possible that it is necessary that p' may be represented by the formula '$\Diamond\Box p$'. In systems of *quantified* modal logic, the modal operators are used in combination with the familiar existential and universal quantifiers ('E' and 'A' respectively) of ordinary, non-modal quantifier logic. So, for instance, the statement 'There is something, x, such that it is necessary that x is F' may be represented by the formula '$(Ex)\Box Fx$'. That statement must, of course, be carefully distinguished from the statement 'It is necessary that there is something, x, such that x is F', which is duly represented by the formula '$\Box(Ex)Fx$'. (In the current terminology, the first of these two statements is a statement of *de re* necessity whereas the second is a statement of *de dicto* necessity, because in the second what falls within the scope of the necessity operator is itself a complete statement, whereas this is not so in the first.) Of course, more complex formulas than these can easily be constructed, using more than one quantifier and symbols for negation, conjunction, disjunction, and so forth.

Notice that the modal statements I have been representing symbolically are ones which make use of the modal sentence-modifiers 'it is necessary that' and 'it is possible that', rather than the modal adverbs or the modal auxiliary verbs mentioned earlier. But this linguistic difference is probably less significant than the difference between all of these familiar ways of expressing modal claims and the language of possible worlds, which is an invention of philosophers and logicians. For instance, it seems relatively uncontroversial that the statement 'There is something which is such that it is possible that it is red' is just a rather stilted way of saying 'There is something which can be/could be/could have been red'—though precisely which auxiliary verb we choose will depend upon what notion of possibility we are trying to express. (Recall here the distinction, introduced at the beginning of Chapter 5, between 'temporal' and 'counterfactual' possibility.) Similarly, 'It is possible that there is something which is red' is just another way of saying 'It can be/could be/could have been the case that there is something which is red'.

Modal logics and their interpretation

A good many different formal axiomatic systems of modal logic have been developed by modal logicians, just as mathematicians have developed various axiomatic systems of geometry, of which Euclid's system is just the best known. Some of these systems of modal logic are 'stronger' than others, in the sense that all the axioms and theorems of one system may be derived from the axioms of another system whereas the second system (the stronger of the two) has axioms and theorems which cannot be derived from the axioms of the first system (the weaker system). Of the many different systems of modal logic that have been developed, four are particularly important, these being known, for historical reasons, as the Lewis systems S4 and S5, the Brouwerian system B, and system T. Of these, S5 is the strongest, because the axioms and theorems of each of the other systems are contained in it, while T is the weakest, because its axioms and theorems are contained in each of the others. S4 and B are of intermediate strength, each being contained in S5 and containing T, but neither containing the other. Each of the stronger systems can be obtained by adding certain axioms to system T. System T itself contains the following two distinctive modal axioms:

(1) $\Box p \to p$

(2) $\Box(p \to q) \to (\Box p \to \Box q)$

(1) states that if it is necessary that p, then it is the case that p and (2) states that if it is necessary that if p, then q, then if it is necessary that p, then it is necessary that q. System B contains, in addition to (1) and (2), the axiom

(3) $p \to \Box \Diamond p$

This states that if it is the case that p, then it is necessary that it is possible that p. System S4 contains, in addition to (1) and (2), the axiom

(4) $\Box p \to \Box \Box p$

This states that if it is necessary that p, then it is necessary that it is necessary that p. Finally, S5 contains, in addition to (1) and (2), the axiom

(5) $\Diamond p \to \Box \Diamond p$

This states that if it is possible that p, then it is necessary that it is possible that p. Axioms (3), (4), and (5) are the 'characteristic' axioms of systems B, S4, and S5 respectively—that is to say, they are the axioms which need to be added to axioms (1) and (2) of system T in order to generate, respectively, systems B, S4, and S5.

Let us now recall how the language of possible worlds is used to characterize possible truths and necessary truths. As I explained in the previous chapter, we need to take into account the *accessibility* relation between possible worlds if we are to do this in a perfectly general way. What we then say is that a proposition is *possibly* true in a given possible world just in case that proposition is true in *some* possible world that is accessible to the given world. Correspondingly, we say that a proposition is *necessarily* true in a given possible world just in case that proposition is true in *every* possible world that is accessible to the given world. And, of course, to say that a proposition, p, is possibly true or necessarily true in a given world is just to say that, in that world, it is possible that p or it is necessary that p. We must remember, however, that we have some room for choice concerning the properties of the accessibility relation between possible worlds. In particular, it is important which of the following properties we take that relation to have: reflexivity, symmetry, and transitivity. The accessibility relation is *reflexive* if it is the case that every possible world is accessible to itself. It is *symmetrical* if it is the case that, whenever a world w_1 is accessible to a world w_2, world w_2 is also accessible to world w_1. And it is *transitive* if it is the case that, whenever a world w_1 is accessible to a world w_2 and world w_2 is accessible to a world w_3, world w_1 is also accessible to world w_3.

Now, it is relatively easy to establish the following relationships between systems T, B, S4, and S5 and certain possible combinations of properties of the accessibility relation between possible worlds. If we specify merely that the accessibility relation is *reflexive*, we get system T. If we specify that the accessibility relation is *reflexive and symmetrical*, we get system B. If we specify that the accessibility relation is *reflexive and transitive*, we get system S4. And if we specify that the accessibility relation is *reflexive, symmetrical, and transitive*, we get system S5. (Note here that no relation can be symmetrical and transitive but not reflexive, so that we also get system S5 if we specify merely that the accessibility relation is symmetrical and transitive.) This explains the relative strengths of the various systems and why they have the characteristic axioms they do. For example, we can explain the characteristic axiom of S5, axiom (5) above, as follows. The axiom states that if it is possible that p, then it is necessary that it is possible that p. In order to see why this is so, observe first of all that what axiom (5) states is logically equivalent to the following: if it is possible that it is necessary that p, then it is necessary that p. That is to say, the formula '$\Diamond p \rightarrow \Box \Diamond p$' of (5) is logically equivalent to the formula '$\Diamond \Box\, p \rightarrow \Box p$'. (To prove this logical equivalence, we need only to draw on the fact that '$\Diamond p$' is, by definition, equivalent to '$\sim\Box\sim p$': to say that it is possible that p is equivalent to saying that it is *not* necessary that it is *not* the case that p.) Suppose, now, that 'It is possible that it is necessary that p' is true in a given w_0. What this means, in the language of possible worlds, is that some possible world, call it w_1, which is accessible to w_0, such that 'It is necessary that p' is true in w_1. This in turn means that p is true in every possible world that is accessible to w_1. However, if we assume that the accessibility relation between possible worlds is reflexive, symmetrical, and transitive (in other words, if we assume that it is an *equivalence relation*), then it is evident that every possible world is accessible to every other possible world. It follows that, since p is true in every possible world that is accessible to w_1, p is true in every possible world that is accessible to w_0, for the worlds that are accessible to w_0 are precisely the same worlds as those that are accessible to w_1, namely, all the worlds there are. But this in turn means that 'It is necessary that p' is true in world w_0. So we have shown that from the fact that 'It is possible that it is necessary that p' is true in w_0, it follows that 'It is necessary that p' is true in w_0, which is precisely what axiom (5) requires.

Accessibility relations and essentialist theses

At this point, it is instructive to recall two controversial issues concerning essentialist theses that were discussed in the preceding two chapters. In Chapter 5, I pointed out that it is possible to accept the thesis of the necessity of identity while rejecting the thesis of the necessity of diversity. And in Chapter 6, I explained how it was technically possible to defend a weakened version of the thesis of the necessity of constitution, allowing that a composite object might have been composed of a slightly, but not a completely, different set of original component parts when it first came into existence. In each case, the tenability of the position in question rests upon the acceptability of a system of modal logic weaker than S5: that is to say, in the language of possible worlds, it rests upon our being able to construe the accessibility relation between possible worlds as failing to have all the properties of an equivalence relation. In the first case, what must be denied is that the accessibility relation is *symmetrical*. In the second case, what must be denied is that it is *transitive*. I hope that I made the latter fact sufficiently clear in my discussion of the second case in Chapter 6. But the former fact is equally easy to appreciate. For suppose that it is maintained that the thesis of the necessity of diversity is incorrect. This is to maintain that even if 'a is not identical with b' is true in a certain possible world, w_0, it may none the less be the case that 'It is possible that a is identical with b' is true in w_0. This in turn means, in the language of possible worlds, that there is some possible world, call it w_1, which is accessible to w_0 and in which 'a is identical with b' is true. Now, however, suppose that the thesis of the necessity of *identity* is correct. This implies that 'It is necessary that a is identical with b' is true in world w_1, which in turn means, in the language of possible worlds, that 'a is identical with b' is true in every possible world which is accessible to world w_1. But we have already assumed that world w_1 is accessible to world w_0, so that if we also assume that the accessibility relation between possible worlds is symmetrical, we must accept that, conversely, world w_0 is accessible to world w_1. However, we have just agreed that 'a is identical with b' is true in every possible world which is accessible to world w_1, so that if world w_0 is indeed one of those worlds, it follows that 'a is identical with b' is true in world w_0. But this contradicts our initial supposition that 'a is *not* identical with b' is true in world w_0. Clearly, then, in order to avoid this contradiction, while accepting the thesis of the necessity of identity but not the thesis of the necessity of diversity, we must deny that world w_0 is accessible to world w_1 and hence deny that the accessibility relation between possible worlds is symmetrical. This means, of course, that we cannot accept either system B or system S5 as our preferred system of modal logic. Similarly, if we deny that the accessibility relation between possible worlds is transitive, in order to uphold a weakened version of the thesis of the necessity of constitution, we cannot accept either system S4 or system S5 as our preferred system of modal logic. But a word of caution is called for here. As I implied when discussing the thesis of the necessity of constitution in Chapter 6, any choice of a system of modal logic weaker than system S5, when we are concerned with the concepts of *metaphysical* possibility and necessity, may be difficult to motivate in a principled way—so that we should not too lightly assume that, where the metaphysical modalities are concerned, we are free to choose our system of modal logic simply with a view to protecting some cherished modal thesis from attack.

How should we understand talk of possible worlds?

I hope that the discussion so far in this chapter has borne out my suggestion that the language of possible worlds is useful and even illuminating for the purpose of studying formal axiomatic systems of modal logic. In essence, the utility of that language in this context arises from the fact that, when we translate into the language of possible worlds modal claims originally stated with the aid of modal operators or their ordinary English equivalents—the expressions 'it is possible that' and 'it is necessary that'—we are able to eliminate those modal operators in favour of *quantifier* expressions whose variables of quantification range over possible worlds. Thus, instead of saying 'It is possible that p', we say 'There is some possible world, w, such that w is accessible and p is true in w', or something to that effect. The second sentence is certainly more long-winded than the first, but, from a logical point of view, it has the great advantage of enabling us to utilize the familiar resources of ordinary, *non-modal* quantifier logic. As far as its *logical form* is concerned, this sentence is indistinguishable from one such as 'There is some wooden box, x, such that x is nearby and y is located in x'. Non-modal quantifier logic is a very well-understood system, so that translating modal claims into a language governed by that logic and devoid of modal operators can, not surprisingly, help us to understand logical relations between modal claims and assist us in formulating and evaluating arguments which involve such claims. But the deeper question which should concern us, from a metaphysical point of view, is whether translating modal claims into the language of possible worlds can help us in any way to understand the *content* or *meaning* of modal claims. How we answer this question will depend on what we think talk of 'possible worlds' itself means, whether we think that there really are any such entities as possible worlds and, if we do, what we think their nature is. In all of these matters, a broad range of options faces us.

A deflationary view

One option would be to maintain that talk of possible worlds is nothing more than a convenient way of rephrasing modal claims which draws its entire meaning from the independently constituted meanings of more familiar ways of expressing modal claims—those which exploit modal auxiliary verbs, modal adverbs, and modal sentence-modifiers. On this thoroughly deflationary view, we should not invest talk of possible worlds with any ontological significance, as though it were a way of talking about some special class of entities whose intrinsic nature awaits further description.

However, against this suggestion it may be urged that if sentences in the language of possible worlds are *true*—which many must be, if such sentences simply paraphrase more familiarly expressed modal claims and many of the latter are true—then possible worlds must surely *exist*: for many such possible-worlds sentences quite explicitly state that *there are possible worlds*. For instance, the possible-worlds sentence which translates 'It is possible that I am rich'—'There is some possible world in which it is true that I am rich'—clearly entails the simpler sentence 'There is some possible world', which says that at least one possible world exists. (Here I am setting aside, for the sake of simplicity, any mention of accessibility between possible worlds.) It seems, then, that possible-worlds talk cannot be construed as being ontologically innocent: by indulging in it, we appear to commit ourselves to acknowledging the existence of a certain class of entities, *possible worlds*—and the only question remaining for us is what these entities are.[2]

But this line of objection is surely too quick and too slick. The view under examination maintains that the possible-worlds sentence 'There is some possible world in which it is true that I am rich' is nothing more than a paraphrase of the more familiar modal sentence 'It is possible that I am rich' and derives its meaning entirely from the meaning of the latter, which itself makes no reference to any entity whatsoever apart from *me*—an object of a perfectly familiar kind. So how can it fairly be alleged that that view *does* after all commit its adherents to the existence of entities of a further and unfamiliar kind? But what, then, it may be asked, does the sentence 'There is some possible world' *mean*, on the view under examination? For that sentence surely is entailed by 'There is some possible world in which it is true that I am rich' and is therefore true if that other sentence is true. This seems a fair question, but it also seems to have an obvious answer: 'There is some possible world' simply means 'It is possible that something is the case'. For the latter, translated into the language of possible worlds, means 'There is some possible world in which some proposition is true' and this is trivially equivalent to 'There is some possible world', because it is trivially true that every possible world is a world in which some proposition is true.

One seeming advantage of the deflationary view of possible-worlds talk now under consideration is that it may appear to eliminate the supposed

---

[2] What is being appealed to here, in effect, is W. V. Quine's criterion of ontological commitment, encapsulated in his famous slogan, 'To be is to be the value of a variable'. See further 'Existence and Quantification', in his *Ontological Relativity and Other Essays* (New York: Columbia University Press, 1969).

problem of *transworld identity* which was discussed in the previous chapter. If, in all ontological seriousness, there are no possible worlds, conceived as real entities of some kind yet to be described—because to say that 'There are possible worlds' is really just to say that it is possible that some propositions are true—then, surely, there can be no problem as to how the same object can exist 'in' different possible worlds and be identified 'across' possible worlds. Let us see how this train of thought might be developed, before we go on to evaluate it.

Transworld identity again

Suppose that we are talking about some actually existing object, such as a certain oak tree, T, which is actually growing in a certain field and is flourishing there. And suppose the question is raised as to whether T could have flourished just as well if it had been growing on higher ground. Expressed in the language of possible worlds, our question is whether there is another possible world, accessible to this, the actual world, in which T is growing on higher ground and is flourishing just as well as it actually is. Now, this may seem to prompt the further question of how we can determine that, in this other possible world, it is indeed T that is growing on the higher ground and not some other, numerically distinct tree. We may be satisfied that there is a possible world in which *an* oak tree, similar in many ways to T, is growing and flourishing on higher ground: but what would make it the case that such a tree is, or is not, identical with T? Don't we need some principle, or criterion, of 'transworld identity' in order to answer such a question—a principle which will tell us, regarding T and some tree existing in another possible world, whether or not they are one and the same tree? Those philosophers who regard talk of possible worlds as no more than a *façon de parler* may want to reply to this question with a firm 'No'. By their account, to ask whether there is another possible world in which T is growing on higher ground and flourishing is to ask nothing more than whether T could have flourished if it had been growing on higher ground. And, in order to understand the latter question, the only question of identity that needs to be settled is the question of which tree T *actually* is. Once this is settled—say, by identifying T as the tree which is actually growing in a certain location—there is simply no further question of identity to be addressed.

Hence, according to this way of thinking, when it is asked how we can determine whether, in some other possible world, it is indeed T that is growing on higher ground and not some other tree, the answer is that this is an entirely spurious question, for the only genuine question of identity concerning T has already been settled by considerations which solely concern its actual properties. Having fixed T's identity in the only sense that is either possible or required, what makes it the case that T is the tree said to exist 'in some other possible world' is simply the fact that this is the tree we have chosen to talk about. In effect, it is we who *stipulate* that the tree in question is T—which we are perfectly entitled to do, because there is no further fact of identity to be established.[3]

One may worry, however, that this short way with the problem of transworld identity is superficial and inadequate, failing to recognize that a genuine difficulty does exist. For one thing, it may be asked how we can be entitled to assume that T could have existed *at all* in a location other than the one in which it actually does exist. Surely, it may be said, we can only inquire into what properties T *could* have had if we are in a position to say in what circumstances T—that very tree—would still have existed. Doesn't this require us to have some grasp of T's 'individual essence'? And doesn't such a grasp amount, in effect, to a grasp of a principle or criterion of transworld identity for objects of T's kind—in this case, oak trees? This seems to be a reasonable objection. The thought that there can be no genuine problem of transworld identity if there really are no such entities as possible worlds does indeed seem mistaken. Certainly, it may be that the problem is not most perspicuously articulated in terms of identity 'across possible worlds'—but that doesn't mean that the questions we may be tempted to articulate in those terms aren't genuine questions which require substantive answers and cannot be settled by mere stipulation. I strongly suspect that this is indeed the case.

Another deflationary view

Now, even if the deflationary view of possible-worlds talk that we have just been examining cannot be credited with dissolving the problem of transworld identity, there may be other reasons for favouring it—not least the fact that it is ontologically parsimonious. But against this view, one may object that it threatens to leave unexplained *why* familiar modal sentences

---

[3] Compare Saul A. Kripke, *Naming and Necessity* (Oxford: Blackwell, 1980), 42 ff.

should be paraphrasable in terms of possible-worlds sentences, especially since this fact is generally unknown to ordinary users of those familiar modal sentences. There is, admittedly, nothing especially strange in the notion that a sentence may be paraphrased, in a way which entirely preserves its meaning, by another sentence with a very different logical structure. Thus, to use a famous example of Frege's, the sentence 'The direction of line a is the same as the direction of line b' may be paraphrased by the sentence 'Line a is parallel to line b', despite the fact that the two sentences seem to be attributing different relations to different pairs of objects.[4] However, this example does not provide a very helpful model for adherents of the view of possible-worlds talk now under examination: for not only will the Fregean paraphrase come as no surprise to users of either of the sentences involved, but also we have no reluctance to say that *directions* exist if *lines* do, and vice versa. The fact that the sentence concerning directions can be paraphrased by one concerning lines is not naturally taken to imply that directions do not really exist, whereas the deflationist is suggesting that, because possible-worlds talk is just a paraphrase of familiar modal language, possible worlds do not really exist.

The view of possible-worlds talk that we have just been examining is not, however, the only deflationary view of such talk that is available. Another deflationary view, in some ways even more extreme than the first, is to regard talk of possible worlds as nothing more than a convenient heuristic device. According to this view, when we 'translate' a familiar modal sentence into a sentence in the language of possible worlds, our 'translation' does not even *preserve*, much less explain, the meaning of our original modal sentence. Rather, it provides us with a *surrogate* for that original modal sentence which is more amenable to the familiar kinds of logical manipulation made available by non-modal quantifier logic. We do not have to ask, and indeed should not ask, what sort of entities are the values of the possible-worlds variables in the surrogate sentences, because those sentences are not to be regarded as literally true or false, but merely as providing convenient linguistic objects for the purposes of formulating and evaluating modal arguments. If, in the course of manipulating such surrogate sentences, we engage in certain flights of fancy, imagining possible worlds as 'alternative realities' of some sort, this is harmless enough and may even help us in our reasonings, rather as coloured beads or

[4] See Gottlob Frege, *The Foundations of Arithmetic*, trans. J. L. Austin (Oxford: Blackwell, 1953), 74.

pebbles may help a child in carrying out arithmetical calculations. But—so it may be urged—such imaginings have nothing to do with the *meanings* of the surrogate sentences formulated in the language of possible worlds, for those sentences do not have determinate meanings at all and do not need to have them in order to fulfil the purposes for which they are constructed. Against this view it may be objected, however, that it leaves us with a mystery as to *why* the language of possible worlds should prove so useful for formulating and evaluating modal arguments, given that possible-worlds sentences are devoid of meanings that are in any way related to the meanings of the familiar modal sentences for which they are supposed to be surrogates.

Modal fictionalism

Both of the deflationary views of possible-worlds talk that we have looked at so far may seem attractive because they are ontologically parsimonious, apparently allowing us to indulge in the convenience of talking in terms of possible worlds but without incurring any obligation to say what possible worlds are, because the term 'possible world' is not taken to express the concept of any distinctive kind of object or entity. However, both of these views should be clearly distinguished from another view which hopes to reap the benefits of possible-worlds talk without incurring any ontological cost—a view which is commonly known as 'modal fictionalism'.[5] According to this view, the term 'possible world' does indeed express the concept of a distinctive kind of object or entity, but one which has no real instances: that is to say, it is the concept of a certain kind of *fictional* entity, somewhat as the concept of a unicorn is the concept of a certain kind of fictional entity. Just as we can say what a unicorn would be, if there were such a thing, we can, on this view, say what a possible world would be, if there were such a thing—but it is just that there are no such things. Even so, it is suggested, the meaning of modal claims can be illuminated by talking in terms of these fictional entities.

However, this view requires that we modify the usual scheme for translating familiar modal sentences into possible-worlds sentences. Instead of saying, for instance, that 'It is possible that p' means 'There is at least one possible world in which p is true', we must say that the former sentence

[5] See especially Gideon Rosen, 'Modal Fictionalism', *Mind* 99 (1990), 327–54. See also John Divers, 'A Modal Fictionalist Result', *Noûs* 33 (1999), 317–46.

means something like this: 'According to the fiction of possible worlds, there is at least one possible world in which p is true'. The reason for this is that the modal fictionalist contends that possible worlds are fictional, non-existent entities, so that, on this view, the sentence 'There is at least one possible world' is simply *false*, just as the sentence 'There is at least one unicorn' is simply false. Therefore, on the fictionalist's view, the sentence 'There is at least one possible world in which p is true' is also false, no matter what proposition p might be—and yet, of course, he does not want to say that the sentence 'It is possible that p' is false, no matter what proposition p might be. So he must deny that the latter sentence is adequately translated by the former. Instead, he must translate 'It is possible that p' by something like 'According to the fiction of possible worlds, there is at least one possible world in which p is true', which, of course, can perfectly well be true—just as the sentence 'According to Greek mythology, there is at least one unicorn' is true, even though the sentence 'There is at least one unicorn' is false.

The contrast between modal fictionalism and the first deflationary view discussed earlier is clearly brought out by the fact that, according to that other view, the possible-worlds sentence 'There is at least one possible world' is not only true, but trivially so, since it means quite simply 'It is possible that at least one proposition is true'. Other things being equal, it would seem that this view is preferable to modal fictionalism, since it does not require us to say what kind of thing a possible world would be and does not require us to modify the usual translation scheme between familiar modal sentences and sentences of the language of possible worlds. However, it may be that modal fictionalism can exploit to its advantage certain features of some *realist* theory of possible worlds, without incurring the ontological commitments of such a theory. This would give it, in the memorable words of Bertrand Russell, all the advantages of theft over honest toil. In particular, it may be urged that there are modal truths which can be adequately articulated only in the terms made available by such a realist theory and which therefore cannot be adequately articulated solely with the aid of the more familiar modal locutions, such as the modal sentence-modifiers 'it is possible that' and 'it is necessary that'.[6] If that were so, modal fictionalism would certainly be preferable to either of the other deflationary views discussed earlier. And if it could achieve all of

---

[6] This is the contention of David Lewis: see his *On the Plurality of Worlds* (Oxford: Blackwell, 1986), 13 ff.

this without incurring the ontological commitments of a realist theory of possible worlds, it would surely deserve our allegiance in preference to any other approach, whether realist or deflationary.

Realist theories of possible worlds

But it is now time that we looked at some realist theories of possible worlds. Recall that when I first began to talk about possible worlds, in Chapter 5, I introduced them as being possible *situations* of a special kind—namely, *maximal* possible situations. It will be remembered that I characterized a possible situation as being maximal just in case it satisfies the following condition: for any proposition, p, either it is the case that p is true in the situation in question, or else it is the case that p is not true (and hence that not-p is true) in the situation in question. I did not say much about the general notion of a 'situation' in that chapter, but, as I was using this term, it is synonymous with the term 'state of affairs'. In what follows, I shall say a little about what metaphysicians have typically conceived states of affairs to be, though without wishing to imply that I endorse the inclusion of such entities in our ontology.

Traditionally, a state of affairs is conceived to be something closely related to, but not the same as, a proposition. In particular, it may be said that a state of affairs which actually obtains is a *fact* and that facts are what make propositions true or false. For example, it may be said that the proposition that Mars is red is made true by the fact that Mars is red. Mars's being red, then, is a state of affairs which actually obtains and is consequently a fact. A state of affairs which does not actually obtain but which could have obtained is not a fact, but it could have been a fact: it is, if you like, a possible fact. An example of such a state of affairs is Mars's having an ocean. Clearly, we have to distinguish carefully between saying that a certain state of affairs *exists* and that it *obtains*. The state of affairs of Mars's having an ocean does not obtain, because it is not a fact that Mars has an ocean: but this does not mean that that state of affairs does not exist. There is a parallel with propositions here: the proposition that Mars has an ocean is not true, but this does not mean that that proposition does not exist. It would seem, then, that states of affairs are, like propositions, *necessary* beings: in the language of possible worlds, any state of affairs which exists in any possible world exists in every possible world. Since we are now treating possible worlds as maximal possible states of affairs,[7] this amounts to saying that any state of affairs which exists in any maximal possible state of affairs exists in every maximal possible state of affairs. This may sound odd, but is not paradoxical. It implies, for instance, that every possible state of affairs exists in the maximal possible state of affairs which actually obtains, that is, in the actual world: but this doesn't mean that every possible state of affairs *obtains* in the actual world, which would imply a contradiction.

States of affairs, if they are indeed necessary beings, would appear to be abstract entities, just as propositions are. So to regard possible worlds as maximal possible states of affairs is to regard them as abstract entities of a special kind. Assuming that one is a realist concerning abstract entities in general, to regard possible worlds as being abstract entities of a special kind is certainly to adopt a realist view of possible worlds. But, on reflection, it may strike one as being an unpalatable and ontologically extravagant view. In the first place, it may be wondered why we should need to include *both* maximal possible states of affairs *and* propositions in our ontology. If possible worlds are abstract entities, like propositions, why don't we simply say that they *are* propositions, or, more precisely, maximal consistent sets of propositions—where a set of propositions is consistent just in case the conjunction of those propositions could be true? In short, why not simply identify a possible world with the set of propositions that are true 'in' it? This would mean identifying the actual world with the set of all propositions that are actually true. And some philosophers have indeed advocated precisely this position. At this point, however, it may strike us forcefully how odd it is to say that possible worlds, including the actual world, are *abstract* entities, whether states of affairs or sets of propositions. Certainly, we may be very resistant to the idea that the world we actually inhabit is an abstract, necessary being. On the contrary, it seems to be a concrete, contingent being, consisting at least in part of numerous objects existing in space and time, including ourselves.

Robust realism and the indexical conception of actuality

This last thought prompts a quite different but robustly realist conception of possible worlds: not as being abstract entities, but as being, as it were,

---

[7] Compare Alvin Plantinga, *The Nature of Necessity* (Oxford: Clarendon Press, 1974), 44 ff.

parallel universes, each quite as concrete as the actual physical universe we inhabit, but each spatiotemporally and causally isolated from all of the others.[8] Against this view, it may be objected that what it offers is not an account of what possible worlds are, but just a grossly inflated account of what physical reality actually includes—in short, that it is a contribution to speculative cosmology rather than to the metaphysics of modality. It may be replied that this objection rests upon a misunderstanding of the meanings of the words 'actual' and 'actually'. In particular, it may be contended that the term 'the actual world' is an *indexical* expression, analogous to the expressions 'now' and 'here'. Just as the word 'now' refers, on any occasion of its use, to the *time* at which it is uttered and the word 'here' refers, on any occasion of its use, to the *place* at which it is uttered, so, it may be said, the term 'the actual world' refers to the *world* in which it is uttered. Consequently, the many concrete worlds being postulated cannot all be seen as parts of one enormous actual world, since *each* of these worlds is 'the' actual world to its inhabitants, just as each time is 'now' to the people existing at that time. On this view, our world's being 'actual' is not a matter of its being somehow more real than other worlds, which are 'merely' possible: rather, it is just a matter of its being *our* world—a fact which does not confer upon it any special ontological status. All possible worlds, then, are ontologically on an equal footing, according to this way of thinking.

If this view of possible worlds is correct, it seems clear that we cannot literally speak of one and the same concrete object existing in two different possible worlds: transworld identity is impossible for concrete objects, because concrete objects exist in space and time—and each possible world has its own space-time, which is spatiotemporally unrelated to the space-time of any other world. The most we can hope to say is that a concrete object existing in one possible world has 'counterparts' existing in other possible worlds—objects which are similar to the object in question in certain especially significant ways.

But this prompts the objection that it is mysterious why modal statements about objects existing in one world should have anything to do with quite different objects existing in other worlds. When it is said, for instance, that a certain oak tree, *T*, which exists in our world *could have been* taller than it is, this is taken to be true in virtue of the fact that *another* oak tree, existing in another space-time continuum but in some ways

---

[8] This is the view of David Lewis, who also inspired the indexical conception of actuality described below and the theory of 'counterparts' as an alternative to the postulation of literal 'transworld' identity: see his *On the Plurality of Worlds*.

similar to T, is taller than T. But why should facts about another tree have anything to do with how *this* tree, T, could have been? It is true enough that the other tree is not just any arbitrarily chosen tree, but is T's 'counterpart' in the world in question. But since the counterpart relation is merely a matter of similarity, not of identity, it is perhaps hard to see how invoking it helps to solve the problem that has been posed. Indeed, how would it make any difference to us, existing in this world—the one we call 'actual'—if none of the other worlds existed at all? We would be none the wiser, since those worlds are, in any case, alleged to be causally isolated from ours, so that their existence or non-existence can have no causal impact on us. If none of those other worlds existed, we would go on believing that objects in our world had certain modal properties—for instance, that a certain tree could have been taller than it is—and these modal beliefs would go on being justified or not, as the case may be, for the same reasons as before. It seems that the existence of other possible worlds, conceived along the lines now under consideration, would simply be irrelevant to the very area of discourse—modal discourse—which talk of possible worlds is supposed to illuminate.

Moderate realism and actualism versus possibilism

Can we combine a moderate realism concerning possible worlds—one sufficient to acknowledge their explanatory usefulness—with the view that the actual world alone contains the whole of concrete reality? Perhaps we can. So far we have looked only at realist views of possible worlds which treat all possible worlds, including this, the actual world, as belonging to the same ontological category. On one view, all worlds are abstract, necessary beings—maximal possible states of affairs, or maximal consistent sets of propositions. On another view, all worlds are concrete beings, each with its own space-time continuum and population of material objects. But what we would like to say, perhaps, is that the *actual* world, and it alone, contains concrete objects existing in space and time, whereas other possible worlds are entities of quite another nature, most probably abstract entities of some sort. If we are content to allow that the actual world includes not only concrete objects existing in space and time, but also abstract entities, such as numbers, sets, and propositions, then we can say, for instance, that other possible worlds are indeed maximal consistent sets of propositions—each of them characterizing, as it were, a way the actual world could have been. One maximal consistent set of propositions is distinctive in that all of the propositions belonging to it are *true*. But this set of propositions cannot, of course, be *identified* with the actual world, because it is only one object amongst many existing in the actual world. This set of propositions characterizes the way the actual world *is*. According to this view, when we say of some actually existing object that it also exists 'in' some other possible world, all we mean is that if all of the members of a certain maximal consistent set of propositions had been true, then that object would still have existed. Put more loosely, we mean that if that possible world had been (or, more strictly, had characterized) the actual world, then the object in question would still have existed. (Recall that I mentioned this sort of proposal in Chapter 3, where I compared it with a proposal that a 'presentist' theory of time might endorse.)

The view just described is a form of *actualism*: that is to say, it is committed to the doctrine that the only entities which exist are entities which *actually* exist. Possible worlds other than the actual world are, on this view, actually existing entities, because they are just parts of the actual world, namely, certain abstract entities which actually exist. Opposed to actualism is *possibilism*, the view that certain possible entities exist which do not actually exist. Why should anyone believe in possibilism? To say that something exists which does not actually exist sounds very close to being self-contradictory—though, of course it isn't, if 'actually' is understood to be an indexical expression. After all, it isn't contradictory to say that something exists which does not exist *now* (provided, of course, that we read the verb 'exists' tenselessly, rather than as being in the present tense), or which does not exist *here*. But it may be doubted whether the indexical interpretation of 'actually' is correct. Of course, we can say, without fear of self-contradiction, that something *could have* existed which does not actually exist, but this is perfectly consistent with actualism (provided, of course, that we don't mean by this that there *is* something which could have existed but which does not actually exist, but only that there could have existed something which does not actually exist). For example, the actualist can allow that there could have existed a tenth planet orbiting the Sun inside the orbit of Mercury, even though no such planet actually exists. The possibilist will maintain, however—with how much plausibility is a matter for debate—that there are modal truths which actualism simply cannot accommodate, because there are more things than are dreamt of in the actualist's ontology: for example, 'alien' properties which no actual object

possesses or could ever have possessed, but which are possessed by obj
in some other possible world.[9] I shall not attempt to resolve this dispute
here, though my own sympathies lie with the actualist.[10]

---

[9] See Lewis, *On the Plurality of Worlds*, 159 ff.

[10] For further discussion of the issues raised in this chapter, see Robert C. Stalnaker, 'Possible Worlds', *Noûs* 10 (1976), 65–75, reprinted in the very useful volume edited by Michael J. Loux, *The Possible and the Actual: Readings in the Metaphysics of Modality* (Ithaca, NY: Cornell University Press, 1979); Colin McGinn, 'Modal Reality', in Richard Healey (ed.), *Reduction, Time and Reality* (Cambridge: Cambridge University Press, 1981); Nathan Salmon, 'The Logic of What Might Have Been', *Philosophical Review* 98 (1989), 3–34; and Graeme Forbes, *The Metaphysics of Modality* (Oxford: Clarendon Press, 1985). For another approach to modality not discussed in this chapter, see David M. Armstrong, *A Combinatorial Theory of Possibility* (Cambridge: Cambridge University Press, 1989).

PART III

CAUSATION AND CONDITIONALS

8
COUNTERFACTUAL CONDITIONALS

Subjunctive versus indicative conditionals

I have spoken a good deal, in recent chapters, about the notion of 'counter-factual possibility', which I first introduced at the beginning of Chapter 5. It is this notion of possibility that is in play when we speak of what properties an object *could* have had, in contrast with the properties that it actually does have. Very often, however, we also want to say what properties an object *would* have had, if circumstances had been in some way different from how they actually are. We may judge, for instance, that a certain oak tree, T, would have been taller if it had been growing in more fertile soil. The conditional sentence used to express this judgement—'If T had been growing in more fertile soil, then T would have been taller'—is a so-called *counterfactual conditional*. The characteristic hallmarks of such a conditional are generally taken to be, first, that its *antecedent* (the if-clause) expresses a state of affairs which is 'contrary to fact', that is, which does not actually obtain, and, second, that the auxiliary verbs appearing in its antecedent and consequent (the then-clause) are 'subjunctive' in mood. For the latter reason, such conditionals are also called 'subjunctive conditionals', in contrast with so-called 'indicative conditionals', whose verbs are in the 'indicative' mood. An example of an indicative conditional would be 'If T has shed its leaves, then winter has arrived'. Someone asserting this conditional would not ordinarily be taken to imply that its antecedent expresses a state of affairs which is contrary to fact—that T has *not* shed its leaves. A few words of caution are in order here, however. First, some logicians and linguists are unhappy with the claim that English possesses a subjunctive mood which is clearly distinguishable from the indicative mood, even though many other languages—such as Italian, French, and Latin—certainly do.[1] Second, there are many so-called subjunctive conditionals which are *not* counterfactuals, as they are typically asserted without any implication that their antecedents express states of affairs which are contrary to fact (such subjunctive conditionals are sometimes called 'open' subjunctive conditionals). And, third, there are some so-called indicative conditionals which, technically, *are* counterfactual conditionals according to this criterion, standard examples being indicative conditionals whose consequents are something like 'I'm a Dutchman' or 'I'll eat my hat' (as in 'If that painting's a Picasso, then I'll eat my hat')—for, in asserting conditionals such as these, a speaker most certainly *does* want to imply that the antecedent of the asserted conditional is false. However, in what follows I shall ignore all of these complications and simply talk about 'counterfactual conditionals' as if this term denoted a perfectly clear-cut class of conditionals, of which a paradigm example would be the conditional cited earlier, 'If *T* had been growing in more fertile soil, then *T* would have been taller'.

There are some very good reasons why a survey of metaphysics, such as the present book is intended to be, should have a close concern with the meaning of counterfactual conditionals. One is simply that, because they are statements which are, in a broad sense, *modal* in character, the proper interpretation of counterfactual conditionals raises important questions in the metaphysics of modality. Even more significant, however, is the fact that many metaphysicians have made use of counterfactual conditionals in their accounts of other metaphysically important notions, especially the notion of *causation*. Some have even maintained that causal statements can be *analysed* in terms of counterfactual conditionals. Whether or not such a view can be sustained is a question which we shall have to postpone until Chapter 10, but it is surely indisputable that counterfactual conditionals and causal statements are at least intimately related to one another. For instance, someone who asserts 'The explosion caused the collapse of the bridge' would normally take this causal statement to imply the counterfactual conditional 'If the explosion had not occurred, then the bridge would not have collapsed'. As we shall see in Chapter 10, matters are not in fact quite so straightforward as this, for in some circumstances the effect of a

---

[1] One such theorist is V. H. Dudman: for his distinctive approach to conditionals, see his 'Interpretations of "If"-Sentences', in Frank Jackson (ed.), *Conditionals* (Oxford: Oxford University Press, 1991). See also Jonathan Bennett, 'Farewell to the Phlogiston Theory of Conditionals', *Mind* 97 (1988), 509–27, although Bennett has since retracted the view expressed in that paper: see his 'Classifying Conditionals: The Traditional Way is Right', *Mind* 104 (1995), 331–54.

given cause would still have occurred even in the absence of that cause, because in its absence something else would have caused the effect in question. But this sort of complication is not something that need concern us at present.

Counterfactual conditionals and possible worlds

So what, then, do we mean when we assert a counterfactual conditional? Let us take as the general form of a counterfactual conditional the sentence-form 'If it had been the case that p, then it would have been the case that q'. This is slightly misleading, in that a sentence of this form is a *past-tense* counterfactual conditional, whereas there can perfectly well be present-tense and future-tense counterfactual conditionals—though in practice most of the counterfactual conditionals which people assert are in the past tense, simply because we know more about the past than we do about the present and the future and are consequently better placed to judge that the antecedents of past-tense conditionals are contrary to fact than that the antecedents of present-tense and future-tense conditionals are. So this is another complication that I shall ignore for the time being. Of course, it is hardly very idiomatic English to say 'If it had been the case that T was growing in more fertile soil, then it would have been the case that T was taller', instead of the much simpler 'If T had been growing in more fertile soil, then T would have been taller'. But the advantage of the more complex mode of expression is that it conforms to an easily generalizable pattern, namely, that exhibited by the general sentence-form presented above—'If it had been the case that p, then it would have been the case that q', where p and q are any two propositions that we may care to choose.

Now, in reply to our question—what do we mean when we assert a counterfactual conditional?—many philosophers have offered answers which appeal to the notion of *possible worlds*, which we have already explored in considerable depth in previous chapters. We shall examine some of these answers in due course. But first let us be clear about what is being looked for as an answer to our question. What we are looking for, primarily, is an account of the *truth conditions* of counterfactual conditionals. That is to say, we are looking for a statement of a logically necessary and sufficient condition for the truth of a sentence of the form 'If it had been the case that p, then it would have been the case that q—

and, moreover, a logically necessary and sufficient condition which can itself be stated without using any counterfactual conditional. This qualification is clearly needed if we are to avoid both triviality and circularity in an account of the truth conditions of counterfactual conditionals. With these desiderata in mind, then, one answer to our question that many philosophers have been inclined to give is, to a first approximation, something like this:[2]

(1) 'If it had been the case that p, then it would have been the case that q' is true if and only if q is true in the closest possible world in which p is true.

This analysis of the meaning of a counterfactual conditional introduces only one notion which we have not hitherto encountered, that of one possible world's being 'closer' to the actual world than another possible world is—and I shall say more about this notion in a moment. Indeed, analysis (1) assumes that, for any proposition p, there is, relative to the actual world, a *closest* possible world in which p is true. But this assumption may certainly be queried. Since, presumably, no world is as close to the actual world as the actual world is to itself, if the actual world is itself a world in which p is true, then there is such a world as the closest world in which p is true—namely, the actual world. But if, as is normally assumed to be the case with a counterfactual conditional, p is not actually true but contrary to fact, then it seems at least conceivable that there should be no closest world in which p is true—either because there are two or more worlds in which p is true that are equally close to the actual world and closer than any other such world, or else because, for any world in which p is true, there is a closer world in which p is true, so that there is an infinite series of ever-closer such worlds.

In order to overcome these potential difficulties, analysis (1) above is rejected by some philosophers and replaced by something like this:[3]

(2) 'If it had been the case that p, then it would have been the case that q' is true if and only if q is true in all of the closest possible worlds in which p is true.

If it should turn out that of all the worlds in which p is true there is just

---

[2] See Robert C. Stalnaker, 'A Theory of Conditionals', in Nicholas Rescher (ed.), *Studies in Logical Theory*, American Philosophical Quarterly Monograph 2 (Oxford: Blackwell, 1968), reprinted in Jackson (ed.), *Conditionals*.

[3] See David Lewis, *Counterfactuals* (Oxford: Blackwell, 1973).

one that is the closest, then analysis (2) effectively reduces to analysis (1). But if two or more worlds in which p is true are equally close and no such world is closer than them, then (2) requires that all of these worlds be worlds in which q is true if the counterfactual conditional in question is to be true. And if there is an infinite series of ever-closer worlds in which p is true, then (2) requires that all of the worlds after a certain point in the series be worlds in which q is true if the counterfactual conditional in question is to be true. One consequence of (2) is that 'If it had been the case that p, then it would have been the case that q' must be deemed true if there is *no* world in which p is true—that is to say, if p is impossible—because in that case it is vacuously true that q is true in 'all' of the closest worlds in which p is true, there being no such worlds. But this seems harmless enough. We can say that the counterfactual conditional itself is vacuously true in such circumstances, to distinguish such a case from the more interesting ones which arise when p is possible.

Conditional excluded middle and 'might' counterfactuals

One important difference between analysis (1) and analysis (2) is that only the former implies the truth of a principle known as 'conditional excluded middle' where counterfactual conditionals are concerned.[4] If we use the formula '$p \,\square\!\!\rightarrow q$' to represent a counterfactual conditional of the form 'If it had been the case that p, then it would have been the case that q', then this principle may be represented as follows:

$$(\text{CEM}) \; p \,\square\!\!\rightarrow q \vee p \,\square\!\!\rightarrow \sim q$$

It is easy to see why (CEM) fails according to analysis (2). For suppose that q is true in some but not all of the closest possible worlds in which p is true, so that not-q is true in all the remaining closest possible worlds in which p is true. In that case, (2) implies that 'If it had been the case that p, then it would have been the case that q' and 'If it had been the case that p, then it would have been the case that not-q' are *both* false, whereas (CEM) requires that if one of these conditionals is false then the other is true.

---

[4] For discussion, see Robert C. Stalnaker, 'A Defense of Conditional Excluded Middle', in the very useful volume edited by W. L. Harper, R. C. Stalnaker, and G. Pearce, *Ifs* (Dordrecht: D. Reidel, 1981).

However, this means that, if we accept analysis (2), we cannot regard a counterfactual conditional of the form '$p \,\Box\!\!\rightarrow q$' as being logically equivalent to the negation of one of the form '$p \,\Box\!\!\rightarrow \sim q$', that is, as being equivalent to a statement of the form '$\sim (p \,\Box\!\!\rightarrow \sim q)$'. But then we may ask whether a statement of the latter form is equivalent to any form of counterfactual conditional at all. Many philosophers think that the answer is 'Yes', calling the kind of counterfactual conditional involved a 'might' counterfactual. This is a counterfactual conditional of the form 'If it had been the case that p, then it *might* have been the case that q', which may be represented by the formula '$p \,\Diamond\!\!\rightarrow q$'. So, the proposal is to accept the following logical equivalence as defining the logical relationship between 'might' counterfactuals and 'would' counterfactuals:

(DMC) $p \,\Diamond\!\!\rightarrow q \leftrightarrow \sim (p \,\Box\!\!\rightarrow \sim q)$

(DMC) defines the 'might' counterfactual 'If it had been the case that p, then it might have been the case that q' as having the same truth conditions as 'It is *not* the case that: if it had been the case that p, then it would have been the case that *not-q*'. Thus, for example, 'If I had tossed this coin, then it might have landed heads' is taken to be logically equivalent to 'It is not the case that if I had tossed this coin, then it would not have landed heads'. Obviously, however, analysis (1) leaves no scope for such a distinction between 'would' and 'might' counterfactuals: effectively, it treats all counterfactuals as 'would' counterfactuals.

The question of transitivity

Despite this important difference between analyses (1) and (2), the two analyses have several other important features in common—which is why I shall focus chiefly on the simpler analysis (1) from now on. In particular, both analyses imply that certain patterns of inference which are arguably valid for indicative conditionals are not valid for counterfactual conditionals. For example, both analyses imply that 'would' counterfactuals are *not transitive*, are *not contraposable*, and are *not* subject to *strengthening*. That is to say, both analyses classify as invalid the following three inference patterns:

(Trans) $p \,\Box\!\!\rightarrow q$, $q \,\Box\!\!\rightarrow r$, therefore $p \,\Box\!\!\rightarrow r$
(Contr) $p \,\Box\!\!\rightarrow q$, therefore $\sim q \,\Box\!\!\rightarrow \sim p$

(Stren) $p \;\Box\!\!\rightarrow q$, therefore $(p \;\&\; r) \;\Box\!\!\rightarrow q$

That (Stren) is invalid is certainly intuitively plausible, as the following apparent counterexample demonstrates: one may surely accept as true the 'would' counterfactual 'If I had struck this match, then it would have caught fire' without having to accept as true the 'would' counterfactual 'If I had struck this match and at the same time held it under water, then it would have caught fire'. Apparent counterexamples to (Trans) and (Contr) can also be constructed, though it is more debatable how plausible these alleged counterexamples are. As we shall see in Chapter 10, the alleged invalidity of (Trans) is crucial for certain counterfactual analyses of caus-ation, so what is at issue here is no mere technicality. What is indisputable, however, is that (Trans) is invalid according to both analysis (1) and analy-sis (2), so that one can uphold the validity of (Trans) only if one is pre-pared to reject both of these analyses and adopt some alternative analysis. Take analysis (1), for instance. According to (1), '$p \;\Box\!\!\rightarrow q$' and '$q \;\Box\!\!\rightarrow r$' are both true just in case q is true in the closest world in which p is true and r is true in the closest world in which q is true. Suppose, then, that both of these 'would' counterfactuals are in fact true. Even so, if the closest world in which p is true is not as close as the closest world in which q is true, it may none the less be the case that r is *not* true in the closest world in which p is true—and if this happens to be the case, then, according to analysis (1), the 'would' counterfactual '$p \;\Box\!\!\rightarrow r$' is not true, contrary to what (Trans) demands.

One of the most famous putative counterexamples to (Trans) is the following, which is due to Robert Stalnaker and concerns J. Edgar Hoover, one-time head of the Federal Bureau of Investigation in the United States: 'If J. Edgar Hoover had been born in the Soviet Union, then he would have been a communist; and if J. Edgar Hoover had been a communist, then he would have been a traitor; therefore, if J. Edgar Hoover had been born in the Soviet Union, then he would have been a traitor'.[5] It may seem plaus-ible to accept the premises of this argument as true and yet to reject the conclusion as false, contrary to what (Trans) demands. And according to analysis (1) the explanation, once again, would be that all the worlds in which Hoover is born in the Soviet Union, including the closest such world—which is a world in which he is a communist—are less close than the *closest* world in which Hoover is a communist: so that even though he is a traitor in the latter world—for it is a world in which he is a United

---

[5] See Stalnaker, 'A Theory of Conditionals'.

States citizen holding a high public office that is incompatible with allegiance to communism—it need not follow that he is a traitor in the closest world in which he is born in the Soviet Union.

Of course, we are not really in a position to evaluate this explanation until we have a clearer idea of what it might mean to say that one world is 'closer' than another to the actual world, which is a matter we shall look into shortly. But, even in advance of doing this, we may suspect that the proposed explanation is incorrect, because we may suspect that what is wrong with the inference under examination is just that it involves an ambiguity. According to this diagnosis, the inference concerning Hoover is not an illustration of the supposed fallacy of transitivity, but simply involves a straightforward fallacy of *equivocation*. Roughly speaking, the suggestion is that the consequent of the first conditional in the Hoover argument does not really express the same proposition as is expressed by the antecedent of the second proposition in that argument, because both of the clauses concerned are elliptical or abbreviated—and are abbreviations of *different* sentences. Thus, it may be said, what we really mean by the first premise of the Hoover argument is something like this: 'If J. Edgar Hoover had been born in the Soviet Union, then he would have been a Soviet citizen and a communist'—whereas what we really mean by the second premise is something like this: 'If J. Edgar Hoover had been a communist and had (still) been a United States citizen, then he would have been a traitor'. If this diagnosis is correct, then, clearly, the fact that the premises of the Hoover argument are plausibly true while its conclusion is plausibly false cannot be taken to show that (Trans) is an invalid form of inference for 'would' counterfactuals, since, on this diagnosis, the Hoover argument does not really constitute an inference of the form specified by (Trans).

However, it may be urged against the foregoing diagnosis of the error in the Hoover argument that it is suspiciously ad hoc and that it gives us no assurance that similar diagnoses will be able to explain away all other putative counterexamples to (Trans). Even if we sympathize to some extent with the diagnosis that has been offered in this case, what we really need to do, if we are to challenge the putative counterexamples to (Trans) in a systematic way, is to advance and defend an alternative analysis of 'would' counterfactuals which does not have as a consequence the invalidity of (Trans). I shall suggest such an alternative analysis later, after we have discussed the notion of closeness between possible worlds. And again I remark that one important reason why we should be concerned with the status of (Trans) is that it bears directly on the adequacy of certain counterfactual analyses of causation.

The notion of 'closeness' between possible worlds

It is now high time that we examined the notion of 'closeness' between possible worlds. Whatever view we may take as to what possible worlds *are*—if indeed we think that they really exist at all—we may agree that worlds may be distinguished from one another in terms of the propositions that are or are not true 'in' them. Clearly, if w_1 and w_2 are two distinct worlds, the same propositions cannot be true in both of them. But, even so, it may be that a vast majority of the propositions that are true in w_1 are also true in w_2 and vice versa—in which case, we may say that w_1 and w_2 are, overall, very *similar* to one another. (Of course, it may still be true that w_1 and w_2 differ from one another in respect of the truth or falsity of *infinitely many* propositions, so that there is a sense in which there are 'no more' propositions in respect of whose truth or falsity these worlds differ than there are propositions in respect of whose truth or falsity they agree. But this is rather like the fact that a line of finite length can have a large part which is very similar in length to the whole line, even though the whole line contains both infinitely many points that are contained within the part and also infinitely many points that are not.) Conversely, it may be that worlds w_1 and w_2 differ with respect to the vast majority of propositions that are true in them, in which case we may say that w_1 and w_2 are, overall, very *dissimilar* to one another. In between these extremes, we can envisage a spectrum of intermediate cases, so that any two worlds can, in principle, be compared with one another as to their degree of overall similarity. And then we can say, quite simply, that one world, w_1, is 'closer' to the actual world than is another world, w_2, just in case w_1 is, overall, more similar to the actual world than w_2 is. Of course, it may be that, in many cases, we cannot easily judge which of two worlds is in fact closer to the actual world—but that, it seems, is a purely epistemological problem, not a metaphysical one. The utility of our talking in terms of closeness between possible worlds does not depend upon our *always* being able to determine which of two worlds is closer to the actual world, but only upon our being able to do this in many of the cases which matter—and perhaps this is an ability we do have.

However, things are not really as simple as I have represented them so far, because not all propositions may be of equal weight when it comes to assessing the overall similarity between different possible worlds. Consider, for instance, those propositions which concern the *laws of nature* which obtain in a certain possible world, and contrast these with the propositions which concern *individual matters of fact* in that world—facts about what individual objects exist, what properties they have, and what relations they stand in to one another. We may be able to envisage two different possible worlds which are very similar to one another in respect of individual matters of fact and yet which differ significantly in respect of their laws of nature. Even more easily, we may be able to envisage two different possible worlds which are very similar to one another in respect of their laws of nature and yet which differ greatly in respect of individual matters of fact. Should we say that a difference between two worlds in respect of their laws of nature is more important than a difference between them in respect of individual matters of fact, when we are judging how similar these worlds are to one another overall? It may seem obvious that our answer to this question should be 'Yes'. But in fact it may be that our answer should depend on the purposes for which we are comparing the worlds in question. In other words, it may be that our judgements of overall similarity between worlds should be sensitive to our motives for making such judgements. That in turn would mean that such judgements do not have a purely objective basis in the nature of the worlds we are comparing, but a partly subjective basis in our motives for wanting to compare them.

The problem of deterministic worlds

An example may help to make vivid what is at stake here. Suppose that I have in my hand a stone and that I am wondering whether or not I should regard as true the following counterfactual conditional: 'If I had let go of this stone a moment ago, then it would have fallen to the ground'. According to analysis (1), what I must do is to consider whether, in the closest possible world in which I let go of this stone a moment ago, the stone fell to the ground—where, by the 'closest' such possible world is meant that world, of all the worlds in which I let go of this stone a moment ago, which is most similar to the actual world in respect of the truth-values of the propositions which matter most for the purposes of this comparison. But which propositions are those? Obviously, there are many possible worlds in which I let go of the stone a moment ago but it did not fall to the ground—

because in these worlds, for example, somebody else caught the stone as soon as I let it go, or the stone was attached by a piece of string to the ceiling, or a net was suspended between my hand and the floor, or . . . . The list of such possibilities is clearly infinite. But, on the assumption that none of the possibilities appropriately listed here obtains in the actual world, it seems natural to say that none of these worlds is the *closest* possible world in which I let go of the stone a moment ago. Notice that all of these possibilities concern individual matters of fact. But consider now the laws of nature which obtain in this and other possible worlds. Clearly, there are possible worlds in which our law of gravitation does not hold and in some of these worlds, too, the stone does not fall to the ground when I let it go, even though no one else catches it, it is not attached to the ceiling by a piece of string, there is no net suspended beneath it, and so on. However, once again, it seems natural to say that none of these worlds, either, is the *closest* possible world in which I let go of the stone a moment ago, because a difference in the laws which obtain in different worlds is a very important difference, outweighing a great deal of similarity between them in respect of individual matters of fact.

But now we begin to approach a difficulty. If the laws of this, the actual world, are deterministic in character, and thus permit no exceptions, then any world which is exactly similar to the actual world in respect of its laws, but which differs from the actual world in respect of any individual matter of fact which obtains at a certain time, must also differ from the actual world in respect of individual matters of fact which obtain at all earlier times—and thus must differ in respect of a great many individual matters of fact. For example, assuming the laws of the actual world to be deterministic, any possible world in which the laws of the actual world obtain but which is unlike the actual world in that I let go of the stone a moment ago must also be unlike the actual world in respect of individual matters of fact at all preceding times. Consequently, if such a world is judged to be the *closest* possible world in which I let go of the stone a moment ago, then analysis (1) is committed to the truth of infinitely many counterfactual conditionals of the form: 'If I had let go of this stone a moment ago, then such-and-such would have been different at an earlier time t'. But it may strike us as being far from natural to say that all of these counterfactuals are true.

The obvious way around this problem is to insist that, when it comes to judging overall similarity between worlds for the purposes of evaluating a counterfactual conditional, the closest possible world in which the antecedent of the conditional is true should be regarded as a world which is indistinguishable from the actual world in respect of individual matters of fact up to the time at which the state of affairs mentioned in the antecedent obtains—thus, in our example, up to the time at which I let go of the stone. However, the consequence of insisting upon this is that one can no longer regard the closest world in which the state of affairs mentioned in the antecedent of the counterfactual obtains as being a world in which the laws of the actual world hold without exception: for, assuming these laws to be deterministic, any world which is indistinguishable from the actual world in respect of individual matters of fact up to the time at which the state of affairs mentioned in the antecedent is supposed to obtain *and* in which the laws of the actual world hold without exception must be a world which is also indistinguishable from the actual world in respect of what *subsequent* individual matters of fact obtain—so that it must be a world in which, as in the actual world, the state of affairs mentioned in the antecedent of the counterfactual conditional does *not* obtain.

It seems, then, that we are compelled to deny that similarity in respect of the laws which hold in the actual world and another possible world always outweighs in importance any amount of difference between these worlds in respect of individual matters of fact when we are concerned to evaluate a counterfactual conditional. It seems that we must say that exact similarity in respect of *past* individual matters of fact (past, that is, with respect to the time of the state of affairs mentioned in the antecedent of the conditional) always outweighs in importance a minor dissimilarity in respect of the laws which obtain in the two worlds, where this dissimilarity is required in order to allow the worlds to differ in respect of the state of affairs mentioned in the antecedent of the conditional.[6]

Backtracking counterfactuals and context-dependency

However, we have not yet reached the bottom of this issue, for it seems clear that *sometimes*, at least, we *do* want to assert as true certain so-called 'backtracking' counterfactual conditionals, of the form 'If so-and-so had

---

[6] See further David Lewis, 'Counterfactual Dependence and Time's Arrow', *Noûs* 13 (1979), 455–76, reprinted in Jackson (ed.), *Conditionals*, and also Jonathan Bennett, 'Counterfactuals and Temporal Direction', *Philosophical Review* 93 (1984), 57–91.

happened at time t, then such-and-such would have been different at a time earlier than t'. For example, we may want to assert as true something like this: 'If I had let go of this stone a moment ago, then I would have decided a little while earlier to do so'. Clearly, though, if we insist that the closest possible world in which I let go of this stone a moment ago must be one which is indistinguishable from the actual world in respect of individual matters of fact obtaining up to a moment ago, then we must maintain that such a world is one in which I did *not* decide a little while earlier to let go of the stone. And according to analysis (1), that will require us to judge the counterfactual conditional now at issue to be *false*, contrary to our original intention. We should not, then, insist on the point in question, but must be prepared to be more flexible.

In fact, matters get even more complex than this. It may be that, for certain purposes, we want to judge as true our original counterfactual conditional, 'If I had let go of this stone a moment ago, then it would have fallen to the ground', while for other purposes we want to judge as true the counterfactual conditional whose consequent is the *negation* of the consequent of the first conditional, namely, 'If I had let go of this stone a moment ago, then it would *not* have fallen to the ground'. Why might we want to judge the latter as true? Well, suppose that the stone is a precious one which is fragile: in that case, we may judge that if I had let go of the stone, I would have made an effort to catch it and would have succeeded in doing so—so that it would not have fallen to the ground. (Indeed, we may judge that I would have made this effort on the grounds that if I had let go of the stone, I would have done so with a prior intention of catching it— this last counterfactual being, of course, a backtracking one.) Now, according to analysis (1), it cannot be the case that *both* of these counterfactual conditionals are true—that is, both 'If I had let go of this stone a moment ago, then it would have fallen to the ground' and 'If I had let go of this stone a moment ago, then it would *not* have fallen to the ground'. At least, they cannot both be true if the *same* possible world is selected as the closest possible world in which I let go of the stone, for the purposes of evaluating these conditionals. But, for different reasons, we may indeed want to evaluate both of these conditionals as true. We may want to judge as true the conditional 'If I had let go of this stone a moment ago, then it would not have fallen to the ground', for the reason that, the stone being precious, I would have made a successful effort to catch it. But, equally, we may want to judge as true the conditional 'If I had let go of this stone a moment ago, then it *would* have fallen to the ground', for the reason that the stone is a heavy object and that heavy objects which are unsupported fall to the ground. It seems silly to insist that I must *choose* between these two judgements, because both of them seem perfectly reasonable things to say in appropriate conversational contexts. Certainly, I shouldn't assert both conditionals in the *same* conversational context. But the lesson seems to be that, when we are concerned to compare possible worlds for overall similarity to the actual world for the purposes of evaluating counterfactual conditionals, *different* features of those worlds count as more important in different conversational contexts.[7]

Thus, in the case of our stone, when the focus of our conversation is the natural behaviour of heavy objects, it is reasonable to use a standard of similarity between worlds which allows us to evaluate the counterfactual conditional 'If I had let go of this stone a moment ago, then it would have fallen to the ground' as being *true*. But when the focus of our conversation is the natural human propensity to save precious objects from harm, it is reasonable to use a standard of similarity between worlds which allows us to evaluate that same counterfactual conditional as being *false*. Now, of course, in a perfectly good sense, this is *not* in fact the 'same' counterfactual conditional in the two conversational contexts: it is the same conditional *sentence* that is being used in the two conversational contexts, but given that in one context it is judged to express a true proposition while in the other it is judged to express a false proposition, we must clearly say that the same conditional sentence expresses different propositions in these different contexts of its use. In short, counterfactual conditional sentences are, in respect of their propositional content or meaning, *context-dependent*. It seems that we must say this whether or not we endorse a possible-worlds analysis of counterfactual conditionals such as analysis (1) or analysis (2). But if we do endorse either of those analyses, we must accommodate the context-dependency of counterfactual conditionals by acknowledging the context-dependency of the standards whereby we judge one possible world to be more or less similar to the actual world than another possible world is. This in turn means that 'similarity' between possible worlds is not a purely objective matter which rests solely on the nature of the worlds in question, but is a partly subjective matter which turns on the conversational purposes for which we assert counterfactual conditional sentences. This is not to say that the *truth or falsity* of a

[7] See further my 'The Truth about Counterfactuals', *Philosophical Quarterly* 45 (1995), 41–59, where the theoretical background to much of what follows is explained in detail.

counterfactual conditional is partly a subjective matter, only that appropriate standards of similarity between possible worlds for evaluating counterfactual conditionals must be selected on a partly subjective basis: once those standards have been selected, however, the question of whether or not a given counterfactual conditional is true by those standards may be a purely objective matter.

The question of transitivity again

We are now in a position to return to some earlier business. Earlier on, I suggested that putative counterexamples to the *transitivity* of counterfactuals—that is, to the inference pattern (Trans)—may be diagnosed as involving a fallacy of equivocation rather than as genuine counterexamples to (Trans). But I conceded that it looks suspiciously ad hoc to press this charge by claiming that, where such putative counterexamples are concerned, some of the counterfactual conditionals involved have elliptical or abbreviated antecedents or consequents. However, we are now able to offer an alternative and more sustainable version of this sort of diagnosis. We can urge that, whenever we are presented with a putative counterexample to (Trans), we are only able to judge the premises to be true and the conclusion to be false if we adopt a shifting standard of similarity between possible worlds for the purpose of evaluating the counterfactual conditionals concerned—and that the use of such a shifting standard amounts to a kind of equivocation.

Consider again the Hoover argument: 'If J. Edgar Hoover had been born in the Soviet Union, then he would have been a communist; and if J. Edgar Hoover had been a communist, then he would have been a traitor; therefore, if J. Edgar Hoover had been born in the Soviet Union, then he would have been a traitor'. If we are to judge the premises of this argument to be true and its conclusion to be false, must we not vary our assumptions as to which features of a possible world are more important for the purpose of assessing its degree of overall similarity to the actual world? For example, in evaluating the first premise as true, we must be regarding as relatively unimportant the fact that, in the actual world, Hoover was a United States citizen: for we are assuming that a world in which Hoover is born in the Soviet Union and remains a Soviet citizen is significantly closer to the actual world than is a world in which he is born in the Soviet Union and later becomes a United States citizen. On the other hand, in evaluating the second premise as true, we must be regarding as far from unimportant the fact that, in the actual world, Hoover was a United States citizen: for we are assuming that a world in which he is a communist and a United States citizen is significantly closer to the actual world than is a world in which he is a communist and emigrates to another country with a communist regime. There is nothing inevitable about that assumption, however: one can perfectly well imagine a conversational context in which it would be natural to judge as true the counterfactual conditional 'If J. Edgar Hoover had been a communist, then he would have emigrated to the Soviet Union'. In fact, for virtually any counterfactual conditional we can envisage *some* conversational context in which it would be natural to judge that conditional as being true. But the point about the Hoover argument is that we cannot—I suggest—envisage a *single* conversational context in which it would be natural to judge its premises to be true and its conclusion to be false. If that is so, then the Hoover argument, construed as having true premises and a false conclusion, does indeed involve a kind of equivocation. And that means that it cannot fairly be represented as constituting a genuine counterexample to (Trans).

An alternative analysis of counterfactuals

However, we cannot leave matters there. If (Trans) is not an invalid inference pattern, then neither analysis (1) nor analysis (2) can be correct, for both of these analyses imply that (Trans) is invalid. We can only uphold (Trans) if we are prepared to uphold an alternative analysis—one which implies that (Trans) is valid. One such alternative analysis that might be proposed is the following:[8]

> (3) 'If it had been the case that p, then it would have been the case that q' is true if and only if (a) in every sufficiently close possible world $p \rightarrow q$ is true and (b) either there is some sufficiently close possible world in which p is true or else in every sufficiently close possible world q is true.

In clause (a), '$p \rightarrow q$' means 'It is not the case that both p and not-q', or, equivalently, 'Either not-p or else q'—that is to say, '$p \rightarrow q$' is a so-called *material* conditional. Analysis (3) may look complicated, but it is not so

---

[8] See again my 'The Truth about Counterfactuals', where I also explain in more detail why we have reason to doubt that there are any genuine counterexamples to (Trans).

really. Clause (b) of analysis (3) requires of a true counterfactual conditional either that its antecedent be, in an appropriate sense, a *possible* truth or else that its consequent be, in an appropriate sense, a *necessary* truth. In most ordinary cases, the first of these alternatives will obtain. As for clause (a) of analysis (3), this requires of a true counterfactual conditional that it implies the corresponding 'strict' conditional, that is, that it implies that the corresponding material conditional be, in an appropriate sense, a necessary truth. The senses of 'possibility' and 'necessity' in operation here are not those of unqualified *metaphysical* possibility and necessity, however, for we are only concerned with truth in 'sufficiently close' possible worlds, not with truth in possible worlds without any restriction (although, in some contexts, every possible world without restriction will count as 'sufficiently close'). But what do we mean by 'sufficiently close'? The answer, of course, is that what counts as sufficiently close depends on the conversational context. For a given conversational context, there will be a single standard of similarity between possible worlds and, relative to that standard, a single measure of sufficient closeness. It is easy to verify that analysis (3) implies that (Trans) is a valid inference pattern. It is also easy to verify that analysis (3) implies that neither (Contr) nor (Stren) is a valid inference pattern, that is, that counterfactual conditionals are not contraposable and are not subject to strengthening. It is worth noting, too, that analysis (3), like analysis (2) and unlike analysis (1), supports the distinction between 'would' and 'might' counterfactuals as defined by (DMC) and does not support the principle of conditional excluded middle, (CEM).

This is not the place for me to mount a full-scale defence of analysis (3). I mention it simply to show that there is a feasible analysis of counterfactual conditionals which represents them as being transitive and which can, with some plausibility, be appealed to in support of a diagnosis of the alleged counterexamples to transitivity as involving, in reality, a fallacy of equivocation. The most important lesson of the present chapter, however, is that counterfactual conditionals have a context-dependent propositional content and that any analysis of such conditionals which appeals to the notion of 'closeness' between possible worlds will have to accommodate this context-dependency by acknowledging the context-dependency of our standards of similarity between possible worlds. To the extent that this implies that there is a subjective element amongst the factors which determine the propositional content of a counterfactual conditional sentence on any given occasion of its use, we may harbour some doubts as to whether counterfactual conditionals provide suitable materials for the analysis of various kinds of statement—such as causal statements and disposition statements—which are ordinarily thought of as reporting purely objective matters of fact. This is an issue to which I shall return in Chapter 10, where we shall be looking at counterfactual analyses of causation.

9

CAUSES AND CONDITIONS

Causal statements and the relata of causation

Early in the previous chapter, I remarked that there seems to be an intimate relation between counterfactual conditionals and *causal* statements—that, for example, someone who asserts 'The explosion caused the collapse of the bridge' would normally take this causal statement to imply the counterfactual conditional 'If the explosion had not occurred, then the bridge would not have collapsed'. Even so, it may be doubted whether the relation between these statements is strictly one of *entailment*—that is, that it is logically impossible that the causal statement be true and the counterfactual conditional be false—and it may also be doubted whether a relation of entailment holds between these statements in the opposite direction. If the two statements entailed one another, it would be open to us to maintain that the causal statement can be *analysed* by means of the counterfactual conditional and thus be regarded as having the same propositional content or meaning as the latter. But it is most implausible to maintain this. As we shall see in the next chapter, this still leaves open the possibility that a causal statement such as this is analysable with the help of counterfactual conditionals in some more complex way. But before looking into that possibility, we need to examine some more general issues concerning the nature of causation and discuss some other views about the meaning or analysis of causal statements.

One very important question that we must ask concerning causation is this: given that causation is a relation, what is it a relation between? In other words, what are the *relata* of the relation of causation?—assuming, indeed, that we can properly speak of *the* relation of causation, for it may be possible to urge, on the contrary, that the verb 'to cause' is not univocal and does not always signify the same relation on every occasion of its use. In the case of the causal statement we considered a moment ago—'The

explosion caused the collapse of the bridge'—it seems clear that the putative causal relata being referred to are particular *events*, the explosion being
said to be the cause, or at least *a* cause, of which the bridge's collapse is said
to be an effect. And, indeed, many philosophical accounts of causation
assume that causal relata—causes and effects—are always and only particular events. But not all philosophers of causation agree with this view.
For instance, as we shall see in Chapter 11, some wish to draw a fundamental distinction between 'event causation', which is a relation between
particular events, and what they call *agent causation*, which they generally
conceive to be a relation between an agent, such as a particular human
being, and a particular event. Other philosophers maintain that causation
is a relation between *states of affairs*, or *facts*, rather than between events, or
at least that 'fact causation' is a basic and irreducible species of causation,
even if event causation should also be recognized as a genuine species of
causation in its own right.[1] In support of their position, such philosophers
would point to our use of such statements as 'The victim died because he
swallowed poison', which entails both 'The victim swallowed poison' and
'The victim died', where each of the latter two statements expresses a state
of affairs which the speaker takes to be a fact. The suggestion, then, is that
what is being stated in such a case is that one fact caused another: that the
fact that the victim swallowed poison caused, or brought about, the fact
that the victim died. Other philosophers, however, would urge that when
such a statement is made, what is really being offered is a causal *explanation* rather than an account of what caused what. For these philosophers,
there is a fundamental distinction to be drawn between causation and
causal explanation, with causation being a relation between particular
events whereas causal explanation typically involves a relation between
sentences, statements, or propositions.[2] On this view, then, we may causally
explain why it is the case that the victim died by stating that the victim
swallowed poison, but should still insist that the reason why the explanation is correct, if it is correct, is that a particular event of the victim's
swallowing some poison caused the particular event of the victim's death.

---

[1] See, for example, D. H. Mellor, *The Facts of Causation* (London: Routledge, 1995) and Jonathan
Bennett, *Events and their Names* (Oxford: Clarendon Press, 1988), 21 ff.

[2] See, for example, Donald Davidson, 'Causal Relations', *Journal of Philosophy* 64 (1967), 691–
703, reprinted in his *Essays on Actions and Events* (Oxford: Clarendon Press, 1980) and also in
Ernest Sosa and Michael Tooley (eds.), *Causation* (Oxford: Oxford University Press, 1993).

Event causation

Later in this chapter, I shall return to the issue of whether or not causation can ever properly be regarded as a relation between facts or states of affairs. For the time being, however, I shall concentrate on issues concerning statements of event causation, that is, statements of the form 'Event c caused event e', where c is said to be the cause, or at least a cause, of e. What does a statement of this form mean? What we are ideally looking for, in answer to this question, is a way of expressing the truth conditions of such a causal statement in terms which do not themselves involve any causal concepts—the point of the latter requirement being that an analysis of causation should not be circular. It may be, of course, that no such answer to our question is possible, because it may be that the concept of 'cause' is basic and unanalysable. But, it seems, the only way to find out whether or not this is so is to try to answer our question: if we discover that, despite our best efforts to do so, we fail, then that will give us some reason to suspect that the concept of 'cause' is indeed basic and unanalysable.

Before we look at some putative answers to our question, I should say something about the distinction, implicit in what I have just said, between speaking of *the* cause of a given effect, e, and speaking of *a* cause of e. Clearly, there is a perfectly good sense in which an effect may have more than one cause, not least because causation is a *transitive* relation: if c caused e and d caused c, then d caused e—and yet c and d must clearly be *different* causes of e in such a case, because no event can be a cause of itself. Of course, on the assumption that a cause must precede its effect, c and d will, in such a case, be events occurring at different times. However, it is also possible for each of two or more events occurring at the same time to be causes of a given effect, e—although, barring some kind of over-determination of e by these causes, no one of these causes will be a *sufficient* cause of e. By a 'sufficient' cause of an event, e, I mean an event, or conjunction of events, whose occurrence *causally necessitates* the occurrence of e. It may perhaps be, of course, that a given event, e, has *no* sufficient cause in this sense, because it is conceivable that some events occur at least partly by chance. But let us ignore this complication for now: we shall return to it later, when we come to consider probabilistic conceptions of causation. Then, one thing that we could mean in speaking of 'the' cause of an event, e, is its sufficient cause at a certain time, t—which might be a single event, c, occurring at t, or might be a conjunction of several different events occurring at t, each of which was only a 'partial' cause of e. There are some further complications involved in this issue, which I shall discuss later. For the moment, however, it will be easier if we restrict ourselves to the notion of one event's being *a* cause of another event, without concerning ourselves with the question of when and in what sense it is proper to speak of 'the' cause of any given event. That understood, our original question reduces to this: what are the truth conditions of a statement of the form 'Event c was a cause of event e'?

The 'Humean' analysis of causation and its problems

Perhaps the most famous answer to this question was given by David Hume, though it is open to debate whether he actually accepted this answer himself.[3] The answer is as follows:

(1) Event c was a cause of event e if and only if (a) c preceded e and (b) c and e are, respectively, events of types T_1 and T_2 such that every event of type T_1 is followed by an event of type T_2.

(1) expresses what is commonly called the 'constant conjunction' analysis of event causation, so called because it implies that what makes one event a cause of another, over and above the fact that the first event precedes the second, is the fact that events of the first kind are 'constantly conjoined' with—universally followed by—events of the second kind. It certainly appears that analysis (1) meets the main desideratum of an answer to our question, because no causal concept is explicitly employed in its explanation of what it means to say that one event was a cause of another, so that the analysis cannot apparently be charged with circularity (unless, perhaps, it can be argued that the analysis implicitly relies in some way upon causal concepts for its interpretation). However, despite this virtue, analysis (1) is faced with many difficulties, some of which appear to be fatal.

One such difficulty is the problem of determining how the *types* of events mentioned in (1) are to be individuated. Clearly, not *every* feature of the particular events c and e can be deemed relevant to determining the

---

[3] See David Hume, *Enquiries Concerning Human Understanding and Concerning the Principles of Morals*, ed. L. A. Selby-Bigge and P. H. Nidditch (Oxford: Clarendon Press, 1975), 76. For doubts about whether Hume accepted this definition himself, see Galen Strawson, *The Secret Connexion: Causation, Realism, and David Hume* (Oxford: Clarendon Press, 1989).

types to which they may be said to belong, for the purposes of the analysis offered by (1). For if we deem every such feature to be relevant, then we must allow that there are types to which c and e can be said to belong of which c and e, respectively, are the *sole members*. And then the truth of clause (b) of (1) will follow trivially from the truth of clause (a), implying, absurdly, that any two events occurring at different times are related as cause to effect. But which features of c and e *can* be deemed relevant to determining to which types they may be said to belong, for the purposes of analysis (1)? This may not be a question that is easy to answer without compromising the analysis of causation that is being offered. Consider, for instance, the fact that if event c is indeed a cause of event e, then one feature of c is that it is a cause of an event of some type to which e belongs. (There must presumably be *some* type to which e belongs—but if there is not, then analysis (1) is doomed in any case.) Suppose, then, that e is an event of a certain type, T_2. That being so, there is a perfectly good sense in which c is an event of the following type: 'event that is a cause of an event of type T_2'. Call this type, to which c belongs, T_1. Now, assuming that a cause always precedes its effects, it is evidently the case that every event of type T_1—that is, every event that is a cause of an event of type T_2—is followed by an event of type T_2, so that clause (b) of analysis (1) is satisfied. However, regarding clause (b) as being satisfied for this sort of reason would obviously render analysis (1) completely trivial and hence incapable of revealing anything interesting about the concept of causation. The root of the problem here lies, of course, in the fact that type T_1 in this case has been individuated in terms of a feature of c which involves its causal relationship to e. So, in order to avoid this sort of problem, we must apparently stipulate that, for the purposes of analysis (1), the types T_1 and T_2 invoked in that analysis should not be individuated in terms of any features of c and e which involve a causal relation between them. In effect, this may be seen as reinforcing the requirement that analysis (1) should not be circular. However, what right have we to assume, quite generally, that any two causally related events belong to types which *can* be individuated without reference to the causal relation between those events?

Even if this potential difficulty with analysis (1) can be overcome, other difficulties remain. In some cases, it seems, clauses (a) and (b) of analysis (1) may be satisfied in respect of a pair of events c and e, even though c and e are causally quite unrelated, because c and e belong, respectively, to certain types T_1 and T_2 which happen to have very few instances, all of which happen, quite accidentally, to stand in the relation of temporal precedence required by clause (b) of (1). For instance, it might be that T_1 is a rare type of subatomic event and T_2 is a rare type of astronomical event, but that it just so happens that every event of type T_1 is followed by an event, somewhere in the universe, of type T_2. The charge being raised against analysis (1) here, then, is that it fails to distinguish between genuinely causal conjunctions of events and purely accidental conjunctions of events. Indeed, the cogency of this charge, while made vivid by examples involving rare types of event, is not dependent upon the availability of such examples. It still has force even if we suppose that the event-types to which c and e belong are frequently instantiated. The objection, in effect, is that analysis (1) misrepresents a causal relation between two events as holding in virtue of what may be nothing more than a cosmic accident or coincidence. The objection may be pressed home by asking why facts concerning *other* pairs of events quite distinct from c and e should have any bearing on the issue of whether or not c and e stand in a causal relation to one another, since causation seems to be a relation which connects a given cause with a given effect quite independently of their relations to other events (unless, of course, those other events are intermediate events in a chain of causation linking the given cause with the given effect, which is beside the point as far as the present objection is concerned). The objection may also be supported by the observation that the analysandum of (1), 'Event c was a cause of event e', plausibly implies the counterfactual conditional 'If c had not occurred, then e would not have occurred', whereas the analysans of (1), 'c preceded e and c and e are, respectively, events of types T_1 and T_2, such that every event of type T_1 is followed by an event of type T_2', plainly does *not* imply that counterfactual conditional. The reason why the analysans of (1) cannot imply that counterfactual conditional is simply that the analysans only has implications regarding what is *actually* the case, whereas the counterfactual conditional concerns what *would* have been the case if the world had been in some respect different from how it actually is.

The counterfactual approach to event causation

In the face of these difficulties, most philosophers now hold out little hope for analysis (1) or anything much like it. But what may be offered in its place? One obvious suggestion would be, quite simply, to appeal to the counterfactual conditional just mentioned, giving us as our sought-for analysis the following:

(2) Event c was a cause of event e if and only if c occurred and e
     occurred and if c had not occurred, then e would not have occurred.

(2) is a *counterfactual* analysis of event causation, but a particularly simple
one which is, fairly evidently, inadequate. It is inadequate not least because,
although in many ordinary circumstances it is plausible to maintain that a
causal statement of the form 'Event c was a cause of event e' implies a
counterfactual conditional of the form 'If c had not occurred, then e would
not have occurred', circumstances can also arise in which, if an actual
cause, c, of a certain event, e, had not occurred, then some *other* event, d,
would instead have caused e and so e would still have occurred. We shall
examine this kind of circumstance and its implications for counterfactual
analyses of causation more fully in Chapter 10. Another difficulty with
analysis (2), however, is that its analysans, 'c occurred and e occurred and if
c had not occurred, then e would not have occurred', does not necessarily
imply its analysandum, 'Event c was a cause of event e', because such a
counterfactual conditional can be true even if c and e are, plausibly, events
which are not related as cause to effect. For instance, let c be the event of
Napoleon's birth and let e be the event of Napoleon's death: the counterfactual conditional 'If Napoleon's birth had not occurred, then Napoleon's
death would not have occurred' is plainly true—and yet it would be
unnatural to say that Napoleon's birth was a *cause* of Napoleon's death.

Of course, it might be urged in reply that although this would not be a
natural thing to say, it may none the less be *true*. Consider, then, another
kind of counterexample to analysis (2). Sometimes, one event is a *part* of
another event: for instance, the event of my arm's going up on a certain
occasion apparently includes, as a part, the event of my hand's going up on
that occasion, since my hand is a part of my arm. Consequently, it seems
that the following counterfactual conditional is true: 'If my arm's going up
had not occurred, then my hand's going up would not have occurred'.
Indeed, the following counterfactual conditional also seems to be true: 'If
my hand's going up had not occurred, then my arm's going up would not
have occurred'. But if both of these conditionals are true, analysis (2)
implies that each of these events is a cause of the other—which cannot be
the case, because causation is an asymmetrical relation. Indeed, it seems
right to say that neither event can be a cause of the other, since, plausibly, a
part cannot be a cause of a whole of which it is a part, nor can a whole be a
cause of one of its own parts. It seems right to insist, in fact, that a cause
and any one of its effects must be wholly distinct events, having no part in

common—and analysis (2) fails to imply this. Of course, this defect could easily be remedied, in one way or another, but since we have reason to believe that (2) has other, fatal flaws, there is little point in making the necessary revision. Notice, by the way, that analysis (1) does not suffer from this particular defect, on the assumption that clause (a) of (1) means '*c wholly* preceded *e*': so one option would be to add this clause to analysis (2). But against that suggestion it may be urged that it cannot be part of the concept of causation that a cause precedes its effects, since 'backward' causation—the causation of an earlier event by a later event—is not inconceivable. Whether or not backward causation is metaphysically *possible* is another matter, however—since not everything that is conceivable is metaphysically possible—and that is a question we shall examine further in Chapter 18.

Probabilistic event causation

One defect from which both analysis (1) and analysis (2) appear to suffer is that they leave no scope for the possibility that at least some causation may be irreducibly *probabilistic* in character.[4] Modern quantum physics seems to require that we admit this possibility, because it implies that the occurrence of subatomic events of various kinds cannot, even in principle, be predicted with certainty from prior states of affairs and the laws of physics. The 'probability' with which such an event may be predicted to occur is not, then, merely a measure of our ignorance of the event's underlying causes, for even if all of the causal factors relevant to its occurrence or non-occurrence could be taken into account, it would still remain to some degree a matter of chance whether or not that event would occur. Moreover, whether or not quantum physics demands that we operate with a concept of probabilistic causation, the idea that a cause might not necessitate its effects but only affect the chances of their occurrence in some way is perfectly intelligible, and so arguably ought to be accommodated by any adequate analysis of causality.

But how might this demand be met? It apparently will not do simply to say something like the following:

---

[4] For two recent accounts of causation which attempt to accommodate probabilistic causation, see Paul Humphreys, *The Chances of Explanation: Causal Explanation in the Social, Medical, and Physical Sciences* (Princeton, NJ: Princeton University Press, 1989) and D. H. Mellor, *The Facts of Causation* (London: Routledge, 1995). For an influential earlier account, see Patrick Suppes, *A Probabilistic Theory of Causality* (Amsterdam: North Holland, 1970).

(3) Event c was a cause of event e if and only if c occurred and e occurred and the occurrence of c made the occurrence of e probable to some degree.

For it might be that c made e probable to a very *low* degree, that is, made e very *im*probable. On the other hand, it surely will not do to insist that c made e probable to a very *high* degree, because e might be an event which, in the absence of c, would have been extremely improbable, but which the occurrence of c made more probable, although still not highly probable— and in that case, it would still seem natural to say that c had a causal influence upon e. So, in place of (3) we might want to propose something like this:

(4) Event c was a cause of event e if and only if c occurred and e occurred and the occurrence of c raised the probability of the occurrence of e by some amount.

But what, exactly, does (4) *mean*? What does it mean to say that 'the occurrence of c raised the probability of the occurrence of e by some amount'? Perhaps it can be taken to mean something like this: 'If c had not occurred, then the probability of e's occurring would have been less than it actually was'. This interpretation effectively makes analysis (4) a more general version of the simple counterfactual analysis of causation, analysis (2). For analysis (2) can then be seen as constituting a special case of analysis (4), arising when it is true that, if c had not occurred, then the probability of e's occurring would have been *zero*, so that e would not have occurred. (Clearly, given that e did in fact occur, the actual probability of e's occurring was not zero: so if it is true that, if c had not occurred, then the probability of e's occurring would have been zero, then it is *a fortiori* true that, if c had not occurred, then the probability of e's occurring would have been less than it actually was—which implies, according to analysis (4) under its present interpretation, that c was a cause of e.) However, if (2) is defective, as we have already seen, then so too, it seems, is (4), because it includes (2) as a special case.

Perhaps, however, the lesson to be learnt here is merely that (4) should not be interpreted in the counterfactual fashion just suggested. As an alternative, we could appeal to the notion of *conditional probability*, interpreting 'the occurrence of c raised the probability of the occurrence of e by some amount' to mean something like this: 'The conditional probability of e's occurring given the occurrence of c was higher than the conditional probability of e's occurring given the non-occurrence of c. The notion of conditional probability in play here is a perfectly familiar one. We frequently talk of the conditional probability of one event's occurring given the occurrence of another event. We say, for instance, that the conditional probability of my throwing a six, given a single throw of a fair die, is one in six, or one sixth. However, there are some difficulties attending the notion of the conditional probability of one event's occurring given the *non*-occurrence of another event: for the non-occurrence of an event is not itself an *event* of any kind. So, if we cannot intelligibly talk of the conditional probability of e's occurring given the *non*-occurrence of c, it seems that we shall have to talk instead of the conditional probability of e's occurring given the occurrence of some alternative event distinct from c, and compare this with the conditional probability of e's occurring given the occurrence of c, in order to judge whether or not the occurrence of c can be said to have 'raised the probability of the occurrence of e by some amount', in the sense now being mooted. This other event will, evidently, have to be some event whose occurrence was incompatible with the occurrence of c, so as to exclude the possibility of both events occurring. However, in any given case we shall be able to envisage *many* other events whose occurrence was incompatible with the occurrence of event c, but which could have occurred instead of c. For instance, if c is a certain event of my throwing a fair die, then, instead of c occurring, any one of the following events, each of them incompatible with the occurrence of c, could have occurred in place of it: I could have left the die untouched on the table, I could have crushed it, I could have put it in my pocket, I could have thrown the die having loaded it beforehand. . . . The list is endless. How, then, do we decide with *which* conditional probability we should compare the conditional probability of e's occurring given the occurrence of c, for the purposes of analysis (4)? Different choices of an alternative event to contrast with c may well result in different verdicts as to whether or not the occurrence of c 'raised the probability' of the occurrence of e by some amount, in the sense now being proposed—and yet it surely cannot be the case that whether or not c was a *cause* of e depends upon such a choice of ours. It may perhaps be that, in every conceivable case, there is just one correct and natural way to make such a choice, but unless that is so, analysis (4), interpreted in terms of the notion of conditional probability, would seem to face a difficult problem. My own suspicion is that this problem cannot be solved in any convincing way. But there, for present purposes, I shall leave the issue of how best to understand the notion of probabilistic causation.[5]

Contributory causes and background conditions

So far, we have chiefly been concerned with the notion of what may be called a 'contributory cause'—an event which is *a* cause of a given effect, but not necessarily its 'complete' cause at any given time. Earlier, I used the term 'partial cause' to express this notion. The 'complete cause' at a given time, t, of a given effect, e, will comprise *all* of e's contributory or partial causes at t. Such a complete cause of e will be a 'sufficient' cause of e, in the sense explained earlier, if its occurrence causally necessitates the occurrence of e. But, in view of the possibility of probabilistic causation, we should allow that even a complete cause of e may leave open some chance of e's not occurring. Now, I have been implicitly assuming that all of the contributory causes which comprise an event's complete cause at any given time are themselves *events* occurring at that time. But this assumption may certainly be challenged. Consider, for instance, the complete cause, at a time t, of a certain explosion, e, occurring immediately after t. Perhaps the explosion occurred because an electric spark occurred at t in a room containing inflammable gas. However, the spark was certainly not a sufficient cause of e, nor, plausibly, was it a complete cause of e: apparently, it was at most a contributory or partial cause of e. Why? Because other causal factors surely played a role in bringing about e—factors such as the presence of both inflammable gas and oxygen in the room. But the presence of inflammable gas in the room and the presence of oxygen in the room do not seem to be aptly described as being *events* of any kind, since they involve no kind of *change*. They are 'static' conditions, or 'standing' conditions, which seem to be more appropriately categorized as 'states of affairs'. Against this, it may perhaps be said that we need to understand the term 'event' in a broad sense when we are dealing with the topic of causation: and that 'events', in a suitably broad sense of the term, include not only changes but also what might be called 'unchanges' or 'non-changes'. A non-change, in this sense, is not to be confused with the non-occurrence of an event, which I earlier declared not to be an event of any kind: rather, it may be said, a non-change consists in some thing or things *continuing to be*

[5] For further discussion of this highly technical area of the philosophy of causation, see Daniel M. Hausman, *Causal Asymmetries* (Cambridge: Cambridge University Press, 1998).

the same in respect of some property or relation, whereas a change consists in some thing or things *becoming different* in respect of some property or relation. Of course, it may be suspected that the dispute here is a merely verbal one without any substantive ontological significance. I am not at all convinced that this is so, but I will not attempt to adjudicate on the matter just now, in view of its controversial nature. Let it simply be said that there is a prima facie case for maintaining that at least some of the contributory causes of an event such as our explosion, *e*, are not events of any kind but entities belonging to a quite distinct ontological category—perhaps, indeed, 'states of affairs'. Later on, I shall look into an important objection to this proposal, but before doing so I want to explore another issue which the example of the gas explosion can be used to raise.

I remarked earlier that we sometimes speak of *the* cause of a particular event, such as our explosion, *e*. I also said that one thing we might mean by this is *e*'s *sufficient* cause at a certain time, *t*, if *e* has one. We might also mean *e*'s *complete* cause at *t*. But, ordinarily, we would mean neither of these things in speaking of 'the' cause of *e*. Rather, we would typically be referring to some particular event or state of affairs which was at most a contributory or partial cause of the given effect—in the case of our explosion *e*, something such as the electric spark. But why should we single out such an event or state of affairs for special treatment in this way, when it is only one of many contributory causes of the given effect? Is there really something distinctive about an event such as the electric spark, in the case of the explosion, which differentiates it objectively from other causal factors equally responsible for that effect, such as the presence of inflammable gas and oxygen in the room?

In answer to this question, one might be tempted to say that these other causal factors were merely 'background conditions', whereas the occurrence of the spark constituted a departure from the natural course of events and thereby 'triggered' the explosion. But in response to this it may be urged that what we regard as 'background conditions' and what we regard as a 'departure from the natural course of events', in any given case, is determined more by our attitudes and interests than it is by any purely objective feature of the situation at hand. A room in which inflammable gas and oxygen are regularly present, such as, perhaps, a chemical laboratory, is one in which every effort will be made to prevent the occurrence of electric sparks. A spark in such a room will be an 'unusual' event and therefore might be singled out by us as 'the' cause of an explosion if one should occur. By singling out the spark in this way, we identify a kind of causal factor over which we can try to exercise more careful control in future, in otherwise similar situations. However, it is easy to envisage another case in which an explosion is caused in exactly the same way, but in a room in which electric sparks are a regular occurrence and the presence of inflammable gas is something 'unusual'—for example, an electronics laboratory into which gas has begun to leak from an underground pipe, despite every effort to prevent this from happening. In such a case, it seems, we would single out the presence of inflammable gas in the room as being 'the' cause of the explosion, in the colloquial sense now under scrutiny. And yet, in respect of the causal factors present just prior to the explosion, it seems that the two cases could be exactly similar to one another. The implication appears to be that our singling out something as being 'the' cause of a given effect, in the colloquial sense, does not reflect any special causal role which the event or state of affairs in question played in bringing about that effect, but merely reflects the practical importance to us of that causal factor as one over which we could have exercised more control.[6] However, it is important not to let this subjective or pragmatic aspect of our talk about 'the' cause of an effect deceive us into imagining that causation itself is not a wholly objective relation between events or states of affairs which obtains quite independently of our attitudes and interests. In order to avoid this danger, it is probably better, in metaphysical and scientific contexts—as opposed, say, to legal and moral contexts— simply to avoid altogether any talk of 'the' cause of an effect, in the colloquial sense, and restrict ourselves to talk of contributory causes and complete causes.

Fact causation

I now want to return to the important question of whether events, or states of affairs, or entities of both of these ontological categories, can be causes and effects. Recalling from Chapter 7 that a state of affairs which obtains is a *fact*, what is at issue here is whether causation is exclusively a relation between events or exclusively a relation between facts, or whether, alternatively, it is a relation in which either a fact or an event can stand to either a fact or an event. However, what I shall focus on, for present purposes, is the narrower claim that at least sometimes one fact can be the cause of

---

[6] See further J. L. Mackie, *The Cement of the Universe: A Study of Causation* (Oxford: Clarendon Press, 1974), 34 ff.

another fact, for this claim has come under severe attack by a number of philosophers.[7] A statement of fact causation, if we can allow such a thing, would be a statement of the form 'The fact that p caused the fact that q', or, equivalently, one of the form 'The fact that p caused it to be the case that q'. These are, admittedly, hardly the sorts of thing that anyone would actually say in everyday speech, but there are everyday statements which do appear to come quite close to these forms. One might say, for instance, something like this: 'It was because I dropped a vase of flowers that water was lying all over the floor', or, in slightly more stilted language, 'What was responsible for the fact that water was lying all over the floor was the fact that I dropped a vase of flowers'. It may seem to be a harmless regimentation of such idioms to recast them in either of the uniform patterns that have just been proposed, giving rise to such sentences as 'The fact that I dropped a vase of flowers caused the fact that water was lying all over the floor' and 'The fact that I dropped a vase of flowers caused it to be the case that water was lying all over the floor'. For the sake of simplicity and despite its ugliness, let us adopt the first of these two forms—'The fact that p caused the fact that q'—as our canonical form for a putative statement of fact causation.

In order to see what is problematic about putative statements of fact causation, we need first to appreciate that causation is, very plausibly, a purely *extensional* relation—by which is meant that it is a relation which holds between two entities, if it holds between them at all, independently of how those entities may happen to be described or designated. Thus, the truth-value of a causal statement should not be affected by the way we choose to refer to the entities which, according to that statement, are related as cause to effect. Consequently, one would suppose that, given a true statement of fact causation of the form 'The fact that p caused the fact that q', one can transform this statement into another true statement of fact causation in accordance with either of the following two principles. First, one ought to be able to replace 'p' by any sentence logically equivalent to 'p'—such as, for example, 'If not-p, then p' (where this is understood as being a material conditional)—and likewise for 'q'. Second, one ought to be able to replace any singular term occurring within 'p' by another singular term having the same reference—and likewise for 'q'. To illustrate the latter principle, consider the following statement of fact causation, which for present purposes we may presume to be true: 'The fact

---

[7] See, for example, Davidson, 'Causal Relations'.

that Napoleon was defeated in battle by the allied armies caused the fact that the First French Empire collapsed'. Now, since 'Napoleon' and 'the victor of Austerlitz' denote one and the same person, the following, according to our second principle, should also be a true statement of fact causation: 'The fact that the victor of Austerlitz was defeated in battle by the allied armies caused the fact that the First French Empire collapsed'. And, indeed, this does seem to be a true statement, given that the first statement was true, so that our second principle seems to be vindicated.

However, it appears that, by suitable applications of our two principles, we can transform any putatively true statement of fact causation, of the form 'The fact that p caused the fact that q', into another statement of fact causation of the form 'The fact that r caused the fact that s', which we would have to regard as likewise being true, where the only constraint on 'r' and 's' is that both of these sentences should themselves be true. In other words, it appears that, if *any* statement of fact causation is true, then *every* statement of fact causation which refers to any two facts whatever is true. Thus, for instance, since it is a fact that grass is green and likewise a fact that the earth is round, we shall have to accept that if any statement of fact causation is true, then so too is the following statement of fact causation: 'The fact that grass is green caused the fact that the earth is round'. And this is plainly absurd. Consequently, it seems that we must deny that there is any such thing as fact causation, for only if we do this can we deny that there are any true statements of fact causation and so avoid the absurdity just described.

The Slingshot Argument

I now need to demonstrate how our two principles give rise to the foregoing surprising result. There are several different ways in which this can be done, but all of them involve a version of what is sometimes called the 'Slingshot Argument', which has wider application than merely to statements of fact causation.[8] Here is one version of that argument, applied specifically to statements of fact causation. Let us start with the assumption that the following is a true statement of fact causation:

---

[8] For a wide-ranging discussion of the Slingshot Argument in its many forms and applications, see Stephen Neale, 'The Philosophical Significance of Gödel's Slingshot', *Mind* 104 (1995), 761–825. See also my *The Possibility of Metaphysics: Substance, Identity, and Time* (Oxford: Clarendon Press, 1998), ch. 11.

(i) The fact that p caused the fact that q.

Now, elementary logic tells us that 'p' is logically equivalent to 'p and a is identical with a', whatever object 'a' may happen to name, because it is a logical truth that everything, and thus also a in particular, is self-identical. Equally, if slightly less obviously, 'p' is logically equivalent to 'a is identical with the object, x, such that p and x is identical with a'. The latter can be written using standard logical notation as '$a = (\iota x) (x = a \,\&\, p)$'. This is an identity statement with the singular term 'a' on one side of the identity sign and a definite description, '$(\iota x) (x = a \,\&\, p)$', on the other side. That 'p' is logically equivalent to '$a = (\iota x) (x = a \,\&\, p)$' can be shown using Russell's Theory of Descriptions, for according to that theory, this identity state-ment is analysable as being logically equivalent to the following statement, again using standard logical notation: '$(Ex) (x = a \,\&\, p)$'. And this in turn is logically equivalent to '$a = a \,\&\, p$', which, as we have already observed, is logically equivalent to 'p'. Hence, applying the first of the two principles discussed earlier, we can say that if (i) is a true statement of fact causation, then so also is the following, for it arises from (i) simply by replacing 'p' in (i) by the logically equivalent sentence '$a = (\iota x) (x = a \,\&\, p)$':

(ii) The fact that $a = (\iota x) (x = a \,\&\, p)$ caused the fact that q.

Now, the second of the two principles discussed earlier permits us to replace, in any true statement of fact causation, a singular term by any other singular term denoting the same object, so as to produce another true statement of fact causation. But it is easy to see that if 'r' is any true sentence whatever, then the definite description '$(\iota x) (x = a \,\&\, r)$' denotes the same object as is denoted by the definite description which appears in (ii), '$(\iota x) (x = a \,\&\, p)$', because both of these definite descriptions denote the object a. For, just as we can prove that 'p' is logically equivalent to '$a = (\iota x) (x = a \,\&\, p)$', so we can prove, in exactly the same way, that 'r' is logically equivalent to '$a = (\iota x) (x = a \,\&\, r)$'. Hence, given that '$p$' and '$r$' are both true, '$a = (\iota x) (x = a \,\&\, p)$' and '$a = (\iota x) (x = a \,\&\, r)$' are likewise both true, whence we can infer that the definite descriptions '$(\iota x) (x = a \,\&\, p)$' and '$(\iota x) (x = a \,\&\, r)$' both denote the same object, namely, a. Con-sequently, our second principle permits us to replace the first of these two definite descriptions in (ii) with the second to produce the following statement of fact causation, which must be true if (ii) is true:

(iii) The fact that $a = (\iota x) (x = a \,\&\, r)$ caused the fact that q.

Finally, drawing on the already established fact that 'r' is logically equivalent to '$a = (\iota x)\ (x = a\ \&\ r)$', we can once again apply our first principle and replace the latter sentence in (iii) with 'r', resulting in:

(iv) The fact that r caused the fact that q.

Obviously, by a similar sequence of transitions, we can replace 'q' in (iv) with any true sentence 's', to produce, as a statement of fact causation which must be true if (i) is true, the following:

(v) The fact that r caused the fact that s.

So what we have shown is that by successive applications of our two principles, we can derive (v) from (i) and therefore if (i) is true so, too, must (v) be true, no matter what true sentences 'r' and 's' may happen to be. Since (i) was any arbitrarily chosen statement of fact causation which we assumed to be true, we have thus established our surprising and seemingly absurd result that if any statement of fact causation is true, then *every* statement of fact causation which refers to any two facts whatever is true.

Possible responses to the Slingshot Argument

Although technically quite complicated, the foregoing argument seems, on the face of it, to be relatively straightforward. Can we then conclude, as some philosophers would like us to, that the notion of 'fact causation' is absurd and hence that facts, unlike events, cannot be the relata of causation? Of course, one alternative possibility might be to deny that causation is an extensional relation. It might even be suggested that causation as a relation between facts is a non-extensional relation, whereas causation as a relation between events is an extensional relation, so that there are really two quite different kinds of causation. But against this it may be protested that any relation deserving of the name 'causation' must be a purely objective relation between entities which holds quite independently of how we describe or refer to the entities in question, and so cannot be a non-extensional relation. The relation of *causal explanation* is non-extensional, it may be said, because an explanation is meant to confer understanding and so may be sensitive to our ways of describing the facts that we seek to explain. That being so, we can happily allow that a Slingshot Argument cannot be used to reduce to absurdity the notion of one fact's *causally explaining* another fact (or of one true proposition's causally explaining another true proposition, if that formulation is preferred). But, according to this way of thinking, causation and causal explanation must be sharply distinguished from one another, with causation being exclusively an extensional relation between events.

Another possibility, however, is to challenge the Slingshot Argument against fact causation while accepting that causation between facts will have to be an extensional relation. The weak point in the Slingshot Argument lies, perhaps, in the transition from (ii) to (iii). For the legitimacy of this step depends upon our assuming that the definite description in (ii) and the definite description in (iii) which replaces it are both singular terms which possess the same reference, namely, the object *a*. However, the reasoning which enabled us to make the earlier transition from (i) to (ii) appealed to Russell's Theory of Descriptions—and according to this theory, as interpreted by Russell himself, definite descriptions are *not* genuine singular terms which refer to particular objects. Rather, Russell maintains that a definite description is an 'incomplete symbol', which has no independent meaning of its own and can only be understood within the context of some sentence in which it appears.[9] On Russell's view, when a sentence which contains a definite description is analysed in accordance with his Theory of Descriptions, the definite description disappears without trace and no singular term remains which could be thought of as preserving any referential role that we might have been tempted to ascribe to the definite description. Thus, for Russell, a sentence of the form 'The object which is *F* is *G*', in which we might be tempted to see the definite description 'the object which is *F*' as a singular term, is analysed as meaning 'There is exactly one object which is *F* and every object which is *F* is *G*', a sentence containing no term which makes singular reference to any object whatever. So, it seems, if we appeal to Russell's Theory of Descriptions in order to legitimate the step from (i) to (ii), we cannot consistently treat the definite descriptions in (ii) and (iii) as co-referential singular terms, as we need to do in order to legitimate the step from (ii) to (iii).

This way of blocking the Slingshot Argument against fact causation does, however, raise some further questions. In particular, how can we now explain why it seemed perfectly satisfactory to make the transition from 'The fact that Napoleon was defeated in battle by the allied armies caused the fact that the First French Empire collapsed' to 'The fact that the victor of Austerlitz was defeated in battle by the allied armies caused the fact that

---

[9] See Alfred North Whitehead and Bertrand Russell, *Principia Mathematica*, 2nd edn. (Cambridge: Cambridge University Press, 1927), introd., ch. III.

the First French Empire collapsed', relying simply on the fact that Napoleon was indeed the victor of Austerlitz? One answer might be that in this case we are assuming that the definite description 'the victor of Austerlitz' is playing a genuinely referential role and nothing more than that, so that the sentence containing it is not to be analysed in accordance with Russell's Theory of Descriptions.[10] Another answer, compatible with the first, might be that we *can* in fact construe these two statements of fact causation in such a way that we might dispute the transition from one to the other—and that we can do this precisely when we construe the definite description 'the victor of Austerlitz' in the second statement as being amenable to Russell's analysis. This is more evident if, in uttering the second statement of fact causation, we stress or emphasize the definite description by our tone of voice, saying 'The fact that *the victor of Austerlitz* was defeated in battle by the allied armies caused the fact that the First French Empire collapsed'—for this then suggests that it was not merely the fact that Napoleon was defeated which brought it about that the Empire collapsed, but rather the fact that he was victorious at Austerlitz and later defeated. Altogether, then, it seems that the Slingshot Argument against fact causation can be effectively challenged or, at the very least, called sufficiently into question for the notion of fact causation to remain worthy of serious consideration alongside the notion of event causation.

[10] For the view that definite descriptions can sometimes play a purely referential role, see Keith Donnellan, 'Reference and Definite Descriptions', *Philosophical Review* 75 (1966), 281–304, reprinted in Stephen P. Schwartz (ed.), *Naming, Necessity, and Natural Kinds* (Ithaca, NY: Cornell University Press, 1977).

10

COUNTERFACTUALS AND EVENT CAUSATION

The simple counterfactual analysis of event causation

We saw in the previous chapter that it is a debatable matter whether causation is exclusively a relation between particular events, since there is something to be said for the view that there can be causal relations between *facts*. However, in the present chapter I shall be concerned solely with the notion of event causation and more especially with the question of whether statements of event causation can be analysed with the help of counterfactual conditionals. We have already looked at one possible counterfactual analysis of event causation, analysis (2) of the previous chapter, which I shall now refer to as the 'simple' counterfactual analysis, namely:

> (SCA) Event c was a cause of event e if and only if c occurred and e occurred and if c had not occurred, then e would not have occurred.

I remarked, when discussing this proposal in the previous chapter, that one of its defects is that it seems to imply that an event which is a part of another event may be a cause of the latter event, and likewise that an event may be a cause of another event which is a part of the former event. So the first amendment that needs to be made to (SCA) is to include on its right-hand side a clause stipulating that c and e are wholly distinct events, to give:

> (SCA+) Event c was a cause of event e if and only if (a) c and e are wholly distinct events, (b) c occurred and e occurred, and (c) if c had not occurred, then e would not have occurred.

Of course, this raises the question of what we mean by describing two events as being 'wholly distinct'. The obvious and correct thing to say is that two events are wholly distinct just in case there is no event which is a common part of both of them. (Here we should understand 'part' in a liberal sense, to mean 'proper or improper part': a proper part of something is not identical with that thing, whereas an improper part of something is identical with that thing—so that there is a trivial sense in which everything is a part of itself, because everything is identical with itself.) But when, exactly, is one event a part of another, distinct event? Clearly, if one event wholly precedes another event, then neither is a part of the other: but this does not get us much further forward, since to say that one event 'wholly precedes' another event is just to say that every part of the first event precedes every part of the second. In any case, we cannot necessarily assume that, when an event c causes an event e, c wholly precedes e—on the one hand because 'backward causation' may be possible and on the other because *simultaneous* causation may be possible. Evidently, we cannot rule out simultaneous causation by claiming that no two wholly distinct events can occur at the same time, for the latter claim is utterly implausible. Indeed, it would seem, on the face of it, that two wholly distinct events could occur not only at the same time but in the same place. Whether or not that is really so is a matter to which we shall return in Chapter 12, when we come to discuss the individuation of events and various different possible criteria of identity for events. For the time being, let us set aside such questions, however, and pretend that we have a sufficiently clear grasp of what is required for one event to be, or not to be, a part of another, distinct event.[1]

Some difficulties for the simple analysis

Even setting aside such questions, the amended simple counterfactual analysis of event causation, (SCA+), appears to have difficulty in distinguishing between cause and effect and also in distinguishing between a pair of events related as cause and effect and a pair of events which are merely different effects of a common cause. The first sort of difficulty, which is more profound than it may initially appear, may be illustrated as

---

[1] For an extensive discussion of part–whole relations amongst events, see Judith Jarvis Thomson, *Acts and Other Events* (Ithaca, NY: Cornell University Press, 1977).

follows. Suppose that a certain bomb contains a reliable mechanism which enables it to be exploded, but only by pressing a certain button, and that, on a certain occasion, the button is pressed and the bomb duly explodes. In that case, the right-hand side of (SCA+) seems to be satisfied where c is the explosion of the bomb and e is the pressing of the button: for these are wholly distinct events, both of which occurred, and it is surely true to say that if the explosion of the bomb had not occurred, then the pressing of the button would not have occurred. (To deny the truth of this counterfactual conditional would be to imply that the pressing of the button might have occurred even if the explosion of the bomb had not occurred, which is incompatible with the assumption that the bomb's mechanism was a reliable one.) But, according to (SCA+), this means that the explosion of the bomb caused the pressing of the button, whereas what we want to say is quite the reverse of this—that the pressing of the button caused the explosion of the bomb. Of course, (SCA+) allows us to say this too, because it is surely also true that if the pressing of the button had not occurred, then the explosion of the bomb would not have occurred (given, as we are, that the bomb could only be exploded by pressing the button). However, we should clearly *not* say that each event caused the other, first because causation is an asymmetrical relation and secondly because we do not want to say, without good reason, that a later event caused an earlier event, since backward causation—even if it is possible—is surely not a commonplace phenomenon.

One answer to this apparent difficulty would simply be to add to the right-hand side of (SCA+) a clause stipulating that c occurred earlier than e: but this would have the disadvantage of ruling out backward causation by definition, which we surely should not do. Another answer would be to stipulate that the counterfactual conditional appearing in (SCA+) should not be a so-called 'backtracking' counterfactual (recalling our discussion of such counterfactuals in Chapter 8). That is to say, in evaluating the counterfactual conditional appearing in (SCA+) as being true or false, in any given case, we should consider whether or not, in the possible world(s) in which c does not occur but everything else happens just as in the actual world up to the time of c's occurrence, e also occurs. In the case of our bomb example, the counterfactual conditional 'If the explosion of the bomb had not occurred, then the pressing of the button would not have occurred' turns out to be *false* according to this method of evaluation: because, according to this method, the following counterfactual conditional, which contradicts the counterfactual conditional just mentioned, is plainly true: 'If the explosion of the bomb had not occurred, then the pressing of the button would (still) have occurred'. However, it is obvious that this answer will again rule out backward causation by definition, which we have already seen to be undesirable. Backward causation will be ruled out because, if c occurs later than e, the proposed method of evaluation will assume that e occurs in the relevant possible world(s) in which c does not occur, for any such world is stipulated to be one in which everything happens just as in the actual world up to the time of c's occurrence—and this will include the occurrence of e, given that e occurs before c. What is required, clearly, is some account of the *direction* of causation which does not simply identify this with the direction of *time*, that is, which explains which of two events that are related as cause to effect is the cause and which is the effect, without simply stipulating that the earlier of the two is the cause and the later the effect. I shall not attempt to provide such an account here, though I shall return to the issue in Chapter 18, when we come to discuss the direction of time. But we should not underestimate the difficulty of providing such an account which is both adequate in itself and capable of being utilized, non-circularly, in a counterfactual analysis of causation.[2]

The other difficulty for (SCA+) mentioned a moment ago is that it will not necessarily distinguish between a pair of events related as cause and effect and a pair of events which are merely different effects of a common cause. Consider, for instance, the following situation. Suppose that we again have a bomb fitted with a reliable mechanism which enables it to be exploded only by pressing a certain button, but that, quite independently, the mechanism also enables a warning light to be activated, once more only by pressing the button. The button is pressed and—either simultaneously or in sequence—the bomb explodes and the warning light flashes. We want to say that the pressing of the button caused both the explosion of the bomb and the flashing of the light, but it seems that (SCA+) commits us to saying, in addition, that the explosion of the bomb caused the flashing of the light and vice versa, which is clearly mistaken. Even if we stipulate that a cause must always precede its effect, we shall still have a difficulty if, say, the flashing of the light precedes the explosion of the bomb: for in that case, it seems, we shall still have to acknowledge the truth of the counterfactual conditional 'If the flashing of the light had not

[2] For more on the direction of causation, see J. L. Mackie, *The Cement of the Universe: A Study of Causation* (Oxford: Clarendon Press, 1974), ch. 7. See also Daniel M. Hausman, *Causal Asymmetries* (Cambridge: Cambridge University Press, 1998).

occurred, then the explosion of the bomb would not have occurred'—and so (SCA+) will still require us to say that the flashing of the light caused the explosion of the bomb, which we know to be false.

However, if we stipulate instead that the counterfactual conditional appearing in (SCA+) should not be a backtracking counterfactual, then it seems that we can escape the difficulty, because this allows us to evaluate as *false* the counterfactual conditional 'If the flashing of the light had not occurred, then the explosion of the bomb would not have occurred', even if we assume that the flashing of the light occurred before the explosion of the bomb. Why? Because if we consider the possible world(s) in which the flashing of the light does not occur but everything else happens just as in the actual world up to the time at which the flashing of the light occurs, we find that such a world is one in which the causal processes leading to the explosion of the bomb are already under way at the time at which the light fails to flash, so that the explosion still occurs.

But it may be doubted whether this solution to the problem really redounds to the credit of the counterfactual analysis of causation that is being proposed. For it will be noted that in explaining how the solution works, I made reference to certain 'causal processes' that were supposedly already under way at a certain time. This suggests that we need an independent grasp of the concept of causation in order to see how the proposed counterfactual analysis of causation can escape the difficulty that was raised earlier. But then the pretensions of that proposed analysis to provide us with a genuine understanding of the concept of causation seem to be undermined. However, this, I think, points to a more general problem afflicting all counterfactual analyses of causation—a problem to which I shall return later in this chapter.

The problem of causal overdetermination

Another serious difficulty, or set of difficulties, facing the amended simple counterfactual analysis of event causation, (SCA+), arises from the possibility of various forms of *causal overdetermination*.[3] I shall distinguish, in particular, three types of cases of causal overdetermination, which I shall call, respectively, cases of *actual overdetermination*, cases of *pre-emption*,

---

[3] See further Marshall Swain, *Reasons and Knowledge* (Ithaca, NY: Cornell University Press, 1981), 65 ff. See also Louis E. Loeb, 'Causal Theories and Causal Overdetermination', *Journal of Philosophy* 71 (1974), 525–44.

and *fail-safe* cases. The three types of cases may be characterized as follows. In each type of case, I am assuming that a certain event, c, is a cause of another event, e.

(1) In a case of *actual overdetermination*, e has another actual cause, d, in addition to c, such that, even if c had not occurred, d would still have occurred and would still have caused e.

For example, suppose that an assassin's shot, c, causes the victim's death, e, but that a second assassin also fires at the same time as the first and that his shot, d, not only also causes e but would still have caused e even if the first shot, c, had not occurred.

(2) In a case of *pre-emption*, another event, d, occurs, such that although d is not actually a cause of e, if c had not occurred, then d would still have occurred and would then have caused e.

Here we may say that d's causation of e was pre-empted by c's causation of e. For example, suppose that the first assassin's shot, c, causes the victim's death, e, but that a second assassin also fires a split-second later than the first and that his shot, d, although not actually a cause of e, would have caused e if the first shot, c, had not occurred.

(3) In a *fail-safe* case, if c had not occurred, then another event, d— which did not actually occur—would have occurred and would then have caused e.

For example, suppose that an assassin's shot, c, causes the victim's death, e, but that there is a second assassin, who does not actually fire but who would have fired if c had not occurred and whose shot, d, would then have caused e.

Clearly, the main difference between the three types of cases lies in the status of event d. In a case of type (1), d is an event which actually occurs and which actually causes e. In a case of type (2), d is an event which actually occurs but which does not actually cause e. In a case of type (3), d is an event which does not actually occur at all. But in all three types of case, if c had not occurred, then d would have occurred and would have caused e, so that e would still have occurred. And this, of course, is why all such cases, if they are possible, provide counterexamples to the amended simple counterfactual analysis of causation, (SCA+): for they are all cases in which the left-hand side of (SCA+) is true, because event c was a cause of event e, and yet the right-hand side of (SCA+) is *not* true, because it is not true that, if c had not occurred, then e would not have occurred (since it is true, on the contrary, that if c had not occurred, then e would still have occurred).

Some possible responses to the problem

Of course, these putative cases of causal overdetermination only provide convincing counterexamples to analysis (SCA+) if we can reasonably suppose such cases really do occur. But perhaps it can be argued that we cannot. For example, it may be objected against putative cases of type (1)—that is, putative cases of actual overdetermination—that the events c and d in such cases, which are purportedly both actual causes of a given event e, are in fact merely parts of a compound event, call it $c + d$, which actually causes e. Now, we must presumably acknowledge that if either c or d had not occurred, then $c + d$ would not have occurred. But we have already been given that if c had not occurred, then d would still have occurred and would have caused e. And we may presume, likewise, that if d had not occurred, then c would still have occurred and would have caused e. So it turns out that if we regard $c + d$ as actually causing e, we are still faced with a problem of overdetermination, albeit now one of type (2), pre-emption. For now, it seems, we must concede that even if $c + d$ had not occurred, either c would still have occurred or else d would still have occurred and that in either case an event would still have occurred which—although not actually a cause of e—would have caused e, so that e would still have occurred. And this implies, according to (SCA+), that $c + d$ was not, after all, a cause of e. It seems, then, that we can save (SCA+) from counterexamples of type (1) in this way only at the expense of generating further counterexamples of type (2). In view of this fact, and because it also seems likely that any defence of (SCA+) against counterexamples of type (2) will equally serve as a defence of it against counterexamples of type (3), it seems sensible to concentrate our attention upon counterexamples of type (2), which is what I propose to do from now on.[4]

One way in which we might attempt to defend (SCA+) against counterexamples of type (2) is to argue that if c, the actual cause of e, had not occurred, then the event that d would have caused would not have been e, but rather some numerically distinct, even though very similar, event.

---

[4] For doubts about the existence of genuine overdetermination of type (1), see Martin Bunzl, 'Causal Overdetermination', *Journal of Philosophy* 76 (1979), 134–50.

Thus, it may be pointed out that if the first assassin had not fired, so that only the second assassin had fired a split-second later, then the victim would have been hit a split-second later than he actually was and would quite probably have been wounded in a slightly different way, albeit still fatally. This may encourage us to suppose that the event caused by the second shot would not have been the very same event as the one that was actually caused by the first shot. It may sound odd to say that the victim would have died 'a different death', but that might literally be true. The issue that confronts us here raises a question of *transworld identity* of the kind discussed earlier, in Chapter 6—although now we are concerned with the transworld identity of events rather than of material objects. We know that such questions are difficult and contentious ones. And as yet we haven't even determined how events are to be individuated or identified in the actual world, let alone 'across possible worlds'—a matter to which we shall turn our attention in Chapter 12. However, a few preliminary observations may be in order here. First of all, it would be implausible to contend that the precise time of an event belongs to its 'individual essence'—that is, that one and the same event could not have occurred slightly earlier or later than it actually did occur. It may be absurd to suppose that the Battle of Hastings—that very conflict—could have occurred during the reign of Queen Elizabeth I instead of in 1066, but it doesn't seem absurd to suppose that it could have occurred a day earlier or later than it actually did. (Of course, this supposition may open the way to a paradox, if we consider a long series of possible worlds, in each successive member of which the Battle of Hastings occurs a day later than in the previous one, for at the end of this series we may have a possible world in which the battle occurs during the reign of Queen Elizabeth I: but there may be a way to block such a paradox, as we saw in Chapters 6 and 7, by denying that the accessibility relation between possible worlds is unrestrictedly transitive.) In any case, however, it would not be impossible, perhaps, to construct a plausible type-(2) counterexample to (SCA+), that is, a pre-emption example, in which, if event c had not occurred, the effect of event d would have occurred at *the very same time* at which event e actually occurred—so that it would be unwise to assume that merely by insisting that the precise time of an event belongs to its individual essence we could defuse all type-(2) counterexamples to (SCA+). (Indeed, if we try to defuse *type-(1)* counterexamples to (SCA+) in the way proposed earlier, we shall be faced precisely with type-(2) counterexamples of the kind now being contemplated.)

Instead of insisting that the precise time of an event belongs to its individual essence, we might think of insisting instead that all of an event's *causes and effects* belong to its individual essence. This would certainly eliminate all putative type-(2) counterexamples to (SCA+), because now we would be saying that event *e* could not have occurred at all if it had not been caused by event *c*—that, for instance, the victim would have died a different death if he had been killed by the second assassin rather than by the first, simply because the death that he would then have died would have been a death caused by a different shot. But the trouble with trying to defuse type-(2) counterexamples to (SCA+) in this way, quite apart from its inherent implausibility, is that it appeals to the very concept of event causation which (SCA+) is intended to analyse. Clearly, we need already to understand what causation is in order to understand what it means to say that all of an event's causes and effects belong to its individual essence. Furthermore, this proposal has the undesirable implication that true propositions concerning causal relations between events are metaphysically necessary truths. That is to say, given that it is true that an event *c* caused an event *e*, it will be metaphysically necessary—true in all possible worlds—that this is so (or, at least, true in all possible worlds in which either *c* or *e* exists). Why? Because if the property of being caused by event *c* is an essential property of event *e*, then it is a property that *e* has in every possible world in which *e* exists, so that in every such world it is true that event *e* is caused by event *c*. But, however much we may disagree with certain aspects of David Hume's philosophy of causation (allowing for the disagreement amongst commentators as to what his true opinions really were), one thing that Hume has surely taught us is that true propositions concerning causal relations between events are *contingent* truths, not metaphysically necessary ones. The necessity which causation involves is at most 'natural' or 'physical' necessity, not metaphysical necessity.[5]

The complex counterfactual analysis of event causation

I shall now turn to a quite different strategy for dealing with type-(2) counterexamples to (SCA+). This strategy accepts that the counterexam-

---

[5] For an opposing view, see Sydney Shoemaker, 'Causal and Metaphysical Necessity', *Pacific Philosophical Quarterly* 79 (1998), 59–77.

ples are fatal to (SCA+) and attempts to replace (SCA+) by an alternative counterfactual analysis of causation. There are many ways in which one might try to carry out this strategy, but I shall focus on one in particular, the key idea of which can be credited to David Lewis.[6] A type-(2) counterexample to (SCA+), that is, a pre-emption example, presents us with a case in which an event c causes an event e, even though it is not true to say that if c had not occurred, then e would not have occurred: e would still have occurred, because if c had not occurred, another event d would have caused e. The lesson is that it is not necessary, for c to have caused e, that it be true that if c had not occurred, then e would not have occurred. Now, let us say that if it *is* true that if c had not occurred then e would not have occurred, then e is 'counterfactually dependent upon' c. Then the lesson is that it is not necessary, for c to have caused e, that e should be counterfactually dependent upon c. However, perhaps what we can propose, in place of (SCA+), is something like the following analysis, which I shall call the 'complex counterfactual analysis of causation':

(CCA) Event c was a cause of event e if and only if (a) c and e are wholly distinct events, (b) c occurred and e occurred, and (c) a chain of counterfactually dependent events linked c to e.

What clause (c) of (CCA) means is this: there was a finite sequence of actually occurring events, with c being the first member of the sequence and e the last, such that each member of the sequence was counterfactually dependent upon the immediately preceding member of the sequence. For instance, suppose that there was a sequence of events of this kind which possessed just three members, with c being the first member and e being the last, and call the intermediate event of the sequence x. Then what is required by clause (c) is that x should be counterfactually dependent upon c and that e should be counterfactually dependent upon x. This in turn means that the following two counterfactual conditionals should be true: 'If c had not occurred, then x would not have occurred' and 'If x had not occurred, then e would not have occurred'. Now, before we try to see how clause (c) is supposed to overcome the problem of pre-emption, we need to appreciate that the solution to that problem which is being offered here rests on the presumption that counterfactual conditionals are *non-transitive* (an issue that we discussed in some detail in Chapter 8). Clearly,

---

[6] See David Lewis, 'Causation', *Journal of Philosophy* 70 (1973), 556–67, reprinted with postscripts in his *Philosophical Papers*, vol. 2 (Oxford: Oxford University Press, 1986). See also Swain, *Reasons and Knowledge*, 47 ff.

if counterfactual conditionals are *transitive*, then the two counterfactual conditionals just cited entail the following counterfactual conditional: 'If c had not occurred, then e would not have occurred'. But this is precisely clause (c) of the now-discredited (SCA+). So, if counterfactual conditionals are transitive, clause (c) of the new analysis, (CCA), entails clause (c) of the old analysis, (SCA+), in which case (CCA) is vulnerable to all the type-(2) counterexamples which afflict (SCA+). Hence, it is crucial for the success of (CCA) that counterfactual conditionals may correctly be regarded as non-transitive. This, however, already presents a difficulty for (CCA), because, as I tried to show in Chapter 8, it is certainly debatable whether counterfactual conditionals are non-transitive, my own view being that they are not. However, I shall set aside such doubts for the time being and assume, for the sake of argument, that counterfactual conditionals are indeed non-transitive.

Pre-emption cases

How, then, is (CCA) supposed to overcome the problem of pre-emption? To see how, consider again our pre-emptive assassination example. We want to say that the first assassin's shot, c, caused the victim's death, e, even though it is true that, if c had not occurred, then the second assassin's shot, d, would have caused e, so that e would still have occurred. However, it seems that (CCA) can accommodate this situation quite easily. According to (CCA), the reason why we can say that c caused e is that there was a chain of counterfactually dependent events linking c to e, which is perfectly consistent with its being true that, even if c had not occurred, e would still have occurred (given the non-transitivity of counterfactual conditionals). Moreover, (CCA) enables us to deny that the second assassin's shot, d, was actually a cause of the victim's death, e: for we may say that there was *not* a chain of counterfactually dependent events linking d to e. At the same time, we may say that there *would have been* such a chain linking d to e if c had not occurred: so that (CCA) licenses us to say, as we want to, that if c had not occurred, then d would have caused e. Finally, (CCA) even allows us to uphold the *transitivity of causation*, which (SCA+), to its discredit, does not (unless, of course, counterfactual conditionals are transitive). For, clearly, even given that counterfactual conditionals are non-transitive, it is still the case that if a chain of counterfactually dependent events links an event x to an event y, and another chain of counterfactually dependent events links event y to an event z, then there is a chain of counterfactually dependent events linking event x to event z.

This way of handling pre-emption cases appears to presume, quite plausibly, that in a case of pre-emption, some effect of the actual cause, c, of event e prevents the completion of what would otherwise have been a chain of counterfactually dependent events linking event d to event e. For example, in the pre-emptive assassination case, we may suppose that the entry of the first bullet into the victim's body not only caused certain fatal tissue-damage but also, by causing the victim's body to move, prevented the occurrence of the fatal tissue-damage that would have been caused by the entry of the second bullet.

However, a problem apparently arises for analysis (CCA) in cases of *late pre-emption*. These are cases in which the only effect of event c that prevents the completion of a chain of counterfactually dependent events linking the event d to event e is the event e itself. The problem now is that, in such a case, it seems that there will not be a complete chain of counterfactually dependent events linking the *actual* cause of e, event c, to event e, so that analysis (CCA) will not license us to describe event c as being a cause of event e. Why? Because if the penultimate event in the putative chain of counterfactually dependent events linking c to e had not occurred, the occurrence of e would not have prevented the completion of such a chain linking d to e, so that e would still have occurred. Hence, e is not counterfactually dependent upon the penultimate event in question, so that these two events do not in fact belong to a chain of counterfactually dependent events linking c to e. Discussion of late pre-emption cases can become extremely complicated, however, so I shall not indulge in further discussion of them here. Suffice it to say that it is generally recognized that such cases present a serious problem for counterfactual analyses of causation along the lines of (CCA). For some philosophers of causation, this difficulty merely provides an incentive to construct yet another, still more elaborate counterfactual analysis of causation which can accommodate cases of late pre-emption.[7] But other philosophers, less enamoured of the counterfactual approach, may be more inclined to see in such problems a

---

[7] For discussion of the problem of late pre-emption and a proposed solution to it, see Lewis, postscript E to 'Causation', *Philosophical Papers*, vol. 2, 193 ff. Lewis now rejects the solution proposed there: see his 'Causation as Influence', *Journal of Philosophy* 97 (2000), 182–97. The issue of the *Journal of Philosophy* in which this paper appears is a special issue on causation and contains several other interesting papers on the subject. For another problem apparently raised for (CCA) by pre-emption, see William K. Goosens, 'Causal Chains and Counterfactuals', *Journal of Philosophy* 76 (1979), 489–95.

sign that we would do better to abandon the counterfactual approach altogether.

General objections to the counterfactual approach

So far, we have been trying to assess the merits of various counterfactual analyses of causation by seeing how well they accommodate certain problem cases. Our strategy has been to try to identify cases in which, plausibly, the truth-value of a causal statement of the form 'Event c was a cause of event e' differs from the truth-value of the statement in terms of which, according to a proposed counterfactual analysis, such a causal statement is to be analysed. So far, we have not discovered a counterfactual analysis of causation which uncontroversially accommodates every problem case that we have been able to construct, but this still leaves open the possibility that some more refined counterfactual analysis will be successful on this score. But now I want to consider some more general reasons for doubting whether any sort of counterfactual analysis of causation could be correct— remembering that a successful analysis of any concept should not even implicitly rely upon the very concept being analysed for its interpretation, since its doing so would render it circular and in this sense unenlightening. Another general constraint which it seems reasonable to impose upon any adequate analysis of causation is that it should represent causation as being a purely objective relation between its relata, that is, as being a relation which obtains between certain entities independently of human interests and independently of how we may choose to describe those entities. However, we have some grounds for suspecting that counterfactual analyses of causation may not be able to meet either of these general constraints, because of the very nature of counterfactual conditionals.

The circularity objection

In the first place, it may plausibly be argued that we very often need to appeal to causal considerations for the purpose of interpreting counterfactual conditionals and evaluating them as being true or false. This may not be immediately obvious if we adopt one popular account of the meaning of a counterfactual conditional which was described in Chapter 6. According to this account, a counterfactual conditional of the form 'If it had been the case that p, then it would have been the case that q is true if and only if q is true in all of the closest possible worlds in which p is true. Nothing in this statement of the truth conditions of a counterfactual conditional seems to make any reference, either explicit or implicit, to causality. However, we also saw in Chapter 8 that it is no simple matter to determine which of various possible worlds in which a proposition p is true is the closest, or most similar, to the actual world, for the purposes of evaluating a counterfactual conditional as being true or false. We need to be able to compare the worlds in question for similarity in various respects—notably, for similarity in respect of certain particular matters of fact and similarity in respect of certain natural laws. (We also, of course, need to make a judgement as to whether similarity in one respect contributes more than similarity in another respect to the overall similarity or dissimilarity between any two worlds—a point to which I shall return shortly.) Now, in many cases, some of the particular matters of fact in question will surely be *causal* matters of fact and some of the laws in question will surely be *causal* laws. And this surely presents a problem for counterfactual analyses of causation, as the following simple example suggests.

Suppose that we seek to evaluate as true or false a counterfactual conditional we discussed in Chapter 8, 'If I had let go of this stone a moment ago, then it would have fallen to the ground'. Then we need to consider whether, in the closest possible worlds in which I let go of this stone a moment ago, it fell to the ground. Which are the closest such worlds? However we decide to answer this question, once we settle upon an answer to it the question will remain as to whether or not, in the worlds in question, the stone falls to the ground. But whether or not it falls to the ground in the worlds in question will clearly depend, at least in part, on what causal matters of fact and what causal laws obtain in those worlds. For instance, it will depend on whether or not, in the worlds in question, the stone is *supported* by another object, whether or not it is *attracted* by the earth's gravitational field, and whether or not the *law of gravitation* holds universally, as we suppose that it does in the actual world. Thus, whether or not the counterfactual conditional in question is actually true or false will depend, at least in part, on whether or not certain *causal propositions* are true in the closest possible worlds in which I let go of the stone. It seems fair to object that, if this is generally the case with counterfactual conditionals—and more specifically with the counterfactual conditionals that are appealed to in counterfactual analyses of causation—then there is an implicit circularity involved in attempting to analyse *causal* statements in terms of counterfactual conditionals. *Is* it the case, then, with the counterfactual conditionals that are appealed to in counterfactual analyses of causation, that their truth or falsehood depends, at least in part, on what causal propositions are true in certain 'nearby' possible worlds? Surely it *is*, at least if the proposed account of the meaning of a counterfactual conditional is accepted. For a counterfactual analysis of a statement of event causation such as 'My letting go of this stone a moment ago was a cause of the stone's falling to the ground' would typically appeal to some such counterfactual conditional as 'If I had not let go of this stone a moment ago, then it would not have fallen to the ground'—and the latter is precisely the sort of counterfactual conditional whose truth or falsehood depends on what causal propositions are true in nearby possible worlds, according to the proposed account of the meaning of a counterfactual conditional. It seems, then, that an implicit circularity is involved in adopting both that sort of account of the meaning of a counterfactual conditional and a counterfactual analysis of statements of event causation. At the very least, it does not appear that someone who did not already grasp the meaning of causal propositions could hope to acquire a grasp of their meaning with the aid of such a combination of doctrines. This still leaves open the question of which of those doctrines we should abandon but, on balance, it seems more reasonable to abandon a counterfactual analysis of causation than to abandon a possible-worlds analysis of counterfactual conditionals, given that we must make a choice between them. I say this because there are other reasons to doubt the adequacy of counterfactual analyses of causation.

The objectivity objection

Another feature of the possible-worlds account of the meaning of counterfactual conditionals which apparently renders these conditionals unsuitable for employment in an analysis of causation is one that was touched on a moment ago. This is that, when determining which of various possible worlds should be deemed the 'closest', for the purposes of evaluating a counterfactual conditional as being true or false, we need to make a judgement as to whether similarity in one respect (say, in respect of certain past matters of fact) contributes more than similarity in another respect (say, in respect of certain natural laws) to the overall similarity or dissimilarity between any of these worlds and the actual world. As we saw in

Chapter 8, such a judgement is not one whose rightness or wrongness turns simply on objective features of the possible worlds that are being compared: it is, rather, a partly subjective judgement, which reflects the conversational purposes for which we assert or deny a particular counterfactual conditional sentence. In different conversational contexts, one and the same counterfactual conditional sentence might justifiably be assigned different truth values by the same speaker, without this indicating any change of opinion on the part of the speaker. Thus, the very same speaker who, in one conversational context, is prepared to assert as true the counterfactual conditional 'If I had let go of this stone a moment ago, then it would have fallen to the ground' might well, in another conversational context, be prepared to assert as true the counterfactual conditional 'If I had let go of this stone a moment ago, then it would *not* have fallen to the ground'. In the first context, he might be making the point that heavy, unsupported objects fall, whereas in the second context he might be making the point that sensible people take pains to catch precious, fragile objects which they let go of. Different ways of assessing members of the relevant range of alternative possible worlds for comparative 'closeness' to the actual world enable one to evaluate both of these counterfactual conditional judgements as being true in the conversational contexts in which they are made. Counterfactual conditional sentences are, as I put it in Chapter 8, highly context-dependent in respect of their propositional content. And, as I also remarked in Chapter 8, the distinctly subjective element which their kind of context-dependency involves suggests that such sentences are ill-suited to capture the propositional content of causal statements, given that the latter purport to be purely objective expressions of matter of fact. At the very least, it seems that one would have to stipulate that the counterfactual conditionals utilized in any proposed counterfactual analysis of causal statements are to be interpreted in a way which is suited to the sort of conversational context in which *causal* matters of an appropriate kind are the subject of discourse. And this would once more indicate that there is an implicit circularity involved in appealing to counterfactual conditionals in order to analyse the content of causal statements. The more general lesson would once again be that, far from it being the case that the meaning of counterfactual conditionals can throw light on the meaning of causal statements, we need *already* to have a firm grasp of the notion of causality in order to be able to interpret counterfactual conditionals in ways that are appropriate to the conversational contexts in which they are used.

Alternative approaches

Where does all of this leave us? It certainly leaves us, so far, without any satisfactory analysis of the meaning of statements of event causation, of the form 'Event *c* was a cause of event *e*'. Might it be possible to analyse such a statement in a way which does not appeal to counterfactual con-ditionals? Perhaps, though I am not optimistic about this. One possibility might be to analyse singular causal statements of this form with the help of statements expressing causal *laws*, the suggestion being that any particular causal relation between events must be an instance of some general causal law. If laws are simply regarded as regularities or 'constant conjunctions' amongst events of certain types, this proposal effectively reduces to the unsatisfactory 'Humean' analysis of event causation that we looked at in Chapter 9. If laws are thought of in some other way—for example, as involving relations of necessitation amongst universals—then the proposal may be more promising.[8] But it apparently still falls foul of the plausible objection that causation is a relation which either holds or fails to hold between certain particular events quite independently of what *general* truths may or may not obtain in the world at large. It still seems perfectly intelligible that there should be cases in which one event causes another even though there is no general causal law whatever under which such a case falls.[9] Yet another possibility might be to analyse singular statements of event causation in terms of statements asserting the transference of some quantity, such as energy, from one object to another, the suggestion being that all causal processes involve some such transference.[10] For example, in the case of a stone whose falling to the ground has amongst its causes the event of its being released, the stone acquires kinetic energy from the earth's gravitational field (although, more strictly, we should say that the stone's potential energy, owing to its position in the earth's gravi-tational field, is converted into kinetic energy). Similarly, thermal energy is transferred from a hot poker to some colder water into which the poker is

---

[8] This is the view of laws favoured by David Armstrong: see his *What is a Law of Nature?* (Cambridge: Cambridge University Press, 1983).

[9] See further G. E. M. Anscombe, 'Causality and Determination', in her *Metaphysics and the Philosophy of Mind: Collected Philosophical Papers, Volume II* (Oxford: Blackwell, 1981), reprinted in Ernest Sosa and Michael Tooley (eds.), *Causation* (Oxford: Oxford University Press, 1993).

[10] For discussion, see Phil Dowe, *Physical Causation* (Cambridge: Cambridge University Press, 2000), ch. 3. Dowe himself distinguishes between a *conceptual* analysis of causation and an *empir-ical* analysis of causation (pp. 1 ff.) and offers an empirical analysis of his own (ch. 5).

plunged. However, these are scientific facts revealed by empirical investigation, rather than suitable ingredients in a conceptual analysis of causation. It is far from evident that 'transference' of some kind, even in the very broadest sense of that term, is involved, as a matter of conceptual necessity, in any process that deserves to be called 'causal'. After all, the 'Cartesian' dualist who conceives of mind and body as substances of utterly distinct natures, which none the less interact causally with one another, is ill-equipped to characterize such causal interactions in terms of the 'transference' of any quantity from mind to body or vice versa—and yet I think it would be unfair to describe the dualist's proposal as being literally *inconceivable* on that account. It may be, in the end, that we must simply accept the notion of causality as being primitive and irreducible, like the notions of identity and existence. Given the fundamental role that it plays in our conception of the world, we should not be altogether surprised if the notion of causality resists analysis in terms of any more fundamental notions—for it may be that the notion of causality is itself as fundamental as any of our other notions are.

PART IV

AGENTS, ACTIONS, AND EVENTS

11

EVENT CAUSATION AND AGENT CAUSATION

Agents and agent causation

So far, our discussion of causation has focused chiefly on *event* causation, although we have also examined the view that *facts* (or states of affairs) can be causes and effects. However, as I mentioned in Chapter 9, many philosophers, particularly those concerned with the philosophy of action, consider that a further important species of causation is *agent* causation, in which the cause of some event or state of affairs is not (or not only) some other event or state of affairs, but is, rather, an *agent* of some kind.[1] An 'agent', in the sense intended here, is a persisting object (or 'substance') possessing various properties, including, most importantly, certain causal powers and liabilities. A paradigm example of an agent would be a human being or other conscious creature capable of performing intentional actions. Indeed, some philosophers of action would like to restrict the term 'agent' to entities such as these and, correspondingly, restrict the term 'agent causation' to cases of intentional action. For present purposes, however, I shall adopt a more liberal view, not least because we are not yet in a position to distinguish clearly between those things that are, and those that are not, capable of performing intentional actions, nor even to say what is distinctive about intentional, as opposed to unintentional, action. But later we shall see that there plausibly is something special about the

[1] See, for example, Richard Taylor, *Action and Purpose* (Englewood Cliffs, NJ: Prentice-Hall, 1966), chs. 8 and 9; Roderick M. Chisholm, 'The Agent as Cause', in Myles Brand and Douglas Walton (eds.), *Action Theory* (Dordrecht: D. Reidel, 1976); and Timothy O'Connor, *Persons and Causes: The Metaphysics of Free Will* (New York: Oxford University Press, 2000), chs. 3 and 4. For an opposing view, see Donald Davidson, 'Agency', in Robert Binkley, Richard Bronaugh, and Ausonio Marras (eds.), *Agent, Action, and Reason* (Toronto: University of Toronto Press, 1971), reprinted in Donald Davidson, *Essays on Actions and Events* (Oxford: Clarendon Press, 1980).

causation of an event by an animate—and, more particularly, by a rational—agent.

It cannot be denied that our ordinary ways of talking about action support, at least superficially, the idea that agent causation is a distinct species of causation. As well as making statements of event causation, such as 'The explosion of the bomb caused the collapse of the bridge', we say such things as '*The bomber* caused the collapse of the bridge'—where, by 'the bomber', we might be referring to an individual human being, or we might be referring to an aeroplane. In short, there is no doubt that the verb 'to cause' may take, as its grammatical subject, a noun phrase referring to a persisting object, either human or inanimate, quite as well as a noun phrase referring to a particular event. Moreover, since events and persisting objects are entities belonging to quite distinct ontological categories, it is strongly arguable that the verb 'to cause' must have a different sense when a term referring to a persisting object figures as its grammatical subject from the sense it has when a term referring to a particular event plays that role. This is brought out by the fact that, whereas it would not be incongruous to say, for example, 'Smith and Jones together caused the collapse of the bridge', it would indeed be incongruous to say, 'The explosion of the bomb and Jones together caused the collapse of the bridge'. The latter sentence appears to involve a category mistake, rather like the one that famously occurs in the sentence 'She came home in a sedan chair and a flood of tears'—the anomaly in the latter case being that the sense in which a person can be 'in' a sedan chair is quite different from the sense in which a person can be 'in' a flood of tears.[2] The lesson seems to be, then, that event causation and agent causation are distinct species of causation, because the sense in which an event can be a 'cause' is quite different from the sense in which an agent can be a 'cause'.

An analysis of agent causation

However, even if we accept this conclusion, that does not prevent us from proposing that one or the other of these species of causation is 'reducible' to, or analysable in terms of, the other—that agent causation is reducible to event causation, or that event causation is reducible to agent causation. A reductionist thesis of this sort would maintain either that any statement of

[2] See Gilbert Ryle, *The Concept of Mind* (London: Hutchinson, 1949), ch. 1.

agent causation can be analysed in terms of a statement in which no notion of causation other than that of event causation is employed, or else, conversely, that any statement of event causation can be analysed in terms of a statement in which no notion of causation other than that of agent causation is employed. Opposing either form of reductionism would be the thesis that both species of causation exist but that neither is analysable in terms of the other. In order to see what is at issue here, let us first look at how one might attempt to reduce agent causation to event causation. And let us take, as the canonical form of a statement of agent causation, the following: 'Agent A caused event e'. (An alternative and perhaps more colloquial formulation would be 'Agent A brought about event e' or 'Agent A made event e happen', but I shall adhere to the preceding formulation because it explicitly employs the verb 'to cause'.) Then the obvious suggestion would be that a statement of this form can be analysed along something like the following lines:

(1) Agent A caused event e if and only if there was some event, x, such that x involved A and x caused e.

Of course, analysis (1) is no clearer than the notion of 'involvement' which it exploits. How, precisely, must an event 'involve' an agent A if, in virtue of that event's causing an event e, A may be said to have caused e? If we cannot spell out an appropriate notion of involvement, or can only do so in a way which appeals, either explicitly or implicitly, to the notion of agent causation, then analysis (1) will have failed. Perhaps, however, we can say something like the following, at least to a first approximation: an event, x, 'involves' an agent, A, in the sense demanded by analysis (1), just in case x consists in some change in one or more of the properties of A. (The properties in question might be, but need not be, intrinsic properties of A: they might equally be relational properties of A.) For example, in the case of an animate agent A, such as a particular living creature, an event which is a *movement* of A is an event 'involving' A because a movement of A consists in A's undergoing changes in the dispositions of its limbs and/or changes in its spatial relations to its environment. Perhaps this will suffice, if only for the time being, to clarify the notion of 'involvement' figuring in analysis (1). (However, I should say that I am rather doubtful whether, in the end, a satisfactory notion of 'involvement' really can be spelled out.)

Causative action verbs and basic actions

In order to appreciate some of the attractions, as well as some of the potential limitations, of analysis (1), it is helpful to observe that many transitive verbs of action have quite specific causal implications. For instance, when we describe one person as having killed another, we imply that the first person—the agent of the action—*caused the death* of the second person. Even if 'killing' cannot be defined as simply meaning 'causing death', 'killing' does at least *imply* 'causing death'. Similarly, 'pushing' implies 'causing motion away from the agent', 'stopping' implies 'causing rest or cessation of motion', 'cutting' implies 'causing separation or division', 'crushing' implies 'causing compression or decrease in volume', and so forth. Some of these *causative action verbs*, as we may call them, also imply the specific *means* by which a certain kind of effect is caused by the agent. For example, 'pushing' implies not merely 'causing motion away from the agent', it implies 'causing motion away from the agent *by the application of pressure*'. Similarly, 'cutting' implies 'causing separation or division *by the transverse movement of a sharp edge*', whereas 'ripping' implies 'causing separation or division *by the application of tension in opposite directions*'. Certainly, we can very often say, when we describe an agent's action by using a causative verb, *by what means* the agent caused the kind of effect which that verb implies, even if the verb that we use does not imply those specific means itself. For example, if we describe an agent as having killed someone, and thus as having caused that person's death, we may well also be able to say *how* the killing was done—say, by shooting, or stabbing, or poisoning, each of which verbs do imply a certain kind of means of causing a certain kind of effect.

However, there is a special class of actions which seem to defy description in these means–end terms. These are the so-called *basic* actions, such as a human agent's spontaneous movement of one of his or her own limbs.[3] For instance, when a human agent is described as having *waved his hand*, it is thereby implied that the agent caused a certain kind of motion in his hand: but nothing is implied as to the means, if any, by which the agent did this. Indeed, if we were to ask such an agent *how*—in the sense of 'by what means', rather than in the sense of 'in what manner'—he waved

---

[3] See Arthur C. Danto, 'Basic Actions', *American Philosophical Quarterly* 2 (1965), 141–8, and also his *Analytical Philosophy of Action* (Cambridge: Cambridge University Press, 1973), ch. 2.

his hand, very likely his reply would be that he didn't do this *by* any means at all: he would probably reply that he *simply waved his hand*. In contrast, a human agent will, in general, know precisely how he pushed, pulled, stopped, cut, crushed, or killed something or someone—that is to say, he will know by what means he caused effects of the kinds implied by these action verbs. It is tempting, then, to define a basic action as an action in which the agent causes an effect of a certain kind, but *not* 'by' any means whatever.[4] (Of course, when a human agent waves his hand, certain muscular and neural events will precede the motion of his hand and be causally related to that motion. But it seems incorrect to say that the agent waves his hand 'by means of' causing these muscular and neural events, of which he is likely to know nothing. Indeed, even if one knows that such events invariably precede hand motions of the kind occurring when one waves one's hand, it seems more natural to say that one can cause the muscular and neural events 'by means of' waving one's hand, rather than vice versa.)

The case for irreducible agent causation

The relevance of these observations to the analysis of agent causation suggested above, analysis (1), is the following. On the one hand, the fact that many causative action verbs imply a means–end structure to the actions they describe seems to favour analysis (1). For the use of such a verb to describe an action very often suggests an appropriate event, 'involving' the agent, which can be appealed to for the purpose of analysing the action in the manner proposed by analysis (1). For instance, suppose we describe a human agent, A, as having killed someone else, B, by poisoning. This is an instance of agent causation: A caused B's death. But we also know by what means A caused B's death, namely, by administering poison to B. But therefore, it seems, we can very easily identify an *event*, involving A, which can be said to have caused B's death, namely, A's administration of the poison to B. So it seems that analysis (1) is vindicated in this instance. For here, it appears, is a case in which it is true to say that the agent, A, caused a certain effect in virtue of the fact that a certain event involving A caused that effect—namely, the event of A's administration of the poison to B. On the other hand, the existence of the class of basic actions threatens to defeat analysis (1), for in the case of a basic action, as

---

[4] I adopt a different definition of basic action in my *Subjects of Experience* (Cambridge: Cambridge University Press, 1996), 151, for reasons I shall not go into here.

we have defined it, there appears to be *no* suitable event involving the agent which can be called upon to provide the cause—in the event causation sense of 'cause'—of the effect which, in performing that action, the agent is said to cause. For example, when a human agent, A, spontaneously waves his hand, what *event*, involving A, can we appeal to, for the purposes of analysis (1), as having been the cause of a certain kind of motion in A's hand? Nothing analogous to the event appealed to in the poisoning case will be forthcoming, it seems, simply because, in a case of 'basic' action, the agent supposedly does not cause the given effect 'by' any means whatever: he simply causes it—that is to say, he causes it *directly*. Moreover, it would appear that there *must* be basic actions, if agents perform any actions at all: for if *every* action had a means–end structure, this would apparently generate a vicious infinite regress, whereby the means of each action is compelled to be the end of another.

However, at least in the case of inanimate agents, there appears to be a way of avoiding such a regress and defending analysis (1). This is because not all actions demand description in terms of causative verbs, that is, in terms which imply that the agent, in performing the action in question, caused some effect. An inanimate object can *push* or *pull* another object and in so doing it causes the latter object to move in certain ways. But when we ask *by what means* an inanimate agent can push or pull another object, our answer is likely to make reference to behaviour of the agent which is not properly described in terms of causative verbs. For instance, an inanimate agent can push another object by *rolling* into it or by *falling* on to it: but 'roll' and 'fall' are not causative verbs, so there is no reason to suppose that the actions which they describe have a means–end structure. Generally speaking, it is inappropriate to ask *by what means* an inanimate object rolled into or fell on to another object. The first object's behaviour will, of course, be subject to causal explanation, but in all probability we shall explain why that object rolled or fell by referring to *another* object's action upon *it*, rather than in terms of some further behaviour of the object in question. Consequently, in the case of inanimate agents, their non-causative behaviour provides an obvious terminus to the threatened regress, and a well-defined class of events 'involving' those agents to which analysis (1) can appeal. For example, if a boulder pushes a tree by rolling into it, providing us with a case in which an inanimate agent (the boulder) causes motion of a certain kind in another object (the tree), we can plausibly reduce this instance of agent causation to one of event causation, in the way proposed by analysis (1), by saying that in this case it was *the rolling of the boulder*—an event involving the boulder—which caused the motion of the tree. And since the boulder's rolling is not itself a matter of the boulder's *causing* anything, because 'roll' is not a causative verb, no further question arises as to 'by what means' the boulder rolled. (Though this, as I have just pointed out, is not to deny that the boulder's rolling can be causally explained by reference to some *other* object's action upon *it*.) Consequently, in such a case, no further fact of agent causation *by the boulder* remains to jeopardize our claim to have analysed the boulder's agency wholly in terms of event causation.

But it will be evident that matters are not so simple when we are concerned with animate agents, such as animals and human beings. When a human agent spontaneously waves his hand, thus causing motion in his hand, this seems not at all like the case of a boulder causing motion in a tree by rolling into it. In describing the spontaneous waving of one's hand as being a 'basic' action, we implied precisely that in such a case motion in the hand was *not* caused 'by' any means whatever: that is, that there was no *behaviour* or *activity* of the agent by means of which the agent caused motion in his hand, in the way that by rolling the boulder caused motion in the tree. Rather, what we seem to have in such a case is an instance of *irreducible* agent causation. Animate agents, we may feel tempted to say, are capable of *spontaneous self-movement*, which involves an agent's causing motion in its own limbs or other body parts *directly*. However, it is likely to be objected that this view of the matter is incompatible with a wholly naturalistic conception of animals, including human beings, and their causal powers. It may be urged that however much it may seem that animals engage in 'spontaneous self-movement', in the sense just proposed, in reality their agency must always be reducible to event causation, just as the agency of inanimate objects plausibly is.

The problem of free will

But why 'must' this be so? There seems to be nothing unintelligible or incoherent about the notion of spontaneous self-movement. Moreover, the idea that there is this kind of irreducible agent causation holds out the prospect of a solution to the problem of free will which dogs the reductionist approach to human action. If all human agency is ultimately just a matter of one event's causing another, then, since the causal history of the events supposedly involved in any instance of human agency will plausibly be traceable back, through prior events, to times before the agent's birth, we seem to lose all sense of the agent's being genuinely responsible for—the author of—his or her own actions.[5] A human agent must then be seen as no freer, in reality, than the boulder which rolls into the tree, its rolling being caused by the action of some other object upon it, which action is in turn caused by yet earlier events—and so on back to the dawn of time. Acknowledging that there is room for a certain amount of probabilistic causation between events provides no escape from this conclusion, since a boulder's behaviour would be no freer on that account than it would be in a perfectly deterministic universe.

But how, exactly, would the existence of irreducible agent causation, in the case of animate agents, provide a solution to the problem of free will? In the following way. Suppose that, on a particular occasion, a human agent, A, caused an event e, such as motion in A's hand, but that this instance of agent causation is not reducible to one of event causation. That is to say, suppose that it is not in virtue of some *event's* causing e that A may be said to have caused e. Now, this still leaves open the question of whether or not some prior event or events were causes of e and, if so, whether or not that prior event or those prior events were causally sufficient for the occurrence of e. However, it is perfectly conceivable that no prior event or combination of events was causally sufficient for the occurrence of e, but that A's agency on this occasion was causally necessary for the occurrence of e. That is to say, it may be the case that if A had not caused e, then e would not have occurred, since prior events alone were not causally sufficient for the occurrence of e. (This is perfectly compatible with the suggestion that certain prior events were, none the less, causally *necessary* for the occurrence of e.) In that case, it seems, e occurred as a consequence of A's agency and yet e was not causally determined by prior events (nor, we may suppose, did e have the probability of its occurrence fully determined by prior events). Hence, A was causally responsible for—was genuinely the author of—e and in causing e acted freely.

But, it may be asked, was not A's causing e itself caused by some prior event or events? If so, then was not the occurrence of e, after all, causally determined by prior events (or, at least, was not the probability of e's occurrence fully determined by prior events)? And if not, then was not A's causing e something quite inexplicable, a matter of pure chance? The

[5] See Peter van Inwagen, *An Essay on Free Will* (Oxford: Clarendon Press, 1983), ch. 3. Although van Inwagen's argument has frequently been challenged, I think that it is basically sound.

proper answer to this question, I suggest, is that if *A*'s causing *e* was, as is being supposed, an instance of irreducible agent causation, then we should not think of it as something which itself had a *cause* of any kind—but that, at the same time, we should not think of it as something which, in lacking a cause, must therefore have been a matter of pure chance.[6] It is open to us to say, instead, that *A*'s causing *e* is subject solely to *rational*, not to *causal*, explanation. That is, it is open to us to say that *A* caused *e for a reason*, while denying that anything *caused A*'s causing *e*. I shall say more about this possibility in a moment.

Mental causation, rational choice, and freedom of action

In the preceding few paragraphs, I have been trying to make out as good a case as I can for the idea that agent causation is irreducible to event causation, on the grounds that there are plausible cases of 'basic' action by animate agents which involve irreducible agent causation—a basic action being an agent's causing a certain event and yet not causing that event 'by' any means whatever. However, an advocate of the thesis that agent causation is always reducible to event causation may urge that, even in what appears to be a case of basic action as defined above, there still is, in fact, an event (or conjunction of events) which causes the event, *e*, which the agent, *A*, is said to cause and which, in the appropriate sense, 'involves' *A*. But, it may be added, the event (or conjunction of events) in question will be a *mental* event (or conjunction of events) of a certain kind—which should not surprise us, since apparently 'basic' action of the sort with which we are now concerned is exhibited precisely by animate agents, such as human beings. In particular, it may be suggested that the events in question will simply be the onsets of certain cognitive and/or affective states of the animate agents concerned—in short, the onsets of certain beliefs, desires, or emotions.[7] Thus, it may be claimed, when a human agent 'spontaneously' waves his hand or otherwise 'spontaneously' moves some part of his body, the bodily event which the agent is thereby said to cause is one which is in fact caused by the onsets of such states as the agent's desire to

---

[6] Compare O'Connor, *Persons and Causes*, 52 ff. and 87.

[7] This, essentially, is the view of Donald Davidson: see his 'Actions, Reasons, and Causes', *Journal of Philosophy* 60 (1963), 685–700, reprinted in his *Essays on Actions and Events*.

attract someone's attention and his belief that by waving his hand he could achieve this. (If one adheres to a psychophysical identity theory of mind, one may also maintain that these mental events are in fact identical with certain physical events in the agent's brain or nervous system, though it is not necessary to make this additional claim.)

However, I imagine that the advocate of irreducible agent causation will object to this proposal on grounds which should now be familiar—namely, that the proposal leaves no room for genuine free will in human affairs and that it distorts the relationship between an agent's actions and his reasons for action. An agent's beliefs and desires may give him a reason to act in a certain way—for instance, to wave his hand—but if we treat those beliefs and desires as *causing* the motion of his hand, we cannot really say that the agent acts 'for' that reason, because to act for a reason is to be *guided* by what one (reasonably) believes and desires but not to be *caused* to behave in a certain way by one's beliefs and desires.[8] In short, the proposal under consideration appears not to leave any room for rational *choice* on the part of the agent as to how to act in the light of his beliefs and desires.

However, if this objection is deemed sound, why shouldn't an opponent of the idea of irreducible agent causation simply say that, in what appears to be a case of 'basic' action as defined above, it is in fact the *choice* or *decision* of the agent—a mental event—which causes the event, *e*, which the agent, *A*, is said to cause? Another term for this kind of mental event would be a 'volition' or 'act of will', according to certain philosophers of action. My own view is that, if one wants to maintain that agent causation is reducible to event causation, then it is indeed preferable to appeal to mental events of this kind, rather than to the onsets of states of belief and desire, for the purpose of analysing apparently 'spontaneous' human action.[9] But it may still be objected that to analyse spontaneous human action in terms of causation by mental events of *any* kind—even the 'choices' or 'volitions' of the agent—is to preclude any satisfactory solution to the problem of free will. This is because an event must either have or lack a cause, which on the view under scrutiny would have to be another event of some kind: and then we are faced with an apparent dilemma—for if our choices are caused, then we lack genuine freedom; and if our choices are uncaused, then they seem to be mere chance happenings, so that we

---

[8] In this way, we may turn on its head Davidson's well-known argument that reasons must be causes: see further my *An Introduction to the Philosophy of Mind* (Cambridge: Cambridge University Press, 2000), 258 ff.

[9] I develop a volitionist theory of action along these lines in my *Subjects of Experience*, ch. 5.

once again lack genuine freedom.[10] In contrast, it seems that the advocate of irreducible agent causation can plausibly resist saying that A's causing e, in a case of basic human action, is itself something which has a cause, without thereby implying that A's causing e is a mere chance happening: for A's causing e is not a *happening*—an event—at all, and is therefore not the sort of thing that is apt to have an event as a cause. Not being the sort of thing that is apt to have an event as a cause, its lack of a cause is only to be expected and can carry no adverse implication that it defies explanation of any kind, since there may be other kinds of explanation than causal explanation—notably, rational explanation.

Basic actions and backward causation

At this point I want to return, briefly, to an issue touched upon earlier, namely the relationship between a human agent's basic actions, such as his spontaneous hand-wavings, and the muscular and neural events that invariably precede and are causally related to the bodily motions involved in such actions, such as the motions of an agent's hand. I remarked that, while most human agents know nothing of such muscular and neural events, even if one does know that such events invariably precede the sort of hand motions that occur when one waves one's hand, it seems more natural to say that one can cause the muscular and neural events 'by means of' waving one's hand, rather than vice versa. Some philosophers find this view puzzling, however, because they think that a kind of backward causation would have to be involved if an agent were to cause a neural event, e_1, 'by means of' causing a bodily motion, e_2—such as a hand-motion—where e_1 occurs *before* e_2.[11] But in fact no backward causation of any kind need be involved here. It is not being proposed that the later event, e_2, *causes* the earlier event, e_1, since we are not concerned here with event causation but rather with agent causation. Indeed, it can readily be accepted that, in such a case, the earlier event, e_1, is a contributory cause of the later event, e_2—for, as I have already made clear, an advocate of irreducible agent causation need not say that *no events whatever* are (contributory) causes of the event which is caused by an agent in a case of basic action: all that is being claimed is that it is not *in virtue of* its causation by any events whatever that

---

[10] But see further my *An Introduction to the Philosophy of Mind*, 254 ff.

[11] See G. H. von Wright, *Explanation and Understanding* (London: Routledge and Kegan Paul, 1971), 76 ff.

the agent may be said to cause that event. Nor can it be complained that backward causation must be involved because the agent's causing of e_2 occurs later than e_1: for, quite apart from anything else, it simply isn't obvious *when*, precisely, the agent's causing of e_2 may be said to occur, if indeed it is proper to describe it as 'occurring' at all. (I say 'if' because it is *events* that are said to 'occur'—and, according to the advocate of irreducible agent causation, an agent's causing of an event is not itself an event of any kind.)

The conceptual priority of agent causation

I hope I have now done enough to explain why some philosophers of action hold, I think with some justification, that agent causation is not universally reducible to event causation, in accordance with analysis (1) or any similar principle. But what about the suggestion that event causation is instead reducible to, or analysable in terms of, agent causation? This is a suggestion that has only rarely been explored—largely, I suppose, because it is commonly imagined that talk of 'agent causation' is appropriate only where the intentional actions of rational, or at least animate, agents are concerned. However, as I explained at the beginning of this chapter, we do not need to use the term 'agent' in a way which restricts its application to such beings. There is a perfectly good sense in which something as insensate as a boulder can be a causal agent. Of course, if agent causation *could* only be exercised by rational or animate agents, then the suggestion that all event causation is reducible to agent causation would amount, in effect, to the doctrine that nothing is caused to occur in the world save through the agency of rational or animate beings. It may be that certain 'primitive' cultures have assumed such a view, attributing all physical events which lack a human or animal origin to the agency of gods or spirits. Equally, certain idealist philosophers, notably George Berkeley, have maintained that only thinking beings can cause anything (but that what they cause are certain purely mental effects in their own or others' minds).[12] Clearly, however, if we are prepared to use the term 'agent' in a broader way, to apply to inanimate as well as animate beings, then there is scope to maintain that event causation is reducible to agent causation without embracing one or other of these more improbable doctrines. But before I

[12] See George Berkeley, *A Treatise Concerning the Principles of Human Knowledge*, paras. 25–6, in his *Philosophical Works*, ed. M. R. Ayers (London: Dent, 1975), p. 84.

explore this possibility, I want to discuss a reason which we might advance for maintaining that the notion of agent causation is at least *conceptually prior* to that of event causation, even if it is doubted whether event caus-ation is *reducible* to agent causation. For this consideration does indeed focus on the special case of the intentional actions of rational agents.

Although, in a metaphysical study such as the present one, our main concern is the nature of certain fundamental features of reality, such as causation, we must inevitably be concerned also with certain epistemo-logical questions: for if we purport to have knowledge of a certain feature of reality, our account of the nature of that feature should not be such as to render our knowledge of it impossible or inexplicable. Consider, then, our claim to have knowledge of at least some relations of causation between events—and consider what mental capacities such a knowledge claim pre-supposes. It is strongly arguable that only a creature capable of intentional action can acquire knowledge of causal relations between events from experience. Such a creature must not only be an agent, but must also be *aware* of being an agent—and so, it seems, must possess the concept of agent causation. The argument for this conclusion is as follows.[13]

A purely passive being that was capable of observing its physical environment—something like, perhaps, an intelligent tree, if such a being is indeed possible—would apparently be incapable of distinguishing between causal sequences of events and purely coincidental sequences of events. Such a being might be able to register the existence of certain regularities or uniformities amongst types of events occurring in its observable environment, but it would be unable to discriminate between those regularities that obtained purely by coincidence and those that obtained in virtue of causal relations between the events concerned. The being might notice, for instance, that night regularly followed day, that thunder regularly followed lightning, and that the extinction of flames regularly followed their dousing by water. All of these sequences, we know, are causal sequences—although not in every case is the first member of such a sequence a cause of the second member, since in some cases the two events are collateral effects of a common cause. But, of course, it is also possible to experience purely coincidental sequences of events on a regular basis. It might be, for instance, that, within one's experience, the fall of a certain kind of object has regularly been followed by a flash of light. How-ever, if one is in doubt as to whether or not such a sequence is causal in

---

[13] Here I follow the lead of G. H. von Wright: see his *Explanation and Understanding*, 60 ff.

nature, one can attempt to resolve that doubt by means of active intervention and experimentation. For instance, one can attempt to interrupt the fall of the next object of the kind in question, to see whether or not a flash of light will still occur even in the absence of the fall. Again, one can attempt to initiate the fall of such an object oneself, to see whether or not such a fall is still followed by a flash of light. Because we are causal agents ourselves and are aware of our ability to intervene in and manipulate the course of nature in such ways, we are able to test causal hypotheses experimentally and thereby hope to distinguish, albeit not infallibly, between causal and non-causal sequences of events. (Clearly, an important component of this ability to intervene in the course of nature is our capacity to move *ourselves* at will about our physical environment in accordance with our desires, at least within certain limits, rather than having our spatial location and orientation determined wholly by external factors.) But it seems that a purely passive creature, however acute its powers of observation, would be incapable of discriminating empirically between causal and non-causal sequences of events—from which it seems reasonable to conclude that it would have no concept of event causation, as it would have no empirical basis upon which to apply that concept. Certainly, it could not acquire the concept of event causation from experience, if the preceding argument is correct, but nor is it reasonable to suppose that it would possess the concept innately, since the possession of a concept which has no application can confer no evolutionary advantage upon a creature.

An analysis of event causation

The lesson of the preceding argument seems to be that the concept of agent causation cannot be derived from that of event causation, because possession of the former concept is a prerequisite of possession of the latter concept. It cannot be that we first learn to apply the concept of event causation to observable events and then learn to conceive of ourselves as agents by grasping the truth of some principle along the lines of analysis (1) above. It really does seem that agent causation must be, in this sense, *conceptually* prior to event causation.

It does not follow from this, however, that agent causation must be *ontologically* prior to event causation: it could still be true that analysis (1), or something like it, tells us correctly what agent causation *consists in*. On the other hand, provided that we do not understand the notion of a causal 'agent' in too restricted a way, there is nothing to stop us from proposing that agent causation is ontologically, as well as conceptually, prior to event causation. Instead of explaining agent causation in terms of event causation, along the lines suggested by analysis (1), we could attempt to explain event causation in terms of agent causation, perhaps along something like the following lines:

> (2) Event *c* caused event *e* if and only if there was some agent, *A*, and some manner of acting, *X*, such that *c* consisted in *A*'s *X*ing and *A*, by *X*ing, caused *e*.

Consider, for instance, one of our earlier examples of a statement of event causation, 'The explosion of the bomb caused the collapse of the bridge'. According to analysis (2), this is true because there was a certain agent (in the broad sense), namely, the bomb, and a certain manner of acting, namely, exploding, such that the event which was the explosion of the bomb consisted in that agent's acting in that manner (that is, it consisted in the bomb's exploding) and the agent, by so acting, caused the collapse of the bridge—that is to say, the bomb, by exploding, caused the collapse of the bridge.

Plausible though analysis (2) may be in this sort of case, it may not be wholly free of difficulties. Some of these difficulties, however, may be relatively easy to deal with. For instance, it may be that where analysis (2) speaks of event *c* as consisting in a *single* agent's acting in a certain way, a more refined version of (2) should allow *c* to consist in *one or more* agents' acting in certain ways, either independently or in unison. But I shall ignore this sort of problem as one of mere detail. Much more serious would be the objection, if it is sound, that there are some events which cause other events and yet which do not consist in *any* agent's or agents' acting in any way. However, I shall not pursue this sort of objection here either, as it raises issues which are more properly the concern of the next two chapters. Instead, I shall focus on an apparent difficulty for analysis (2) which arises from my earlier proposal that one can cause the muscular and neural events which typically precede certain movements of one's hand 'by means of' waving one's hand. We want to say that such muscular and neural events are *causes* of the hand movements, rather than their *effects*. Now, if my earlier proposal was correct, what we have in such circumstances is a human agent, *A*, and a manner of acting, namely, waving one's hand, such that *A*, by acting in that manner, caused a certain muscular or neural event,

e_1. But we also want to say that e_1 caused, rather than was caused by, the hand movement, e_2, which occurred on this occasion. Will analysis (2) allow us to say this? Not if we want to say that e_2 *consisted in* A's waving his hand. For if the hand movement, e_2, consisted in A's waving his hand and (as we have just proposed) A, by waving his hand, caused the muscular or neural event e_1, then analysis (2) implies that e_2 caused e_1 rather than vice versa—it implies that the hand movement caused the muscular or neural event, whereas the truth is the reverse of this.

Fortunately for an adherent of analysis (2), it seems clear that we should not say that the hand movement, e_2, consisted in A's waving his hand. A's waving his hand was an *action* of A's—it was A's *causing* a certain kind of movement in his hand and so certainly cannot be identified with just such a movement of his hand. The hand movement, e_2, rather than consisting in A's waving his hand, in fact consisted in A's *hand's* moving in a certain way. We may be confused about this if we do not distinguish, as we clearly should, between transitive and intransitive senses of the verb 'to move'.[14] In talking of a 'hand movement', we might either mean to talk of someone's moving (in the transitive sense) his hand or alternatively mean to talk of someone's hand's moving (in the intransitive sense): but, in the present context, we should evidently mean the latter. Obviously, a 'hand movement' in the *latter* sense can occur even if the person whose hand it is does not move it—that is, even if a 'hand movement' in the *former* sense is not performed. A's waving his hand is a 'hand movement' in the former sense and, clearly, in no way can the hand movement which consists in A's hand's moving also be said to consist in A's waving his hand.

So, it may be asked, how *does* analysis (2) enable us to account for the causal relation between the muscular or neural event, e_1, and the hand movement, e_2? The answer is quite straightforward. Provided that we can say, as we plausibly can, that the muscular or neural event, e_1, consisted in some body part's acting in a certain way—for instance, it might have consisted in a certain muscle fibre's contracting or in a certain neuron's firing—and that that body part, by acting in that way, caused (albeit indirectly) the hand movement, e_2, then analysis (2) allows us to say, as we want to, that e_1 caused e_2. But notice that the 'agent' to which we must now appeal, for the purpose of analysing this relationship of event causation, is not the human agent, A, who waved his hand and, in so doing, performed a basic action. Rather, the 'agent' in question is merely an organic part of A's

---

[14] See further Jennifer Hornsby, *Actions* (London: Routledge and Kegan Paul, 1980), ch. 1.

body and so not a rational agent or even an 'animate' agent, in the sense in which an entire living organism is an animate agent. However, we need see no conflict here between the agency of the human being, A, and the agency of A's body parts, such as particular muscle fibres or neurons of A's. On the contrary, human agency, while not reducible to the agency of human body parts, clearly depends upon the latter, in the sense that our possession of a body in working order is a necessary condition of our ability to exercise physical agency on our own account.

Whether there are any inescapable problems besetting analysis (2), or any similar attempt to analyse event causation in terms of agent causation, I leave for others to judge. But in favour of the ontological primacy of agent causation over event causation I would urge just this. It seems proper to say that events of themselves possess no causal powers. Only persisting objects—that is, individual 'substances'—possess causal powers and, indeed, causal liabilities. It is such objects that we describe as being magnetic, corrosive, inflammable, soluble, and so forth. Objects manifest or display their causal powers and liabilities by acting on things, or being acted upon, in various appropriate ways—by attracting, corroding, burning, dissolving, and so forth. In describing such activities we use, of course, the language of agent causation, rather than the language of event causation. We resort to the latter, I suggest, primarily when we are at least partially ignorant about the causal agents that are at work. Analysis (2) explains this, for we could be sure that the right-hand side of (2) was satisfied in certain circumstances, and hence that its left-hand side was true, even though we could not identify a specific agent and manner of acting in virtue which the right-hand side of (2) was satisfied on that occasion. It may be suggested, then, that those philosophers who accord ontological primacy to event causation are tempted to do so by the fact that events seem to be, in general, more epistemically accessible than substances are. In short, their approach may simply be the legacy of an empiricist epistemology which distrusts all talk of causal machinery at work in the real world behind the shifting scenes of appearance.

Implications for the notion of causality

If we take agent causation to be both conceptually and ontologically prior to event causation, what bearing does this have on the question of whether the notion of causality is ultimately analysable or definable in non-causal terms? At the end of the preceding chapter, I surmised that the notion of causality might in fact be primitive and irreducible. But nothing that I have said in this chapter encourages me to think otherwise. First of all, although, as I remarked earlier in this chapter, many transitive verbs of action are causative verbs, I see no reason to suppose that the actions which such verbs describe are simply *definable* in terms of a generic notion of agent causation. For instance, although 'killing' clearly implies 'causing death', it is very doubtful that 'killing' just *means* 'causing death'.[15] Why? Because it seems proper to say that an agent may cause the death of a living creature without *killing* that creature—for example, by causing another agent to kill that creature. Thus, if a would-be assassin cannot bring himself to kill his intended victim himself, he may induce someone else to kill the victim for him—in which case, it seems, the would-be assassin is a cause of the victim's death even though he does not kill the victim himself. (This isn't to say, of course, that such a course of action need be any less reprehensible than killing.)

Rather than saying that every causative verb is synonymous with some verb phrase in which the verb 'to cause' (in its agent-causation sense) appears, I am inclined to reverse the direction of semantic explanation and say that our grasp of the concept of agent causation is, as it were, a distillation of our grasp of a multiplicity of more specific action-concepts—concepts such as those of killing, pushing, stretching, attracting, corroding, burning, and dissolving. These and related action-concepts form a family, whose members bear 'family resemblances' to one another but possess, I suggest, no common and clearly definable 'essential core'.[16] Certainly we may say that the actions in question are all ways in which an agent may cause something to happen: but I think that this observation, rather than helping to elucidate the nature of such actions, better serves to elucidate what it means to speak of an agent's causing something to happen—for we very arguably have a much firmer grasp on the nature of these and similar specific actions than we do on the generic notion of agent causation. However, clearly, we cannot hope to *define* agent causation by reference to any class of such specific actions, given that they form an open-ended family whose members bear only family resemblances to one another and

---

[15] See the editor's introduction in Pieter M. Seuren (ed.), *Semantic Syntax* (Oxford: Oxford University Press, 1974), 8 ff., and Judith Jarvis Thomson, *Acts and Other Events* (Ithaca, NY: Cornell University Press, 1977), 128.

[16] See Renford Bambrough, 'Universals and Family Resemblances', *Proceedings of the Aristotelian Society* 60 (1960/1), 207–22.

share no common essence. So I conclude, albeit somewhat tentatively, that the concept of agent causation is primitive and indefinable, but that it is at the same time the product of our grasp of an open-ended multiplicity of specific ways in which individual objects can act upon one another.

12

ACTIONS AND EVENTS

Do events exist?

The previous chapter inevitably involved us in a good deal of talk about actions and events, but left unaddressed certain fundamental ontological questions concerning the existence and nature of such entities. Must we really include 'actions' and 'events' in our ontology, as entities in their own right, in addition to—or perhaps even instead of—persisting objects (or 'substances') which act in various ways and undergo various kinds of change? Assuming that they exist, are actions just a species of events, or are they items belonging to an altogether different ontological category? And how are actions and events to be individuated? What are their identity conditions? Need we and can we frame satisfactory *criteria of identity* for such entities? These are the main questions that I shall examine and, to some extent, try to answer in this chapter.

Presented with the general question 'Do events exist?', one's immediate response might well be to say, 'Yes, of course they do—for we are constantly referring to them'. Here one might have in mind both certain famous events of history, such as the Battle of Hastings or the Boston Tea Party, and more mundane events of one's own personal experience, such as the wedding of a sister or the death of an uncle. We have familiar ways of constructing certain singular noun-phrases whose function seems to be to secure reference to particular events, which must therefore exist if such reference is successful. However, we should be wary of assuming that a singular noun-phrase whose function appears to be referential really does function in a referential way. Consider, for example, a singular noun-phrase such as 'the average British citizen', as used by some statistician in describing certain demographic trends: it would surely be naïve to suppose that such a statistician uses this phrase with an intention to *refer* to any particular entity and that his statistical account fails if there is no such thing as 'the average British citizen'. Rather, the statistician's use of this phrase is part of a convenient way of summing up certain general information about a large population of individual human beings—to no one of which, in particular, is he referring. What we seem to need at this point is a viable *criterion of ontological commitment*—a principle which will reliably tell us what kinds of entities a theorist is committed to acknowledging as existent, in virtue of his acceptance of the truth of a given theory. And what we have just discovered is that we cannot regard as particularly reliable the principle that the *singular noun phrases* which are standardly used in the expression of a theory reveal its ontological commitments. In a moment, I shall discuss another and much more widely endorsed criterion of ontological commitment, but before doing so I want to consider a second possible response to our original question, 'Do events exist?'

This second response is, disconcertingly, the very reverse of the previous one. Faced with the question, 'Do events exist?', some philosophers are inclined to reply with an emphatic 'No', even while conceding quite readily that we do indeed *refer* to particular events constantly, both in everyday speech and in scientific discourse. The point of such a denial, however, would not be to suggest that events are 'not real', or not genuine features of the world, but rather that the verb 'exist' is not one which properly expresses their distinctive 'mode of being'. According to this way of thinking, we should say that events *occur* or that they *happen*, rather than that they *exist*; whereas, conversely, we should say of persisting objects (or 'substances') that they *exist*, but not that they *occur* or *happen*. We should not dismiss this suggestion too lightly, as one resting merely upon an idiosyncrasy of everyday language. For the point is not just that it 'sounds odd' to say such things as 'The Battle of Hastings *existed* in 1066'. Rather, the view in question may be motivated by a carefully considered metaphysical doctrine which denies that entities of different ontological categories all share some single 'mode of being'.

Advocates of this doctrine may urge that our use of the verb 'to be' is systematically ambiguous, with its sense depending upon the category of entity being referred to by the subject of that verb on any given occasion.[1] Thus, just as the sense in which *exercise* may be said to be 'healthy' is different from, but closely related to, the sense in which a *person* (or other living being) may be said to be 'healthy', so it may be contended that the

---

[1] This approach is Aristotelian in its inspiration: for discussion, see Michael J. Loux, 'Kinds and Predications: An Examination of Aristotle's Theory of Categories', *Philosophical Papers* 26 (1997), 3–28.

sense in which an *event* may be said to 'be' is different from, albeit related to, the sense in which a *substance* may be said to 'be'. In particular, it may be suggested that, just as the primary sense of the adjective 'healthy' is that in which a person (or other living being) may be said to be healthy, so the primary sense of the verb 'to be' is that in which a substance may be said to be or exist—and that the secondary or derivative sense in which an event may be said 'to be' has its subordinate status in virtue of the ontologically dependent nature of events in relation to substances. This doctrine, which is more or less Aristotelian, undeniably has some attractions. However, I am not convinced that one can only adequately recognize the ontological primacy of substances—if, indeed, such recognition is due—without accepting that the verb 'to be' is ambiguous in the way being proposed. Consequently, I shall assume in what follows that, contrary to this proposal, a perfectly proper way to acknowledge the reality of events is to say that they *exist* and, indeed, that all real beings or entities 'exist' in precisely the same sense of that verb, which I shall henceforth take to be perfectly univocal. (I acknowledge that the proposal which I am now dismissing merits more discussion than I can afford to give it here, but I would also urge that the position which I favour is, as it were, the 'default' position, which should be presumed correct unless it can be shown to be mistaken.)

An argument for the existence of events

I mentioned, a little while ago, a certain criterion of ontological commitment which has received widespread endorsement in recent times. This is W. V. Quine's criterion, encapsulated in his famous slogan 'To be is to be the value of a variable'.[2] According to this criterion, we may discover the ontological commitments of a theory by first expressing the theory in the language of first-order predicate logic and then determining what kinds of entities must be admitted as possible values of the bound variables used in thus expressing the theory, if the theory is to be deemed true. (A 'bound variable' is a variable bound by a quantifier, as the variable 'x' is bound by the existential quantifier 'E' in the formula '$(Ex)Fx$'; the latter formula means, quite simply, 'There is at least one thing, x, such that x is F', where 'F' is any predicate one may care to choose.) Thus, for example, given that

[2] See, for example, W. V. Quine, 'Existence and Quantification', in his *Ontological Relativity and Other Essays* (New York: Columbia University Press, 1969). In that paper, Quine discusses the significance of so-called 'substitutional' quantification, referred to later in this paragraph.

elementary arithmetic—which is, of course, just a particular mathematical theory—includes such relatively uncontested truths as 'There is a prime number greater than 4 and less than 7' and 'Every natural number has a successor which is a natural number', Quine's criterion implies that elementary arithmetic is committed to the existence of *natural numbers* and, indeed, to the existence of infinitely many of them. This becomes obvious once we express such purported truths in standard logical form—for instance, when we express the first of the two purported truths just cited in the form '(Ex) (x is a natural number and x is prime and x is greater than 4 and x is less than 7)'. For the latter sentence plainly entails '(Ex) (x is a natural number)', which must therefore likewise be deemed true, according to elementary arithmetic, given that the sentence entailing it is deemed true. However, '(Ex) (x is a natural number)' can be true only if its bound variable, 'x', can take as a value something to which the predicate 'is a natural number' applies: in other words, it can be true only if natural numbers exist. (The argument here presumes, of course, the correctness of a certain way of interpreting the so-called 'existential' quantifier, 'E'—a way which has, to be fair, been challenged by some logicians who favour a so-called 'substitutional' interpretation of the quantifiers and who, as a consequence, may regard the epithet 'existential' as tendentious in this context. But I shall not pursue this debate here, since my main concern at present is to describe rather than to defend Quine's criterion of ontological commitment.)

Quine's criterion of ontological commitment may evidently be invoked in defence of a positive answer to the question 'Do events exist?'. One such line of argument is famously due to Donald Davidson and runs roughly as follows.[3] In everyday speech, we frequently assert *action sentences* which we take to be uncontentiously true. Such a sentence typically consists of a subject term denoting an agent, a verb of action, and one or more adverbs or adverbial phrases expressing the time, manner or place at or in which the agent acted. For example, 'Jones climbed slowly, steadily, at dawn, on the north face of Everest' is a typical action sentence. Evidently, there is no limit to the number of adverbial qualifiers which can be attached to the verb in an action sentence. Equally evidently, from any such adverbially

---

[3] See Donald Davidson, 'The Logical Form of Action Sentences', in Nicholas Rescher (ed.), *The Logic of Decision and Action* (Pittsburgh, Pa.: University of Pittsburgh Press, 1966), reprinted in Donald Davidson, *Essays on Actions and Events* (Oxford: Clarendon Press, 1980). For discussion, see Lawrence Brian Lombard, *Events: A Metaphysical Study* (London: Routledge and Kegan Paul, 1986), 9 ff.

qualified sentence we can validly infer a sentence from which one or more of the adverbial qualifiers has been detached. For instance, the action sentence just cited plainly entails all of the following simpler action sentences: 'Jones climbed slowly, steadily, at dawn', 'Jones climbed slowly, steadily', 'Jones climbed slowly', and 'Jones climbed'. But how can we explain these entailments? First-order predicate logic will not help us to do so if we leave these sentences in their present grammatical form, because first-order predicate logic does not recognize the grammatical phenomenon of adverbial qualification. As far as that system of logic is concerned, 'Jones climbed slowly' and 'Jones climbed' are simply two quite distinct atomic predicative sentences with the same subject term, as logically unrelated to one another as are 'Jones climbed' and 'Jones laughed'.

However, if we are prepared to recognize in action sentences an underlying logical form which differs from their superficial grammatical form, then we can indeed appeal to first-order predicate logic for an explanation of the problematic entailments. All we need to do is to construe each action sentence as involving an implicit existential quantification, with the variable of quantification taking *events* as its possible values. For example, we may construe our original action sentence, 'Jones climbed slowly, steadily, at dawn, on the north face of Everest', as implicitly having the following logical form: '(Ex) (x was a climbing and x was by Jones and x was slow and x was steady and x was at dawn and x was on the north face of Everest)'. Then we can explain, for example, the entailment of 'Jones climbed' by 'Jones climbed slowly' in terms of the laws of first-order predicate logic, since it amounts simply to the entailment of '(Ex) (x was a climbing and x was by Jones)' by '(Ex) (x was a climbing and x was by Jones and x was slow)'.[4] The latter entailment holds purely in virtue of the truth-functional properties of the conjunction 'and'. And now, to complete the argument for the existence of events, we can appeal to Quine's criterion of ontological commitment: having expressed what we take to be true action sentences in the language of first-order predicate logic, in the manner just prescribed, we see that their truth requires the existence of *events* as possible values of the variables of quantification used in thus expressing action sentences. For instance, in the case of our sample action sentence, its truth requires the existence of something to which the

---

[4] As Davidson himself would readily acknowledge, this particular example is complicated by the fact that 'slow' is a so-called *attributive* adjective—the complication being that an event that is slow for a climbing might be fast for, say, a climbing in poor weather: see his *Essays on Actions and Events*, 106–7.

predicate 'is a climbing' applies: and *climbings*, it seems clear, are simply (a species of) events.

Is the foregoing argument open to any serious objection? Perhaps so. In the first place, what entitles us to assume that the entities that we must call upon as possible values of the variables of quantification in this case are indeed *events*? Shouldn't we say, rather, that they are *actions*? Of course, it may be held that actions just are (a species of) events: but that is a further claim, which is not established simply by the argument that has been developed so far. Secondly, and more fundamentally, why should we suppose, just because the problematic entailments can only be explained by means of first-order predicate logic when action sentences are taken to involve existential quantification over events (or actions), that therefore we should indeed take action sentences to involve such quantification? Why shouldn't we maintain instead that first-order predicate logic provides an inadequate means of representing the logical relationships between action sentences, with the implication that what we really require is a way of extending first-order predicate logic so as to accommodate the phenomenon of adverbial qualification?[5] After all, what is so sacrosanct about first-order predicate logic in its standard form? Perhaps the response to this objection will be that if we can avoid having to extend first-order predicate logic, by quantifying over some suitable category of entities, then we should certainly do so, because it is more extravagant, in general, to revise one's logic than to augment one's ontology. How satisfactory such a response would be, I leave others to judge for themselves. Suffice it to say that it is not uncontentious that the argument developed earlier is a good way of defending a positive answer to the question 'Do events exist?' On the other hand, perhaps it will be felt that we don't really need an *argument* to justify our belief in the existence of events quite generally, any more than we need an argument to justify our belief in the existence of *things* quite generally, because we can't really make sense of the idea of there being *no events or things whatever*. Whether or not that is so I shall not attempt to determine now, but for the time being I shall simply assume that we are indeed entitled to believe in the existence of events, and turn instead to questions concerning their nature.

---

[5] For such an approach see, for example, Terence Parsons, 'Some Problems Concerning the Logic of Grammatical Modifiers', in Donald Davidson and Gilbert Harman (eds.), *Semantics of Natural Language* (Dordrecht: D. Reidel, 1972).

Criteria of identity

It may be urged, with some plausibility, that we do not really grasp the nature of entities of a given category until we have a firm grasp of the *identity conditions* of entities of that category—and that what is needed for such a grasp is an understanding of a suitable *criterion of identity* for such entities. To cite another famous slogan of Quine's: 'No entity without identity'.[6] There has been much debate on the logical form and status of identity criteria, but for present purposes I shall assume that a criterion of identity for entities of a given kind, k, is a statement of the following form:[7]

> (C_k) If x and y are entities of kind k, then x is identical with y if and only if x and y stand in the relation R_k to one another.

Clearly, if (C_k) is to be neither trivial nor circular, then the relation R_k must be neither the relation of identity itself nor any relation which presupposes or depends upon the identity of any entity of kind k. For example: in the mathematical theory of sets, we can formulate a criterion of identity for sets which states that x and y are the same set if and only if x and y have exactly the same members. This criterion is neither trivial nor circular, because it can be determined whether or not x and y have the same members without first determining whether or not x and y are identical and without having to presuppose the identity of any *set*. Of course, we must allow that a set may have other sets amongst its members, but, where this is so, we can apply the given criterion to the sets in question to determine *their* identity by reference to *their* members, and so on repeatedly, if need be, until we eventually arrive at sets which have *no* sets amongst their members—and *their* identity we can determine, by means of the given criterion, without presupposing the identity of any set whatever. (One such set will be the *empty* set, which has no members at all, but other such sets will have as members only entities which are *non*-sets—for instance, concrete objects, such as trees, planets, and ships.)

It might be thought at this point, in view of the foregoing remarks, that what we need in order to understand better the nature of events is an acceptable *criterion of identity for events*. And, indeed, in due course I shall look at some proposed criteria of identity for events. But, as a matter of

---

[6] See, for example, W. V. Quine, 'Speaking of Objects', in his *Ontological Relativity and Other Essays*.

[7] See further my 'What is a Criterion of Identity?', *Philosophical Quarterly* 39 (1989), 1–21.

fact, I have some doubts as to whether it even makes sense to propose a criterion of identity for events *quite generally*, as opposed to criteria of identity for this or that *kind* of events, for the same reason that it may be doubted whether it makes sense to propose a criterion of identity for *things* quite generally, as opposed to criteria of identity for various different kinds of things. The point is that the distinction between events and things is a distinction between two different *categories* of entities—and it seems that entities of many different kinds, with different identity conditions, can very often belong to one and the same ontological category. For example, the category of *things*—even if we restrict our attention to concrete, as opposed to abstract, things—includes items as different from one another as living organisms, artefacts, and lumps of matter, all of which very plausibly have quite different criteria of identity. (Of course, 'thing' is a slippery term, and in one very broad sense it is just synonymous with 'entity'—but more commonly it is used in a more restricted sense, as it is when 'things' are contrasted with such items as events, processes, properties, and relations.) Why, then, should we assume that different *kinds* of events do not have different identity conditions, in the way that different kinds of things plainly do? If this assumption is mistaken, then the search for a criterion of identity for events quite generally will be entirely misguided. None the less, this is what many recent philosophers concerned with the ontology of events have tried to seek. All that I can suggest, then, is that we approach their proposals with some caution and even some scepticism.

The individuation of actions and events

One quite popular idea is that actions and events are to be individuated and identified at least in part by reference to their time and place of occurrence. Certainly, if we are talking about *individual* or *particular* actions or events, as opposed to the types or kinds which these individuals exemplify or instantiate, then it seems indisputable that one and the same action or event cannot recur at different places and times. If the Battle of Hastings took place at Hastings in 1066, then that very event cannot also have taken place elsewhere at a different time—although, of course, another very similar battle could have taken place in another place at a different time. We do sometimes talk of events 'recurring'—for instance, we may talk of a 'recurring headache'—but what I think we mean (or *should* mean) by this is just that a number of *different* individual events of the same kind (or of very similar kinds) can sometimes occur in succession. It might be suggested, then, that if x and y are individual events of the same kind (for example, if x and y are both battles, or are both headaches), then x and y are one and the same individual event of that kind just in case x and y occur at the same place and at the same time. Unfortunately, however, this proposal is plainly flawed: for even if two different *things* of the same kind cannot exist in the same place at the same time (for example, two different trees, or two different statues), it would appear that two different *events* of the same kind can indeed occur in the same place at the same time, even if such a coincidence is not a particularly common occurrence. We can even make sense of such a coincidence in the case events such as battles and headaches. For example: three opposing armies might be fighting pairwise with one another on the same battlefield during the same period of time, in which case one might say that three different battles were being fought simultaneously in the same place. Again: in a case of so-called 'multiple personality syndrome', two distinct 'persons' associated with the same human body might complain of having suffered a headache at the same time, in which case (since we do not regard headaches as being shareable between different persons) one might say that two different headaches occurred in the same place (namely, in the same head, or part of a head) at the same time. I concede that these examples are a little far-fetched, but that doesn't matter: if they even make sense, as they seem to, we cannot say with any confidence that it is *impossible* for different events of the same kind to occur in the same place at the same time—in which case, the proposal now under scrutiny cannot be endorsed. And, in any case, with other, more esoteric kinds of events the possibility of coincidence is even more easily envisaged. For instance, if three point particles, P_1, P_2, and P_3, collide simultaneously, then three different collisions occur in the same place at the same time—the collision between P_1 and P_2, the collision between P_2 and P_3, and the collision between P_3 and P_1. (A 'point particle' would be a particle with certain physical properties and capable of motion, but possessing no spatial extension.)

Are actions events?

So far, in discussing the individuation of actions and events, I have made no distinction between actions and events and, indeed, it is widely assumed that actions just *are* (a species of) events—for which reason it is also widely assumed that actions and events are to be individuated in the same fashion. But already in the previous chapter I paved the way for a challenge to these assumptions. Suppose that we take seriously the notion of agent causation proposed in that chapter—and suppose we say, accordingly, that certain actions consist in *an agent's causing some event*. Then we may very well want to resist, with good reason, the suggestion that such actions are themselves *events* which *occur* at certain times and places. For how could the *causing* of an event—whether by an agent or by another event—itself be an *event*, with a specific location and time of occurrence?[8] Consider, for instance, Smith's action of killing Jones by administration of a slow-acting poison. Since Smith's action was his killing Jones, it follows that Smith, in performing this action, caused Jones's death, which presumably occurred at a specific time and place—for example, on Tuesday afternoon in Jones's bedroom. But perhaps Smith administered the poison much earlier, Jones ingesting it on Monday in his dining room. So when and where did Smith kill Jones? On Monday in the dining room, or on Tuesday in the bedroom, or over the course of both days and partly in each location? I am inclined to say that the question is a misplaced one, because Smith's action is not itself an event at all, but the causing of an event. In my view, it would be just as silly to ask *where* and *when* an explosion caused the collapse of a bridge: the explosion occurred in a certain place at a certain time, as did the collapse—but the explosion's *causing* the collapse did not (or so I am inclined to say). For the same reason, I am reluctant to speak of actions *occurring*: I prefer to say that, whereas events occur, actions are *performed*. If it is still insisted that we may always quite sensibly ask where and when an action was performed, then I will still urge that we should not attempt to answer such a question as if actions were a species of events. Where an action consists in an agent's causing some event by means of causing various other, intermediary events, then the question of where and when the action was performed can, I suggest, only be answered by saying where and when all of these constituent events occurred—which implies that there is no such time as 'the' time at which the action was performed and no such place as 'the' place at which it was performed.

I must acknowledge at once that my preferred way of talking about where and when an action was performed is not shared by a good many other modern philosophers of action—notably, of course, many of those

[8] See further Kent Bach, 'Actions Are Not Events', *Mind* 89 (1980), 114–20, and Maria Alvarez and John Hyman, 'Agents and their Actions', *Philosophy* 73 (1998), 219–45. See also my *An Introduction to the Philosophy of Mind* (Cambridge: Cambridge University Press, 2000), 240 ff.

who assimilate actions to events. According to one view of these matters, a human action—such as Smith's action of killing Jones—is in fact nothing else than a certain bodily event: in this case a certain movement of Smith's body, namely, the movement involved in Smith's administration of the poison as, say, he tipped the poison bottle with his hand.[9] According to this view, all that human agents ever *do*, really, is to undergo certain bodily movements: the events that follow these movements, such as the motion of the poison bottle and, ultimately, the death of Jones, are just *consequences* of the actions in question. So is it incorrect, on this view, to say that Smith killed Jones, or even that he tipped the poison bottle? By no means. For, according to this view, we very often *describe* our actions, quite legitimately, in terms of their more or less remote effects. An action which, in itself, is merely a bodily movement, such as a certain motion of Smith's hand, may be variously redescribed as a tipping of a poison bottle or as a killing of a victim, just so long as it has, amongst its effects, events of certain appropriate kinds—in this case, a tipping motion of a poison bottle and the death of another human being.

Philosophers who espouse this sort of view must say, it seems, that Smith's action of killing Jones took place on Monday in the dining room, assuming that this is when and where the crucial movement of Smith's hand occurred. But to other philosophers this verdict sounds distinctly odd and even absurd: for how can Smith have killed Jones a day before Jones died, while Jones was still hale and hearty—and how can Smith have killed Jones far from the place in which Jones died? No doubt we can make sense, of a kind, of such odd ways of talking—but the fact that we find them so odd strongly suggests that any theory of action which requires us to talk in these ways rests upon some sort of mistake. In my view, the mistake is one of assimilating actions to events, and the remedy is explained above.

A causal criterion of identity for events

Setting aside these concerns, however, let us return now to the question of how events—whether or not these should be taken to include actions—are to be individuated. The one proposal that we have looked at so far—that

---

[9] See, for example, Donald Davidson, 'Agency', in Robert Binkley, Richard Bronaugh, and Ausonio Marras (eds.), *Agent, Action, and Reason* (Toronto: University of Toronto Press, 1971), reprinted in Davidson, *Essays on Actions and Events*.

spatiotemporal location serves to individuate events of any given kind—turned out to be flawed, since numerically distinct events of the same kind can plausibly coincide in space and time. But another and seemingly more promising proposal appeals instead to causal considerations, on the plausible assumption that all events have causes and/or effects. (Even if some events have no causes—such as, perhaps, a putative 'first' event—and some events have no effects, it seems safe to say that we can have no evidence of there being any event which has no causes and no effects whatever: for unless an event has either causes or effects, it seems that it cannot make itself known to us in any way, however indirect.) Putting the proposal in the form of a putative criterion of identity for events, along the lines of the schema (C_k) presented earlier, it amounts to the following principle:[10]

> (C_e) If x and y are events, then x is identical with y if and only if x and y have the same causes and effects.

Those who typically espouse this principle presume that all causation is event causation, so that the causes of any event are always themselves events (rather than, say, *agents* of any kind). But this presumption also seems to lead to the principle's downfall, because it appears to condemn the principle to a fatal circularity. Recall that, when introducing schema (C_k), I remarked that the relation R_k must be neither the relation of identity itself nor any relation which presupposes or depends upon the identity of any entity of kind k. But, it would seem, principle (C_e) violates the latter requirement. For to say that events x and y have the *same* causes and effects is, given the presumption just mentioned, simply to say that *the same events* that cause and are caused by x likewise cause and are caused by y, which surely presupposes the identity of certain entities of the very kind for which principle (C_e) is supposed to provide a criterion of identity—namely, certain *events*.[11] This appears still more evident if we rephrase (C_e) in the following way:

> $(C_e{}^*)$ If x and y are events, then x is identical with y if and only if (i) for any event z, z is a cause of x if and only if z is a cause of y and (ii) for any event z, x is a cause of z if and only if y is a cause of z.

[10] See Donald Davidson, 'The Individuation of Events', in Nicholas Rescher (ed.), *Essays in Honor of Carl G. Hempel* (Dordrecht: D. Reidel, 1969), reprinted in Davidson, *Essays on Actions and Events*.

[11] See further W. V. Quine, 'Events and Reification', in Ernest LePore and Brian McLaughlin (eds.), *Actions and Events: Perspectives on the Philosophy of Donald Davidson* (Oxford: Blackwell, 1985). Replying to Quine in the same volume, Davidson concedes the difficulty and in consequence abandons the criterion.

Although neither clause (i) nor clause (ii) of (C_e^*) contains any explicit expression of identity between events, both of these clauses contain a repeated variable, 'z', which takes events as its possible values. And when a variable is repeated in this way, it must be implicitly understood that it takes the *same* value at both of its occurrences. Thus, in each of these clauses, the variable 'z' must be understood to take the *same event* as its value at both of its occurrences, which appears to presuppose the identity of some event, contrary to our requirement on non-circularity. To put the point another way: to say, as in clause (i), that an event z is a cause of x if and only if z is a cause of y is just to say that an event z is a cause of x if and only if *that same event* is also a cause of y.

Some responses to the circularity objection

At this point, it is worth comparing the apparently defective criterion of identity for events, (C_e), with the perfectly acceptable criterion of identity for *sets* cited earlier, for they are superficially similar.[12] The latter criterion states that if x and y are sets, then x is identical with y if and only if x and y have the same members. Now, it is true that some sets may have other sets amongst their members: but we saw earlier that, whenever this is so, it is possible, by repeated applications of the stated criterion of identity, eventually to determine whether or not a set x is identical with a set y without presupposing the identity of any set whatever. This is because all sets are ultimately founded upon entities which do not themselves have members in the set-theoretical sense—that is, they are all ultimately founded upon entities which are either *non*-sets or else identical with the empty set. (The stated criterion itself implies that there is only one empty set, because if sets x and y both have no members, then, quite trivially, they have *the same* members and so are identical according to the criterion.) However, it seems improbable that anything like this situation can be supposed to obtain in the case of *events*, given the presupposition that the only species of causation is event causation. It is true that criterion (C_e) implies that there is at most one event which has no causes and effects—and such an event, if it could reasonably be supposed to exist, would be in some ways analogous to the empty set of set theory. (Clearly, if events x and y both

---

[12] For more on the points about to be made, see my 'Impredicative Identity Criteria and Davidson's Criterion of Event Identity', *Analysis* 49 (1989), 178–81.

have *no* causes and effects, then, quite trivially, they have *the same* causes and effects, so that x and y are identical according to criterion (C_e).) However, in the first place, as we saw earlier, we have no reason to suppose that *any* event has no causes and effects and, secondly, even if such an event did exist, it plainly could not play a role in the theory of events similar to that of the empty set in set theory, because whereas the empty set can be *a member of* other sets, the putative event with no causes and effects plainly cannot be *a cause or effect of* any other event. Of course, we could save criterion (C_e) from circularity if we could suppose that certain entities other than events could be causes or effects of events—for instance, if we could maintain that there is agent causation as well as event causation and that agent causation is irreducible to event causation. For then we could hope to identify certain events by reference to their agent causes and then to identify other events by reference to these previously identified events. But this would be too high a price to pay for most philosophers who are inclined to espouse a causal criterion of identity for events along the lines of (C_e).

Couldn't we perhaps hope to save criterion (C_e) from circularity in the following way, without either supposing that there is an event which has no causes and effects or giving up the presupposition that the only species of causation is event causation? Suppose that the universe began with the occurrence of a finite number of uncaused events, each of which caused various subsequent events. Call the supposed uncaused events e_1 and e_2 and suppose, say, that e_1 was an immediate cause of events e_3 and e_4, while e_2 was an immediate cause of events e_4 and e_5. If we like, we can suppose that this is all that happens in the very simple universe under consideration. Now it might seem that each of the five events occurring in that universe is distinguishable in terms of its causes and/or effects and consequently that principle (C_e) suffices as a criterion of identity for events in such a universe. Thus, e_1 is the event which has no causes and is a cause of events e_3 and e_4, e_2 is the event which has no causes and is a cause of events e_4 and e_5, e_3 is the event which is caused by e_1 but not by e_2, e_4 is the event which is caused by both e_1 and e_2, and e_5 is the event which is caused by e_2 but not by e_1. It might seem that, in this way, we have specified the causal relations between the events in our five-event universe so as to assign to each of those events a unique causal role which serves to distinguish it unambiguously from all of the other events.

However, symmetry considerations reveal that, in fact, the only event which is uniquely identified by its causal role in these circumstances is the event e_4, which is distinctive in being the only event which has two causes and no effects. Of the remaining events in our five-event universe, e_1 is just like e_2 in having no causes and two effects and e_3 is just like e_5 in having one cause and no effects. Unless we have some further way of distinguishing e_1 from e_2 and e_3 from e_5, then, we have not yet managed to identify every event in this imaginary universe unambiguously. I am prepared to grant that, in certain other very simple universes of an asymmetrical character, criterion (C_e) may indeed serve its intended purpose of unambiguously identifying every event non-circularly. But I see no reason to suppose that the universe which we actually inhabit is one in which criterion (C_e) can serve its intended purpose in the way it might in such an imaginary universe. Apart from anything else, we have no compelling reason to suppose that our actual universe contains a finite number of events or that it began with a finite number of uncaused events. Here I should make it plain that the objection to criterion (C_e) is not so much that it is *impractical*—that it would be impossible in practice to use it in order to identify and distinguish between events, in a universe as complex as ours is—but rather that it fails in principle to determine unambiguously the relations of identity and diversity between events in any but certain unrealistically simple universes.

Events as property exemplifications

Our search for a general criterion of identity for events has not proved fruitful so far, which may perhaps confirm my suspicion that we shouldn't expect events of every kind to be individuated in the same general way. But another suspicion that may be encouraged by this failure is that we have been approaching matters from the wrong direction: instead of attempting to cast light on the nature of events by trying to formulate a satisfactory criterion of identity for events, perhaps we should first endeavour to say what events *are*—which should then help us to understand what their identity conditions might be. So far, in this chapter, we haven't advanced much beyond saying that events are things that *happen* or *occur* (using the word 'thing', here, in its broadest sense, to mean 'entity' or 'item'). This tells us, indeed, that events are *temporal* entities and hence that it doesn't make sense to talk of 'timeless events'. But it leaves practically everthing else about their nature undetermined, apart from their *particularity*—the fact that they are individual entities of some sort. Thus far, then, we have said little more than that an event is a *temporal particular*: an item which happens or occurs at a particular time and is not repeatable. And some philosophers, it seems, would be happy to leave matters at that, perhaps even considering that nothing more than this can be said about events in general. But others would urge that events, as a category, are by their very nature related not only to particular times, but also to particular concrete objects and their properties. One suggestion, for instance, is that an event just *is* the exemplification of a property by an object at a time, so that every event can be represented by (though not necessarily be identified with) an ordered triple of an object, a property, and a time.[13] (An ordered triple is simply a set of three items taken in a particular order—a mathematical example being the ordered triple of the first three positive integers taken in ascending order of magnitude, $\langle 1, 2, 3 \rangle$.)

In many familiar cases, this proposal has a good deal of plausibility. For instance, the death of Julius Caesar is an event which can plausibly be thought of as Caesar's exemplifying the property of dying on the Ides of March 44 BC and thus as being representable by the ordered triple $\langle$Caesar, dying, Ides of March 44 BC$\rangle$. If this conception of the nature of events is correct, it seems to provide us immediately with a corresponding account of the identity conditions of events. The obvious thing to say is that if x and y are events, then they are the same event if and only if they are represented by the same ordered triple—that is to say, if and only if they are exemplifications of the *same* property by the *same* object at the *same* time. This, of course, still leaves open the question of how we are to individuate properties, objects, and times: but since none of these are events, it is not obvious that the proposed criterion of identity for events can be convicted of circularity or triviality.

I shall say more about this and related conceptions of events in the next chapter, but for present purposes I should just point out a few potentially vulnerable features of it. One possible problem is that there may perhaps be some events which do not involve the existence of any particular object at all. Think of an event such as a sudden flash of light, perhaps one occurring during an early phase of the universe, before any material objects such as stars had formed.[14] Whereas a flash of light from a light-house can perhaps be thought of as being the lighthouse's exemplifying the

[13] See Jaegwon Kim, 'Events as Property Exemplifications', in Myles Brand and Douglas Walton (eds.), *Action Theory* (Dordrecht: D. Reidel, 1980).

[14] See P. F. Strawson, *Individuals: An Essay in Descriptive Metaphysics* (London: Methuen, 1959), 46.

property of flashing at a particular time, it is not so clear what we can say in this vein about the putative flash of light in the early universe. (We might be tempted to say that in this case the 'object' exemplifying the appropriate property is the *universe* itself: but this looks suspiciously ad hoc and little more than a verbal trick.)

Another possible problem concerns the nature of the supposed 'properties' whose exemplification by objects at times events are alleged to be. Talk of 'properties' is often extremely obscure, as we shall see more fully in Chapter 19. Too often, philosophers make the careless assumption that any meaningful predicate expresses a property which something can possess: but, in fact, even if we can justify the inclusion of properties in our ontology, it is a far from trivial matter to determine which predicates express properties and equally problematic to determine when two predicates express the *same* property. Even setting aside these general difficulties concerning properties, however, it may be doubted whether the appeal to properties in characterizing the nature of events really can always avoid implicit circularity. For instance, when I said, a moment ago, that a flash of light from a lighthouse can perhaps be thought of as being the lighthouse's exemplifying the property of flashing at a particular time, this may prompt the question of what, precisely, we should understand by the property of 'flashing' in this context. If, by 'flashing', we simply mean 'emitting a flash'—as seems plausible—then it appears that what we are talking about in speaking of a lighthouse's 'flashing' is just a species of *agent causation* (in the very broad sense of that term discussed in the previous chapter). In other words, according to this interpretation of the verb, for a lighthouse to 'flash' is for it to cause, produce, or bring about *a flash*, that is, an *event* of a certain kind. If that is so, then it is blatantly circular to characterize *a flash* as an object's exemplifying the property of flashing at a particular time, for this then just amounts to saying that *a flash* is the exemplification of the property of producing *a flash* by an object at a time. Indeed, the latter pronouncement seems not only circular but actually false, since it is hard to see how one could *identify* an event with an object's exemplification of the property of producing just such an event. At the very least, then, adherents of the proposal now under consideration must take great care about which property they choose to include in the ordered triple supposedly representing a given event, making sure that it is not a property which an object possesses only in virtue of producing an event of the very kind in question.

My conclusions in this chapter have mostly been negative: that we have found no satisfactory general argument for the existence of actions or events, that actions are plausibly not events, that we have found no satisfactory general criterion of identity for events, and that, so far, nothing much more can confidently be said about events in general but that they are temporal particulars ('things which happen'). Given the evident importance of events for contemporary metaphysics, these conclusions may be disappointing. However, in the next chapter I hope to be able to say something rather more positive about the nature of events.

13

EVENTS, THINGS, AND SPACE-TIME

Event-ontologies versus thing-ontologies

We came to no very positive conclusion in the preceding chapter as to what, exactly, events *are*, beyond saying that they are temporal particulars—'things which happen'. Although events, for the most part, appear to be things which happen *to* persisting objects (or 'substances')—as, for example, a death is something which happens to an animal or human being—we did not even arrive at any very clear conception of *how* events are related to the persisting objects, if any, to which they happen, or which 'participate' in those events. We briefly considered the view that an event just *is* the exemplification of a property by an object at a time, but saw that it is apparently vulnerable to certain difficulties. In the present chapter, I want to inquire more deeply into how we might conceive of the ontological relationship between entities in the category of *event* and entities in the category of *persisting object, substance*, or *thing*—in the narrow sense of 'thing', in which we restrict this term to such items as trees, rocks, animals, stars, and atoms. (Some philosophers prefer to call items belonging to these two categories 'occurrents' and 'continuants' rather than 'events' and 'things', which has the advantage of avoiding some unwanted connotations associated with everyday terms but the greater disadvantage of artificiality.)[1] I also want to raise the question of how things and events are related ontologically to the *places* and *times* in which they are situated or at which they occur and, indeed, how the existence of space and time quite generally is related to the existence of the concrete

---

[1] The terminology of 'continuants' and 'occurrents' is due to W. E. Johnson: see his *Logic, Part I* (Cambridge: Cambridge University Press, 1921), 199.

occupants of space and time, both things and events. Can we, for instance, make sense of the notion of a perfectly 'empty' space or time—regions of space, or even an entire space, in which no concrete object exists and periods of time, or even an entire time, in which no event occurs? If so, what does this imply for our conception of how space and time in general are related, ontologically, to concrete things and events capable of occupying them?

On the question of how events and persisting objects, or 'things' (in our narrow sense), are related ontologically to one another, several different positions have been advocated at one time or another. Some philosophers invite us to be either *reductionists* or *eliminativists* about either things or events, while others invite us to be *non-reductive pluralists*. The reductionists attempt to reduce either things to events or else events to things (and their properties or relations), whereas the eliminativists argue that either things or events may be excluded, without any real loss, from our ontology. The non-reductive pluralists, in contrast, maintain that we need to include both things and events in our ontology as items belonging to two mutually irreducible and equally fundamental categories. Let us call an ontological theory which attempts to reduce things to, or eliminate them in favour of, events an *event-ontology*. And let us correspondingly call an ontological theory which attempts to reduce events to, or eliminate them in favour of, things (and their properties or relations) a *thing-ontology* (or *substance-ontology*). These may be described as *monistic* ontologies, as far as the thing/event distinction is concerned, in contrast to any *pluralist* ontology which admits both things and events as items of equally fundamental ontological status. With these distinctions in mind, we are in a position now to examine some of the attractions and weaknesses of the various types of ontology just mentioned.

Event-ontologies and modern physics

It is sometimes said that modern physics requires us to espouse an event-ontology. According to this way of thinking, the physical world as described by modern physics is a four-dimensional space-time manifold, each point of which may be designated by an ordered set of space-time coordinates of the form $\langle x, y, z, t \rangle$, the first three co-ordinates specifying a spatial location and the fourth a moment of time, relative to some suitable frame of reference. A complete description of the physical world, it is then suggested, can in principle be supplied by specifying what is happening at each such point of space-time, that is, in terms of the events occurring at all such points. What we ordinarily think of as being a persisting object, such as a rock or a tree, is, it may be urged, just a series of events—a *process*—which occupies that object's so-called 'world-line', its path through space and time. Another way of putting this is to say that what we ordinarily think of as a persisting object or thing is just the 'material content' of a region of space-time and as such is not in reality distinct from the collection of events occurring in that region.[2] This, of course, is a reductionist rather than an eliminativist event-ontology: it admits that persisting objects or things exist, but contends that they are nothing 'over and above' the events occurring in the space-time regions occupied by them. If, however, it is objected that to reduce things to events in this way is to commit some sort of 'category mistake'—on the grounds, for instance, that persisting objects, unlike events, cannot properly be said to 'occur'— then an alternative option is an eliminativist event-ontology, according to which talk of persisting objects should be replaced by, rather than reduced to, talk of events and processes, at least in a fundamental scientific description of the physical world.

Those who say that modern physics prescribes an event-ontology of either of these kinds are rather overstating their case.[3] Modern physics is perhaps consistent with such an ontology, but does not appear to entail it. Some philosophers and philosophically-minded physicists may have been misled on this score by their allegiance to an excessively positivistic epistemology of science. In particular, they may have been swayed by the thought that all that empirical science reveals to us, finally, are the results of certain actual or possible measurements and observations which can be made in the physical world—and that measurements and observations are, after all, just *events*. If we think, in a positivistic spirit, that measurements and observations are all that physical science is really concerned with, then we may be led to imagine that all that may legitimately be said to *exist*, for scientific purposes, are measurements and observations occurring at various points of space-time. However, the naïveté of such a stance is striking. Apart from anything else, it ignores the fact that scientific measurements

---

[2] See W. V. Quine, 'Identity, Ostension, and Hypostasis', in his *From a Logical Point of View*, 2nd edn. (Cambridge, Mass.: Harvard University Press, 1961), and also his *Word and Object* (Cambridge, Mass.: MIT Press, 1960), 171. For another scientifically inspired event ontology, see Alfred North Whitehead, *The Concept of Nature* (Cambridge: Cambridge University Press, 1920).

[3] See further D. H. Mellor, *Real Time* (Cambridge: Cambridge University Press, 1981), 127 ff.

and observations are made by *people* and very often with the indispensable aid of scientific *instruments*. Both people and instruments are persisting objects or things, which we cannot without argument presume to be 'nothing over and above', or reducible to, mere collections of events of measurement and observation. The impersonal and abstract character of much official scientific discourse may partially disguise the metaphysical inadequacy of the view now under scrutiny: using verbs expressed in the third-person and passive voice, such discourse tends to describe measurements and observations as 'being made', almost as if this activity were somehow disembodied, rather than being carried out in real laboratories by real people using real instruments.

A rather more compelling—though still far from conclusive—argument for saying that modern physics prescribes an event-ontology is that quantum physics demands an event-ontology and all physics is ultimately reducible, at least in principle, to quantum physics. According to this line of thinking, talk of fundamental physical 'particles'—such as protons, neutrons, electrons, and the like—is misleading in its suggestion that these entities are at all like the persisting objects which we ordinarily take to populate the macroscopic world of tables, rocks, and trees. Once we appreciate the partially 'wave-like' character of these sub-atomic entities, which permits them to be 'spread out' and 'entangled' with one another in states of 'superposition', we can see that the ontology of quantum physics cannot be, in any straightforward sense, a thing- or substance-ontology— or so it may be said.

The proper response to this sort of observation is, I think, as follows. First, even if it turns out to be the case that some sort of 'field' interpretation of quantum phenomena is preferable to any kind of 'particle' interpretation, it doesn't follow that such an interpretation would commit us to a thoroughgoing event-ontology.[4] Even before quantum physics was on the scene, some scientists and philosophers considered that we should ultimately describe all physical phenomena in terms of the propagation of disturbances in fields of force or energy rather than in terms of interacting particles of matter in relative motion. But such a 'field'-ontology is perfectly compatible with a 'substance'-ontology of sorts, namely, with a substance-ontology which holds the physical world to consist, not of a plurality of distinct material substances, as the Greek atomists believed,

---

[4] For the 'field' versus 'particle' distinction, see Michael Redhead, 'A Philosopher Looks at Quantum Field Theory', in Harvey R. Brown and Rom Harré (eds.), *Philosophical Foundations of Quantum Field Theory* (Oxford: Clarendon Press, 1990).

but rather to be in its entirety a single and indivisible substance, as Spinoza contended. This single substance might be identified with space-time and the various 'fields' be regarded as, in Spinozistic terms, highly complex 'modes' of that single substance. A field of force or energy is, after all, something that is characteristically conceived of as being extended in space and persisting over time, though not qualifying as a 'substance' in its own right because it has an ontologically dependent status, only existing so long as its existence is sustained by the activity of something more fundamental—something that we might call the field's 'substrate'. This, for instance, is how we ordinarily think of the magnetic field of an electromagnet, which is sustained only so long as an electric current passes through the magnet's coils. If we think of *matter* as being, ultimately, a kind of field-effect, then it seems that we must conceive of the field in question as having as its 'substrate' nothing less than space-time itself, which thereby acquires the status of a singular and fundamental substance.

Secondly, however, even setting aside these esoteric issues concerning the ontology of quantum physics, we may challenge the idea that if the ontology of quantum physics turns out not to be a thing- or substance-ontology, then this implies that a reductionist or eliminativist conception of macroscopic physical objects must be espoused. The thought behind this idea is, presumably, that if macroscopic objects, such as rocks and trees, are ultimately composed entirely of quantum 'particles', and quantum 'particles' are not really 'things' or 'persisting objects' in any recognizable sense, then it follows that rocks and trees cannot be things or persisting objects either: so that we must either deny that they really exist or else regard them as being reducible to non-things of the same category—whatever it may turn out to be—that quantum entities should properly be said to belong to (perhaps, indeed, the category of events). Now, it is true enough that our everyday conception of composition is such that an entity of a given category can only be composed by other entities of the same category—a larger thing by smaller things or a larger event by smaller events, for instance. This may imply that we should not, strictly, speak of a macroscopic physical object, such as a rock, as being *composed* of quantum entities, if we want to regard the rock as being a genuine 'thing' or 'substance' and the quantum entities as being 'non-things' of some kind. However, nothing in quantum theory itself appears to require us to see the relationship between a rock and the quantum entities which 'underlie' it as being literally one of composition in this familiar sense. It seems open to us to regard the rock as having the status of an 'emergent' entity, arising out of a complex array of quantum phenomena but belonging to an altogether different ontological category, one which is only exemplified on the macroscopic scale. Certainly, the coherence of this view would have to be successfully challenged by anyone seeking to undermine our allegiance to the reality of persisting objects or 'substances' merely by appeal to the putative ontology of quantum physics.

Events and change

Having considered what appear to be the somewhat dubious prospects of defending an event-ontology on scientific grounds, let us look next at a converse point of view—one which takes a reductionist or eliminativist stance towards events in favour of the ontological primacy of things or substances. This, of course, is a much more traditional position—one which may loosely be described as being 'Aristotelian' in spirit. Now, whereas one might aspire to *identify* a 'thing', such as a rock or a tree, with some collection or series of events (though perhaps only on pain of being accused of committing a category mistake), it is clear that there is no prospect whatever of our saying, with any degree of plausibility, that an event—such as the Battle of Hastings—just *is* (identical with) some collection of things or persisting objects. The most obvious reason for this is that events occur *at times*, often of fairly short duration, whereas the persisting objects which 'participate' in events—such as the soldiers who fought at the Battle of Hastings—typically have careers which transcend the times of those events. Rather, what we might more plausibly contend is that any event is a *change* in the properties of or relations between some thing or things. For instance, a death, we might say, is a change in the vital properties of a living organism (understanding its 'vital' properties to be those in virtue of which it qualifies as a living thing). Similarly, a marriage, we might say, is a change in the legal relationship between two persons. That events are changes does indeed seem a sensible—perhaps even platitudinous—thought. And that changes are at least very often changes in the properties and relations of things seems equally uncontentious. But this account of the nature of events is only as clear as the notion of 'change' to which it appeals. What *is* a change? If all that we can say is that a change is an *event*, or a *happening*, or an *occurrence*, then we shall not have made much progress at all.

But perhaps we can say something more illuminating about the nature of change. In the broadest possible sense of 'change', we may say, perhaps, that a change occurs at a time *t* just in case something begins to be the case at *t* which was not the case prior to *t*. For example, a change in the colour of an object, *O*, occurs at a time *t* if, say, *O* is green prior to *t* but *O* begins to be red at *t*. (*O* here might be something like a traffic light.) In this case, it seems clear, the change in question is a change in the object *O* itself, since it is a change in the colour-properties of *O*. But consider now another kind of case such as the following: the change which occurred when Xanthippe became a widow upon the death of her husband, Socrates. Here we may be reluctant to say that the change in question was really a change in *Xanthippe*. Or, again, consider the change which occurs when Mary (who has stopped growing) becomes shorter than her brother, Tom, because Tom has suddenly grown. We do not, perhaps, want to say that this is really a change in *Mary*, or that Mary herself has really changed. Even so, in both these cases, it seems, we want to say that *something* has really changed: Socrates in the first case—for he has died and to die is certainly to suffer a kind of change, indeed a very radical one—and Tom in the second case. Some philosophers say that, in these cases, Xanthippe and Mary have undergone a 'mere Cambridge change'—a term whose historical roots need not concern us here—but perhaps we can say more perspicuously that Xanthippe and Mary have undergone a *purely relational* change, as opposed to an *intrinsic* change. They have changed only inasmuch as something to which they are somehow related has undergone an intrinsic change: independently of their relationship to the thing in question, Xanthippe and Mary have not (or need not have) undergone any change at all.

Is it the case, though, that non-intrinsic change in an object always and only arises in virtue of some relationship it bears to another object which is itself the subject of an intrinsic change? Perhaps not, for consider the following kind of case. Today every object that existed yesterday is older than it was yesterday. Tom, for instance, is perhaps 4,961 days old today, whereas he was 4,960 days old yesterday. According to the definition of change proposed earlier, this implies that a change has occurred: for today it began to be the case that Tom is 4,961 days old, which was not the case yesterday. But is this a change in *Tom*—and if so, is it an *intrinsic* change in Tom? No doubt Tom will indeed have changed in some way since yesterday and, indeed, changed intrinsically in some way: but not, surely, purely in virtue of being one day older. We can perfectly easily conceive of an object which gets one day older without changing intrinsically in any way at all. So it seems that an object's merely getting older is not in itself a matter of that object's undergoing some kind of intrinsic change. But equally, it seems, an object's merely getting older is not in itself a matter of that object's being somehow related to something which *does* undergo some kind of intrinsic change: for, quite apart from anything else, we seem to be able to conceive of a world of objects *all* of which get one day older without any of them undergoing any kind of intrinsic change. (This is a putative possibility to which I shall return later in this chapter.)

One thing that emerges from this example is how very broad the conception of 'change' is that was defined earlier. This is an advantage of that conception for our present purposes, because it means that it is a conception which does not presuppose much, if anything, about the ontological relationships between change, events, and things. Employing this notion of change, there will be nothing circular or question-begging in our proposing, as we did earlier, that an event is a *change* in the properties of or relations between some thing or things. Of course, if we are right in saying that something's getting older is not in itself a matter of that thing (or anything else) undergoing any kind of intrinsic or relational change, then it will follow, according to our proposal, that Tom's becoming a day older today is not an *event*. But that, if anything, seems to be to the credit of our proposal, since it sounds distinctly odd to speak of Tom's becoming a day older as being an event. Apart from anything else, we expect events to have causes and effects, but it is not clear that Tom's becoming a day older, as such, has either. All that is required for Tom to become a day older today is that nothing should have caused his death yesterday. But the non-occurrence of any event causing Tom's death yesterday is not a *cause* of Tom's becoming older today, since a 'non-occurrence' is not some strange kind of 'negative' event. Indeed, there are no negative events, in the way that there are negative facts.[5]

It is true, of course, that various events cause Tom to go on living from yesterday to today—and it might be thought that these are the causes of Tom's becoming a day older today. However, we are not obliged to say the latter. We may concede that the events in question provide a causal explanation of the fact that Tom is still alive today and hence a day older, without conceding that Tom's becoming a day older today is itself an event which the events in question cause. The mere passage of time, it seems, is not properly conceived as consisting in a succession of events, each requiring a prior cause. And Tom's becoming a day older today is merely a logical

---

[5] See further D. H. Mellor, *The Facts of Causation* (London: Routledge, 1995), 133 f.

consequence of the passage of time, together with the fact that his death did not occur yesterday. It does not appear to be something which can properly be described as an 'effect', in the causal sense of this word, and consequently does not seem to be something belonging to the category of *events*.

Are there any 'subjectless' events?

There is, however, one apparently very serious difficulty facing the proposal that an event is a change in the properties of or relations between some thing or things—a difficulty which we touched upon in the previous chapter. This is that there would at least appear to be some events which have no thing or things as their 'subject'. As was noted in that chapter, Peter Strawson makes the point in one place that 'There was a flash' does not entail 'Something flashed'.[6] That is perfectly correct. However, it does not immediately threaten our proposal. Consider, for instance, a flash of lightning, which is certainly an event. A child who asked, upon seeing a flash of lightning, 'What was it that flashed just then?', would have to be told that *nothing*—no *thing*—flashed. A flash of lightning is not like the flash of a lighthouse. Had the child's question concerned a flash of the latter kind, we could quite properly have answered 'It was a lighthouse that flashed'. But none of this goes any way at all toward showing that a flash need not be a change in the properties of or relations between some thing or things. In the case of a lightning flash, indeed, it seems entirely correct to say that it is just such a change, the things in question being various charged particles in the clouds, changes in whose electrical properties constitute the kind of electrical discharge which science reveals a lightning flash to be. These particles do not literally 'flash', in the way that a lighthouse flashes, but they do undergo certain intrinsic and relational changes which may be said to constitute an event of the kind we describe as a 'lightning flash'.

This sort of case makes it clear that genuine counterexamples to the proposal that an event is a change in the properties of or relations between some thing or things may not be all that easy to come by. Even so, we did meet a putative counterexample of this sort in the previous chapter, when we considered the case of a flash of light occurring in the early universe,

---

[6] See P. F. Strawson, *Individuals: An Essay in Descriptive Metaphysics* (London: Methuen, 1959), 46.

before the formation of any material particles. If photons, as quantum entities, are not really 'things', for reasons adumbrated earlier, then there would seem to be little scope for identifying any *thing* or *things* as the 'subject' of such a change, other than, perhaps, the physical universe as a whole, conceived as a singular and indivisible substance along Spinozistic lines. However, the very fact that even this option remains as a way of saving the proposal from counterexamples demonstrates, perhaps, its versatility and strength as a metaphysical hypothesis. (Opponents might say, contrariwise, that it demonstrates the vacuity of the hypothesis, by exhibiting to us its apparent unfalsifiability: but although unfalsifiability is very arguably a defect in scientific hypotheses, because it deprives them of empirical content, it seems rather to be a virtue in a metaphysical hypothesis.)

Reductionism versus eliminativism

Incidentally, our proposal that an event is—is 'nothing but'—a change in the properties of or relations between some thing or things may be given either a 'reductionist' or an 'eliminativist' gloss. We might see this proposal, in line with my implicit assumption so far, as telling us what events *are*, by 'reducing' them to—or explicating them in terms of—changes in the properties of or relations between things. This, then, is not to deny that events exist, only to contend that they are ontologically dependent entities, depending for their existence and identity upon the things, properties, and relations in terms of which they are to be explicated. It is a view which still permits us to quantify over and refer to events with impunity. But an eliminativist would prefer to see in such a proposal a way of excluding events from our ontology altogether: according to this way of reading it, the proposal is that we can, and in principle should, replace all of our talk about events and their properties and relations by talk of change in the properties and relations of things (remembering here that talk of 'change' in the sense now being understood is not just trivially equivalent to talk of the occurrence of events).[7]

How should we choose between the reductionist and eliminativist options? Perhaps, applying Occam's infamous razor, we should adopt the

---

[7] For one recent defence of eliminativism regarding events, see Michael Tye, *The Metaphysics of Mind* (Cambridge: Cambridge University Press, 1989), ch. 2.

eliminativist option if and only if we can find no honest work for events to do. If we are convinced, for instance, that events need to be included in our ontology to serve as the relata of causal relations, then we should choose the reductionist option in preference to the eliminativist one. And note here that even if we believe in the ontological primacy of agent causation over event causation (see Chapter 11), we may still need to include events in our ontology as *effects*, even if not as *causes*. All things considered, however, it would seem that the eliminativist option is unduly austere and I shall continue to assume as much from now on.

Is motion change of distance?

One kind of change which we have not yet properly considered is the kind of change which occurs when two persisting objects or things *move* relative to one another. Such a change, which would seem to qualify quite unproblematically as an event, is apparently a kind of relational change, for the objects in question clearly undergo a change in respect of the degree of spatial separation or distance between them—and distance is a relation. But this kind of change may not, on the face of it, seem to be what I earlier described as a *purely* relational change, that is, a change which an object undergoes only inasmuch as something to which it is somehow related undergoes an intrinsic change—such as Xanthippe's becoming a widow or Mary's becoming shorter than Tom. If two objects move relative to one another, it is not clear that we should want to say that just one of these objects is undergoing an intrinsic change while the other is undergoing a purely relational change. Indeed, it may be held that motion just *is* change of distance between two objects, in which case it does not essentially involve any kind of intrinsic change in the objects in question—that is to say, any change in their intrinsic properties—but only a change in a contingent relation between them. (An intrinsic property of an object is one which it possesses independently of any relation that it may bear to any other object.) This, certainly, seems to be the conception of motion that is assumed by modern physics. However, it is a conception which is not invulnerable to challenge, as we shall now see.

Common sense suggests that sometimes, at least, relative motion between two objects does indeed constitute a purely relational change on the part of one of these objects. For example, if an astronaut separated from his ship in deep space fires a bullet from his space gun, he and the bullet will move away from one another: but the astronaut will also move relative to his ship and his ship relative to him—and yet we intuitively want to say in this case that it is *the astronaut*, not his ship, which is 'really' moving, because the initiating cause of the change of distance between them was a force acting upon the astronaut, not upon the ship. In this case, it seems, the ship's 'movement' relative to the astronaut is a purely relational change, arising from an intrinsic change involving the astronaut. Perhaps, indeed, we can say that the intrinsic change in question is not a change in any intrinsic property of the astronaut, but only a change in an intrinsic property of a pair of objects consisting of the astronaut and the bullet or (if this way of putting it is preferred) a change in an intrinsic *relation*—namely, distance—between the astronaut and the bullet. (An intrinsic relation between two objects is a relation which holds between them independently of any relation that either object may bear to any third object.) This would allow us to preserve the 'orthodox' scientific conception of motion as change of distance between objects, supplemented merely with the observation that when such change occurs we are not obliged to say that *both* of the objects concerned are 'really' moving.

However, a more radical but apparently quite coherent alternative would be to conceive of 'real' motion as being a kind of *intrinsic property* of the moving object—a property which may help to *cause* changes of distance between that object and others, but which does not *consist in* its undergoing such changes of distance. (Note, though, that talk of such causation will not fit comfortably with the idea that all causes are events.) According to this way of thinking, both the astronaut and the bullet are 'really' moving, but not *in virtue of* the change of distance between them, this merely being an *effect* of their (oppositely directed) motions, just as the change of distance between the astronaut and his ship is an effect of the astronaut's motion in a certain direction. Motion in an object, on this conception, is something like a 'directional tendency', of variable magnitude, which is intrinsic to the moving object and helps to cause, in appropriate circumstances, changes of distance between it and other objects, the other contributory causes being the 'directional tendencies' of the other objects in question.[8] (In fact, the mathematical conception of velocity as a vector is perfectly consistent with this view of motion, even though the view is at

---

[8] Compare Michael Tooley, 'In Defense of the Existence of States of Motion', *Philosophical Topics* 16 (1988), 225–54, and Denis Robinson, 'Matter, Motion and Humean Supervenience', *Australasian Journal of Philosophy* 67 (1989), 394–409.

odds with the 'orthodox' idea that motion simply consists in change of distance between objects—an idea which arises, perhaps, from a confusion between what motion is and how it may be measured. I shall return to these matters when I say more about the nature of motion in Chapters 14 and 16.)

Prospects for a non-reductive pluralism of things and events

So far in this chapter we have been considering strategies and arguments for reducing things to, or eliminating them in favour of, events or for reducing events to, or eliminating them in favour of, things (and their properties or relations). But, as I indicated at the outset of the chapter, a possible alternative position to adopt would be a form of *non-reductive pluralism* with respect to the distinction between things and events.[9] To the extent that there are difficulties besetting the reductivist and eliminativist positions, non-reductive pluralism may emerge as the victor by default. According to this view, the world contains things (persisting objects, or substances) and it also contains events, but both are types of 'basic particular'. Things and events, being particulars of different basic types, have different sorts of properties and enter into different sorts of relation—but, according to the view under scrutiny, little more than this can be said, quite generally, about the distinction between them. We can remark, indeed, that events occur at times or last through periods of time, whereas things persist over time or from one time to another; that events happen to or 'befall' things, whereas things 'participate' in events; and that events may uncontentiously have temporal parts or stages—earlier and later phases— whereas things apparently do not. Such remarks, however, almost plati- tudinous as they seem to be, do not amount to anything deserving the title of a *theory* of the distinction between things and events. Indeed, they seem to leave inherently mysterious the relationship between an event and the things which 'participate' in it—for example, the relationship between a battle and the men fighting it or between a marriage and the two people getting married. If things and events are items of two basic and mutually irreducible ontological categories, it would seem that the relationship of

---

[9] This would appear to be Donald Davidson's position: see his 'The Individuation of Events', in Nicholas Rescher (ed.), *Essays in Honor of Carl G. Hempel* (Dordrecht: D. Reidel, 1969), reprinted in Donald Davidson, *Essays on Actions and Events* (Oxford: Clarendon Press, 1980).

'participation' between things and events must itself be something basic and incapable of analysis or explication. If so, this is a deeply unsatisfactory feature of the non-reductive pluralist's position. For this reason, I am inclined to view non-reductive pluralism as being a position of last resort, to be adopted only if no reductive or eliminative position proves to be tenable. As will be clear from the preceding discussion, my own preference is for a conception of events which reduces them to, or explicates them in terms of, changes in the properties of or relations between things. In short, I am in favour of a thing- or substance-ontology.[10] Such a view renders entirely unmysterious the relationship between events and the things which 'participate' in them, for on this view those things' participation in the events in question consists in their being the very things changes in whose properties or relations constitute those events. Thus, for example, by this account a living creature 'participates' in the event of its death simply in virtue of being the thing a change in whose vital properties constitutes that event.

Can there be time without change?

We have thought a good deal, in this chapter, about the relationship between things and events, but rather less about the relationship between items in these categories and the *places* and *times* which, in some sense, they 'occupy'. Both things (in the narrow sense currently intended) and events are necessarily inhabitants of time and may also be inhabitants of space. We should probably not insist, without qualification, that things and events are *necessarily* inhabitants of space, because we can at least coherently conceive of spatially unlocated things and events, such as 'Cartesian' egos and their cognitions. Things and events *of certain kinds* clearly are necessarily inhabitants of space—for example, material bodies are, as are explosions and collisions. We can make no coherent sense of the notion of a spatially unlocated material body, nor can we intelligibly conceive of an explosion or collision which does not occur *somewhere*. But this holds on account of the *kinds* of things and events that we are considering here, not simply on account of their being things and events as such. Partly in view of this element of contingency in the relationship between things and events, in general, and space or place, I shall concentrate in what follows on

[10] See further my *The Possibility of Metaphysics: Substance, Identity, and Time* (Oxford: Clarendon Press, 1998).

issues concerning time—though in the next chapter I shall consider in some depth the question, mentioned at the outset of this one, of whether space, or even merely some region of space, could exist wholly devoid of physical objects.

The corresponding question concerning time is this: could time in its entirety, or even merely some period of time, exist wholly devoid of events, that is, without anything at all *happening* during that time? This is sometimes broached as the question of whether there could be (a period of) *time without change*. However, that way of putting the question is potentially misleading since, as we have already seen, the term 'change' admits of many subtly different interpretations. In the most general sense of the term that I defined earlier, according to which a change occurs at a time t just in case something begins to be the case at t which was not the case prior to t, it is perfectly clear that there cannot, on pain of contradiction, be time without change. For if a period of time exists, it must have earlier and later parts, and of any time t during the period it will consequently be true to say that something begins to be the case at t which was not the case prior to t—namely, it begins to be the case at t that the part of the period earlier than t is past. This kind of 'change' is simply the so-called 'passage' of time itself, which must take place if time is to exist at all. A more interesting question, then, is whether there could be a period of time during which no *event* occurred—though this question obviously depends for its interpretation upon what conception is adopted of an event. Suppose, however, that we adopt the conception recommended earlier, that an event is a change in the properties of or relations between some thing or things. Then our question amounts to this: could there be a period of time during which nothing—no *thing*—underwent any change in its properties or relations to other things?

Earlier in this chapter, I gestured towards a positive answer to this question, when I said that we seem to be able to conceive of a world of objects *all* of which get one day older without any of them undergoing any kind of intrinsic change. But we should be wary of assuming that what we are able to 'conceive' therefore constitutes a genuine metaphysical possibility. In such a world, what would *make it the case* that objects got 'older' by a day? Certainly, nothing and no-one in such a world would be able to record or measure the passage of time during the period of non-change—for people, clocks, and even atomic processes would all remain 'frozen' for that period. However, we should resist applying a verificationist criterion of meaning at this point, contending that, because the passage of time would be unobservable and unmeasurable during the supposed period of non-change, such a period could therefore not meaningfully be said to exist. Moreover, it is at least arguable that an observer inhabiting such a world could, in principle, have good *indirect* evidence for believing that a period of time had elapsed during which no event (in our sense) had occurred.

Shoemaker's argument

Exploiting a famous thought experiment of Sydney Shoemaker's designed for this purpose, we could suppose that the observer's world is divided into three distinct regions, A, B, and C, each one of which is observed by inhabitants of the others to go, periodically, into a 'frozen' state, in which nothing happens in the region in question.[11] Observation over many years might indicate that the three regions each go into a 'frozen' state of a year's duration after a fixed number of 'unfrozen' years, the number being different for each region. For region A, a 'freeze' appears to occur once every three years; for region B, it appears to occur once every four years; and for region C, it appears to occur once every five years. There are many opportunities for the inhabitants of any two different regions to communicate with one another during periods in which both of their regions are 'unfrozen', so that the complete evidence for the regular cyclical pattern of the 'freezes' can be made available to an inhabitant of any one of the regions. However, it takes only elementary reasoning to see that, if the cyclical hypothesis is correct, then once every sixty years all three regions must simultaneously undergo a 'freeze', so that for one year in every sixty the whole world is 'frozen'.

Of course, an alternative hypothesis would be that a more complicated pattern of 'freezes' occurs, missing out the total 'freeze' in every sixtieth year. But, quite generally, it is preferable to adopt a simpler hypothesis rather than a more complicated one in order to explain a given set of empirical data: and the cyclical hypothesis is clearly simpler than its rival which omits the total 'freeze' in every sixtieth year. So, it seems, the cyclical hypothesis offers the best, because the simplest, explanation of the empirical data in question and is therefore supported by those data more

---

[11] See Sydney Shoemaker, 'Time Without Change', *Journal of Philosophy* 66 (1969), 363–81, reprinted in his *Identity, Cause and Mind: Philosophical Essays* (Cambridge: Cambridge University Press, 1984). The discussion that follows cannot do full justice to the subtlety of Shoemaker's arguments, given the limited space available.

strongly than is its rival. It seems that inhabitants of the world in question ought, accordingly, to accept the cyclical hypothesis and therewith its implication that a period of time can elapse in which nothing at all happens.

Here, however, it may be objected that we are putting the cart before the horse in suggesting that empirical evidence could support the cyclical hypothesis when what is at issue is whether the cyclical hypothesis even states a *possibility*. Empirical evidence may help us to choose between rival scientific hypotheses, as may considerations of simplicity, but a precondition for any such hypothesis even to be considered eligible as an explanation for certain empirical data is that it should express a possible state of affairs. Any hypothesis which entails an impossibility itself expresses an impossible state of affairs. But the cyclical hypothesis entails that a period of time elapses in which nothing at all happens in the three-region world, so unless it is *possible* for nothing at all to happen for a period of time, the cyclical hypothesis expresses an impossible state of affairs and is ineligible for the purposes of scientific explanation. Hence, empirical evidence can only count in favour of the cyclical hypothesis on condition that it really is possible for nothing at all to happen for a period of time, which is the very point at issue. Thus it appears that the thought experiment involving the three-region world cannot in any way help to establish this possibility, that is, provide rational grounds for thinking that it really is a possibility.

Besides, there is another problem with the cyclical hypothesis, even assuming that it is possible for nothing at all to happen for a period of time. If the three-region world were ever to enter into a total 'freeze', why should any part of it subsequently become 'unfrozen' again? According to the cyclical hypothesis, all of the three regions become 'unfrozen' following each year of total 'freeze': but what could possibly *cause* the regions to become 'unfrozen' again, given that nothing at all happens—no event whatever occurs—during the period of time immediately preceding the time of 'unfreezing'? If causes are events, then the only events capable of causing the 'unfreezing' of the regions following a total 'freeze' would be events which occurred at least one year prior to the time of 'unfreezing'. But to suppose that any such event could cause the 'unfreezing' is to suppose that there can be *causation at a temporal distance*, that is, that an event occurring at an earlier time can cause an event occurring at a later time 'directly', without that earlier event causing any event which occurs at an intermediate time and which in turn causes the later event. The trouble (or, at least, one trouble) with the notion of causation at a temporal distance is that it is hard to see how the supposed cause could cause its supposed effect to occur *at the time it did*—in this case, at least one year later—rather than at some earlier time. Of course, it might still happen *by chance* that all three regions of the three-region world become 'unfrozen' precisely one year after the beginning of some total 'freeze'. But if that is what happens, rather than the 'unfreezing' after a total 'freeze' always being brought about by prior causes, then there would be no reason to expect there to be a regular cycle of 'freezes' of the kind proposed by the cyclical hypothesis, since the length of any period of total 'freeze' would be a matter of pure chance—and so there would be no reason to believe the cyclical hypothesis to be true.

As for the more fundamental question of whether, indeed, it is possible for nothing at all to happen for a period of time, it would seem that we cannot hope to provide a principled answer to this question unless or until we possess a satisfactory theory of the nature of time itself. Some steps towards the construction of such a theory will be taken in the course of the next five chapters.

PART V

SPACE AND TIME

14

ABSOLUTISM VERSUS RELATIONALISM

Dimensionality and the structure of space

What *are* space and time? And how are they related to one another? Space, as far as we know, is three-dimensional. Is time just a fourth dimension which, together with the three dimensions of space, helps to comprise a unitary four-dimensional manifold in which all physical objects and events somehow reside? Or is it a mistake to think of time as being any kind of dimension in which physical reality is extended or 'spread out', in the way in which physical things are extended in space? Certainly, we do not, in our everyday concerns, normally think of time as being anything like space, even though the mathematical representation of time in theoretical physics may tempt us assimilate time to the three dimensions of space. Physicists often represent spatiotemporal relations graphically by means of (two-dimensional) space-time diagrams, in which one axis represents time, t, and the other represents the three dimensions of space, s (see Fig. 14.1). But it is equally common to use such two-dimensional graphical representations to convey information about relations between, for instance, the pressure and temperature of a gas—and no one imagines that pressure and temperature are literally dimensions of reality in which physical things are extended. So the mathematical representation of time implies nothing, in itself, about the similarity or lack of it between time and the three dimensions of space. However, since the nature of time is, if anything, even more problematic than the nature of space, let us, for the present, focus on space—even though it may turn out, eventually, that space can only properly be conceived of as a part or aspect of an all-embracing space-time. (I shall return to this issue at the end of the chapter.)

Space, it seems, has parts. Some of these parts are three-dimensional,

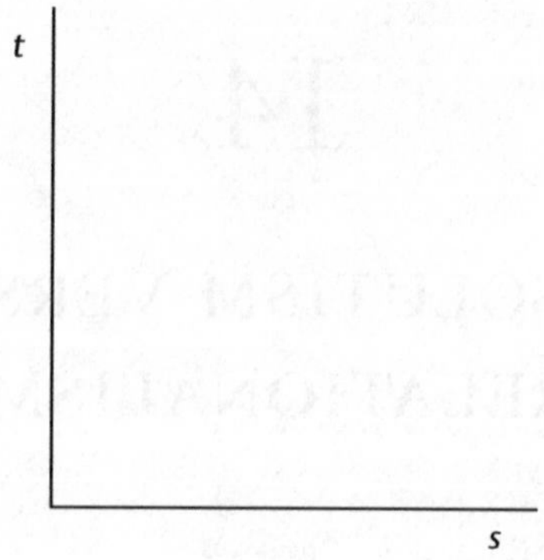

Fig. 14.1

like space as a whole: these we may call *volumes* of space or, more colloquially, 'regions'. But regions of space have two-dimensional boundaries—their *surfaces*—which may also seem to be parts of space. Surfaces in turn have one-dimensional or linear boundaries and these *lines* have zero-dimensional boundaries, otherwise known as *points*. Some philosophers and most modern mathematicians take a 'bottom-up' view of three-dimensional space and its various lesser-dimensional parts or features, maintaining that space as a whole is ultimately *composed* of points—that it is just an aggregate or multiplicity of points. Against this view, other philosophers contend that no plurality, however large, of zero-dimensional entities can possibly add up to or collectively constitute a three-dimensional entity—not even if the plurality question is uncountably infinite. According to many of these philosophers—who take instead a 'top-down' view of the relation between space as a whole and its lesser-dimensional features—surfaces, lines, and points are not, strictly speaking, *parts* of space at all, but just 'limits' of certain kinds and as such 'abstract' entities (in one sense of the term 'abstract', which we shall explore further in Chapter 20).[1]

These are matters that we shall discuss in more detail in Chapter 16. For the time being, let us just take note of the fact that the only parts of space that we can uncontentiously regard as such are its three-dimensional regions or volumes. However, even if it is uncontentious that space as a whole has three-dimensional parts, it is questionable whether space as a whole is *composed* of those parts, because to suppose that it is may seem to

---

[1] See further Joshua Hoffman and Gary S. Rosenkrantz, *Substance among Other Categories* (Cambridge: Cambridge University Press, 1994), 107 ff. and 188 ff.

concede too much to the 'bottom-up' view of space. Composition is normally conceived of as a relation which obtains between a whole and parts of that whole which could, in principle, exist independently of the whole of which they are parts. But, very arguably, no region of space could exist independently of space as a whole. Not even God, it may seem, could obliterate all of space except for a certain three-dimensional region of it. Perhaps He could *shrink* the whole of space to what was formerly the size of a small region of it—on the assumption that space as a whole is not necessarily infinite in extent—but that is a very different thing for Him to do. If this line of thinking is correct, then space as a whole has a unitary or singular nature which is inconsistent with our regarding it as being 'made up' of lesser parts of any kind—even if we accept, as we surely must, that space contains many quite distinct regions, some of which are contiguous with one another and others of which are widely separated.

We have arrived by degrees at a conception of space as a singular three-dimensional entity which, while exhibiting internal geometrical complexity, is, ontologically speaking, a simple and indivisible whole. Considered a priori, it may seem that space as a whole may be either finite or infinite in extent, and if finite then either bounded or unbounded. If it is finite but unbounded, then it cannot be 'flat', as Euclid supposed, but must be positively 'curved', having a topology in three dimensions which is analogous to that of the surface of a sphere. (The surface of a sphere is not infinitely extended, but it does not have any 'edge' or boundary.) Non-Euclidean 'curved' space may be difficult or even impossible for us to imagine, but seems to be, metaphysically speaking, perfectly possible—and many modern cosmologists think it likely that space actually is 'curved' in this way. It would be a mistake, incidentally, to suppose that if three-dimensional space is positively 'curved', then there must be some fourth spatial dimension *in which* it is curved, in the way in which the two-dimensional surface of a sphere is curved in the third dimension. This is simply a point at which the analogy breaks down. The 'curvature' of space—whether it is of 'positive', 'negative', or, indeed, 'zero' value—is an internal or intrinsic feature of space itself, not a feature which it possesses only in virtue of its relation to some higher-dimensional space in which it is 'embedded'. And, clearly, its curvature must have *some* value, even if that value is zero, as Euclid effectively assumed.

Space as 'the void' versus space as a 'plenum'

But how is space, thus conceived, related to the physical objects which seemingly occupy its various regions and move about within it? We may be strongly tempted to think of space as a kind of 'container' for physical objects, but this can at best only be a metaphor and may well be a misleading one. 'Containers', after all, are, literally speaking, just various types of physical object. For instance, a fish tank is a container for water and the fish that live in it. Some philosophers, convinced that space itself is distinct from any material entity residing in it, have thought of space as 'the void'—a kind of emptiness which material bodies can partly fill. But it is hard to see how 'the void' can be anything at all—how it can differ from mere nothingness or absence of being—in which case it is hard to see how anything material can 'occupy' it. It seems that 'the void' could have no features or nature of its own, for only that which *is* something—a real entity—can have features or a nature. And space, we have seen, does have features and so, presumably, a nature. Space is *something*, not nothing. But what sort of something? That is the chief question.

Contrary to the conception of space as 'the void', there is the conception of space as a 'plenum'—as something that is, quite literally, 'full'. Full of what? Full, perhaps, of matter—or of its modern equivalent, energy (the equivalence being underwritten by Einstein's famous equation, $E = mc^2$). Modern physics teaches us that even the 'vacuum' is, in reality, a highly energetic state.[2] We have good empirical reason to suppose that there is no part of space which is not suffused with energy, even though the energy-density of some parts of space is clearly much higher than that of others. Even so, we may wonder whether it is not at least metaphysically possible for there to be regions of space that are perfectly empty of matter and energy. If that is possible, then, it seems, space cannot simply be identified with the spatially extended material universe as a whole. And, indeed, the so-called field equations of Einstein's general theory of relativity—which forms the basis of modern scientific cosmology—admit of solutions in which space is entirely devoid of matter and energy.[3] So, mathematically, at least, it seems that the notion of perfectly 'empty' space is perfectly coherent.

[2] For an interesting discussion of some of the possible implications of this, see John Leslie, *The End of the World: The Science and Ethics of Human Extinction* (London: Routledge, 1996), 108 ff.

[3] See further J. D. North, *The Measure of the Universe: A History of Modern Cosmology* (Oxford: Clarendon Press, 1965), 87 ff.

We thus arrive at a puzzling conclusion: that space cannot be mere emptiness and yet could be perfectly empty. Space seems to teeter uncomfortably on the boundary between being nothing and being something. It is that in which all material things have their existence while itself being somehow immaterial. Perhaps this makes more intelligible Sir Isaac Newton's suggestion that space is God's 'sensorium' (as it were, the theatre of His mind), or it may recall to us St Paul's famous remark (a favourite one of Berkeley's) that it is in God that we 'live, move, and have our being'.[4] Seen in such a light, space presents itself as a unitary and indivisible immaterial substance, possibly infinite in nature—which makes it not far removed from God Himself, as He is conceived by traditional theism. Indeed, from a theological point of view, space thus conceived even seems to pose something of a dilemma: for either space threatens to constitute an infinite and uncreated substance which rivals God, or else, to eliminate the threat of such rivalry, God is to be identified with space, which means that He is spatially extended and, quite literally, 'omnipresent' (located everywhere)—and neither alternative sits altogether comfortably with traditional theological doctrines. Spinoza adopts something like the second option, speaking as he does of the one substance of his monistic metaphysics as *Deus sive Natura* ('God or Nature'). Newton, by contrast, very often seems committed, whether he likes it or not, to something more like the first option, through his allegiance to an 'absolute' conception of space. Setting aside, however, all of the murkier theological complications, let us now inquire more closely into this Newtonian conception of space, considered from a purely scientific and metaphysical point of view—for not only is it metaphysically interesting in its own right, but also it has been immensely influential in the history of science, owing to the enormous and long-lasting success of Newtonian physics.

Newtonian absolute space

Newton arrives at his conception of space as 'absolute'—in the sense to be explained shortly—through a number of considerations concerning the nature of motion. Motion, intuitively, either consists in or at least necessarily involves change of place or position. When we attempt to *measure*

---

[4] See Sir Isaac Newton, *Opticks* (New York: Dover, 1952), query 28, p. 370, and George Berkeley, *A Treatise Concerning the Principles of Human Knowledge*, para. 149, in his *Philosophical Works*, ed. M. R. Ayers (London: Dent, 1975), p. 234. For St Paul's remark, see Acts 17: 28.

motion, however, we inevitably have to do so relative to some identifiable material object, whose position we regard as fixed for the purposes of measurement: this object we may regard as determining a 'frame of reference' for our measurement. To use one of Newton's own examples, one may measure the speed—or, more properly speaking, the velocity—of a sailor as he walks along the deck of his ship by taking the deck as our frame of reference: but since the ship itself may be moving relative to the sea bed, we may find that the velocity of the sailor as measured by taking the surface of the earth as our frame of reference has a quite different value.[5] Now, of course, the Earth in turn is moving relative to the Sun and this moves relative to the other stars of our galaxy, the Milky Way, while the Milky Way in turn is moving relative to other distant galaxies. But then what? Although Newton himself did not know this (being unaware of the existence of distant galaxies), we now know that all of the galaxies in the universe (or, at least, localized clusters of them) are moving away from one another at an immense velocity, in a process known by modern cosmologists as 'the expansion of the universe'. So what are *the galaxies* moving relative to—apart from each other, of course? It is very tempting to answer that every galaxy must be moving relative to *something else*—something which is not itself a galaxy nor, indeed, any other aggregation of matter.

This something else, according to Newton's conception, is *space itself*, which is immaterial. A material object's velocity relative to space itself is its *absolute* velocity, which cannot be measured by us simply because space itself, being immaterial, is imperceptible. When a material object is moving absolutely, it is undergoing a change of its absolute position—that is, it is moving from one part of space to another, the parts of space themselves being necessarily immovable. Mere relative motion, such as the motion of the sailor relative to the deck of his ship, is mere change of relative position, which need involve no change of absolute position at all.

But why should we believe in the existence of this 'absolute' space? Why shouldn't we just say that the galaxies are moving away from each other and leave it at that? This would mean that all motion is relative motion— motion relative to some material object or other which can be taken to determine a frame of reference. After all, Newton concedes that absolute velocity cannot be measured, because the parts of space as he conceives of

[5] See Isaac Newton, *The Principia: Mathematical Principles of Natural Philosophy*, trans. I. Bernard Cohen and Anne Whitman (Berkeley and Los Angeles, Calif.: University of California Press, 1999), Scholium to the Definitions, pp. 409–10. The thought experiments described later are introduced in this scholium.

it are imperceptible. To this it may be replied that we should not apply at this point some crude verificationist criterion of meaning and say, just because absolute velocity is not empirically measurable or observable, that it therefore cannot meaningfully be said to exist. However, our question is whether we should believe that absolute velocity—and therewith absolute space—really does exist and it is not enough, to justify a positive answer to this question, to point out that absolute velocity and space *could* exist, consistently with empirically known facts. We want to know what sort of *empirical* evidence, if any, could justify a belief in absolute space—and if it should turn out that no such evidence ever could justify that belief, then we had better not hold it.

Newton, to his credit, is sensitive to this requirement and attempts to satisfy it. His contention is that, although absolute *velocity* is not empirically measurable, absolute *acceleration*—that is, the *rate of change* of absolute velocity—certainly is empirically detectable. Because we can, as he believes, detect absolute acceleration empirically, we are entitled to believe in the existence of absolute velocity—absolute change of position—and therewith in the existence of absolute space. And to convince us that absolute acceleration is empirically detectable, he presents us with some thought experiments. One of these is his famous example of the rotating bucket, which may be described as follows.

The rotating bucket experiment and Mach's objection

Imagine a bucket, half-full of water, suspended by a rope from a hook. In stage 1 of our thought experiment, the bucket is hanging undisturbed with the water lying stationary with respect to the bucket. Here there is no relative motion between the water and the bucket, a fact which may be ascertained empirically by noting that a small test particle lying on the surface of the water—such as a scrap of paper—does not move relative to an ink mark inscribed on the inside wall of the bucket just above the waterline. In stage 2 of the thought experiment, the rope is twisted a number of times and then released, so that the bucket rotates rapidly about its vertical axis. In this stage of the experiment, there is relative motion between the bucket and the water, as can be seen from the fact that the scrap of paper, which remains stationary with respect to the water, moves relative to the ink mark inscribed on the bucket's inside wall. Finally, in stage 3 of the thought experiment, the water has picked up the rotational motion of the bucket through friction between it and the bucket's wall, so that now there is no longer any relative motion between the water and the bucket—and the scrap of paper accordingly now remains stationary with respect to the ink mark.

We see, thus, that, in respect of the presence or absence of relative motion between the bucket and the water, stage 1 of the experiment is exactly like stage 3, for in both of these stages there is no relative motion between the water and the bucket, whereas in stage 2 there is. However, there is, none the less, an important physical difference between stage 1 and stage 3 which is empirically detectable: this is that in stage 3, but not in stage 1, the surface of the water exhibits a concave form—whereas in stage 1, it is perfectly flat. Why is this? Newton has a simple answer to the question. In stage 3, but not in stage 1, the water is *really* rotating—it is rotating 'absolutely'. By contrast, in both stage 1 and stage 2 the water is *not* really rotating, even though in stage 2 there is relative rotational motion between the water and the bucket. The physical evidence of the water's real rotation in stage 3 is the water's recession from the centre of the bucket, which results in its rising up the bucket's inside wall, thereby making the surface of the water concave.

It is important to appreciate at this point that a rotating object is an object whose velocity is constantly changing and which is therefore *accelerating*: for, velocity being a vector, a change in the direction of an object's motion is a change in its velocity—and acceleration is, by definition, rate of change of velocity. However, according to Newton's own celebrated laws of motion, an object only deviates from its state of rest or uniform motion in a straight line if it is acted upon by a force—a force whose magnitude is directly proportional to the product of the object's mass and its acceleration. Rotational motion in an object, therefore, implies the imposition of some 'centripetal' force upon it—a fact which is borne out in experience when one swings a stone around one's head at the end of a rope, for one soon finds that, the faster one swings the stone, the greater the tension is in the rope. If it were not for the tension in the rope—a kind of force operating on the stone—the stone would fly off at a tangent and move in a straight line, just as Newton's laws of motion prescribe. So it is with the water in the bucket, only here it is the wall of the bucket which is imposing a force upon the water which constrains it to undergo a circular movement: if the wall of the bucket were to break, the water would fly outwards and cease to rotate.

The supposed lesson of the thought experiment is this, then. Mere relative motion—change of distance between one material object and another—must be distinguished from *real* motion in an object, even if we cannot always detect real motion directly. For what we can always detect, at least indirectly, is real *acceleration*, since this is caused by real physical forces which have real physical effects, such as the recession of the water from the centre of the bucket. The physical forces in question are often quite easily measurable: for instance, when one swings a stone around one's head on the end of a rope, one can measure the tension in the rope by incorporating a spring balance into the rope and noting the position of the pointer on the scale of the spring balance.

However, an obvious objection comes to mind at this point. The bucket and rope of our thought experiment are not the only material objects in the world. The rope is attached to a hook, which is presumably fixed to the ceiling of a laboratory, which is in turn built upon the surface of the Earth—and the Earth, we know, is surrounded by many other material objects, including distant stars and galaxies. Certainly, there is a physically detectable difference in the water as it is in stages 1 and 2 of the experiment from how it is in stage 3—and, if we like, we can say that this is because, in stage 3, the water is 'really' rotating, whereas in stages 1 and 2 it is 'really' undergoing no rotation. But what entitles us to say that the water's 'real' rotation does not consist in its rotating relative to any material object? It may be, indeed, that the water's 'rotating' relative to the wall of the bucket in stage 2 of the experiment does not qualify as a 'real' rotation: but how can we legitimately conclude that its 'real' rotation in stage 3 is not merely relative, but 'absolute', in Newton's terms? For why shouldn't we infer from the experiment that the sort of relative rotational motion which gives rise to such characteristic physical effects as the recession of the water from the centre of the bucket is precisely rotation relative to *the rest of the material universe*—the stars and galaxies surrounding us? As the nineteenth-century Austrian physicist and philosopher Ernst Mach pointed out, if we were to increase the thickness of the bucket's wall so that it extended to the distant stars and galaxies, would we not expect the water's surface to become concave in *stage 2* of the experiment, when the water is undergoing a mere relative rotation with respect to the bucket? For, after all, what is the difference between supposing that all of the material universe is rotating around the water and supposing that the water is rotating in the midst of the material universe? As Mach says, we seem not to be presented here with two genuinely distinct alternatives, just two different ways of describing the same set of phenomena.[6]

The two-globes thought experiment

As if to counter this sort of objection, Newton presents another famous thought experiment. He asks us to imagine a universe whose sole material occupants are two exactly similar globes, attached to one another by a straight length of string. Initially, one might suppose that there would be no way of telling whether or not these globes were rotating about the midpoint of the string, for there would be no other material object relative to which their rotational motion could be measured. In this universe, no material object undergoes any change of distance from any other material object. Nevertheless, it seems that there would be a physically detectable difference between the case in which the globes are stationary and the case in which they are rotating about the midpoint of the string, for in the latter case there would be a tension in the string proportional to the rate of rotation of the globes—a tension which could, in principle, be indicated by the position of the pointer of a spring balance incorporated into the string. Since, in this case, there would be a real rotation undergone by the globes, but no merely relative motion with respect to any material object, such real motion must be 'absolute' motion in Newton's sense, that is, change of position in *space itself*, which must therefore be something immaterial.

However, the trouble with this second thought experiment is that it is entirely counterfactual in character. What entitles Newton to assume that, in the very different physical circumstances of the universe that he describes, the string connecting a pair of rotating globes would be under tension, as it would be in our own universe, in which such globes are surrounded by vast quantities of distant matter? In assuming that there would be a physically detectable difference, in the sort of universe he describes, between rotating and non-rotating pairs of globes, he seems to be assuming something for which he ought really to provide independent justification if he is to make good his case for the existence of absolute space. Furthermore, there is, as Einstein observes, something metaphysically questionable about Newton's proposal that, in his two-globe universe, rotation of the globes makes for a physically detectable difference in terms

---

[6] See Ernst Mach, *The Science of Mechanics* (La Salle, Ill.: Open Court, 1960), 279 ff.

of the magnitude of the tension in the string.[7] For the implication is that a real physical effect is associated with the 'absolute' rotation of the globes and hence that Newton's 'absolute' space—an immaterial entity—can interact causally with matter. However, we are already familiar, from the infamous mind–body problem, with the fact that causal interaction between material and immaterial entities is not something whose possibility can lightly be assumed.

Objections to Mach's position

So far, Newton seems to be getting the worst of this argument. Neither of his thought experiments provides, upon reflection, a compelling reason to believe in absolute motion or absolute space. On the other hand, his opponent's position, as exemplified by Mach, is not altogether comfortable either. It may indeed be a mystery, as Einstein suggests, why 'absolute' rotation—rotation with respect to a supposedly immaterial entity— should give rise to any distinctive physical effect. But, equally, it may seem mysterious why, if Mach is right, rotation relative to the distant masses of the universe should give rise to any distinctive physical effect. After all, those distant masses are so far away from us that any causal influence they may have on earthbound objects must have taken many millions of years to reach us—assuming, of course, that Einstein was correct in holding that no causal influence can be propagated at a velocity greater than the speed of light. Would it make any immediate difference to us, here on earth, if all the distant stars and galaxies were annihilated overnight? Everything would surely seem just the same for several years, when we would begin to see the nearest stars disappear. But if it would make no immediate difference to us, how can Mach be right, after all, to suppose that 'real' rotation—rotation that has detectable physical effects, such as the recession of the water from the centre of Newton's bucket—is rotation relative to the distant stars and galaxies? For these physical effects would presumably persist even if the distant stars and galaxies were annihilated overnight. According to Mach's way of thinking, the distant stars have an immense influence upon what happens here on earth—a doctrine which sounds uncomfortably close to that of some astrologers and mystics. Indeed, according to Mach's way of thinking, it would seem, material

---

[7] See Albert Einstein, 'The Foundation of the General Theory of Relativity', in H. A. Lorentz, A. Einstein, H. Minkowski, and H. Weyl, *The Principle of Relativity* (New York: Dover, 1952), 113.

bodies here on earth only possess *mass* (that is, so-called 'inertial' mass) because they are surrounded by the distant stars and galaxies. For it is an object's mass which makes it something upon which a force must be imposed in order to give it acceleration—so that if, as Mach would have to say, a single globe in an otherwise empty universe could not be given an acceleration by the imposition of any force, the implication seems to be that such a globe could have no mass. But then it becomes mysterious how, according to Mach's way of thinking, the material universe as a whole can have any mass, or how, lacking any mass as a whole, its material parts may none the less possess mass and somehow confer the property of mass upon each other. It is natural to assume that a material object's mass (or, at least, its so-called 'rest mass') is an intrinsic property of the object, which it possesses independently of any relation which it may bear to any other object. This, certainly, seems to have been Newton's assumption. But if Mach is correct, it seems that the assumption is fundamentally mistaken and mass turns out to be a relational property which objects can possess only in virtue of being parts of a complex dynamical system.

Some varieties of relationalism

It is hard, then, to say who emerges more intact from this encounter between Newton the 'absolutist' and Mach the 'relationalist'. (I prefer the term 'relationalist' to the more usual 'relationist' for purely stylistic reasons.) Each seems to be committed, even if only implicitly, to some metaphysically mysterious contentions. However, while it is clear enough what the relationalist is opposing—namely, the idea that space exists as an immaterial entity in its own right, independently of any material objects which may occupy it—it may not yet be sufficiently clear what alternative position is being proposed. According to one—very extreme—form of relationalism, space as such does not exist at all, only spatial relations between material objects. However, one serious difficulty with such a view is that it is not at all evident, according to it, what one could possibly mean by saying that there is a place which is actually unoccupied by any material object. And yet it does seem perfectly possible that there should be such a place, even if it is assumed that it is impossible that *every* place should be unoccupied by any material object. A less extreme form of relationalism might maintain, instead, that space—including, possibly, some materially unoccupied places—does indeed exist, but depends for its existence and properties entirely upon the material objects which occupy it and the spatial relations in which those objects stand to one another. Thus, on this view, space is an ontologically dependent entity—unlike the absolute space of Newton—and yet, like Newtonian space, is something that is distinct from any material object or sum of material objects, because it has properties of its own which no material object could possess (for instance, the property of having parts which are possibly materially unoccupied).

Concerning such a view, however, the following query may be raised. If space exists but depends for its existence and properties entirely upon the material objects which occupy it and the spatial relations in which those objects stand to one another, what determines, for instance, whether space is bounded and, if it is, where its boundaries lie? Suppose that the only existing material objects were three particles arranged in an equilateral triangular formation, each particle lying a mile away from each of the other two. Presumably, there would be unoccupied space between the particles. But would there be unoccupied space outside the triangle formed by the particles? And if so, how far would it extend? Would it extend to infinity in all directions? If so, why? If, as this version of relationalism maintains, space depends entirely upon the existence of material objects and their spatial relations, then it would seem that facts about material objects and their spatial relations should determine the answers to questions like those that have just been raised. And yet it is not at all clear that such facts could do so, for in the case that has just been described it is not at all clear, even given those facts, what the answers should be. I am inclined to conclude that this version of relationalism is not much better than the more extreme version described earlier.

Perhaps, however, it is open to the relationalist to adopt something like the following view of the nature of space. Space, the relationalist may say, consists of all the places in which it is *possible* for a material object to be located—and such a place exists if and only if it lies at some distance from a place in which some material object is *actually* located, that is, if and only if it is possible for some material object to move that distance in the appropriate direction. (Hence, it may be contended, all reference to 'places' can ultimately be cashed out in terms of possible movements amongst material objects.) So, for example, according to this way of thinking, if it is *possible* in the three-particle universe just described for one of the particles to move a certain distance away from the midpoint of the triangle while remaining equidistant from the other two particles, then there *actually* exists an unoccupied place in the space of that world at that distance from the midpoint in the direction just specified. What, then, determines whether the space of this universe is bounded and, if so, where its boundaries lie, according to this 'modal' version of relationalism (as we may call it)? The answer, presumably, is that the *natural laws* of the universe in question determine these matters, for these laws determine how—and how far—the particles can move with respect to one another. So space, on this view, depends for its existence and properties not just on what material objects there are and how they are *actually* spatially related to one another, but also upon the laws which govern how these objects may change their spatial relations to one another.

The general theory of relativity and the nature of space

This, or something very like this, it seems to me, is the only version of relationalism that is at all likely to be defensible. But whether this modal version of relationalism is superior to the sort of absolutism favoured by Newton seems still to be an open question. Moreover, how that question is to be resolved, if indeed it can be resolved—for instance, whether it can be resolved by philosophical argument or only by empirical science—also seems to be an open question. It certainly isn't just obvious that the dispute between relationalism and absolutism can only be resolved by empirical science, much less that empirical science has already resolved it in favour of relationalism. Some philosophers and scientists are inclined to assume the latter on the grounds that Einstein's general theory of relativity is superior to Newton's theory of gravitation and is committed to relationalism. But, although Einstein's theory is undoubtedly superior to Newton's, in terms of its compatibility with the empirical evidence and its predictive accuracy, it is not so clear that it is committed to relationalism— even if Einstein himself was, as we have seen, critical of Newtonian absolutism.

It may be wondered how Einstein's theory could be consistent with absolutism, given that the absolutist conceives of space as an immaterial entity which is ontologically independent of any material occupant of it— that is, in effect, as an immaterial substance. Perhaps, however, Einstein's theory is strictly only incompatible with Newton's *dualism* of 'matter' and 'space' and, more specifically, with Newton's conception of *matter*. (We know for sure, of course, that Newton's conception of *mass* is incompatible with Einstein's—and since one's conception of mass is essential to one's conception of matter, it follows that their conceptions of matter are likewise incompatible.) One way of interpreting the conception of 'material bodies' implicit in Einstein's theory is to regard the theory as treating such 'bodies' as being, in effect, local deformations in the fabric of space (or, more strictly, of space-time). Einstein's theory treats space itself as having, or at least as being capable of having, a *variable 'curvature'*, in the sense of 'curvature' discussed earlier. In Einsteinian space, light rays follow the shortest path between any two points and, according to the general theory of relativity, the presence of gravitational mass (that is, a 'material body') in a region of space makes a difference to the path taken by light rays in that region—something that has been well-confirmed by astronomical observation. But, rather than seeing the presence of gravitational mass—a 'material body'—as being something which *causes* a local variation in the curvature of space, it is ontologically more economical and metaphysically less mysterious simply to *identify* the presence of gravitational mass with the presence of such a local variation. According to this way of thinking, 'matter' becomes 'dematerialized' and is treated as being a purely geometrical feature of space itself. However, the consequence is that the conception of *space* that we are left with seems to be very close, ontologically speaking, to Newton's conception, although it is a space of variable curvature, unlike Newton's 'flat', Euclidean space.

Curious though it may seem on first reflection, it is possible, then, to regard Einstein's theory as agreeing with Newton's on the fundamental nature of space—that is, as being absolutist in spirit—while differing only on the nature of *matter*. Just because Einstein's theory advertises itself as the general theory of *relativity*, we shouldn't assume that it is committed to a *relationalist* theory of space. Indeed, as we noted earlier, the field equations of Einstein's theory admit of solutions in which the density of matter is everywhere zero, that is, in which space contains no gravitational mass, or is perfectly 'empty'. This is a possibility which any absolutist may readily accept but which no self-respecting relationalist can countenance: so those who think that Einstein's theory is committed to relationalism owe us an explanation of what it is about the theory which rules out this possibility— and it is not clear what they can say, given that the mathematical principles which lie at the very heart of the theory do not rule it out.[8]

---

[8] For further discussion of the debate between absolutism and relationalism, see John Earman, *World Enough and Space-Time: Absolute versus Relational Theories of Space and Time* (Cambridge, Mass.: MIT Press, 1989).

The special theory of relativity and the nature of time

This may be a good point at which to reintroduce *time* into our discussion. Famously, according to Einstein's *special* theory of relativity (as opposed to the general theory, which he developed later and which incorporated an account of gravitation), events which are simultaneous—that is, which occur 'at the same time'—with respect to one frame of reference may not be simultaneous with respect to another.[9] This is the notorious *relativity of simultaneity*. And Einstein's thinking on this issue is certainly at odds with Newton's, which is committed to an absolute conception of simultaneity and therewith an absolute conception of time. However, the distinction here is between absolutism and *relativism*, not between absolutism and *relationalism*. The chief significance of this difference between Newton and Einstein concerning the nature of simultaneity seems to be that for Newton, but not for Einstein, space and time can be regarded as quite independent aspects of reality. For Einstein, physical reality as a whole is a unitary, four-dimensional space-time manifold and events which have a purely space-like separation with respect to one frame of reference may have a time-like separation with respect to another: the only kind of 'separation' between events whose measure is not frame-relative is neither purely space-like nor purely time-like—it is their *space–time* separation.[10]

This feature of Einstein's theory arises from the fact that one of its basic postulates is the constancy of the velocity of light (*in vacuo*) in all frames of reference. The theory, including the consequences of this postulate, has undoubtedly been strongly confirmed by experiment and observation. For example, the so-called 'time-dilation' effect—whereby a clock with a high velocity (an appreciable fraction of the velocity of light) with respect to a given frame of reference appears to 'run slow'—has been confirmed by the observation that the half-lives of radioactive particles with high velocities are measurably longer, by an amount predicted by the theory, than those of similar particles moving at lower velocities. However, the postulate of the

---

[9] See Albert Einstein, 'On the Electrodynamics of Moving Bodies', in Lorentz *et al.*, *The Principle of Relativity*, 42–3.

[10] See H. Minkowski, 'Space and Time', in Lorentz *et al.*, *The Principle of Relativity*, where Minkowski's famous words appear: 'Henceforth space by itself, and time by itself, are doomed to fade away into mere shadows, and only a kind of union of the two will preserve an independent reality' (75).

constancy of the velocity of light is just that—a postulate—and not itself capable of direct empirical verification. What *can* be directly confirmed empirically is the constancy of the *average* speed of light for a round trip from *A* to *B* and back to *A* again—which, of course, is entailed by, but does not entail, the constancy of the velocity of light. It would be possible, therefore, for a theorist to postulate, contrary to Einstein, that simultaneity is absolute and explain the 'time-dilation' effect in a way which would imply that this effect does not reveal anything about the nature of *time* itself (and so is ill-named), but only something about certain distorting influences on our *measurement* of temporal duration, arising from variations in the speed of light as it travels in different directions (with respect to a given frame of reference). It would then be possible for such a theorist, consistently with all the empirical evidence currently taken to support Einstein's theory, to reject the Einsteinian view that space-like and time-like separation between events are always frame-relative, along with its implication that space and time are not wholly separate and independent aspects of physical reality.[11]

Of course, it might be objected that this new theory would be inferior to Einstein's in being less simple and economical. However, simplicity and economy are not the only criteria by which to judge the relative merits of scientific theories which have the same empirical consequences. There may be metaphysical considerations which favour the ontology of one theory over that of another and which outweigh any considerations of simplicity or economy. After all, we have no evident right to *expect* reality to be 'simple' by our standards. In any case, the criteria by which we judge whether one theory is 'simpler' than another are themselves open to dispute and are often far from obvious.[12] Moreover, on the question of economy, there is in fact a clear sense in which the new theory would be more economical than Einstein's, in that the postulate of the constancy of the velocity of light, to which Einstein's theory is committed, is stronger than—entails but is not entailed by—the principle that the average speed of light for a round trip is constant, which is all that the new theory is committed to.

None of this is to say that we should reject Einstein's theory in favour of the new theory. It is just to point out that an empirical scientific theory such as Einstein's, no matter how strongly it may be confirmed by

---

[11] A theory along these lines is developed and defended by Michael Tooley in his *Time, Tense, and Causation* (Oxford: Clarendon Press, 1997), ch. 11.

[12] See further Elliott Sober, *Simplicity* (Oxford: Clarendon Press, 1975).

observation and experiment, does not necessarily have the last word on such fundamental metaphysical issues as the nature of space and time and their interrelationship. It is perfectly conceivable that a philosopher should devise a metaphysical argument which so compellingly demonstrates that simultaneity, properly conceived, must be absolute, that we would be obliged to prefer the new theory to Einstein's. I do not claim to have such an argument myself, but I do urge that we retain an open mind about its possibility.

15

INCONGRUENT COUNTERPARTS
AND THE NATURE OF SPACE

Substantivalism, relationalism, and transcendental idealism

In the previous chapter, the dispute between absolutist and relationalist accounts of the nature of space was left unresolved, as was the question of whether this is an issue which is to be resolved, if at all, by empirical science or by philosophical argument. According to absolutism, space is an immaterial and (in a strong sense) a unitary or singular entity which does not depend for its existence or properties upon the material objects, if any, which may happen to occupy it. In describing space as being, on this view, 'unitary' or 'singular', I mean that it is conceived as a whole which has ontological priority over its parts—that is, as a whole which, while it undoubtedly *possesses* parts (at least, the three-dimensional parts that are its 'regions'), is not in any sense *composed* of those parts, since its parts cannot exist independently of space as a whole. Thus, for the absolutist, space is no mere aggregate or plurality of entities, in the way that a heap of sand is an aggregate or plurality of grains, something whose existence and identity depend upon the existence and identity of the things which constitute its parts. This is because, according to the absolutist, the parts of space are necessarily related to one another in an unchangeable order or arrangement, unlike the grains in a heap of sand—and the very identity of each part of space depends upon its position in this order or arrangement of all the parts, rather in the way in which the very identity of a natural number depends upon its position in the entire series of natural numbers. In sum, for the absolutist, space is a *substance*, in one technical metaphysical sense of the term in which it denotes an entity which does not depend for its existence or identity upon the existence or identity of any other entity.[1] Hence, the absolutist conception of space may also—and perhaps more perspicuously—be called a *substantivalist* conception of space.

According to the opposing *relationalist* conception of space, space—to the extent that the relationalist acknowledges its real existence at all—is an ontologically dependent entity, depending for its existence and properties at least in part upon the material objects occupying it and the spatial relations in which those objects stand to one another. I say 'at least in part' because, as we saw in the previous chapter, the most plausible version of relationalism—the 'modal' version—holds that space depends for some of its properties upon the laws of nature which govern how material objects occupying it can move with respect to one another. The relationalist, clearly, must deny that it is possible for space to exist entirely devoid of any kind of object occupying it, since in the absence of occupying objects and their spatial relations to one another, space is deprived of the very entities upon which its existence allegedly depends.

In view of the dependent ontological status that space has according to relationalism, it is evident that relationalism is diametrically opposed to substantivalism. One might think, therefore, that these two approaches leave available no other conception of the nature of space. But that would apparently be a mistake, because Immanuel Kant has famously offered us what would seem to be a third: the conception of space as 'transcendentally ideal'.[2] Kant presents this conception as constituting the only one that is philosophically defensible, given what he sees to be the fatal flaws in the substantivalism of Newton and the relationalism of Leibniz. According to Kant, things 'as they are in themselves'—what he calls *noumena*—are not occupants of space and stand in no spatial relations to one another: space belongs, rather, to the realm of sensible appearances or *phenomena* and as such is an aspect of the constitution of the human mind rather than an aspect of mind-independent reality. If it is true that substantivalism and relationalism are both fatally flawed, then indeed it would seem that something like Kant's view must be accepted: but, on the face of it, his view is extravagant and only to be adopted as a last resort.

---

[1] For more on this conception of substance, see my *The Possibility of Metaphysics: Substance, Identity, and Time* (Oxford: Clarendon Press, 1998), chs. 6 and 7.
[2] See Immanuel Kant, *Critique of Pure Reason*, trans. Norman Kemp Smith (London: Macmillan, 1929), pp. 67 ff.

The argument from incongruent counterparts

Before he converted to the doctrine of transcendental idealism, Kant adhered to a substantivalist view of space inspired by Newton. In defence of substantivalism, he offered a particularly interesting argument known as the *argument from incongruent counterparts*.[3] The fact that he later tried to use this argument in support of a transcendental idealist conception of space may appear to weaken its force as an argument for substantivalism.[4] Perhaps, however, the argument can at best only be used in support of transcendental idealism on the assumption that substantivalism is fatally flawed, in which case there is no inconsistency in his using the argument in support of each of these mutually incompatible positions. For present purposes, however, I shall only consider the argument in its original role of providing a putative defence of substantivalism against relationalism.

Incongruent counterparts are asymmetrical objects which are mirror images of one another, such as a left hand and an otherwise exactly similar right hand. The objects are 'incongruent' because they cannot be brought into congruence—that is, cannot be made to coincide with one another exactly—simply by moving them around and without in any way distorting their shapes. Of course, even two exactly similar left hands cannot *literally* be made to coincide, inasmuch as they are material objects and any portion of matter excludes any other from the space that it occupies—matter is, as we say, 'impenetrable'. However, this consideration is irrelevant to our present purposes. The incongruence of a left hand and an otherwise exactly similar right hand manifests itself in the fact that a glove which exactly fits the right hand will not, without distortion, fit the left hand.

What is the explanation for the possibility of this kind of incongruence? More particularly, how can a relationalist explain it? According to relationalism, all of the properties of space derive from facts concerning the objects which occupy space, including, most importantly, facts about actual and possible spatial relations between these objects. So the fact that space can contain incongruent counterparts seemingly ought to be

---

[3] See Immanuel Kant, 'Concerning the Ultimate Foundation of the Differentiation of Regions in Space', in his *Selected Precritical Writings*, trans. G. B. Kerferd and D. E. Walford (Manchester: Manchester University Press, 1968).

[4] See Immanuel Kant, *Prolegomena*, trans. Peter G. Lucas (Manchester: Manchester University Press, 1953), sects. 11–13, pp. 39 ff.

explicable, according to relationalism, in terms of facts about the actual and possible spatial relations between objects. Is it? Well, the relationalist might perhaps urge that one of these facts is that certain objects, such as a left hand and an otherwise exactly similar right hand, cannot be made to coincide simply by moving one of them relative to the other and without distorting the shape of either (waiving the irrelevant point about the impenetrability of matter)—and that this is why space can contain incongruent counterparts. However, this is plainly a circular explanation and so no explanation at all: it simply tells us that space can contain incongruent counterparts because incongruent counterparts can exist—and, for the relationalist at least, the fact that space can contain incongruent counterparts is nowise distinct from the fact that incongruent counterparts can exist. We want to know *why* it is that incongruent counterparts can exist—how it is possible for there to be pairs of objects, such as a left hand and an otherwise exactly similar right hand, which cannot be made to coincide. However, the relationalist may perhaps now urge that there is simply no explanation of this fact to be had—that it is just a 'brute fact'—pointing out that explanations must end somewhere. If explanation is an asymmetrical relation, so that circular explanations are not allowed, then, on pain of an infinite regress, some facts must not admit of explanation—and perhaps the fact that incongruent counterparts can exist is one such fact. After all, is the substantivalist in any better position to explain this fact? Well, that remains to be seen. But if the substantivalist *can* offer an explanation where the relationalist can offer none, this would certainly seem to count in favour of substantivalism.

Kant's example of the solitary hand

Now, however, Kant presents what may seem to be a crucial challenge to relationalism by asking us to envisage a world whose sole material occupant is a single hand. Such a hand, one may be inclined to suppose, must either be a left hand or else be a right hand. It surely cannot lack handedness altogether. For, after all, if a second hand (of exactly the same size as the first hand) were subsequently to be created in this world (without in any way disturbing the first hand), then it would have either to be congruent with the first hand or else to be an incongruent counterpart of it—in other words, the two hands would have either to have the same handedness or else to be of opposite handedness. And this apparently means that the first hand must have had one or the other handedness even before the second hand was created—for, by hypothesis, nothing was done to the first hand in creating the second. It may be, indeed, that it is arbitrary which handedness is called 'left'-handedness and which is called 'right'-handedness, but all that matters for present purposes is that a solitary hand would have one or other handedness and not lack handedness altogether. In other words, it seems that handedness is an *intrinsic* property of something like a hand or, at the very least, that it is not a property which something like a hand has only in virtue of some relation that it bears to other objects which occupy space. This, however, creates what appears to be a severe difficulty for the relationalist. For if a solitary hand would have a handedness, what would determine which handedness it had? According to the relationalist, it seems, this could only be determined by facts about the actual and possible spatial relations between the *parts* of the hand, these being the only objects occupying space other than the hand itself. And yet it seems that these relations would be exactly the same for a solitary hand of either handedness, in which case the relations in question could not determine which handedness the solitary hand had.[5] (The parts of each hand would stand, it seems, in exactly similar geometrical relations to one another: for instance, the relative lengths of thumb and forefinger would be the same, as would be the angle between forefinger and little finger when each hand was spread out to the same extent.) Thus the relationalist seems to be forced either to deny that the solitary hand would have a handedness, or else to say that its handedness would be a brute fact without explanation.

But how is the substantivalist in any better position to explain what would determine the handedness of a solitary hand? In something like the following way, perhaps (which is what Kant himself suggests). If, as substantivalism maintains, space exists independently of any material object that may occupy it, then we may speak of there being relationships between a material object and space itself which do not reduce to relationships between that material object and other material objects. And it may be that an asymmetrical object such as a hand admits of two quite different relationships to space itself, each of which gives rise to a different handedness. We may perhaps think of these relationships as two different ways in which something like a hand may be 'oriented' with respect to space itself.

<hr />

[5] For a challenge to this claim, however, see Peter Alexander, 'Incongruent Counterparts and Absolute Space', *Proceedings of the Aristotelian Society* 85 (1984/5), 1–21.

On this view, then, handedness is not, strictly speaking, an intrinsic property, because it is a property which something has in virtue of its 'orientation' to space itself—though, for that very reason, it is not a property which something has in virtue of any relation that it bears to other objects which occupy space. This would explain why it is a property which relationalism finds inexplicable.

A two-dimensional analogy

We may illustrate the foregoing approach to the explanation of handedness with the help of the following example. So far, we have only been considering three-dimensional objects, such as hands. But a problem like that of the left and right hands arises in two dimensions as well. Imagine cutting out of thin paper two shapes in the form of a letter 'R' and then placing these shapes on the surface of another sheet of paper. In placing the shapes on the surface, two options would present themselves to us. We could either place both of the R-shapes on the surface 'the same way round', or else we could place each of them on the surface 'a different way round'. In the latter case, one of the shapes would be 'back to front' and each would appear as the mirror-image of the other. In this second case, it would be impossible to make the two R-shapes exactly coincide just by moving them around on the surface of the paper—although, of course, one could easily do so by flipping over one of the shapes. Now, this example is only intended for purposes of illustration. In reality, our paper R-shapes are three-dimensional objects, albeit very thin ones. But it seems that one can at least conceive of a world in which space and all the objects that it contains really are purely two-dimensional. In such a world, it seems, R-shapes would come in two different varieties which were incongruent counterparts of each other. But the suggestion is that what would *explain* this variety would be the fact that there were two different ways in which an R-shape could be oriented with respect to the two-dimensional space which it occupied, rather as there are two 'different ways round' in which a cut-out R-shape of our illustrative example may be placed on the surface of the sheet of paper. And, of course, the same sort of thing might equally be said about *three*-dimensional incongruent counterparts, such as left and right hands, and the three-dimensional space which they occupy.

However, it may be wondered whether our illustrative example is really of much use in helping to us to understand the notion of 'orientation' which is central to the explanation of handedness now being offered on behalf of the substantivalist. For we cannot seriously suppose that something like a hand can *literally* be 'placed' in three-dimensional space either 'one way round' or 'the other way round'. The metaphor or analogy seems to break down precisely at the point at which it is supposed to help us. It is not as though something like a hand can somehow be 'taken out' of space and 'put back' there 'the other way round', because hands are objects which depend for their very existence upon their continuous occupancy of space. Indeed, talk of 'taking something out of space'—construed literally, rather than just as tantamount to talk of annihilating the object in question—is surely incoherent, since it seems to imply a kind of change of place which can only occur *within* space. Our illustrative example perhaps misleads us in this respect, because the sheet of paper on which our cut-out R-shapes can be placed itself exists *within* space—so that the R-shapes can be removed from it and replaced on it simply by making them undergo a temporary change of place—whereas *space itself* plainly does not exist *within* space and so lacks a crucial point of resemblance with the sheet of paper.

We see, then, that the illustrative example of the sheet of paper and the cut-out R-shapes can at best provide a somewhat dubious metaphor or analogy for the notion of 'orientation' that is central to the substantivalist explanation of handedness now under scrutiny. Lacking a non-metaphorical elucidation of that notion, we cannot really claim to understand it satisfactorily. Moreover, to the extent that the metaphor or analogy serves any purpose at all, it may actually seem to play into the hands of the relationalist. For the relationalist may now emphasize the point that, in our illustrative example, the two cut-out R-shapes are not really incongruent counterparts at all, since they can easily be made to coincide by flipping one of them over. If the analogy has any value at all, then, the implication might seem to be that a left and a right hand in three-dimensional space are not really incongruent counterparts either, since they could in principle be made to coincide by 'flipping one of them over' in a *fourth* spatial dimension.[6] The fact that no such dimension actually exists may perhaps be deemed irrelevant, provided that it is metaphysically *possible* for one to exist—as it would appear to be—for then there would seem to be only a merely contingent obstacle to our making the two hands coincide and

---

[6] This is Ludwig Wittgenstein's verdict in the *Tractatus Logico-Philosophicus*, trans. D. F. Pears and B. F. McGuinness (London: Routledge and Kegan Paul, 1961): see 6.36111.

hence no real difference between them. But if being incongruent counterparts is not, after all, a real difference between two objects, such as a left and a right hand, then it is surely not a defect in relationalism that it allegedly cannot explain this 'difference'.

Moebius bands and the topology of space

Another consideration which seems to lead towards the same conclusion is the following. Contrary to what we have been implicitly assuming so far, it should be pointed out that a two-dimensional space *could* in fact have a topology (that is, an overall structure) of such a kind that R-shapes in it would *not* come in two different varieties, so that it would be possible for any R-shape to be made to coincide with any other R-shape merely by moving them around within the two-dimensional space and without distorting either of the shapes. This possibility can be illustrated in terms of our paper cut-out R-shapes as follows. Let the sheet of paper on which the cut-out R-shapes are placed be given the form of a long, narrow strip, which is given a half-twist before its ends are joined together, thus making what is known as a *Moebius band.* Of course, our Moebius band, being made out of paper, is a three-dimensional object, owing to the thickness of the paper. But a Moebius band of zero thickness would be a truly two-dimensional entity and, curiously enough, a *single-sided* one, unlike a band of zero thickness whose ends have been joined without giving it a half-twist. If we place two cut-out R-shapes side by side somewhere on the surface of our paper Moebius band, with one of the shapes seemingly 'back to front' with respect to the other, then simply by moving one of the shapes right around the band and without removing it from the surface of the paper, we can bring it back to a position directly behind the other R-shape, in such a way that the two R-shapes now exactly overlie each other. And, of course, with a Moebius band of *zero* thickness, this would mean that any two R-shapes confined to its single surface could be made to *coincide* exactly, just by moving one of them around the band and without distorting the shape of either. In other words, a two-dimensional space with the topology of a Moebius band is a space in which there are no incongruent counterparts. There seems to be no reason, in principle, why a *three*-dimensional space should not have a similar topology, in which case one could turn what appeared to be a 'left' hand into what appeared to be a 'right' hand simply by transporting it around the universe and bringing it back to its original location. This too, then, would be a universe in which there were no incongruent counterparts. However, rather as before, it may now be urged that, even if the space of our own universe does not *in fact* have a Moebius-like topology, so that a 'left' and a 'right' hand cannot *actually* be made to coincide, our space *could have had* such a topology: so that its lacking such a topology is, once more, only a merely contingent obstacle to our making the two hands coincide, implying that there is no real difference between them and hence no difference which relationalism can be criticized for failing to explain.

Whether the foregoing considerations really help the case for relationalism and undermine that of substantivalism is a matter to which we shall return shortly. But before we do so I want to draw attention to a way in which the possibility of space's having a Moebius-like topology may be deemed to undermine an assumption that is crucial to Kant's thought experiment of the solitary hand. Suppose it were to turn out that space actually did have something like the topology of a Moebius band, in three dimensions. In that case, what we call a 'right' hand and a 'left' hand would not in fact be incongruent counterparts, since either could be made to coincide with the other merely by moving them around in space and without distorting the shape of either. In a sense, this would mean that handedness would not really exist (though I shall qualify this remark later). But this possibility, it seems, immediately undermines one of the assumptions that we made in discussing Kant's example of the solitary hand, for in discussing that example we maintained that the hand would *have* to have a handedness. We now see that this assumption was unwarranted, for if the space in which the solitary hand existed had a Moebius-like topology, then the hand would not have a handedness. However, even though a crucial assumption of Kant's argument is thus undermined, it is not immediately apparent that this fact necessarily assists the case for relationalism, because the explanation for the lack of handedness in such a solitary hand would lie solely in the topology of the space it occupied—that is to say, it would lie in a fact about *the nature of space itself* rather than in any fact about the nature of the sole object which supposedly occupies space: and this seems, if anything, to help the case for substantivalism.

Actual space versus possible spaces

In reply, it is perhaps open to the relationalist to object that the imaginary world of the solitary hand residing in a space whose Moebius-like topology is not determined by facts concerning the material occupant of that space is merely imaginary and does not constitute a genuine metaphysical possibility. The relationalist may urge that worlds with three-dimensional spaces having a Moebius-like topology are genuinely possible, but that these are all worlds in which the topology is determined by facts and natural laws concerning the material inhabitants of those worlds. And, it may further be urged, these will all be worlds which are far more complex than the imaginary world of the solitary hand.

Now, whatever we make of this reply, we do at least need to be clear as to whether the dispute between the substantivalist and the relationalist is supposed to be a dispute about the nature and ontological status of space in the *actual* world or a dispute about the nature and ontological status of space in *any possible world*. The reply just offered on behalf of the relationalist assumes that the dispute is about the nature and ontological status of space in any possible world. However, one might suppose that most relationalists would be happy to concede that absolute space is *metaphysically* possible—that substantivalism is a correct doctrine about the spaces of *some* possible worlds—while denying that substantivalism is true of *our* world. And such relationalists, one might think, are in a position to dismiss as simply *irrelevant* thought experiments, such as Kant's, which involve radically counterfactual states of affairs: they need not take a stance on the question of whether or not such counterfactual states of affairs are genuine metaphysical possibilities. On the other hand, if relationalists are entitled to dismiss as irrelevant an appeal to such a radically counterfactual state of affairs as the existence of a solitary hand, then substantivalists are surely equally entitled to dismiss as irrelevant appeals to such radically counterfactual states of affairs as the existence of a fourth spatial dimension or the existence of a Moebius-like topology, which were earlier made on behalf of relationalism. So if the dispute is construed as being solely about the nature and ontological status of space in the *actual* world, it may seem that none of the considerations so far raised really helps either party. But this presumes, of course, that the dispute can indeed be construed in either of the two ways just described—a presumption which would be undermined if it could be argued that space cannot have a different nature and ontological status in different possible worlds. Whether such an argument is available is a matter to which I shall return later, but for the time being I shall assume that it is not.

Let us take stock of what we may suppose to have been established so far. First, it certainly seems that there *could* be universes with spaces—even three-dimensional spaces—in which incongruent counterparts would not exist, because a 'left' and a 'right' hand in such a universe could be made to coincide exactly, without distorting the shape of either, simply by transporting one of the hands right around the universe. However, it appears most unlikely that the space of our own universe actually has such a topology. Second, it also seems that there could be universes with *four*-dimensional spaces, in which two three-dimensional objects, exactly like a 'left' and a 'right' hand in our universe, could be made to coincide exactly, without distorting either, simply by 'flipping one of them over' in the fourth dimension. Again, however, it appears most unlikely that our own universe actually has such a fourth spatial dimension. On both counts, then, it seems that, however matters may be in other possible universes, in our universe a left hand and an otherwise exactly similar right hand really are incongruent counterparts. Furthermore, it should be noted that even in a universe with four spatial dimensions—unless it had a Moebius-like topology—certain *four*-dimensional objects could still exist which would be incongruent counterparts. More generally, even in a universe with any finite number of spatial dimensions, incongruent counterparts could still exist, unless the space of that universe had a Moebius-like topology. So, it seems, the supposed possibility of making any two n-dimensional objects which appear to be incongruent counterparts coincide exactly simply by 'flipping one of them over' in an $(n+1)$-dimensional space does nothing, in itself, to eliminate the possibility of there being objects which are genuinely incongruent counterparts—since congruence between the two n-dimensional objects can be achieved only at the expense of introducing the possibility of incongruence between certain pairs of $(n+1)$-dimensional objects.

The upshot of all this is that only the possession of a Moebius-like topology by a space genuinely eliminates the possibility of there being pairs of objects in that space which are incongruent counterparts. The space of our universe is almost certainly not Moebius-like and consequently it is at least *physically* (even if not *metaphysically*) impossible to make a left and a right hand of our world coincide exactly without distorting their shapes. The question then is whether this is a fact which is in any way an embarrassment to a philosopher who favours a relationalist conception of the space of our universe. The answer would seem to be that such a philosopher need find this fact no embarrassment if he could hope to explain why the space of our universe lacks a Moebius-like topology by appealing to facts and natural laws concerning the actual and possible spatial relations between material objects in our universe. There seems to be no reason, in principle, why such an explanation should not be available—though this, of course, is very far from saying that such an explanation does in fact exist. But, as far as I am aware, current physical science does not provide any such explanation—and this may give some encouragement to the substantivalist. For if it should emerge that the fact that the space of our universe lacks a Moebius-like topology *cannot* be explained by appeal to facts and natural laws concerning the actual and possible spatial relations between material objects in our universe, then this would imply that the space of our universe has properties which are independent of any facts concerning its material occupants and hence that it has at least some features of a substance.

I say only 'at least some features of a substance' because, even if the space of our universe has some *properties* which are independent of any facts concerning its material occupants, this does not imply that it has an *existence* which is altogether independent of its material occupants: it does not imply, for instance, that the space of our universe could have been entirely devoid of material occupants—but only if this is the case can the space of our universe truly be described as being a 'substance', in the fullest sense of the term. However, if it should turn out that the space of our universe could not have been entirely devoid of material occupants and yet that it has some properties (such as, perhaps, its lack of a Moebius-like topology) which are independent of any facts concerning its material occupants, then *neither* substantivalism *nor* relationalism will turn out to provide a correct account of the nature and ontological status of the space of our universe. Thus we see that Kantian transcendental idealism is not in fact the only alternative to substantivalism and relationalism, since there is a possible position intermediate between these two extremes.[7]

---

[7] For further discussion of handedness and its implications for the nature of space, see Graham Nerlich, *The Shape of Space*, 2nd edn. (Cambridge: Cambridge University Press, 1994), ch. 2, and John Earman, *World Enough and Space-Time: Absolute versus Relational Theories of Space and Time* (Cambridge, Mass.: MIT Press, 1989), ch. 7.

How many dimensions could space have?

There are many issues which our discussion so far has left unresolved or insufficiently explored. One relatively minor issue concerns the number of spatial dimensions actually possessed by the space of our universe, which we have so far assumed to be three. We should remember here that *time*, even if it is in some sense a 'fourth dimension' (though this itself is highly contestable), is certainly not a fourth *spatial* dimension, on a par with our three familiar spatial dimensions of length, breadth, and height. If our universe contained a fourth spatial dimension on a par with these three, then it would be possible to escape from a room whose ceiling, floor, and four walls contained no door or window, without forcing an exit—simply by moving in a direction at right angles to the length, breadth, and height of the room—and this, as far as we know, is *not* possible. It is true that some contemporary physicists postulate the actual existence of more than just three spatial dimensions, maintaining that the additional dimensions manifest themselves only on the ultra-subatomic scale: but such speculations, even if they turned out to be correct, would apparently have no direct bearing on the main issues with which we are concerned in this chapter, relating as they do to the realm of macroscopic objects, including ourselves.

A rather more interesting question is whether space—either the space of our universe or at least the space of some possible universe—is really capable of having more than three spatial dimensions, all on a par with our three familiar dimensions of length, breadth, and height (not, that is, merely in such a way that all but three of these dimensions manifest themselves only on the ultra-subatomic scale). Indeed, is space really capable of having two or fewer dimensions, in the way we assumed earlier when discussing a supposedly two-dimensional space with a Moebius-like topology? Or is there some deep reason for the three-dimensionality of space that we find it to have?[8] Kant evidently thought so, for he considered that the three-dimensionality of space was a necessary feature of it, being bound up with what he regarded as its transcendentally ideal status. Other philosophers have contended that universes in which space is not three-dimensional would not be capable of sustaining intelligent life, so that we

---

[8] For the contrasting views of two leading twentieth-century philosopher-scientists, see Hermann Weyl, *Space-Time-Matter* (New York: Dover, 1952), 283–5, and Hans Reichenbach, *The Philosophy of Space and Time* (New York: Dover, 1957), 279–80.

have at least an 'anthropic' argument for the three-dimensionality of space—an argument to the effect that space must be three-dimensional because, if it were not, we would not be here (as we plainly are!) to acknowledge its existence.[9] Thus it is said, for instance, that complex life-forms would be impossible in a two-dimensional universe, because a complex life-form requires something like an alimentary canal which enables it to ingest matter from its environment and excrete it—and such a 'canal' in a two-dimensional life-form would simply divide it into two separate entities, whereas in a three-dimensional life-form the canal is merely a tube through the life-form which does not disrupt its physical integrity as a single living entity. Again, it is said that complex life-forms would be impossible in a universe with four or more spatial dimensions, because in such universes planets could not form with stable orbits around stars in the way in which they do in our universe, in which an inverse square law of gravitation generates such orbits. Whatever we make of such arguments, however, they do not have much metaphysical depth: they do not go any way towards showing that it is metaphysically necessary for space to be three-dimensional on a macroscopic scale. To that extent, they do nothing to undermine the thought experiments deployed earlier in this chapter, which invoked the possibility of spaces with more or fewer dimensions than the three with which we are familiar.

Does 'space' denote an ontological category?

This is a convenient point at which to address another issue which we earlier left aside: namely, the question of whether space can have a different nature and ontological status in different possible worlds. Of course, it is plausible to contend that *the space of our universe* could not have had a nature and ontological status different from those it actually has: that if it is, say, a *substance* in actuality, as substantivalists believe, then it is a substance in any possible world in which it exists. This is simply because *any* entity's ontological category is very plausibly one of its essential features. In the same way, it is plausible that I am a *person* in any possible world in which I exist—that there is no possible world in which, say, I am a poached egg or the positive square root of four. But a rather more difficult question

---

[9] See further John D. Barrow and Frank J. Tippler, *The Anthropic Cosmological Principle* (Oxford: Clarendon Press, 1986), 258–76.

to answer is whether there can be, in two different possible worlds, two different entities, each of which may properly be described as being the 'space' of its world, but each of which possesses a nature and ontological status different from those of the other. Thus, for example, could the space of one possible world conform to the substantivalist's conception of space while the space of another possible world conforms to the relationalist's? To suppose so is to assume, in effect, that the term 'space' does not denote an ontological category, in the way, say, that 'substance' does.

It might be thought obvious that 'space' cannot denote an ontological category, given that there can be—as we have seen in the course of this chapter—an intelligible dispute between substantivalists and relationalists concerning what ontological category the space of our world should be held to belong to. However, we cannot assume, just because this dispute is intelligible, that things of quite different ontological categories genuinely *could* quite equally merit the title of 'space' (albeit only in different possible worlds). It could be, for instance, that nothing genuinely meriting that title could fail to be a substance—in which case it would seem that 'space' would denote a sub-category of substance and hence an ontological category (albeit not a fundamental one). However, I confess that I know of no convincing argument to this effect. It may seem odd that we should, in some sense, know what space is and yet not know for sure to which ontological category it belongs, nor even whether things of quite different ontological categories could equally merit the title of 'space' (in different possible worlds). But such seems to be our epistemic predicament where space is concerned. (It is a predicament that some philosophers have held us to be in even regarding *ourselves*, maintaining that although we know, in some sense, what we are, we do not know for sure to which ontological category we belong—whether, for instance, we are immaterial souls, living organisms, or bundles of psychological states. In which case, we can hardly complain that it is impossible that we should be in such a predicament regarding space.)

Is handedness a property?

Another important issue left over from earlier discussion, which needs to be considered, is this. I remarked that in a world whose space had a Moebius-like topology, there would be no incongruent counterparts and that this implied that, in a sense, handedness would not exist in such a world. Certainly, in such a world, a 'left' hand could be made to coincide exactly with a 'right' hand, simply by transporting one of them around the universe. But, it might be protested, our very description of this process belies the suggestion that in such a world there would be no difference between 'left-handedness' and 'right-handedness'. Rather than describing a world in which such handednesses do not exist at all, we seem to be describing one in which an object's handedness can be *changed*, simply by transporting it around the universe—which implies, it would seem, that the object does indeed have a handedness at all times, albeit a different one at different times. However, matters cannot be as simple as this, for we can hardly suppose that the transported hand suddenly undergoes a change of handedness somewhere along its journey around the universe—nor can we suppose that the change of handedness is gradual, because handedness does not come in degrees. All we can say is that, while the hands are in close proximity to one another prior to the transportation of one of them, they cannot be made to coincide with each other simply by moving them around *locally*, whereas, after one of them has been transported around the universe and brought back into close proximity with the other, they *can* be made to coincide with each other simply by moving them around locally. Something, clearly, has changed: but it is not clear that what has changed is a *property* of one of the hands. Rather, it seems, a certain *relationship* between the hands has changed.

Even so, it is difficult to resist our inclination to say that some property of one of the hands has changed, so as to make it match the other in a way in which it did not match it before. For, before one of the hands was transported around the universe, the two hands *looked* different, whereas afterwards they do not. How can two things look different, though, without differing in some property? Well, they could do so if the observer is subject to some illusion, or if the objects are observed under different conditions—as, for example, two mountains with the same shape may look different when viewed from different sides. But nothing like this seems to apply in the case of a 'left' hand and an otherwise exactly similar 'right' hand lying in close proximity to one another. It is not as though we are seeing the two hands in two quite different 'perspectives', as in the case of the two mountains. For, while our perspective on each hand will be slightly different, we can easily switch their positions so that we now see each in the perspective in which we formerly saw the other—but this obviously does not have the effect of changing their apparent handedness.

The nature of handedness thus still seems to be something of a mystery.

In some sense, handedness still has objective existence even in a world in which, owing to the Moebius-like topology of its space, incongruent counterparts (as we have defined them) do not exist. Handedness is no mere illusion, it seems, produced by the conditions under which we observe objects residing in space. Even so, one can perhaps see why Kant should have thought that the phenomenon of handedness is evidence of the transcendental ideality of space—its mind-dependent status as the form under which objects manifest themselves to our visual perception, rather than an arena in which those objects reside or a system of relations in which they stand to one another. In fact, though, it seems that handedness is built deeply into the nature of matter, at least in our world. Thus, complex organic molecules of the same composition but different handedness may undergo quite different kinds of chemical interactions—a fact which would make life difficult, or even impossible, for any human being unfortunate enough to have the handedness of his body completely reversed (unless objects in his environment also underwent such a change). Even at the level of subatomic particles, handedness appears to make a difference to the prevalence of certain types of interaction: nature at this level is not blind to differences of handedness, any more than it is blind to differences of electrical charge—which suggests that handedness is a natural phenomenon at least as fundamental as electrical charge.[10] But as long as our understanding of the origin and character of handedness remains clouded, its implications for the nature and ontological status of space will also remain somewhat obscure.

[10] See Martin Gardner, *The New Ambidextrous Universe: Symmetry and Asymmetry from Mirror Reflections to Superstrings*, 3rd edn. (New York: W. H. Freeman, 1990), ch. 22.

16

THE PARADOXES OF MOTION AND
THE POSSIBILITY OF CHANGE

Reality and the appearance of change

The concepts of space, time, and motion are mutually dependent, although the precise nature of their relationship is contentious. One of the purposes of the present chapter is to examine that relationship by studying certain logical and metaphysical problems besetting the concept of motion. When an object moves, it undergoes a change of its spatial location during an interval of time. Movement, thus, is a species of change—and the notion of change, as we saw in Chapter 13, is far from straightforward, admitting as it does of many important distinctions. How any kind of change at all is possible is something of a mystery, rooted partly in the mysterious nature of time itself. It is little wonder, then, that in all ages there have been philosophers who have denied the reality of change, maintaining that it belongs only to the realm of appearances. But even this claim harbours a paradox, for even if only the appearances change, *something* changes and so change is real. To deny the reality of change altogether, it seems, one must deny even the appearance of change—unless, as I very much doubt, one can make clear sense of a distinction between appearance of change and change of appearance. And yet to deny even the appearance of change is to repudiate the very phenomena which have led philosophers to suppose that there is a problem about change in the first place. There cannot even appear to be a problem, it seems, unless change in some sense is real. For this reason, we are likely to find any argument which purports to show that change is impossible especially perplexing.

Motion presents a crucial challenge for the thesis that change is not illusory, for no change seems more real than movement and if movement can be shown, for any reason, to be impossible, then it will be difficult to resist the perplexing conclusion that change in general is impossible. This helps to explain the importance and abiding interest of the famous paradoxes of motion that we owe to Zeno of Elea, which are the central concern of the present chapter. The paradoxes are four in number and go by various names, but, following venerable precedent, I shall call them the Racecourse, the Achilles, the Arrow, and the Moving Blocks. I shall not be at all concerned with the history of the paradoxes or the ancient textual evidence for their provenance, their original form, and the intended purpose of the philosopher who allegedly first thought of them.[1] The first two paradoxes, as we shall see, are really just variants of a single paradox, while the other two are genuinely distinct both from the first two and from each other. It is generally considered that the first two paradoxes present a greater challenge than do either the third or the fourth, which are regarded by some philosophers—wrongly, I think—as trifling or obviously confused. However, because the first two paradoxes have received considerably more attention than the others, I shall spend rather more time discussing them.

The Paradox of the Racecourse

The Paradox of the Racecourse may be set out as follows. A runner, A, has to run a finite distance—say, of 400 metres—in a finite time, by running from a point X to a point Y. He sets off at a certain time, t_0, aiming to arrive at the later time t_1. Clearly, however, before A can arrive at his ultimate destination, Y, he must first run half of the distance between X and Y, reaching the midpoint, Z, at time $t_{1/2}$, which is intermediate between t_0 and t_1. But, on arriving at Z, A still has the second half of his total distance yet to run. Before A can reach Y, then, he must first run half of that remaining distance, reaching the midpoint between Z and Y—call it Z'—at time $t_{3/4}$, which is intermediate between $t_{1/2}$ and t_1. But even on arriving at Z', A still has a quarter (half of one half) of his total distance yet to run, the first half of which (one-eighth of the total) he must run before he can reach Y, as is depicted in Fig. 16.1. Now, in our description of the runner's task, we have obviously set out upon an infinite regress. For, however close to Y the runner gets, some distance between himself and Y will still remain and he

[1] For more on the historical context of Zeno's paradoxes, see Richard Sorabji, *Time, Creation and the Continuum: Theories in Antiquity and the Early Middle Ages* (London: Duckworth, 1983), ch. 21. See also Gregory Vlastos, 'Zeno of Elea', in Paul Edwards (ed.), *The Encyclopedia of Philosophy* (New York: Macmillan, 1972), vol. viii, pp. 369–79.

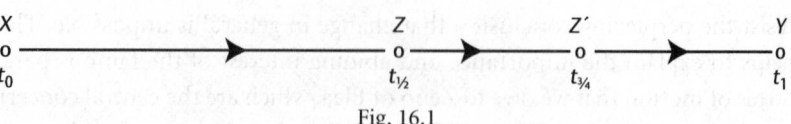

Fig. 16.1

will have to complete the first half of that distance before he completes all of it: but, having completed the first half of it, he is then just faced once more with a task of completing some distance between himself and Y. Thus, he cannot, it seems, complete his original task of reaching Y, because his completion of that task requires his prior completion of an infinite series of similar tasks.

Here it may be objected that there is no reason why the runner should not complete his original task of reaching Y within a finite period of time, because each remaining half-distance is shorter than the previous one and so will take him less time to complete. If the time he takes to run the first half-distance—the distance from X to Z—is, let us say, half a minute, then the time he will take to run the next half-distance, from Z to Z', will be just a quarter of a minute (assuming that he runs at a constant speed). The next half-distance will take him one-eighth of a minute and the half-distance after that only one-sixteenth of a minute—and so on. Thus the sum of the times he takes to run the ever-decreasing half-distances may be expressed as the sum of a converging infinite series, $\frac{1}{2} + \frac{1}{4} + \frac{1}{8} + \frac{1}{16} + \frac{1}{32} + \ldots$, and it can be proved mathematically that this infinite series of ever-decreasing quantities has a sum equal to 1. In short, it can be proved that the runner will take exactly one minute to arrive at his ultimate destination and so will certainly arrive there after a finite period of time.

However, this response arguably does not go to the heart of the problem. For the problem is not to explain how the runner can arrive at his ultimate destination in a finite period of time, given that he can indeed reach that destination, but rather to explain how he can ever arrive there *at all*. For, in order to arrive there, it seems that he must complete an infinite series of tasks—running the first half-distance (from X to Z), then running the second half-distance (from Z to Z'), then running the third half-distance (from Z' to the midpoint between Z' and Y), then running the fourth half-distance, and so on ad infinitum. But it is impossible, surely, to complete an infinite series of tasks, since such a series has, by definition, no last member. I shall return to this claim in due course, for despite its intuitive appeal, it may rest on a confusion. But before doing so,

I want to consider some other possible responses to the Paradox of the Racecourse.

Is the paradox self-defeating?

One response which is quite tempting is to say that the paradox is self-defeating, for the following reason. In describing the task confronting the runner, we began by pointing out that before A can arrive at his ultimate destination, Y, he must first run half of the distance between X and Y. However, it may now be objected that the paradox only works on the assumption that A can at least run that first half-distance, from X to Z, since only if A can reach Z can there be a time at which half of the total distance still remains for him to run. And the same applies to all the other half-distances in the series. But if A can indeed run from X to Z, then he can complete a distance between two points, which is all that his original task amounts to. Hence, it seems, the way in which the paradox is set up concedes the very thesis that it is supposed to undermine, namely, that movement by an object from one point of space to another is possible.

However, this response, too, is questionable. For, very arguably, we should see the propounder of the paradox as presenting a *reductio ad absurdum* argument against the possibility of movement. That is to say, we should see him as presenting an argument which shows how, if we assume that movement is possible, we run into a contradiction, thus demonstrating that movement is not in fact possible. The propounder of the paradox need not be seen as conceding that it really *is* possible for A to run from X to the first midpoint, Z, but merely as assuming that this is possible for the sake of argument, in order to show that movement between one point of space and another is in fact *im*possible, with the implication that A cannot, after all, really run from X to Z.

An inverted version of the paradox

If this objection to the proposed response is not found convincing, it may be urged that there is, in any case, another way of propounding the Paradox of the Racecourse which entirely escapes the alleged difficulty. In this version, what the paradox is designed to show is not that A cannot ever reach his ultimate destination, Y, but rather that A cannot even *begin* to move—that he cannot leave his starting point, X. This alternative version of the paradox may be described as follows. As in the first version, it is pointed out that before A can arrive at his ultimate destination, Y, he must first run half of the distance between X and Y, reaching the midpoint, Z, at a time $t_{1/2}$ which is intermediate between t_0 and t_1. But now it may be remarked that, likewise, before A can reach Z, he must first reach the midpoint between X and Z—call it Z'—at a time $t_{1/4}$, which is intermediate between t_0 and $t_{1/2}$, as depicted in Fig. 16.2.

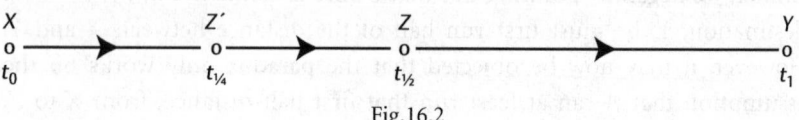

Fig.16.2

In our new description of the runner's task, we again seem to be faced with an infinite regress: before A can arrive at his ultimate destination, Y, he must first complete half of the distance from X to Y; but before he can do that, he must complete half of that half-distance; and before he can do that, he must complete half of that half-half-distance—and so on ad infinitum. But how, then, can A even begin to move? For in order to move any distance at all, A must already have moved a lesser distance: so he now seems to face an infinite series of tasks with no *first* member rather than, as in the original version of the paradox, an infinite series of tasks with no *last* member.

A common-sense objection to the paradox

Given the availability of this inverted version of the paradox, it might seem that we lose nothing by concentrating on the original version, which has the added advantage of a certain intuitive appeal. (I shall, though, return to the inverted version of the paradox later, since we shall discover reasons for doubting whether the two versions can be resolved in the same way.) Now, concerning the original version of the paradox, we must be on guard against those unphilosophically minded individuals who may be inclined to dismiss it in the style of Samuel Johnson. Boswell describes a conversation between himself and Johnson on the topic of Berkeley's view that perceptible objects are merely collections of ideas, and reports Johnson as giving a large stone an enormous kick, expostulating 'I refute it thus!'[2] The

[2] See James Boswell, *The Life of Samuel Johnson* (London: Dent, 1906), vol. i, p. 292.

implication of Johnson's remark is that everyday experience and common sense sufficiently demonstrate that stones are not merely collections of ideas; and, no doubt, he would urge with equal vehemence that they demonstrate that movement is possible. After all, it may be said, we can quite plainly *see* that people can run from one place to another, so where is the difficulty? If our runner, A, has a race of 400 metres to run and has a stride of two metres, then there will come a moment in the race at which he needs just one more stride to complete it—and he can surely take that last stride. What was represented as constituting an infinite series of tasks seems, to common sense, to amount in fact to a merely finite series of tasks consisting of 200 successive strides, which is easily completable by taking the final stride. However, matters are unfortunately not quite as simple as common sense suggests—and even if common sense is right in insisting that motion is possible, that in itself does nothing to remove the paradox. To take even a single stride, A must move his leg from one point of space to another and this is a task which is fundamentally no different in nature from the task of moving himself from X to Y. The fact that we can divide his run into 200 successive strides makes the underlying problem no easier to solve. And, in any case, exactly the same problem would arise if, instead of having A run from X to Y, we had him freewheeling a bicycle from X to Y, in which case we couldn't divide the continuous forward movement of the bicycle's frame into a finite series of sub-movements analogous to the successive strides of a runner.

Infinite series and supertasks

It seems, then, that we must take the Paradox of the Racecourse seriously. But perhaps it still admits of a solution which does not require us to deny the possibility of continuous movement. Recall that I suggested earlier that the root of the difficulty presented by the paradox is that it is apparently impossible to complete an infinite series of tasks, since such a series has, by definition, no last member. And we cannot deny, it seems, that the runner has to complete an infinite series of tasks—unless, of course, we deny that space is infinitely divisible. Certainly, if space is *not* infinitely divisible, then there will be a point in the race so close to Y that the distance between that point and Y is not divisible into two half-distances. And perhaps A will be able to move from that point to Y discontinuously and instantaneously. However, as we shall see when we come to discuss the

Paradox of the Moving Blocks, the notion of such discontinuous and instantaneous motion raises new problems, so it would be better not to assume that this is possible if we can resolve the Racecourse Paradox without doing so.

Let us then focus attention instead upon the claim that, because an infinite series of tasks has, by definition, no last member, it is therefore impossible to complete such a series of tasks. Much depends here on what exactly is meant by 'completing an infinite series of tasks'. If by this is meant 'completing the last task in the series after completing all of its predecessors', then, of course, we must say that it is impossible to complete an infinite series of tasks, simply because such a series has no last member. But if, as seems altogether more sensible, what we should mean by 'completing an infinite series of tasks' is just 'completing all of the tasks in the series in the order in which they occur in the series', then it is far from obvious that this is impossible. Indeed, we have already noted that we can calculate how long it will take to complete an infinite series of tasks, each of which takes half as long as the preceding one. Provided that space and time are both continuous and thus infinitely divisible, there is no problem in supposing that such an infinite series of tasks may exist, and that one does indeed exist in the case of the movement of a point-particle from one point of space to another. Our imaginary runner is no point-particle, of course, which is partly why the Paradox of the Racecourse seems so contrary to common sense and everyday experience. And, indeed, modern physics leads us to believe that point-particles do not actually exist. But these merely contingent facts have no bearing on the question of whether the paradox has any logical force. What I am now suggesting is that it does not, after all, have any logical force, but only appears to do so owing to a confusion over what should be understood by 'completing an infinite series of tasks'.

Against this suggestion, it may be urged that the notion of completing an infinite series of tasks, even if understood in the way recommended earlier, is still problematic. Consider, for instance, the well-known *Thomson's lamp* paradox, which involves such an infinite series of tasks and is thus often described as being concerned with a so-called 'supertask'.[3] The lamp possesses a button which, if pushed, will turn the lamp on if it is already off and turn it off if it is already on. Initially, the lamp is off and the

---

[3] See James F. Thomson, 'Tasks and Super-tasks', *Analysis* 15 (1954), 1–13, reprinted in Richard M. Gale (ed.), *The Philosophy of Time: A Collection of Essays* (Garden City, NY: Anchor Doubleday & Co., Inc., 1967).

'supertask' is to push the button an infinite number of times during the course of one minute, this being accomplished by pushing it for the first time at the beginning of the minute, for the second time after half a minute has elapsed, for the third time after three-quarters of a minute has elapsed, for the fourth time after seven-eighths of a minute has elapsed—and so on ad infinitum. We may add that no button-pushing is to occur that does not belong to this sequence. After each odd-numbered push of the button, the lamp will be on and after each even-numbered push of the button, it will be off. The problem is to say whether the lamp will be on or off when exactly one minute has elapsed. Of course, a physically real lamp would either burn out before the minute had elapsed or simply go on shining continuously after a certain point—and, in any case, there is a physical limit to how rapidly a material object like a lamp's button can move. But we are supposed to be considering the problem from a purely logical point of view, abstracting away from the constraints of physical law, which are merely contingent. This understood, it seems that we have to say that the lamp will be either on or off when exactly one minute has elapsed—there is no other state in which it can be—and yet it also seems that its being in one of those states at that time cannot be the result of any of the button-pushings in the series, because for any such button-pushing which results in the lamp's being on there is a subsequent button-pushing which results in its being off, and vice versa.

This is, indeed, a most peculiar state of affairs but not, it seems, a logically impossible one. We simply have to conclude, I think, that a world in which the 'supertask' is completable is a world in which causal determinism does not reign universally. At the end of the minute, the lamp will be either on or off, but not as a result of any button-pushing in the series. Since, as we have described the supertask, all of the button-pushings that occur do so in the course of the series, the state of the lamp at the end of the minute will not be determined by any button-pushing at all. If we also assume that only a button-pushing can causally determine the state of the lamp at any time, then it follows that the state of the lamp at the end of the minute is causally undetermined. It is important to appreciate here that every button-pushing in the series occurs *before* one minute has elapsed: there is no button-pushing in the series which occurs when exactly one minute has elapsed and so, given that the only button-pushings that occur do so in the course of the series, there is no button-pushing at all that occurs when exactly one minute has elapsed. The reason, of course, why no button-pushing in the series occurs when exactly one minute has elapsed is that the series has no last member. For, since every button-pushing in the series must occur during the course of the minute, no button-pushing in the series can occur *after* the minute has elapsed, whence it follows that if there were a button-pushing in the series which occurred when exactly one minute had elapsed, that button-pushing would have to be the last in the series—and there is no such last member.

Why does the paradox seem so compelling?

My tentative verdict concerning the Racecourse Paradox is, then, that it fails to demonstrate the impossibility of continuous motion because it is erroneously assumed that it is logically impossible to complete an infinite series of tasks, when in fact it is logically possible to complete an infinite series of tasks even within a finite period of time. As we have seen, one reason why the paradox may seem compelling is that one may have a confused understanding of what should be meant by 'completing an infinite series of tasks', taking this to mean 'completing the last task in the series after completing all of its predecessors'. But why should anyone make this mistake—why should anyone suppose that the infinite series of tasks to be completed by the runner *has* a 'last member'? For the following reason, perhaps. Clearly, in order to complete the task of running from X to Y, A must actually arrive at Y: arriving at any other point between X and Y, no matter how close it is to Y, will not suffice. But *every one* of the infinite series of tasks that A must complete in order to arrive at Y involves his arrival at a point between X and Y which is distinct from Y. It may seem, thus, that, even having completed all of those infinitely many tasks, there is still something remaining for A to do, namely, arrive at Y itself: and this, it may seem, is his 'last' task, which succeeds all his infinitely many previous tasks. But, in fact, it would seem that the proper thing to say is that, although there is no *single* task in the infinite series of tasks by completing which A arrives at Y, none the less, by completing *all* of these infinitely many tasks, A arrives at Y—there is nothing further that A need do in order to arrive there than to complete every task in the series. Thus, the *whole* task of running from X to Y, the performance of which results in A's arrival at Y, is just the sum of the infinitely many subtasks in the series, even though no one of those subtasks is such that, by performing it, A arrives at Y. This fact—if we accept that it is a fact—is sufficiently surprising, however, to make entirely understandable one's temptation to suppose, erroneously, that there must be a 'last' task for the runner to complete in order to arrive at Y. Hence, it is perfectly understandable why we should seem to be faced with a paradox, drawn as we are both to saying that the runner must have a 'last' task to complete and to saying that, because the series of tasks which he has to complete is infinite, there can be no such 'last' task for him to complete.

More on inverted versions of the paradox

It may be wondered whether this resolution of the Paradox of the Race-course also works for the inverted version of the paradox, which is intended to demonstrate that the runner cannot even *begin* to move, because he has an infinite series of tasks to complete which has no *first* member. One reason why the inverted version of the paradox may seem to be more difficult to resolve in the foregoing fashion is this. In the original version of the paradox, the propounder of the paradox grants us—if only for the sake of argument—that the runner can complete any single subtask in the infinite series of subtasks confronting him. But then it is open to us to maintain, as we did above, that the runner's *whole* task of running from X to Y is just the sum of all those subtasks and is hence completable by him simply in virtue of his completion of each subtask in the series. But in the inverted version of the paradox, the propounder of the paradox does *not* grant us, even for the sake of argument, that the runner can complete *any* of the subtasks in the infinite series of subtasks confronting him: rather, he lets the burden of proof for this lie with us. Consequently, he will not simply allow us to assume that each of these subtasks is completable and then argue that we can, without contradiction, identify the whole task with the sum of all the subtasks. Moreover, and even more importantly, there is a significant disanalogy between the two versions of the paradox in the following respect. In the original version of the paradox, in which the question is how the runner can ever arrive at his ultimate destination, Y, the problem seems to arise because *none* of the subtasks which the runner is taken to be able to complete involves him arriving at Y. But in the inverted version of the paradox, in which the question is how the runner can ever leave his point of departure, X, *all* of the subtasks which he is required to be able to complete involve him leaving X. Hence, since the very question at issue is how the runner can ever leave X, it doesn't help us answer this question to say that his whole task of running from X to Y is the sum of infinitely many subtasks each of which involves him leaving X.

What we *could* say, though, by analogy with what we said regarding the original version of the paradox, is that the runner's whole task of running from X to Y is the sum of *another* infinite series of subtasks *none* of which involves him leaving X. Each of these subtasks has a starting point, but none of them has the same starting-point as the starting point, X, of the whole task which is the sum of all these subtasks. The starting point of the 'first' subtask in the infinite series that I now have in mind is the midpoint between X and Y, point Z; the starting point of the 'second' subtask in the series is the midpoint between X and Z, point Z' of Fig. 16.2; and so on. And the reason why I put the words 'first' and 'second' in quotation marks here is that the 'first' subtask (that of completing the distance from Z to the ultimate destination, Y) is performed *later* than the 'second' subtask (that of completing the distance from Z' to Z), and so on. To divide up the runner's whole task in this way is, indeed, just to reverse the way in which it is divided up in the original version of the paradox. In effect, it is to take the first of our two earlier diagrams, Fig. 16.1, exchange X for Y, and read time as running from right to left in the diagram, as in Fig. 16.3.

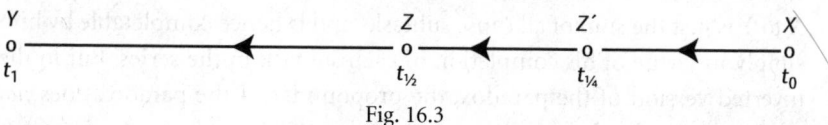

Fig. 16.3

Now, it may be noticed that this third diagram looks as though it is simply the mirror image, reflected from left to right, of our second diagram, which was this:

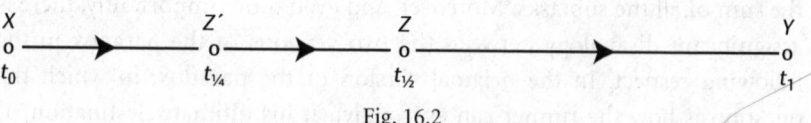

Fig. 16.2

But in this case appearances are misleading. For, as we are interpreting these two diagrams, Fig. 16.3 represents the following two subtasks of the runner: to run from Z to Y and, prior to that, to run from Z' to Z. In contrast, the subtasks that Fig. 16.2 represents are: to run from X to Z and, prior to that, to run from X to Z'. Thus, the supertask of which Fig. 16.2 is a partial representation is one in which all of the runner's subtasks are nested within the interval between X and Z, whereas the supertask of which Fig. 16.3 is a partial representation is one in which all of the runner's subtasks are strung out in a non-overlapping fashion between Y and X. Consequently, we can resolve the version of the Racecourse Paradox represented by Fig. 16.3 in a way which is modelled on our resolution of the original version of the paradox, as represented in Fig. 16.1 (of which Fig. 16.3 is merely a relabelled version). But we cannot construct a solution to the version of the paradox represented by Fig. 16.2 in exactly the same way.

So what *can* we do to resolve the version of the paradox represented by Fig. 16.2? One problem posed by this version of the paradox is that, if the runner is to move any distance at all, he must *already* have moved some (lesser) distance: if space and time are continuous, then there is no least distance for him to move and so no distance which he moves before he moves any other distance. However, our solution to the version of the paradox represented by Fig. 16.3 shows us how it can be possible for the runner to move in such a way that, for any distance that he has moved, he has already moved a lesser distance. So this problem cannot be what is distinctive of the version of the paradox represented by Fig. 16.2. In fact, I think that all that is truly distinctive of this version of the paradox is that it raises the problem of how something can *begin* to move—that is (as we might be tempted to put it), how it can be the case that at a certain instant of time an object is moving, even though it is not moving at any prior instant of time. And at the root of this problem, I think, is the more general problem of how something can be moving *at an instant of time* at all. But this, as we shall see, is the problem raised by the third of Zeno's paradoxes, the Arrow, which we shall examine shortly.

The Achilles Paradox

Before examining the Arrow Paradox, I should briefly mention the second of Zeno's four paradoxes of motion, the Achilles. This, as I mentioned earlier, is really just a variant of the Racecourse Paradox and may be set out as follows. Achilles, A, runs faster than the Tortoise, T, and accordingly A gives T a head start in a race between the two of them. Suppose that T starts at time t_0 and A starts at the later time t_1. Let P_1 be the point in the race at which T arrives when A starts to run, that is, at t_1. By the time, t_2, that A has arrived at P_1, T will have moved on to a point, P_2, some way ahead of A. Similarly, by the time, t_3, that A has arrived at P_2, T will have moved on to another point, P_3, which is still some way ahead of A. And so on ad infinitum (if space and time are continuous and thus infinitely divisible). At each successive time in this infinite series of times, T is ahead of A by a smaller distance—but T is always ahead of A by *some* distance, however small. How, then, can A ever catch up with T? Of course, it can be pointed out that the intervals of time between successive times in the series are progressively smaller, so that if A can catch up with T, he can do so in a finite period of time, since the sum of an infinite converging series of finite quantities can, as we noted earlier, be finite. But, as in the Paradox of the Racecourse, the prior question to be answered is how A can catch up with T *at all*. In effect, indeed, the Achilles Paradox is just a version of the Racecourse Paradox in which the runner, Achilles, has a moving finishing-post instead of a fixed one. That being so, however, the paradox can be resolved in the same way as we resolved the original version of the Racecourse Paradox, and for that reason I shall give it no further attention here.

The Paradox of the Arrow and instantaneous velocity

I turn next, then, to the Paradox of the Arrow. Suppose an arrow to be moving through the air. At any instant of time during its passage from one place to another, the arrow will occupy a part of space which fits it exactly. As it is sometimes put, the arrow will always take up, at any instant of time, a place exactly equal to itself. But how, then, can the arrow ever be *changing* its place—since at any instant of time it is wholly in just *one and the same* place? It is true that the arrow is supposedly in different places at different instants of time, for it must be if it is to move at all. But the problem is that we can apparently never catch it in the act of *changing* its place at any instant of time—and if it never changes its place at any instant of time, how can it be anything other than a purely stationary arrow?

One response that is often made to this supposed paradox is to say that it rests upon a misunderstanding of the nature of motion and, more especially, a misconception of what it is for an object to have a velocity *at an instant of time*. Thus, it may be said, because velocity simply *is* rate of change of distance with respect to change of time, we can only define velocity at an instant of time in terms of distance moved during periods of time surrounding that instant. More precisely, it is proposed that we should define an object's velocity at an instant of time, t, as having the limiting value towards which an infinite series of ratios converges, each member of the series being the ratio of a distance moved by the object to the amount of time taken by it to move that distance, the periods of time in quesion being smaller and smaller intervals surrounding the instant t. We can think of it in something like this way: as a rough approximation of the object's velocity at t, we can say that the value of its velocity at t, in metres per second, is equal to the distance in metres moved by the object during a period of one second which has t as its midpoint, divided by one second. A somewhat less rough approximation would be provided by reducing the period to half a second. A still less rough approximation would be provided by reducing the period to a quarter of a second. And so on ad infinitum. If we now take this infinite series of ratios of distance to time, we shall find that the successive values of the ratios converge upon a limiting value, which may be defined as the object's instantaneous velocity at t.

How is this supposed to dissolve the Paradox of the Arrow? In the following way. If instantaneous velocity should be conceived in the foregoing fashion, then it cannot make sense to ascribe a velocity—and hence motion—to an object *at an instant of time* unless the object undergoes a change of position during a period of time including that instant. No object could acquire an instantaneous velocity of, let us say, 10 metres per second, at an instant of time t, while having zero velocity at all times surrounding t and thus failing to move any distance. Clearly, an object with an instantaneous velocity of 10 metres per second at t does not move any distance at all *at t*. But it must, according to the foregoing conception of instantaneous velocity, move some distance over a period of time which *includes t*. Now, the problem supposedly raised by the Paradox of the Arrow was this. The arrow never appears to be, at any instant of time, *changing* its place—that is, moving at that very instant. But if it never moves at any instant of time, how can it be anything other than a purely stationary arrow? However, according to the conception of instantaneous velocity that has just been advanced, it is simply a mistake to suppose that what distinguishes a moving arrow from a stationary arrow at an instant of time is something that only concerns how the arrows are at that instant. So we should not be at all surprised by the fact that there is no *apparent* difference between a moving and a stationary arrow at an instant of time—and certainly should not infer that, because there is no apparent difference between them, there can be no real difference between them. For, if the foregoing proposal is correct, the real difference between the arrows at an instant of time, *t*, arises from real differences between them at *other* instants of time before and after *t*—in particular, from the fact that the moving arrow is, but the stationary arrow is not, in different places before and after *t*.

However, the foregoing conception of instantaneous velocity is not invulnerable to challenge (as we began to see in Chapter 13). One problem with it is this. Because, on this conception, the velocity of an object at an instant is *defined* in terms of distances moved by the object during periods of time surrounding the instant, it seems that we cannot explain *why* an object changes its position over a period of time by reference to the velocity which it possesses during that period—for any such explanation would be circular. We would just be saying, in effect, that the object changes its position over a certain period of time because it moves a certain distance during that period, which is just to say that it moves a certain distance because it moves a certain distance. But, very plausibly, we *can and should* explain why an object changes its position over a period of time by reference to the velocity which it possesses during that period. It may be true that we can only *measure* the object's velocity at any time by measuring the distance that it moves during a period which includes that time: but this doesn't imply that we should think of the fact that the object has that velocity as simply *consisting* in the fact that the ratio of the distance moved by the object to the length of time it takes to move that distance has a certain value.

Does this mean that the Paradox of the Arrow remains unresolved? Not necessarily. For, drawing on a proposal first sketched in Chapter 13, we can perhaps say that an instantaneous velocity of an object at a time *t* is a *directional tendency* which it possesses at *t*, in virtue of which, if it continues to possess it, it will undergo a subsequent change of spatial position. On this conception, the object's change of position is a consequence of its velocity, not something in terms of which its velocity is defined. But we can still say that there is a real difference, at an instant of time, between a moving and a stationary arrow—a difference which, moreover, does *not* concern how those objects are at other times. For we can say that the arrows differ in respect of their directional tendencies. This is not a difference between them that one could hope to *observe* at *t*, because dispositions—of which tendencies are a variety—are not straightforwardly observable. What we can observe are their *manifestations*. We can observe, for instance, the *dissolving* of the sugar, but not its *solubility*. But its solubility is quite as real a feature of the sugar as is its dissolving. And its solubility explains *why* it dissolves, when it is immersed in an appropriate solvent. In a similar fashion, we may maintain, an object's instantaneous velocity explains why it undergoes a change of spatial position. But it is because an instantaneous velocity is a species of disposition and hence not straightforwardly observable that a moving and a stationary arrow may not *appear* to differ at any instant of time—a fact which the propounder of the Arrow Paradox relies upon in order to perplex us. An instantaneous 'snapshot' of the two arrows at an instant of time would reveal no difference between them: but that, according to the view now being recommended, is because the difference between them, real though it is, is simply not the sort of difference that could be revealed by a snapshot.

How can something begin to move?

We can draw on this alternative conception of an instantaneous velocity to say something about the inverted version of the Paradox of the Racecourse, represented in Fig. 16.2. The problem posed by this version of the paradox is how the runner can even *begin* to move, that is (as we put it), how it can be the case that at a certain instant of time an object is moving, even though it is not moving at any prior instant of time. If an instantaneous velocity is a 'directional tendency', then there seems to be no reason why an object should not acquire this at an instant of time and thus *before* the object has moved any distance at all. By contrast, if an instantaneous velocity can only be ascribed to an object at an instant of time, t, in virtue of distances moved by the object during periods of time surrounding t, then it might appear to make no sense to ascribe an instantaneous velocity to an object at a time, t, before the object has moved any distance at all. However, it may be urged on behalf of the latter conception of instantaneous velocity that, at the instant at which the runner starts the race, his instantaneous velocity should be *zero*—and that this is, in fact, the value of the velocity assigned to him by the method of computation associated with this conception. Indeed, according to this conception of instantaneous velocity, the solution to the inverted version of the Racecourse Paradox is to say that the runner does *not* in fact 'begin to move', in the sense suggested earlier: that is to say, it is not the case, according to this conception, that an object can acquire, at an instant of time, t, a non-zero velocity even though it has zero velocity at all instants of time prior to t. Rather, it will be said, this is how we should understand what it is for an object to 'begin to move' at an instant of time, t: it is for the object to have zero velocity at t but a non-zero velocity at all instants of time succeeding t (until the object stops moving). However, it must still be acknowledged that this account of what it is for an object to 'begin to move' has the counterintuitive consequence that an object cannot acquire a *non-zero* velocity until it has already moved some distance, which prompts the question: how did the object manage to move that distance? That we should find this puzzling provides further evidence, I think, that we do intuitively think of an object's velocity as being something which *explains* why it undergoes a change of position—a notion which, as we have seen, appears to be incompatible with the conception of instantaneous velocity now under scrutiny. But the question of which of the two conceptions is ultimately superior is not one that I shall attempt to settle definitively here.

The Paradox of the Moving Blocks and discrete space-time

The fourth and last of Zeno's four paradoxes of motion is the Paradox of the Moving Blocks, the exact purport of which is somewhat obscure. However, I shall present what seems to be one quite plausible and interesting reconstruction of it. Suppose we have three rows of moving blocks (all of the same size), row A, row B, and row C, with row A moving from east to west at a certain speed and row C moving from west to east at the same speed, while row B, which lies between the other two, is stationary. And suppose we consider a moment of time, t_1, at which the faces of all the blocks are exactly lined up with each other, as is depicted in Fig. 16.4. Now consider a later moment of time, t_2, at which the trailing face of block A_3 is exactly lined up with the leading face of block C_1, as in Fig. 16.5.

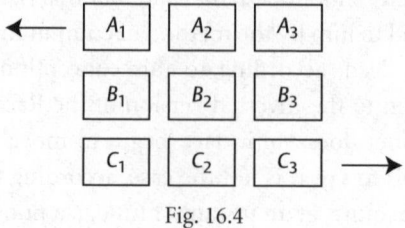

Fig. 16.4

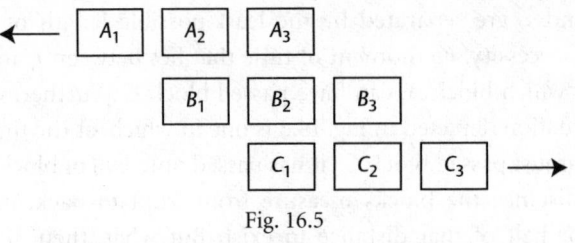

Fig. 16.5

The puzzle is supposed to be this: how can it be the case that, during the interval between t_1 and t_2, block A_3 has passed by *two* complete C blocks while, in the same amount of time, it has passed by only *one* B block—despite the fact that all of the blocks are of exactly the same size?

One's initial thought may be that there is nothing very puzzling about this. Because the A blocks and the C blocks are travelling at the same speed but in opposite directions, their velocity relative to each other is twice the velocity of an A block relative to a B block, since the B blocks are stationary. Perhaps the original propounder of the paradox did not fully comprehend the fact that one and the same object may have two different velocities relative to two different objects which are themselves moving relative to each other. Be that as it may, the example of the moving blocks does appear to create a problem if one supposes that space and time are *discrete* rather than continuous—as one might be tempted to suppose in order to overcome Zeno's other paradoxes of motion (assuming that one is not satisfied with the solutions of these that were proposed earlier). If space and time are discrete, then there is a least possible distance and a least possible length of time, neither of which is divisible. And then the problem posed by the moving blocks is this. Suppose that the moments of time t_1 and t_2 are separated by the least possible length of time, so that block A_3 passes two C blocks, C_3 and C_2, in the least possible length of time. At what time, then, did block A_3 pass block C_3? It must, surely, have passed it at some time *between* t_1 and t_2, when the blocks were spatially related to one another in the way depicted in Fig. 16.6.

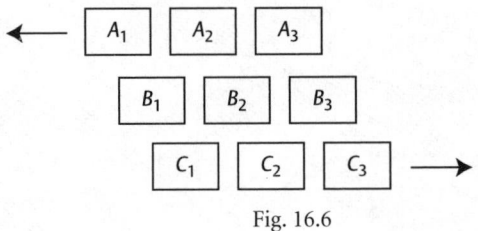

Fig. 16.6

But if t_1 and t_2 are separated by the least possible length of time, then there is, of necessity, *no* moment of time that lies between t_1 and t_2 and so no time at which block A_3 can have passed block C_3. Furthermore, we see that the situation depicted in Fig. 16.6 is one in which, at the time at which block A_3 has just passed block C_3, it has passed only *half* of block B_3, so that, whatever distance the blocks measure from front to back, it should be possible for half of that distance to exist. But what, then, if the blocks measure the least possible distance from front to back? The implication of all this seems to be that there cannot, after all, be either a least possible distance or a least possible length of time, so that space and time must be continuous rather than discrete. But how good the reasoning is for this conclusion I leave to the reader to judge for him or herself.[4]

---

[4] For further discussion of Zeno's paradoxes see, in addition to items already referred to in this chapter, Max Black, *Problems of Analysis: Philosophical Essays* (London: Routledge and Kegan Paul, 1954), Part 2; Adolf Grünbaum, *Modern Science and Zeno's Paradoxes* (London: George Allen and Unwin, 1968); and R. M. Sainsbury, *Paradoxes*, 2nd edn. (Cambridge: Cambridge University Press, 1995), ch. 1.

17

TENSE AND THE REALITY OF TIME

The A series and the B series

The paradoxes of motion that we discussed in the preceding chapter were designed to persuade philosophers that there is something suspect about our conception of change and our apparent experience of it. Motion is perhaps the most obvious and fundamental species of change and so, if the concept of motion can be convicted of harbouring a contradiction, making real motion impossible, we may have to conclude that reality itself is unchanging. This in turn would have a severe impact upon our conception of time as a pervasive feature of reality, especially if we take the view that time without change is impossible (a view that we examined in some detail in Chapter 13). If time without change is impossible and change is impossible, it follows that time itself is impossible—that is to say, it follows that temporality cannot be a genuine feature of reality, in the sense that elements of reality cannot genuinely stand in temporal relations to one another (relations such as *being earlier than* or *being simultaneous with*).

Of course, nothing that we concluded in the preceding chapter gives support to the foregoing line of argument against the reality of time, for we were not persuaded by the alleged paradoxes of motion that even motion—let alone change in general—is impossible. In the present chapter, however, I shall examine another and perhaps more compelling way in which this line of argument against the reality of time may be pursued—one which we owe to the Cambridge philosopher J. M. E. McTaggart, who wrote extensively on this topic in the early years of the twentieth century.[1] (Of course, if McTaggart's argument is correct, he really did no such thing, since there are in reality no 'years' and 'centuries'—but let us pass over the

---

[1] See J. M. E. McTaggart, *The Nature of Existence*, vol. 2 (Cambridge: Cambridge University Press, 1927), ch. 33.

irony of this observation.) In order to understand McTaggart's argument against the reality of time, however, we must first understand an important distinction that he makes between two ways in which events seem to be ordered in time so as to constitute a temporal series. In fact, he speaks of two different temporal series, which he calls the 'A series' and the 'B series', although it is clear that the elements of the series are the same and only the ordering relations between the elements differ, so that we might better speak of two different ways of characterizing a single series rather than of two different series. (In what follows, I should emphasize, I shall be presenting a relatively simple reconstruction of what I take to be the essential features of McTaggart's argument, avoiding detailed matters of textual exegesis and disputes between commentators over finer points of interpretation.)

The difference between McTaggart's A series and his B series is best explained by appeal to two different classes of temporal expression, which we can accordingly call 'A-series expressions' and 'B-series expressions'. A-series expressions include such words and phrases as 'today', 'tomorrow', and 'five weeks ago', while B-series expressions include such words and phrases as 'simultaneously', 'two years earlier than', and 'ten minutes later than'. The important difference between the two classes of expressions is this: a sentence containing an A-series expression may be true at one time but false at another, whereas a sentence whose only temporal expressions are B-series expressions is true at all times if it is true at any time. For instance, the sentence 'It is raining today' may be true on one day but false on the next. By contrast, the sentence 'The Battle of Hastings took place 749 years earlier than the Battle of Waterloo' is true now, will always be true, and, indeed, was even true, it seems, at all times before 1066, the date of the Battle of Hastings. (I acknowledge that not all philosophers would concede this last claim, but for the time being let us not regard it as open to challenge: I shall return to the issue at the end of the chapter.) Of course, no one living earlier than 1815, the date of the Battle of Waterloo, was in a position to *know* that this sentence is true (unless gifted with precognitive powers) or even in a position to refer the Battle of Waterloo, which for any such person was still a future event. But we must distinguish between what is true at a time and what is known to be true at that time. And, given that we now know it to be true that the Battle of Hastings took place 749 years earlier the Battle of Waterloo, we apparently have to conclude that, even before any human being at all existed, it was true that the Battle of Hastings would take place seven hundred and forty-nine years earlier than the Battle of Waterloo.

Here it may be objected that, even if we accept that at all times before 1066 it was true that the Battle of Hastings would take place 749 years earlier than the Battle of Waterloo, it does not follow that the sentence 'The Battle of Hastings took place 749 years earlier than the Battle of Waterloo' was true at those times, for this sentence is expressed in the *past tense*. What was true at those times, rather, was the *future-tensed* sentence 'The Battle of Hastings will have taken place 749 years earlier than the Battle of Waterloo'—or, rather less convolutedly, 'The Battle of Waterloo will take place 749 years later than the Battle of Hastings'. This, after all, is what a soothsayer might have pronounced at such a time. The complication that we are running into here is that *tensed verbs* themselves qualify as A-series expressions and tensed verbs are pretty well ubiquitous in everyday language. If we want to construct a sentence which genuinely contains only B-series temporal expressions, then we must construct one whose verbs are *tenseless*. Such sentences do occasionally occur even in everyday language, examples being the sentences 'Two plus two is four' and 'Courage is a virtue', in which the verb 'is' does not have a present-tense sense. However, nothing prevents us from making much more extensive use of tenseless verbs. Rather than saying 'Rain is now falling in Durham', for example, I could say 'Rain falls in Durham on 12 November 2000', in which the verb 'falls' is tenseless, like the 'is' in 'Two plus two is four'. I am not claiming here that 'Rain is now falling in Durham' has exactly the *same meaning* as—is synonymous with—'Rain falls in Durham on 12 November 2000': patently, it does not. But 'Rain falls in Durham on 12 November 2000' does provide an example of a sentence containing no A-series expressions and consequently one whose truth or falsity is (plausibly) invariable over time. If this sentence is true today, it is (plausibly) true at all times. By contrast, 'Rain is now falling in Durham', while it may be true today (12 November 2000), may yet be false tomorrow (since the sun may be shining in Durham on 13 November 2000).

With these clarifications and qualifications in mind, let us return now to the A series and the B series themselves. The temporal order of events may be described using either A-series expressions or B-series expressions. Consider, for instance, the following three events: the Battle of Hastings, the Battle of Agincourt, and the Battle of Waterloo. Using only B-series expressions, we may say that the Battle of Hastings takes place earlier than the Battle of Agincourt, which in turn takes place earlier than the Battle of

Waterloo (noting that 'takes place' here is to be understood as tenseless). Given that this is true—as it is—it is always true. But we can also say, for instance, that the Battle of Agincourt took place longer ago than the Battle of Waterloo and that the Battle of Hastings took place even longer ago than that. In saying this, we attribute the same temporal order to the three events as we do when we describe their temporal order using only B-series expressions, but now we do so using A-series expressions. Although it is now true to say that the Battle of Agincourt took place long ago, it was not always true to say this, for at one time it was still a future event. At one time, indeed—before 1066—it would have been true to say the following: the Battle of Agincourt will take place in the more distant future than the Battle of Hastings and the Battle of Waterloo will take place in the still more distant future. This way of describing the temporal relationships between the three events would have put them in the same temporal order (the correct one) but by using different A-series expressions. It is no longer true, however, to say that the Battle of Agincourt will take place in the more distant future than the Battle of Hastings and that the Battle of Waterloo will take place in the still more distant future. Now we have to say that the Battle of Agincourt took place longer ago than the Battle of Water-loo and that the Battle of Hastings took place even longer ago than that. This, of course, is because all of these events, which were once future events, are now past events, owing to the so-called *passage of time*. So, in short, events fall into the A series in virtue of occurring in the present or in the more or less distant past or future, whereas events fall into the B series in virtue of standing in earlier/later relations to one another. Both series confer the same temporal order upon events, but do so in quite different ways. And, crucially, the A-series 'position' of an event—its status as a past, present, or future event—is itself subject to change, even though this change does not affect its place in the temporal order of all events.

Change and the passage of time

McTaggart believes that temporality cannot be adequately described using B-series expressions alone. He believes that time essentially involves change and that change cannot be adequately characterized without using A-series expressions. That time essentially involves change follows, it seems, from the fact that time just is the dimension of change—from the fact, that is, that it is *in* time that change necessarily occurs. Of course, we do also speak of non-temporal 'change', as when we describe the width of a river as 'changing'—'getting bigger'—as it approaches the sea. But this would appear to be a purely metaphorical use of the word 'change'. Change in the literal sense is change *in time*, not in space or in any other 'dimension of variation'. But, even accepting this, why does McTaggart believe that change cannot be adequately characterized without using A-series expressions? Chiefly, it would seem, because he considers the *passage of time* itself to involve a species of change which is a prerequisite of any kind of temporal change at all.

Here it is important to appreciate that the passage of time is supposed to be a process which concerns, primarily, *events* and *times*, rather than persisting objects—although it may also be taken to concern the latter derivatively, in virtue of the events in which such objects participate and the times at which they exist. A persisting object, which exists at different times, may undergo a change of its properties or qualities over time (as we saw in Chapter 3, though we also saw there that such change raises problems of its own). For instance, a banana may change in colour from being green to being yellow. As time passes, the banana will also 'get older' and this is, indeed, a kind of 'change' which befalls it as a consequence of the passage of time. But whereas the banana's turning yellow clearly constitutes an event, which occurs at a certain time, it is much more questionable whether we should say that the banana's getting a day older is really an 'event' of any kind (as we saw in Chapter 13). However—and this is the important point—events themselves and the times at which they occur appear to undergo *genuine* change purely as a consequence of the passage of time: a kind of change which persisting objects cannot really be said to undergo. For events and times, it seems, change from being future to being present and from being present to being past. Persisting objects, by contrast, do not literally change from being future to being present or from being present to being past—although, indeed, the *times at which such objects exist* may be said to change in this way. And yet, in McTaggart's view, it is only if events and times do indeed undergo this special sort of change that we can say that time itself really exists and that persisting objects may consequently undergo the characteristic sorts of changes that they are thought to undergo, such as changes in their properties or qualities. In short, it is McTaggart's opinion that genuine change of any kind, including the sorts of changes that persisting objects are thought to undergo, cannot be explained without resort to A-series expressions.

But why, it may be asked, can't we adequately characterize and explain the sorts of changes that persisting objects are thought to undergo purely by recourse to B-series expressions? Consider again, for instance, the banana which undergoes a change of colour from being green to being yellow. Why can't we adequately characterize this change simply by saying that at one time the banana is (tenselessly) green whereas at a later time it is (tenselessly) yellow—employing a sentence containing only tenseless verbs and the B-series expression 'later than'? Well, this characterization would perhaps be adequate if the *times* to which it refers could themselves be characterized without even implicit recourse to A-series expressions— but it is questionable whether this can be done. One way in which the difficulty here can be brought out is this. Recall our earlier example of the river which 'changes' in width along its length, a fact which we may describe by saying that at one place the river is narrow whereas at another place the river is broad. Why doesn't this difference qualify as a literal *change* in the river, of the sort that we would have if the river were (in the same place) narrow on one day and broad on the next day? Simply because in the former case the ascriptions of width are made with respect to *place* rather than with respect to *time*. But this means that, unless we *already* have some satisfactory way of distinguishing time from space as a 'dimension of variation', we cannot distinguish between the literal change of the banana in colour and the merely metaphorical 'change' of the river in width. And, in McTaggart's opinion, this prior distinction can only be captured by drawing on the fact that we think of time, but not space, as being the dimension in which events (and times themselves) undergo change from being future to being present and from being present to being past—a species of change which can only be described using A-series expressions. In short, without calling upon A-series expressions, we have no principled way of distinguishing between time and space as dimensions of variation and so no way of characterizing adequately even the kinds of change which it is thought that persisting objects can genuinely undergo.

McTaggart's argument for the unreality of time

What we need to discuss next is why McTaggart thought that time must be unreal. As we shall soon see in more detail, his reason is that, in his opinion, our use of A-series expressions inevitably involves us in contradiction, so that such expressions cannot be taken to describe anything existing in reality. Thus, in summary, his argument for the unreality of time has the following form:

(1) Time essentially involves change.

(2) Change can only be explained in terms of A-series expressions.

(3) A-series expressions involve contradiction and so cannot describe reality.

Therefore,

(4) Time is unreal.

And what we now need to do is to focus on McTaggart's reasons for maintaining premise (3) of this argument. For the argument would certainly appear to be valid and hence the only way of avoiding its apparently unwelcome conclusion is to challenge one or more of the premises. My own opinion is that, of these premises, premise (3) is the one most open to challenge, although there are a good many other philosophers who think otherwise.[2] Indeed, contemporary philosophers of time are customarily divided into two classes—'A theorists' and 'B theorists'—the first of whom typically accept premise (2) and deny premise (3) while the second typically deny premise (2) and accept premise (3). This is a division to which I shall return later, however, after we have examined the putative grounds for holding premise (3).

Does the A series involve a contradiction?

McTaggart's reason for holding premise (3) is this. He contends, on the one hand, that the A-series expressions 'past', 'present', and 'future', used to characterize the A-series 'positions' of events, are mutually incompatible, inasmuch as it is contradictory to describe one and the same event as being both a past event, a present event, and a future event. If an event is a past event, then, *ipso facto*, it is *not* either a present event or a future event. Similarly, if it is a present event, then it is neither a past nor a future event, and if it is a future event, then it is neither a past nor a present event. And yet, it seems, the passage of time requires that one and the same event can,

[2] See further my 'The Indexical Fallacy in McTaggart's Proof of the Unreality of Time', *Mind* 96 (1987), 62–70, and my 'McTaggart's Paradox Revisited', *Mind* 101 (1993), 323–6. For a contrary view, see D. H. Mellor, *Real Time* (Cambridge: Cambridge University Press, 1981), ch. 6, and *Real Time II* (London: Routledge, 1998), ch. 7.

and indeed must, be past, present, and future: for the passage of time is precisely the process whereby an event changes from being future to being present and from being present to being past—and if an event *changes* in these respects, then it must indeed be characterizable as future, present, and past, in that order.

Now, the obvious response to this apparent problem is to point out that, in order to participate in the passage of time, an event does not have to be future, present, and past *all at the same time*: it only has to be *successively* future, present, and past. That is to say, an event only has to be future at one time, present at a later time, and past at a still later time. Contradiction would only arise, it may be urged, if we had to say that one and the same event must be future, present, and past at one and the same time—but we do not have to, and indeed should not, say this. However, McTaggart does not think that this move will enable us to escape the threat of contradiction. For, so far, we have only characterized the *successive* nature of an event's being future, present, and past *in B-series terms*, that is, in terms of an event's being future at one time, present at a later time, and past at a still later time. In order to characterize this succession as being truly temporal in nature, we need to be able to characterize it in A-series terms as well. What we must say, then, is something like this: an event which is future at the present moment of time is present at a future moment of time and past at a still more distantly future moment of time. However, moments of time, like events, participate in the passage of time: each moment of time, just like each event, is future, present, and past. Once again, we can attempt to avoid the threat of contradiction which this imposes by saying that each moment of time is only *successively* future, present, and past. But, once again, we have to be able to characterize this succession in A-series terms. We seem, thus, to have embarked upon an infinite regress, at each step of which we can only attempt to avoid a threat of contradiction by invoking the next step, at which an exactly similar threat of contradiction arises.

Tenses and the regress problem

On the face of it, this is a rather compelling argument for the truth of premise (3). But perhaps it is not as conclusive as it may at first appear to be. It may be that an A theorist—someone who accepts premise (2), that change can only be explained in terms of A-series expressions—can resist McTaggart's reasoning, perhaps by rejecting certain assumptions that

McTaggart makes. We have been assuming so far, along with McTaggart, that moments of time participate in the so-called passage of time, just as events do. But perhaps it is a mistake to *reify* moments of time—to treat them as real entities, to be included in our ontology along with events and persisting objects. Suppose we exclude moments of time from our ontology: how, then, can we hope to characterize, in A-series terms, the successive nature of an event's being future, present, and past? We shall no longer be able to characterize this in terms, say, of the event's being future at the present moment of time, present at a future moment of time, and past at a still more distantly future moment of time. What could we say instead? We could say, perhaps, that an event which is *presently* future will *futurely* be present and *still more futurely* be past. Similarly, we could say that an event which is *presently* past was *pastly* present and was *still more pastly* future. This is hardly an everyday way of talking, invoking as it does the unfamiliar A-series adverbs 'pastly' and 'futurely', modelling these on the existing adverb 'presently'. However, it seems perfectly intelligible. But where now, exactly, is the threat of contradiction supposed to arise, allegedly only to be deflected by embarking, futilely, upon an infinite regress?

Perhaps it will be urged that the seeds of the regress can already be seen in the use of the past, present, and future *tenses* in the sentences just used to characterize, in A-series terms, the successiveness of an event's being future, present, and past. I said, thus, that an event which *is* presently future *will* futurely be present and *will* still more futurely be past, and that an event which *is* presently past *was* pastly present and *was* still more pastly future. However, it seems to me that this charge is unfounded because, in these sentences, the various tenses of the verbs do not appear to contribute anything to the meaning of the sentences over and above what is contributed by the A-series adverbs which qualify them. To say, for example, that a certain event 'is presently future'—where the 'is' is *present-tensed* rather than tenseless—is to say nothing more than that the event 'is future', where the 'is' is present-tensed, or that it 'is presently future', where the 'is' is tenseless. Similarly, to say, for the purposes that I did, that an event 'was pastly present' is to say no more than that it 'was present', or that it 'is pastly present', where the 'is' is tenseless. This is not to deny that, for certain *other* purposes, one can use the construction 'was pastly' to mean something like 'is pastly past', where the 'is' is tenseless. This, in effect, is what the pluperfect tense achieves when we say something like 'John had already eaten when Mary arrived', meaning that his eating was already past when the past event of Mary's arrival occurred. My point is merely that, in the sentences used earlier to characterize, in A-series terms, the successive-ness of an event's being future, present and past, the tenses were *not*, in fact, contributing anything to the meaning of the sentences over and above what was contributed by the A-series adverbs qualifying them. That being so, those sentences exhibit, after all, no signs of the feared regress.

Perhaps, however, the threat of a regress will instead be raised in the following way. Perhaps it will now be said that, in order to account, in A-series terms, for the way in which events participate in the passage of time, we shall have to say not merely that every event is successively future, present, and past, but also that every event is successively *futurely present, presently present*, and *pastly present*. However, it does not seem to me that these two successions are in any way different. For an event to be 'futurely present'—for it to be going to happen—is just for it to be a *future* event. Every event is inevitably 'present' when and only when it takes place. But another possible objection, which is superficially more substantial, is this. Every event, it would seem, is *at some time X-ly Y*, where 'Y' stands for any one of the A-series adjectives 'past', 'present', and 'future' and 'X-ly' stands for any one of the A-series adverbs 'pastly', 'presently', and 'futurely': and yet no event, on pain of contradiction, can be characterized in all of these nine ways at *the same* time—whence, if one is an A theorist, one must distinguish between the times at which the same event can be character-ized in all these different ways by introducing a *third* level of A-series expressions and thereby embarking once more upon the feared regress.[3]

The first thing to be said about this objection is that it once again invokes *times*, which, on behalf of the A theorist, we had decided to exclude from our ontology. But let us set that issue aside now. The second and more important thing to be said is that, even if it is true that (as I put it) every event is at some time *X-ly Y*, it seems that this is really nothing more than an innocuous consequence of the original point that every event is successively future, present, and past: it is certainly not clear that it involves us either in contradiction or in a vicious infinite regress. Consider, for instance, the Battle of Hastings. At one time—for example, in 1050—it was futurely future, because at the then future time of 1060, it was still a future event. Equally, however, in 1050 the Battle of Hastings was also futurely past and futurely present: it was futurely past, because at the then future time of 1070, it was a past event; and it was futurely present, because at the

---

[3] See further Michael Dummett, 'A Defence of McTaggart's Proof of the Unreality of Time', *Philosophical Review* 69 (1960), 497–504, reprinted in his *Truth and Other Enigmas* (London: Duckworth, 1978).

then future time of 1066, it was a present event. Now, there was also a time at which the Battle of Hastings was pastly future—for example, in 1080, because at the then past time of 1060, it was a future event. At that time, 1080, the Battle of Hastings was also pastly past and pastly present, for reasons which should now be obvious. It is true that in 1050, when the Battle of Hastings was futurely future, futurely present, and futurely past, it was *not* also pastly future, pastly present, and pastly past, as it was in 1080. But none of this is particularly surprising or perplexing, once we understand how these A-series expressions work. Moreover, there seems to be no reason, in principle, why we should object to the use of third-level (and higher) A-series expressions. These would only pose a problem for the A theorist if it could be argued that the A theorist can neither make sense of nor apply first- and second-level A-series expressions until he has already made sense of and can apply A-series expressions of every higher level. But I see no reason to suppose that the A theorist is in this predicament.

Note also that there are significant differences between the objection that we have just been examining and the problem that McTaggart originally raised. The problem that he raised drew on two considerations. The first was that the A-series expressions 'past', 'present', and 'future', used to characterize the A-series 'positions' of events, are mutually incompatible, inasmuch as it is contradictory to describe one and the same event as being a past event, a present event, and a future event. The second was that the passage of time apparently requires that one and the same event can, and indeed must, be past, present, and future—a point to which we envisaged the A theorist responding by saying that an event which is presently future is not also presently present and presently past (which would indeed involve a contradiction), but only futurely present and still more futurely past. Now, however, regarding the nine second-level A-series expressions of the form '*X*-ly *Y*', we have just seen that these are *not* all mutually incompatible. For instance, in 1080, it was correct to describe the Battle of Hastings as being pastly future, pastly present, and pastly past and, indeed, also as being presently past. And, while it may be conceded, as we have just seen, that every event is *at some time X-ly Y*, for each possible value of '*X*' and '*Y*', there is no suggestion that every event must *successively* take on each of these second-level A-series characteristics, one at a time and in a certain order, paralleling at a higher level the way in which each event, through the passage of time, must be successively future, present, and past. Rather, the order in which an event takes on certain combinations of the second-level characteristics simply duplicates the order in which it takes on the first-level characteristics: first of all the event is presently future but also futurely future, futurely present, and futurely past; then the event is presently present; and finally the event is presently past but also pastly future, pastly present, and pastly past. What we see here is simply the ordinary effect of the passage of time, from future to present to past. Altogether, then, it would seem that the attempt to argue that the A theorist's conception of time and its passage forces him into either a contradiction or a vicious infinite regress is ultimately confused and unconvincing. Its superficial appeal arises, I suspect, chiefly from the delight that philosophers seem to take in concocting what appear to be paradoxes. When we press them to explain in detail how the alleged contradiction arises, we all too often find that the seeming paradox crumbles in their hands. That, I think, is what we find in the case of McTaggart's reasoning in defence of premise (3) of his argument against the reality of time.

A diagnosis of McTaggart's mistake

Lest it be suspected that I have escaped from McTaggart's conclusion by sleight of hand, let me say quite explicitly where I think that his argument falls down. It does so, I believe, at the point at which he maintains that, in order to account for the passage of time, we must say that every event is past, present, and future. My response is that we need not, and should not, say any such thing. What we *should* say, and what it suffices for us to say in order to account for the passage of time, is something rather more complicated, but at the same time something which poses no threat whatever of harbouring a contradiction. It is this.[4] Every event is such that it is (i) either pastly past or presently past or futurely past and (ii) either pastly present or presently present or futurely present and (iii) either pastly future or presently future or futurely future. What we have here is a *conjunction of disjunctions*. Some of the nine disjuncts are, indeed, mutually incompatible. For instance, an event which is futurely present cannot also be pastly present. However, each event needs to be characterizable by at most *one* disjunct from each group of three in order for it to satisfy the principle—and this it can be without being characterized by mutually incompatible disjuncts. Consider, for instance, the Battle of Hastings. For

---

[4] See further my 'Tense and Persistence', in Robin Le Poidevin (ed.), *Questions of Time and Tense* (Oxford: Clarendon Press, 1998), or my *The Possibility of Metaphysics: Substance, Identity, and Time* (Oxford: Clarendon Press, 1998), 91.

reasons explained earlier, this event is pastly past, presently past, and futurely past (thus satisfying conjunct (i)), it is pastly present (thus satisfying conjunct (ii)), and it is pastly future (thus satisfying conjunct (iii)). But it is not presently present or presently future (which would conflict with its being presently past) and it is not futurely present or futurely future (which would conflict with its being pastly past and pastly present). My suggestion, then, is that McTaggart confuses the untenable claim that every event is past, present, and future with the more complicated but perfectly tenable claim that I have just articulated. And the latter claim is all that is needed to sustain the A theorist's notion of the passage of time.

The B theorist's conception of time and tense

If the foregoing diagnosis is correct, we need not conclude, with McTaggart, that time is unreal, because we can reject premise (3) of his argument. However, this alone does not suffice to show that the A theory of time is correct. The A theorist still has to contend with the B theorist's claim that premise (2) of McTaggart's argument—that change can only be explained in terms of A-series expressions—is false. (We have already noted McTaggart's reasons for believing (2) to be true, but perhaps those reasons can be challenged.) The B theorist's view is that A-series expressions—expressions such as 'yesterday', 'now', and 'two years ago'—do not serve to characterize features of mind-independent temporal reality. As it is sometimes put, the B theorist holds that there are no 'tensed facts', only 'tenseless' ones. At the same time, the B theorist maintains (if s/he is sensible) that sentences containing A-series expressions cannot simply be translated, without alteration of meaning, into sentences whose only temporal expressions are B-series expressions. To use an earlier example, the B theorist will accept that 'Rain is now falling in Durham', even when spoken on 12 November 2000, does not simply *mean* 'Rain falls in Durham on 12 November 2000'. So what kind of meaning *do* A-series expressions have, according to the B theorist, given that they do not have the same meaning as B-series expressions and do not serve to characterize features of mind-independent temporal reality? The answer is that the B theorist regards A-series expressions as being merely a species of *indexical* or *token-reflexive* expression, exactly on a par with such spatial expressions as 'here' and 'twenty miles away'. What makes the sentence 'Newcastle is twenty miles away' true, when that sentence is spoken in Durham, is the fact that

Durham is twenty miles away from Newcastle. Similarly, according to the B theorist, what makes the sentence 'The Battle of Waterloo took place 185 years ago' true, when that sentence is spoken in 2000, is the fact that 2000 is 185 years later than the year of the Battle of Waterloo, 1815. This fact, which is here reported using only the B-series expression 'later than', is a 'tenseless fact'. So, more generally, according to the B theorist it is always and only tenseless facts that make tensed sentences true (where by 'tensed sentences' I mean sentences which contain A-series expressions). From this the B theorist concludes that a perfectly adequate ontology of time has no need of A-series expressions, for everything that we can meaningfully say about time and temporal relations has its truth or falsehood determined by purely tenseless facts. For the B theorist, A-series expressions have only practical, not theoretical, value. If I need to catch a train at noon on 12 November 2000, I need to know whether *today* is 12 November 2000 and whether it is *now* earlier or later than noon. But what I know when I know that today is 12 November 2000 is not, according to the B theorist, a tensed fact—the fact that today is 12 November 2000—for, according to the B theorist, there is no such fact for me to know.

Is the passage of time illusory?

Whether or not we can ultimately make sense of the B theorist's view of these matters, the A theorist will still complain that the B theory of time treats the passage of time as being at best an illusion. It is questionable whether what remains, when we strip away the notion of the passage of time from our everyday conception of time, still deserves to be called a conception of *time*. In any case, very arguably we should only strip away that notion if it is, for some reason, incoherent or otherwise defective. But is it? McTaggart's argument does not seem to show that it is. However, perhaps there are other and better arguments for thinking that the passage of time is illusory. One consideration that is sometimes advanced is this.[5] If time passes, then there must, presumably, be some *rate* at which it passes, but what could that rate possibly be? We do, of course, sometimes speak of time as passing 'quickly' or 'slowly'—slowly, for instance, when we have a

[5] See further D. C. Williams, 'The Myth of Passage', *Journal of Philosophy* 48 (1951), 457–72, reprinted in Richard M. Gale (ed.), *The Philosophy of Time: A Collection of Essays* (Garden City, NY: Anchor Doubleday & Co., Inc., 1967).

tedious or monotonous task to complete. But here, clearly, we are referring to a subjective feature of our experience of temporality rather than an objective feature of temporality itself. How could it make sense to speak of an *objective* rate, or 'speed', at which time passes? Well, we could of course respond by saying that time passes objectively at the rate of one second per second, or one hour per hour—in other words, at the uniform rate of one unit of time per unit of time. This response seems to be technically unimpeachable but at the same time oddly vacuous. Another thing that we could say, in my view quite correctly, is that it is wrong to think of the passage of time as a kind of *motion*—an error fostered, no doubt, by our use of the verb 'pass' to describe this phenomenon. Metaphors of motion abound in our talk about time: we speak, for instance, of time as a 'river' and of its 'flowing'. But we should not be tempted to construe these metaphors literally. If the passage of time really were a kind of motion, then, since motion involves change of position with respect to time, it seems that we would have to think of the passage of time as involving a change of 'position' of the moments of time with respect to some second-order or second-level dimension of time. In other words, it seems that we would have to suppose there to be two different kinds of time, or at least two different temporal dimensions—and if two, then presumably more than two and perhaps even infinitely many. This is not, perhaps, inconceivable: but we do not want to be driven to embrace this idea for the wrong or bad reasons.[6] A bad reason for embracing it, it seems to me, would be the belief that the passage of time is literally a kind of motion. In the end, maybe the A theorist should simply say this: the passage of time is something that is objectively real, but is at the same time a feature of reality that is so fundamental that we should not try to reduce it to or model it on any other kind of feature of reality. There is nothing defeatist or intellectually cowardly about taking such a stance. Some features of reality, after all, must be fundamental and irreducible: and the passage of time, if it is real, has as good a claim as any to have this status.

[6] For discussion, see Murray MacBeath, 'Time's Square', in Robin Le Poidevin and Murray MacBeath (eds.), *The Philosophy of Time* (Oxford: Oxford University Press, 1993).

Dynamic conceptions of time and the reality of the future

The distinction between those theories of time which hold the passage of time to be real and those which do not is often described as a distinction between 'dynamic' and 'static' conceptions of time—although these terms, depending as they do on metaphors of motion, harbour certain dangers, for reasons that have just been indicated. Static conceptions of time are often said to represent all the moments of time as being 'stretched out' in a 'line', all the parts of which are equally real—whereas dynamic conceptions of time are often said to represent different parts of time as having a different ontological status, depending on whether they are past, present, or future. Thus many dynamic conceptions of time treat the future—and sometimes also the past—as being 'unreal', or at least as being 'less real' than the present, which is treated as being pre-eminently 'real'. The doctrine of *presentism*, indeed, regards *only* the present as being real (see Chapter 3). It is sometimes objected against such views that they are inconsistent with the doctrine of the relativity of simultaneity, which is a consequence of Einstein's special theory of relativity—the problem being that if, as the doctrine implies, events that are 'past' or 'present' relative to one frame of reference may be 'future' with respect to another frame of reference, and yet the future (unlike the past or present) is unreal, then reality itself must be frame-dependent or relative, which seems absurd.[7] However, as we saw in Chapter 14, the doctrine of the relativity of simultaneity, consistent though it is with the available empirical evidence, is not altogether unassailable and it is possible, in principle, to reconcile an absolute theory of time with the very empirical evidence that appears to support the doctrine of the relativity of simultaneity. It is not inconceivable that a compelling metaphysical argument for the reality of the passage of time could exist, which would rationally commit us to denying the doctrine of the relativity of simultaneity and therewith Einstein's special theory of relativity—though I do not claim to be in possession of such an argument myself.

The question of whether the future is 'real' has an obvious, if also rather

---

[7] See, for example, Hilary Putnam, 'Time and Physical Geometry', *Journal of Philosophy* 64 (1967), 240–7, reprinted in his *Mathematics, Matter and Method: Philosophical Papers, Volume 1* (Cambridge: Cambridge University Press, 1975). For an opposing argument, see J. R. Lucas, *The Future: An Essay on God, Temporality and Truth* (Oxford: Blackwell, 1989), 7–8 and 219–20.

contentious, connection with the truth or falsehood of the doctrine of *determinism*—to the extent, indeed, that some philosophers consider that an acceptance of the static conception of time is logically incompatible with a belief in the existence of genuine choice or 'free will'. Earlier, it may be recalled, I assumed that a tenseless sentence, such as 'Rain falls in Durham on 12 November 2000', is, if true at any time, then true at all times. Certainly, a typical B theorist would be happy to say this. But consider what an A theorist should say regarding the truth or falsehood of the future-tensed sentence 'Rain will fall in Durham on 12 November 2000', spoken, say, on 12 November 1995. If such a theorist regards the future as unreal, should he not say that this sentence, spoken on that date, is *neither true nor false*—the reason being that, according to the dynamic conception of time, reality apparently does not include, at that date, any future facts which can make the sentence true or false? Perhaps so.[8] However, against this suggestion it may be remarked that, after the passage of five years, one of the following two present-tensed sentences will be true and the other one false: 'Rain is falling in Durham on 12 November 2000' and 'Rain is not falling in Durham on 12 November 2000'. Suppose, then, that the first of these two sentences turns out to be true. Then will it not have been *true*, five years earlier, to assert 'Rain will be falling in Durham on 12 November 2000'? But, equally, if the second of the two present-tensed sentences turns out to be true, will it not have been *false*, five years earlier, to assert 'Rain will be falling in Durham on 12 November 2000'? Either way, then, it seems that the future-tensed sentence 'Rain will be falling in Durham on 12 November 2000', spoken on 12 November 1995, must have a truth value, even if that truth value is unknowable at the time.

I shall not attempt to resolve this dispute here, turning as it does quite as much on the nature of truth as on the nature of time. But I might remark that it doesn't seem to me at all inevitable that an A theorist—that is, a philosopher who adheres to the dynamic conception of time—should regard the future as being unreal; nor does it seem to me that a rejection of the doctrine of determinism requires one to regard the future as being unreal.[9] Indeed, if, as I have been assuming hitherto, an A theorist is someone who thinks that the passage of time is a process through which

---

[8] For discussion, see Michael Tooley, *Time, Tense, and Causation* (Oxford: Clarendon Press, 1997), 307 ff.

[9] See Storrs McCall, *A Model of the Universe: Space-Time, Probability, and Decision* (Oxford: Clarendon Press, 1994), 194 ff., and, for discussion of McCall's position, Tooley, *Time, Tense, and Causation*, 239 ff.

events change from being future to being present and from being present to being past, then it might be urged that such a theorist had better *not* deny the reality of the future—for unless future events are in some sense real, how can one regard them as *changing* from being future to being present and from being present to being past? If one denies the reality of the future, then, it seems, one can at best adhere to a rather different sort of A theory—one which holds that the passage of time is a process through which, in some mysterious way, the sum total of reality is continually being 'added to', with events first springing into existence as present events and then 'receding' into the ever-growing past.[10] How far one can make sense of such a conception of time and existence I leave for the reader to judge for him or herself.[11]

[10] See C. D. Broad, *Scientific Thought* (London: Routledge and Kegan Paul, 1923), ch. 2, and Tooley, *Time, Tense, and Causation*, ch. 2.

[11] For further material on the topics of this chapter see, in addition to the items already mentioned, L. Nathan Oaklander and Quentin Smith (eds.), *The New Theory of Time* (New Haven, Conn: Yale University Press, 1994).

18

CAUSATION AND THE DIRECTION
OF TIME

Temporal asymmetry and the structure of time

Even if we assume time to be a dimension of reality, comparable in some respects with the three (known) dimensions of space—although this assumption is itself open to challenge—it seems manifest that time differs radically from any of the spatial dimensions in being intrinsically *directed*. More precisely, all events and moments in time would appear to be ordered, by certain intrinsically asymmetrical temporal relations in which they stand to one another, so as to fall into a single temporal sequence. (Here I ignore, for the time being, considerations arising from Einstein's special theory of relativity which may lead us to suppose that events do not all occur in a unique temporal sequence, on the grounds that events which are simultaneous with respect to one frame of reference may not be so with respect to another.) An 'A theorist', as we saw in the previous chapter, would say that events and moments in time are ordered by being (more or less) *past* or (more or less) *future* relative to the present moment. In contrast, a 'B theorist' would say that events and moments in time are ordered by being *earlier* than or *later* than one another—'simultaneous' events being those which stand in exactly the same 'earlier than' or 'later than' relations as each other to all other events (again ignoring, for the time being, the supposed relativity of simultaneity). Whichever description we prefer, however, the important point is that these asymmetrical temporal relations confer both a 'forward' and a 'backward' direction on the temporal sequence of events and moments—the 'forward' direction being from *past to future* or from *earlier to later* events and moments, the 'backward' direction being from *future to past* or from *later to earlier* events and moments. When philosophers and scientists talk of 'the' direction of time, they ordinarily intend to refer to its 'forward' direction, although often they also mean to allude to the very fact that time is directed or asymmetrical in the ways that we have just described. It might be clearer, then, if we alluded to the latter fact by speaking of the *directedness* or *asymmetry* of time and if, when speaking of temporal *direction*, we referred, quite explicitly, either to the 'forward' or to the 'backward' direction of time, thereby acknowledging that time strictly has *two* directions.

Now, of course, we should acknowledge that there is also a perfectly good sense in which each *spatial* dimension may be said to have two 'directions', simply because all of the points in any straight line are positioned relative to one another in a unique order, as we saw when discussing Zeno's paradoxes of motion in Chapter 16. Thus, for example, all of the points in a straight line between any two given points, X and Y, are ordered by being *further from*, or *less far from*, one of the points X and Y: for instance, the midpoint of the line is less far from X than is the point Y. None the less, it seems clear that there is no intrinsic difference between the two different 'directions' of a line—between, say, the *east-to-west* direction and the *west-to-east* direction, or the *north-to-south* direction and the *south-to-north* direction—in the way in which there appears to be an intrinsic difference between the two different directions of time. It is true that it might turn out, purely as a matter of contingent fact, that a particular spatial direction has some special physical significance—as we discover when we find that a compass needle naturally points north. However, this sort of phenomenon, we assume, arises not from some internal asymmetry in space itself or in the spatial relations between points of space, but only from some contingent asymmetry in the distribution or orientation of some physical entity existing in space, such as the direction of the earth's magnetic field. The asymmetry of time, we suppose, is internal to time itself, rather than just being a matter of the asymmetrical distribution or orientation of physical entities existing in time. So we suppose. But we might be mistaken—and this is a possibility that we shall have to contemplate in due course. For the time being, however, I shall continue to accept the supposition.

Another thing that we commonly assume concerning the nature of time is that, although 'linear', it is not 'circular' or 'closed'. That is to say, if an event e_1 is earlier than another event e_2, then it is not also the case that e_2 is earlier than e_1. We do not so readily assume that the equivalent principle holds for space: for although the space of Euclidean geometry is not closed, we can certainly envisage the possibility that physical space might be 'curved', so that by travelling continuously in a 'straight' line— understanding this to be the shortest route between any two points—one might eventually return to one's point of departure (a possibility that we considered when discussing the problem of incongruent counterparts in Chapter 15). But even if time were circular, this would not prevent it from being 'directed', in the sense explained earlier. There could—and plausibly would—still be both a 'forward' and a 'backward' direction of time, even though every event would be in the future of every other event and also in the past of every other event: for instance, my birth would lie both in the past, relative to the present moment, and also in the future (albeit, presumably, only in the very distant future). Again, however, I shall assume for present purposes that time is not circular, interesting though it might be to speculate on the implications of its being so.[1]

To accept that time is not 'circular' or 'closed' is not, incidentally, to assume either that time does, or that it does not, have a 'beginning' or an 'end'. Nor is it to assume that time does, or that it does not, have infinite duration. If time were non-circular and of infinite duration in both 'directions' (that is, if both past and future were of infinite duration), then, of course, time would have neither a beginning nor an end. But a non-circular time of *finite* duration could equally lack either a beginning or an end, or both. This is because time could be topologically analogous to a line of finite length which lacks an endpoint at either or both of its extremities. Think, for instance, of a finite line between (and including) two points X and Y, and then 'delete', as it were, the points X and Y: what one is then left with is a line which has the same length as the original line, but which lacks any endpoints. For any point on the line west (let us say) of the line's midpoint, there is another point on it *further west* of the midpoint: there is no point on the line which is the point *furthest west* of the midpoint and, similarly, no point on it which is the point *furthest east* of the midpoint. I shall not assume, for present purposes, either that time does, or that it does not, have a beginning or an end; nor shall I assume either that it is, or that it is not, of infinite duration. Indeed, it is difficult to see how we could determine, whether by metaphysical argument or by empirical scientific means, either that time has or lacks a beginning or an end, or that time is of finite or infinite duration. It is true that many modern cosmologists favour the hypothesis of the so-called 'Big Bang', a

---

[1] See further W. H. Newton-Smith, *The Structure of Time* (London: Routledge and Kegan Paul, 1980), ch. 3.

supposedly 'first' event which brought into existence not only the entire physical universe but space and time themselves. According to this hypothesis, then, nothing whatever happened 'before' the Big Bang, because time itself began at the moment of the Big Bang.[2] However, it would seem that any empirical evidence which is consistent with this hypothesis must also be consistent with the hypothesis that there were in fact times *before* the physical universe came into existence, even supposing it to have come into existence through the occurrence of some singular event like the 'Big Bang'. It would seem, indeed, that we could have no physical evidence of the existence of times before such an initial event, assuming one to have occurred, because, by hypothesis, nothing physical now existing could be a relic of such earlier times. But, quite generally, the fact that we can have no evidence for the existence of some state of affairs provides no compelling reason for us to believe that such a state of affairs does *not* exist. It seems best, then, to remain agnostic on the question of whether or not time had a beginning or will have an end.

Temporal asymmetry and the passage of time

These considerations in place, let us turn to the somewhat easier—but still very difficult—question of why time, unlike space, should be 'directed'. That is to say, why should time have both a 'forward' and a 'backward' direction which are significantly different from one another, unlike the two different 'directions' of any straight line in space? What, if anything, gives time these directions and what makes the directions different? Some A theorists may be inclined to answer that time has a distinguished direction from past to future because the passage of time actually consists in the 'growth' of reality itself, which is continually being 'added to' by the successive coming into being of new events—each event subsequently 'receding' into the ever-growing stock of past events.[3] This was a view that I briefly considered at the end of the previous chapter, although I confess that it is one which I find it difficult to make clear sense of. For that reason, I shall say nothing much more in the current chapter about this view of time, with its implication that only the present and the past are fully 'real'.

[2] For extended discussion, see William Lane Craig and Quentin Smith, *Theism, Atheism, and Big Bang Cosmology* (Oxford: Clarendon Press, 1993).

[3] See, for example, C. D. Broad, *Scientific Thought* (London: Routledge and Kegan Paul, 1923), 66–7.

If it were correct, though, it would certainly seem to explain, after a fashion, the directedness of time and time's fundamental difference, in this respect, from space. For, according to this view, the difference between the past-to-future direction of time and the future-to-past direction of time is fundamentally an *ontological* one: the former being grounded in a relation between what is fully real and what is *not* (yet) fully real, the latter being grounded in a converse relation between what is not (yet) fully real and what *is* fully real—if, indeed, one can properly speak of 'relations' between existent and non-existent entities. If one doesn't like talk of such 'relations', however, perhaps one can say instead that the two different directions of time are, on this view, differentiated by the fact that one of them (the forward, or past-to-future direction) is that in which reality's 'growing edge' advances, whereas the other direction (the backward, or future-to-past direction) is that in which reality's stock of events is continually being 'added to'. Again, I don't pretend to be able to make complete sense of these suggestions, resting as they seem to do on dubious metaphors of growth.

Causation and temporal asymmetry

But let us set aside, from now on, any idea that the difference between past and future rests on a distinction between what is and what is not fully 'real'. And let us see whether, none the less, we can come to some understanding of the nature and ground of the directedness of time. One obvious and quite promising suggestion is that the directedness or asymmetry of time is grounded in the asymmetry of *causation*. (Causation itself is very plausibly an asymmetrical relation: if an event, e_1, is a cause of another event, e_2, then it is *not* the case that e_2 is also a cause of e_1.) According to this suggestion, what distinguishes the past-to-future or earlier-to-later direction of time from its future-to-past or later-to-earlier direction is the fact that it is always *earlier* events that are causes of *later* events, never later events that are causes of earlier events. There are various ways in which one might draw on this suggestion in order to define more precisely what it is for one event to be 'earlier' than another. One might propose, for example, that an event, e_1, is *earlier* than another event, e_2, if and only if e_1 is at least a potential cause of e_2. I say only 'is at least a potential cause' rather than simply 'is a cause' because, obviously, we cannot with any degree of plausibility maintain that, whenever one event, e_1, is earlier than another event,

e_2, e_1 is *actually* a cause of e_3; nor, indeed, can we rule out the possibility of there being some events which either actually lack any cause whatever or else actually lack any effect whatever. What is now being proposed, though, is that e_1 is earlier than e_2 if and only if it is *metaphysically possible* for e_1 to be a cause of e_2—that is to say, if and only if there either is or could have been a chain of causation leading from e_1 to e_2—the presumption being that it is metaphysically *im*possible for an effect to precede, or even to be simultaneous with, one of its causes. It is also being presumed—perhaps more contentiously—that if e_1 is actually later than e_2, then e_1 could not have been earlier than e_2: for if it could have been, then, clearly, e_1 could have been a cause of e_2 without violating the prohibition on an effect's preceding one of its causes. Yet another presumption—though this time a rather more plausible one—is that it is never metaphysically necessary that an event should have any of the causes and effects that it actually has (that is, in the terminology of Chapter 6, that it is not part of the 'individual essence' of any event that it has any of the causes and effects that it actually has).

Now, if we adopt anything like the foregoing suggestion, then we obviously cannot hope to account for the asymmetry of causation itself in temporal terms: we shall not be able to say that, given any two events that are related to one another as cause and effect, what determines which of these events is the cause and which the effect is their *temporal order*—the cause being the earlier event and the effect the later one—for this would involve us in a blatant circularity. However, a frequently voiced objection to any such account of the asymmetry of causation is that it is implausible, in any case, to insist that a cause *must* precede its effect in time, either as a matter of definition or as a matter of metaphysical necessity. That is to say, it is often urged that 'backward' causation—the causation of an earlier event by a later event—is at least metaphysically *possible*, even if such causation never actually takes place.[4] But, of course, no one who maintains this can also support our earlier proposal that the earlier-to-later direction of time simply *is* the direction of causation—the proposal, as I expressed it, that for one event to be earlier than another is just for that first event to be at least a potential cause of the second event. However, what such a person might, perhaps, be able to maintain instead is that the earlier-to-later

---

[4] See, for example, Michael Dummett, 'Bringing About the Past', *Philosophical Review* 73 (1964), 338–59, reprinted in his *Truth and Other Enigmas* (London: Duckworth, 1978) and in Robin Le Poidevin and Murray MacBeath (eds.), *The Philosophy of Time* (Oxford: Oxford University Press, 1993).

direction of time is the direction in which *most* causation necessarily takes place—the idea being that backward causation, even if it is metaphysically possible, could only ever be an exceptional phenomenon rather than one that is commonplace (as commonplace as forward causation, at any rate). As for the question of what determines the asymmetry of causation, though, it may be claimed with some plausibility that this is an intrinsic feature of the causal relation and that any theory of causation which needs to explain the asymmetry of causation in terms of the temporal order of cause and effect is, for that very reason, a defective theory.[5]

So far, I have suggested two different possible causal accounts of the directedness or asymmetry of time: the first account holding that the earlier-to-later direction of time simply *is* the direction of causation, the second holding that it is the direction of *most* causation. On the second account, how might we define more precisely what it is for one event to be 'earlier' than another, given that we could not now say, as on the first account, that it is for that first event to be at least a potential cause of the second event? Perhaps, if we are still allowed to presume that cause and effect are never simultaneous and that every event has at least some causes or effects, we could say something like the following. First, we could say that those events are *simultaneous* which necessarily stand in no relation of cause and effect to one another. Then we could say that an event, e_1, is *earlier* than another event, e_2, if and only if *most* events that are simultaneous with e_2 are effects of events that are themselves simultaneous with e_1. This formulation suggests, incidentally, an alternative and perhaps better way of defining, on behalf of our first causal account of the directedness of time, what it is for one event to be earlier than another. Rather than saying that it is for the first of those events to be at least a potential cause of the second, we could simply say instead that an event, e_1, is earlier than another event, e_2, if and only if at least *some* event that is simultaneous with e_2 is an effect of events that are themselves simultaneous with e_1. This definition has some advantages over the previous one, but also, perhaps, some disadvantages of its own; I leave to the reader the task of seeing what some of these advantages and disadvantages might be.

[5] For discussion, see J. L. Mackie, *The Cement of the Universe: A Study of Causation* (Oxford: Clarendon Press, 1974), ch. 7, and Michael Tooley, *Causation: A Realist Approach* (Oxford: Clarendon Press, 1987), ch. 7.

Backward causation and time travel into the past

Of course, if a causal account of the directedness of time is what we seek, then we shall only need to appeal to the second sort of causal account just described if we are persuaded that backward causation is indeed metaphysically possible. If we are persuaded that it is indeed possible, then, in order to sustain such an account, we shall also need to be able to argue that backward causation cannot be commonplace. But let us provisionally set aside that further concern now, in the hope that it will not arise, and concentrate on the prior question of whether or not backward causation really is possible. How, though, should we attempt to settle this question? Is it a question to be settled, if at all, only by a priori metaphysical argument—or is it, rather, a question which empirical science alone can hope to answer satisfactorily? My own view—held for reasons explained more fully in Chapter 1—is that empirical science alone cannot definitively determine the answer to a question concerning metaphysical possibility, such as the one with which we are now concerned, although I do not wish to deny that scientific theorizing and empirical data can throw useful light on a question like this. The key point is that empirical data can only be taken to be good evidence for the truth of a scientific theory if its hypotheses are already entitled to be viewed as expressing metaphysical possibilities: that they can be so viewed is not, thus, something that can be determined on merely empirical grounds. With this point in mind, let us then see what purely philosophical reasons there might be for admitting or disallowing the metaphysical possibility of backward causation, before we try to take into account any of the claims of current scientific theory.

One very useful philosophical strategy for exploring whether or not backward causation is possible is the construction of thought experiments involving 'time travel' into the past. Time travel into the *future*, of course, is something that we all engage in all of the time, the only interesting question being whether the 'speed' at which we travel can be varied. If Einstein's special theory of relativity is correct, then it would appear that this 'speed' is indeed variable, in the following sense: the lapse of time between two events, as measured by a traveller moving at a high velocity relative to a given frame of reference, may be appreciably less than it is as measured by an observer who is stationary with respect to that frame of reference. This is the so-called 'time-dilation' effect, which becomes noticeable only for relative velocities which are an appreciable fraction of the speed of light. Thus, for example, someone who travelled between the earth and a nearby star in a time period of twenty years or so, as measured by a clock which he carried with him, might be judged to have spent eighty years or more on his journey by an observer on Earth who used an earth-bound clock to measure the traveller's journey time. During that interval, the traveller will appear to himself to have aged somewhat, but nothing like as much as the observer on earth will appear to himself to have aged. However, Einstein's theory may seem to present an insuperable obstacle to time travel into the *past*, because it prohibits any object from moving faster than the speed of light (or, more exactly, it prohibits any object from accelerating from a velocity which is less than the speed of light to one which is greater than the speed of light).

The difficulty can be seen immediately if we represent the space-time trajectory of a moving object on a space-time diagram of the kind described in Chapter 14, in which the vertical axis represents time, t, and the horizontal axis represents the three dimensions of space, s, as measured relative to some selected frame of reference. For, in such a diagram, the trajectories of two light rays emitted in opposite directions at a point represented by the origin of the axes, O, will be represented by a pair of diagonal lines through O of a certain steepness, as is depicted in Fig. 18.1. (These diagonal lines represent a cross-section through what is commonly called O's 'forward light cone'.) And any object moving away from O at a subluminal velocity in that frame of reference will obviously have to have a trajectory which is represented by a *steeper* diagonal line (and thus a trajectory which is confined within O's forward light cone). However, any such object which supposedly *changes* from moving 'forward' in time to moving 'backward' in time, to arrive at its final destination earlier than the start of its journey, will apparently have to have a trajectory represented by a line whose steepness at some point *is less than* that of one of the diagonal lines representing the trajectory of a light ray (because it will have to 'break through' O's forward light cone). For example, in Fig. 18.1, let O represent the place and time of the 'start' of the time traveller's journey and let the point X represent the place and time of the finish of his journey (where X is, of course, earlier than O). Then, clearly, even though the time traveller begins his journey by travelling forward in time at a velocity less than the speed of light, his complete trajectory can only be represented on the diagram by a line which at some point *crosses* one of the diagonals which represents the trajectory of a light ray emitted at O, implying that he must

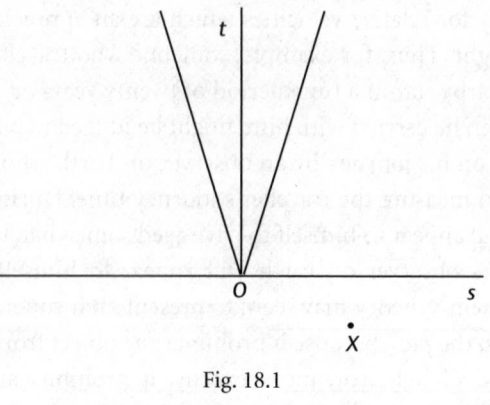

Fig. 18.1

at some time during his journey exceed the speed of light. (I shall explain shortly why the time traveller *must* begin his journey by travelling forward in time at a velocity less than the speed of light.)

However, I undertook to discuss philosophical reasons for and against the possibility of backward causation without prior reference to the claims of current scientific theory, so let us ignore, at least for the time being, the apparent conflict between the notion of time travel into the past and Einstein's special theory of relativity (bearing in mind too that, for reasons given in Chapter 14, as metaphysicians we are not absolutely committed to the truth of Einstein's theory). The relevance of such time travel to the issue of backward causation is simply that time travel into the past inevitably involves backward causation. And, indeed, it might with some plausibility be argued that, conversely, if backward causation is possible, then time travel into the past must also in principle be possible, so that the possibility of each phenomenon stands or falls with the possibility of the other. Clearly, the mere fact that the time traveller succeeds in travelling from a later to an earlier time entails that an earlier event can have a later event amongst its causes, for his success partly consists in the fact that the event of his arrival at his destination has, amongst its causes, the event of his embarking upon the journey at a later time. It is impossible, then, to engage in time travel into the past without causally affecting the past.

Affecting the past versus changing the past

It is important here not to confuse the notion of causally *affecting* the past, which may or may not constitute a genuine possibility, with the manifestly incoherent notion of *changing* the past. If a time traveller from the twenty-first century succeeds in travelling back to the time and place of the Battle of Hastings, in 1066, then it follows that there must be events which occurred in 1066 which had amongst their causes events which occurred in the twenty-first century—notably, the event of the time traveller's arrival at the time and place of the Battle of Hastings. But we cannot coherently think of the time traveller as *changing* what happened in 1066. If he succeeds in travelling back to the time and place of the Battle of Hastings, then it was a *fact* that he was present at the Battle of Hastings long before he set out on his journey: it cannot somehow be a fact that he was *not* there before he set out on his journey and yet be a fact that he *was* there after he arrived—for history is not given twice over, once in a version in which the time traveller is absent from the Battle of Hastings and once in a version in which he is present. However, by being careful to distinguish between the notion of affecting the past (which simply involves backward causation) and the notion of changing the past (which involves incoherent double-talk), we can dismiss as misconceived some superficial attempts to discount the possibility of time travel into the past.

'Personal' time versus 'external' time

Another overly simplistic way to challenge the possibility of time travel into the past is to maintain that the notion of such time travel involves contradictory claims about the amount of time separating two events. Consider again the person who supposedly travels back to the time and place of the Battle of Hastings, starting his journey one thousand years later, in 2066. How long will his journey take him? Presumably, that will depend on how 'fast' he travels—but if he travels quite fast, one may suppose that he might take at most only a few years. Suppose, then, that he takes three years to complete his journey. This means that three years separate the event of his departure, in 2066, and the event of his arrival, in 1066. But, it may be protested, these two events are separated by *one thousand* years, so how can they also be separated by a mere *three* years? The answer, of course, is to distinguish between the lapse of time as measured by a clock which the traveller carries with him and the lapse of time as measured by clocks which are simply travelling forward in time in the normal way.[6] As measured by the traveller's own clock, his journey takes him a mere three years, during which period he will have aged a corresponding amount (for instance, if he doesn't shave during his journey, he will have accumulated a normal three-years' growth of beard). But as measured by 'earthbound' clocks, the traveller's journey takes one thousand years—and during this period he will appear to have grown *younger* by three years (for instance, in 1066 he had three years' growth of beard, but one thousand years later, in 2066, he is clean-shaven). In making this distinction between what we may call the time traveller's own 'personal' time and the 'external' time of ordinary historical records, it seems that we are merely extending a distinction which, as we saw earlier, is endorsed in any case by Einstein's special theory of relativity, which treats the measure of elapsed time as being dependent upon the choice of a frame of reference.

Problems of multiple location and multiple occupancy

Yet another sort of problem which, in the opinion of some philosophers, makes time travel into the past impossible is that which arises when the time traveller supposedly travels back to a time and place at which his 'younger self' was present. Suppose, for instance, that the traveller embarks upon his journey as a middle-aged adult and travels back to the time and place at which he was born. There he will encounter a baby which is, in fact, *himself.* But this seems to imply that at that time and place there exist *two* people—a middle-aged man and a newborn baby—who are in fact *one and the same* person. We appear, thus to have a conflict with the very laws of identity, which do not allow two different things to be one. But if, in response to this difficulty, we simply deny that we have two different things in this case—maintaining that the middle-aged man and the newborn baby really are strictly *identical* persons—then we seem to be faced with

---

[6] See further David Lewis, 'The Paradoxes of Time Travel', *American Philosophical Quarterly* 13 (1976), 145–52, reprinted in his *Philosophical Papers*, vol. 2 (New York: Oxford University Press, 1986) and in Le Poidevin and MacBeath (eds.), *The Philosophy of Time.* I am indebted to Lewis's paper for several of the points concerning time travel made in the present chapter.

the equally unpalatable implication that one and the same person can be in two different locations at exactly the same time (for the middle-aged man cannot literally *coincide*, spatially, with the newborn baby). However, this sort of problem can be relatively easily overcome if we are prepared to adopt the doctrine of 'temporal parts', described in Chapter 3. (Even if we are *not* prepared to adopt that doctrine—and for my own part I am inclined not to—we may still be able to overcome the problem, but not, I suspect, so straightforwardly.) For what we can then say is that it is only a *middle-aged temporal part* of the time traveller which encounters an *infant temporal part* of himself when he travels back to the time and place of his birth. These temporal parts are numerically distinct three-dimensional objects, each of which is a different temporal segment of the four-dimensional entity which constitutes the time traveller 'as a whole' (that is, as a temporally persisting object extending from birth to death). Hence, we have no violation of the laws of identity on our hands. And the principle that one and the same object cannot be in two different locations at exactly the same time must—but plausibly can—be reconstrued as implying only that one and the same *temporal part* of an object cannot be in two different locations at exactly the same time, in which case we have on our hands no violation of that principle either.

One particular variant of the foregoing sort of problem may not appear to be quite so easy to resolve, however. I have in mind a difficulty which seems to attend the very notion of the time traveller reversing his direction of travel through time, from forward to backward.[7] For is he not bound to 'collide' with his earlier self? Suppose, for instance, that he embarks upon his journey at exactly 10.00 a.m., at which time he occupies a certain spatial location. Where, then, will he be located at exactly one second before 10.00 a.m.? If we suppose that he did not change his spatial location for a few seconds before embarking upon his journey, then a younger temporal part of himself will be in exactly the same spatial location as the location occupied by him at the time of his departure, 10.00 a.m. (ignoring, for present purposes, the fact that the Earth is moving on its axis and in its orbit around the Sun). But since the traveller is supposed to travel *backward* in time, beginning at 10.00 a.m., it seems that an *older* temporal part of himself will also have to occupy exactly the same spatial location, at one second before 10.00 a.m., as is occupied by the *younger* temporal part of

---

[7] See Michael Dummett, 'Causal Loops', in Raymond Flood and Michael Lockwood (eds.), *The Nature of Time* (Oxford: Blackwell, 1986).

himself of which we have just spoken. And this conflicts with the principle, which we surely ought to accept, that two different temporal parts of the same object cannot be in the same location at exactly the same time. However, this difficulty, too, seems to have a relatively straightforward solution: we must simply recognize that there can be no travel backward in time which is not accompanied by movement *in space*. The time traveller cannot simply reverse his direction of travel in time while staying in exactly the same spatial location. In fact, it seems, if he is to avoid 'colliding' with his younger self, he must first move very rapidly *in space*, but still forward in time, eventually exceeding the speed of light and only after that beginning to travel backward in time. This should be evident if we attempt to represent his trajectory on the space-time diagram provided earlier (Fig. 18.1 above), making sure that we draw this trajectory as a smooth curve.

The Grandfather Paradox and the problem of causal loops

So far, we have discovered no insuperable obstacle, from a purely logical or metaphysical point of view, to the notion of time travel into the past. But, in the opinion of some philosophers, the serious difficulties attending this notion really only begin to arise when we consider in detail the kind of backward causation which time travel into the past must apparently involve. Perhaps the best-known problem of this kind is that confronting the time traveller who is presented with an opportunity to prevent his own birth from occurring—say, by travelling back to a time before his birth and killing his own grandfather before his parents were conceived. The problem is that if he were to perform this act, then he would bring it about that he never existed—and yet the very act requires his existence. Clearly, we must say that, for some reason, the time traveller *cannot* kill his own grandfather. But it may be hard to see *why* he cannot. That is to say, it may be hard to see what *prevents* the time traveller from performing this act, for he may apparently have both the necessary means for carrying it out and the opportunity to do so: for instance, he may be equipped with a loaded gun and be standing only a few feet away from his grandfather.

However, this, too, does not really present a serious difficulty for the notion of time travel into the past. What we should evidently say is that, *for some reason or other*, the time traveller must in fact fail to kill his grandfather, despite his best efforts to succeed in doing so. His failure to do so will not simply be a miracle. It will have a perfectly ordinary causal explanation of some kind, even if we cannot specify, in advance of knowing the details of the specific case, what this explanation will be. Perhaps the gun will jam, or perhaps the time traveller will suddenly be distracted, or perhaps the person whom he takes to be his grandfather will not in reality be his grandfather. The possible explanations of his failure are infinite in number and hence most of them will never be thought of by anyone. But all that is required is that *one* of them is correct as a matter of fact—and it is not required that this one be known by the time traveller or anyone else. In this respect, the time traveller who attempts, vainly, to kill his own grandfather is in somewhat the same position as someone who has been told by a reliable oracle that he will not perform a certain act in the future, even though that act appears to be perfectly within the agent's power. If the oracle tells the agent that, for instance, he will not eat an egg for breakfast the next day, even though it would seem to be perfectly within the agent's power to do so, then the agent knows—if he knows that the oracle is reliable—that he will indeed not eat an egg for breakfast the next day, no matter what steps he may take to try to do so. The agent knows that, *for some reason or other*, his attempt to eat an egg for breakfast the next day will be frustrated. His failure will have a perfectly ordinary causal explanation, even though the explanation may come as a complete surprise when (and if) it becomes known to the agent.

The foregoing problem seemed to involve the notion of time travel into the past in a potential contradiction, whereby a time traveller might be able to bring about an event which would result in his own non-existence. We have just seen that, although the time traveller might indeed be said to have this 'ability' in the sense of possessing both the *necessary means* and the *opportunity* to bring about such an event, there is also a perfectly clear sense in which he *cannot* bring about such an event and in that sense lacks the 'ability' to do so. But since the two senses of 'ability' are quite distinct, there is no inconsistency in our description of the time traveller's predicament. We can simply conclude that the time traveller will never in fact succeed in bringing about the event in question (the death of his own grandfather), but that this fact may still have a perfectly ordinary causal explanation.

However, a much more worrisome sort of time travelling scenario, I think, is that which involves a *causal loop* of some kind—this being more worrisome precisely because it does not even appear to involve any kind of logical inconsistency but none the less defies certain principles of causal explanation and thus plausibly involves a *metaphysical* impossibility.

An example of such a scenario is one in which the time traveller acquires the plans for his time machine from his older self, who, having built the machine from the plans, has travelled back in time to meet his younger self, precisely in order to give his younger self the plans from which to build the time machine.[8] The problem is that the plans appear to come from nowhere: even though every event in their circular history may seem to be causally explicable in terms of other such events, the 'explanations' involved are ultimately circular and hence not genuine explanations at all (assuming, as we seem entitled to do, that explanation is an asymmetrical relation). Notice that it is not being suggested here that the paper on which the plans are drawn somehow materializes out of nothing and that this is why the scenario involves a metaphysical impossibility—only that the *information* contained in the plans seems to have no origin. In this scenario, no one ever *invented* the time machine. But that is enough to make the scenario at least extremely puzzling and, very arguably, metaphysically impossible, even though it does not appear to involve a logical inconsistency. The problem, then, is this. If the scenario is logically consistent— unlike one in which a time traveller supposedly kills his own grandfather—then what, exactly, is there to prevent such a scenario from being realized, if time travel into the past is genuinely possible? Why *shouldn't* the time traveller's older self be able to hand over the plans for the time machine to his younger self and his younger self be able to use them to construct the time machine? In this case, it doesn't appear that we can simply insist, as in the case of the time traveller who attempts to kill his own grandfather, that, *for some reason or other*, any attempt to enact this scenario will inevitably fail, even if we cannot say in advance what, precisely, the reason will be in any specific instance. That being so, it is very tempting to conclude that what the metaphysical impossibility of the scenario implies—assuming that it is indeed metaphysically impossible— is that time travel into the past is itself metaphysically impossible, whether or not the time traveller actually attempts to enact the scenario in question.

[8] See further Murray MacBeath, 'Who was Dr Who's Father?', *Synthese* 51 (1982), 397–430.

Time travel, general relativity, and informational loops

Our tentative conclusion so far is that the only purely philosophical reason for supposing time travel into the past to be metaphysically impossible is that it would potentially involve the time traveller in a metaphysically impossible causal loop. But let us now try to reconnect our discussion of these matters with some of the doctrines of modern physical science. Earlier in the chapter, I implied that time travel into the past is incompatible with Einstein's special theory of relativity and, more particularly, with that theory's prohibition on any object's accelerating from a subluminal to a superluminal velocity. However, it is worth pointing out that in the wider context of Einstein's *general* theory of relativity, applied on a cosmological scale, time travel into the past does not appear to be completely ruled out. It has been shown, indeed, that there are solutions to the field equations of Einstein's general theory which do permit such time travel, in principle.[9] These are solutions according to which space-time as a whole has a peculiar kind of internal 'curvature', as a consequence of which a traveller could arrive at a space-time destination which was earlier than his point of departure, without ever transcending the speed of light in any locally determined frame of reference. However, one might still worry that this would potentially involve the time traveller in puzzling causal and informational 'loops' of the sort we have just been considering.

In scientific terms, a serious difficulty with such loops is that they seem to involve a violation of the basic laws of thermodynamics—more particularly, the second law, which states that entropy in a closed physical system generally increases with the lapse of time.[10] (The physical universe as a whole, many scientists and philosophers would say, is a 'closed system' *par excellence*, being necessarily immune to any 'outside' interference.) The 'entropy' of a physical system can be thought of as a measure of its 'disorder' and *increase* of entropy is accordingly associated with *decrease* of

---

[9] See Kurt Gödel 'A Remark about the Relationship between Relativity Theory and Idealistic Philosophy', in P. A. Schilpp (ed.), *Albert Einstein: Philosopher-Scientist*, 3rd edn. (La Salle, Ill.: Open Court, 1970). For discussion, see Paul Horwich, *Asymmetries in Time* (Cambridge, Mass.: MIT Press, 1987), ch. 7, and Palle Yourgrau, *The Disappearance of Time: Kurt Gödel and the Idealistic Tradition in Philosophy* (Cambridge: Cambridge University Press, 1991).

[10] This is a concern that Einstein himself raises in connection with Gödel's proposal: see Schilpp (ed.), *Albert Einstein: Philosopher-Scientist*, 687–8. For more on entropy and temporal asymmetry, see Horwich, *Asymmetries in Time*, ch. 4.

'information'. For we can only encode information in a physical form by imposing some order on a physical system—say, by inscribing ink marks on a piece of paper—and if this system becomes increasingly disordered over time (in the case of a piece of paper, through normal processes of wear and tear), the encoded information will correspondingly become increasingly degraded and ultimately lost. Consequently, a causal and informational 'loop'—even one which is consistent with Einstein's general theory of relativity in the manner indicated above—appears to defy the laws of thermodynamics, since information cannot consistently decrease *all the way round* such a loop. It is true that, since these laws are ultimately only statistical or probabilistic in character, they do allow for the possibility of occasional anomalies: it is possible, for instance, if very highly improbable, that all of the fragments of a shattered glass vase should come together again in exactly their original arrangement (without anyone deliberately making this happen). But time travel into the past would apparently open the door to systematic and regular violations of the laws of thermodynamics, which are scientifically very difficult to countenance.

The laws of thermodynamics and the 'arrow' of time

Some physical scientists consider, indeed, that it is the very laws of thermodynamics, and these laws alone, that hold the key to the problem of the directedness or asymmetry of time: the idea being that the forward direction of time just *is* the direction in which entropy generally increases. But this, I think, is going too far. Here we should appreciate that the basic idea behind the second law of thermodynamics is just that, of all the possible ways in which a system of elements can be arranged, there are many more which are very similar than are very dissimilar. For instance, if we think of all the possible distributions of several million particles of blue and red dye in a tank of water, most of these distributions will be ones which make the water look uniformly purple, rather than red in one part of the tank and blue in the other. Hence, if we start with a tank in which the dye particles are segregated—for instance, by inserting a dividing plate between the two halves of the tank and adding blue dye to the water in one half and red dye to the water in the other half—and then leave the particles to move freely throughout the tank (in the case described, simply by removing the plate), the chances are extremely high that a few hours later the water will look uniformly purple in colour. (The assumption here is that the particles are moving randomly in virtue of the thermal energy of the water, so that any one possible distribution of the particles is just as probable as any other.) None the less, if we left the tank long enough without in any way interfering with its contents—and 'long enough' would doubtless be a very long time indeed—there would be nothing to prevent the particles from eventually regaining a segregated distribution once more.

Now, applying this last thought to the case of the entire physical universe, it would seem that, as far as the laws of thermodynamics are concerned, there is nothing to prevent the universe as a whole from eventually entering a phase in which its entropy *decreases* and processes which we normally associate with the forward direction of time all occur in reverse—the fragments of smashed glass vases coming together again, people growing 'younger' rather than 'older', and so forth. But it would surely be mistaken—indeed, simply incoherent—to describe such a phase of the universe as being one in which *time itself* is reversed, because this would imply, absurdly, that there could be three distinct events, e_1, e_2, and e_3, such that e_1 is a little earlier than e_2 and e_3 is also a little earlier than e_2 and yet e_2 occurs at a time which lies *between* the times at which e_1 and e_3 occur. (Let e_2 be an event occurring at the time at which the universe undergoes a phase change, let e_1 be an event occurring near in time to e_2 during one of the phases, and let e_3 be an event occurring near in time to e_2 during the other phase.) Indeed, it would seem that the fact that it is in the *forward* (earlier-to-later) direction of time that entropy generally increases can only be a contingent one, depending on the contingent fact that the *early* universe was in a state of markedly low entropy—that is, was in a highly ordered state. If the 'Big Bang' hypothesis is correct, this has something to do with the circumstances in which the physical universe came into being. But, for our purposes, the important point is that we apparently cannot simply *define* the earlier-to-later direction of time as being the direction in which entropy generally increases.

In saying that, *as far as the laws of thermodynamics are concerned*, there is nothing to prevent the universe from eventually entering a phase in which its entropy decreases and processes which we normally associate with the forward direction of time all occur in reverse, I should stress that I do not mean to imply that such an eventuality is a genuine metaphysical (or even causal) possibility, much less that it will sooner or later actually happen.

That these laws do not preclude it from happening merely demonstrates their predictive limitations. Above all, these laws plausibly *do not*, as some scientists and philosophers seem to think, hold the key to the problem of the 'arrow' of time. I strongly suspect that the key to that problem lies, rather, in the asymmetry of causation. From our examination of the question of whether time travel into the past is possible, we have seen that the main obstacle to such time travel—and therewith to the backward causation that such time travel would inevitably involve—is its potential to give rise to causal loops. Events caught up in such loops would not be amenable to causal explanation, because genuine explanations cannot be circular. And while we cannot reasonably insist that every event whatever is amenable to causal explanation, it is, I think, unreasonable to suppose that large tracts of spatiotemporal reality might exist which are unamenable to causal explanation on account of the presence within them of widespread and systematic causal loops. If this reasoning is sound, then even if we are inclined to admit that backward causation and causal loops are in principle *possible*, we have grounds for supposing that these phenomena are necessarily extremely rare, thus enabling us at least to endorse some version of the *second* of the two causal accounts of the asymmetry of time described earlier—the account according to which the earlier-to-later direction of time may be identified with the direction of *most* causation.[11]

[11] For rather more advanced discussion of some of the topics covered in this chapter, see Steven F. Savitt (ed.), *Time's Arrow Today: Recent Physical and Philosophical Work on the Direction of Time* (Cambridge: Cambridge University Press, 1995).

PART VI

UNIVERSALS AND PARTICULARS

19

REALISM VERSUS NOMINALISM

The distinction between universals and particulars

In this chapter I shall examine one of the most fundamental of all ontological distinctions: the distinction between *universals* and *particulars*. Although discussion of this distinction has a very long history, there continues to be controversy both about how the distinction should be drawn and about whether it has genuine application. That is to say, there is still disagreement as to what should be understood by the terms 'universal' and 'particular' and even some disagreement as to whether anything is usefully describable by either of these terms. However, it is widely assumed amongst modern metaphysicians, I think rightly, that if the distinction ought to be drawn at all then it ought to be drawn in such a way that the terms denote mutually exclusive and jointly exhaustive ontological categories—that is, in such a way that every entity whatever is either a universal or a particular, but not both. But even those philosophers who accept this assumption are divided over the question of whether both of these categories are actually occupied—some holding that both universals and particulars exist, others that only universals exist, and yet others that only particulars exist. Moreover, those who hold that both universals and particulars exist are further divided over the question of whether entities in one of these categories are reducible to entities in the other, and if so, which. Some philosophers hold that universals and particulars are mutually irreducible and thus that these two ontological categories are equally fundamental. Others hold that universals are somehow reducible to particulars or else, conversely, that particulars are somehow reducible to universals. But before we can more fully describe and attempt to evaluate some of these rival ontological doctrines, we need to consider how, precisely, the distinction between the universal and the particular should be drawn.

A spatiotemporal account of the distinction

An approach favoured by some philosophers is to attempt to draw this distinction in spatiotemporal terms. The idea here is, roughly speaking, that particulars are distinctive in being individuated by their spatiotemporal locations, so that no two particulars (or, at least, no two particulars of the same kind) can exist in exactly the same place at the same time and no single particular can exist in two wholly distinct places at the same time. (Two places are 'wholly distinct' just in case they share no common spatial part, that is, just in case they do not 'overlap' spatially.) A single universal, by contrast, is said by such philosophers to be capable of existing in two wholly distinct places at the same time and any number of universals are said to be capable of existing in exactly the same place at the same time.

Some illustrative examples of paradigm instances of the two categories will be helpful here. Consider, then, a paradigm particular such as a particular material object of a certain kind—for example, a particular chair made entirely of some uniformly blue plastic material. And suppose that this chair fully and exactly occupies a certain region of space at a certain time, so that the region of space in question has exactly the same shape and size as the chair. Then, it seems correct to say, this very chair cannot *also* fully and exactly occupy some other, quite distinct region of space at this same time. Furthermore, it would seem that it cannot be the case that another chair, exactly like this one, simultaneously occupies the very same region of space which this one occupies at the time in question. By way of contrast, consider a paradigm universal, such as the property of blueness that is possessed by the particular chair just mentioned. Then it will be said, by the philosophers in question, that although this blueness—like the chair itself—fully and exactly occupies the region of space which is occupied by the chair, the very same blueness may *also* at the same time occupy an entirely distinct region of space, such as the region of space occupied at that time by any other particular chair made of plastic material of exactly the same shade of blue. Furthermore, it will be said that many other universals may exist in the very same regions of space as are occupied by this blueness, such as the various other properties of any of these particular blue chairs.

There is a technical difficulty with the foregoing proposal, however, which emerges from our discussion in the previous chapter of the possibility of time travel. If time travel into the past is possible, then it should be possible, in principle, for a particular blue chair to be 'sent back in time' to a time and place at which it formerly existed. Of course, it plausibly cannot be sent back to *exactly* the same place as the place it occupied at some earlier time, because then it would 'collide' with its earlier self. But it could perhaps be sent back to another nearby place which was not then occupied by any other material object. In that case, however, one and the same particular chair would exist in two wholly distinct places at the same time—which, according to the foregoing proposal, is something that only a universal can do. One solution, it would seem, is to modify the proposal in line with the doctrine of temporal parts (see Chapter 3) and say only that a particular cannot be *wholly present* in two different places at the same time—implying by this that if a particular is in two wholly distinct places at the same time, then this can only be in virtue of the fact that one part of the particular is in one of those places while another part of it is in the other. (Conveniently, this caters not only for the possibility of time travel just mentioned, but also for the case of 'scattered' objects, which have different *spatial* parts—rather than different *temporal* parts—in two or more wholly distinct places at the same time: an example being, perhaps, a temporarily dismantled watch. Indeed, of course, even ordinary, *un*scattered particulars, such as a fully assembled watch, have different spatial parts in two or more wholly distinct places at the same time.) By way of contrast, it may now be said that what is distinctive of a universal is that it can indeed be wholly present in two different places at the same time.[1]

But even with this amendment, the foregoing way of trying to distinguish between universals and particulars is open to serious objection, especially if one considers that there can be entities belonging to either of these categories which do not exist in space or time at all. Some philosophers, for instance, believe in the existence of particular 'Cartesian egos', or immaterial souls, which exist in time but not in space. And many philosophers believe in the existence of *abstract* particulars, such as particular mathematical objects (numbers and sets, for example) and particular propositions, which they conceive of as existing neither in space nor in time. (I shall say more about the distinction between 'abstract' and

---

[1] See further D. M. Armstrong, *Universals: An Opinionated Introduction* (Boulder, Colo.: Westview Press, 1989), 98–9.

'concrete' entities in the next chapter.) Furthermore, many philosophers who believe in the existence of universals—such as the property of blueness—consider that all universals are themselves abstract entities and consequently do not exist in space or time. And even if one believes that the properties of material particulars, such as the blueness of a blue chair, exist in space and time, one can hardly suppose that this is true of the properties of abstract particulars—if there are such particulars—such as a particular number's property of being a prime or a particular proposition's property of being true (assuming truth to be a property of propositions). Accordingly, one cannot consistently adhere to a spatiotemporal account of the distinction between universals and particulars, of the sort outlined earlier, unless one holds that everything that there is *or could be* necessarily exists in space and time—in other words, unless one holds that only *concrete*, not abstract, entities can exist. Notice that it is not enough merely to hold that only concrete entities *do* exist, for once one admits that it is so much as *possible* for there to be either universals or particulars which do not exist in space or time, one cannot regard a spatiotemporal criterion of the distinction between universals and particulars as being adequate. But, surely, it cannot be right to insist upon an account of this distinction which imposes such a strong constraint on what is held to be metaphysically possible. To insist upon such a criterion would be to raise an insuperable barrier to discussion and argument between oneself and a large number of other philosophers whose metaphysical views cannot be dismissed out of hand. I conclude that we are obliged to seek some alternative and metaphysically more neutral way of drawing the distinction between universals and particulars, if this is a distinction that we wish to endorse.

Instantiation and an alternative account

One such alternative is to define the distinction between universal and particular in terms of the relationship of *instantiation* in which one entity may stand to another.[2] Every particular, it may be said, instantiates—is an instance of—some universal. For example, a particular chair is an instance of the kind *chair* or (if one prefers this way of putting it) instantiates the property of *being a chair*. Universals may themselves be instances of other,

---

[2] This is the view I favour myself: see my *The Possibility of Metaphysics: Substance, Identity, and Time* (Oxford: Clarendon Press, 1998), 155.

'higher-order' universals. For example, we might plausibly say that the property of blueness is an instance of the second-order property of *being a colour property*. After all, just as it is true of a particular chair that it *is a chair*, so it is true of blueness that it *is a colour property*. Accordingly, if we may take the predicates 'is a chair' and 'is a colour property' to denote certain properties—universals—then it would seem that the first of these predicates denotes a 'first-order' property (a property which may be possessed only by particulars) while the second denotes a 'second-order' property (a property which may be possessed only by a first-order property). Suppose we accept all this. Then, it seems, we can define the distinction between universal and particular in the following way. A *particular* is an entity which, although it can instantiate (be an instance of) another entity, cannot itself be instantiated by any other entity (cannot have instances). By contrast, a *universal* is an entity which can not only instantiate (be an instance of) another entity, but can also be instantiated by another entity (can have instances).

There may appear to be a technical difficulty with this proposal too. Some philosophers want to maintain that there can be properties—that is, universals—which lack any instances, not just contingently but *necessarily*. Contingently uninstantiated universals pose no problem for the proposal, for the proposal was only that any universal *can* have instances, unlike any particular. It could allow, therefore, for the existence, say, of colour properties which no object, as a matter of contingent fact, has ever possessed— just so long as some object *could* possess them. But if a philosopher wants to say that there exists, for example, such a universal as the property of *being both round and square*, then he must concede that there are universals which *necessarily* lack instances (because, obviously, no object can be both round and square). Hence, such a philosopher could not endorse the proposal now under consideration. Perhaps, however, he could say instead that a universal is something which either can have instances itself, or else is somehow entirely 'composed by' or 'constructed out of' entities which can have instances. This would allow him to acknowledge that the property of being both round and square is a universal, on the grounds that it is a 'conjunctive' property whose conjuncts (the property of being round and the property of being square) are both universals according to the modified criterion (because *they* can both have instances). Of course, this solution will not work for 'simple' universals which necessarily lack instances, though it is hard to see why anyone should think that such properties exist.

On the face of it, the foregoing modification gets around the difficulty, although it might seem to exchange that difficulty for another one. This is because there are some philosophers who maintain that particulars are reducible to combinations (or 'bundles') of universals. The problem is that such a combination of universals would appear to be something which is, as I put it a moment ago, entirely 'composed by' or 'constructed out of' entities which can have instances—so that, according to the modified proposal, it will qualify as a *universal*, rather than as a particular. However, perhaps this problem could be circumvented by distinguishing two different ways in which something can be entirely composed by or constructed out of entities which can have instances—one way which is exemplified in the case of the property of being both round and square, and a different way in which particulars are supposedly 'composed by' or 'constructed out of' universals—and by then insisting that only the first of these ways is to be invoked for the purposes of the modified proposal. Alternatively, perhaps it could be urged, quite plausibly, that the philosophers who maintain that particulars are 'reducible' to combinations of universals are simply committed, whether they like it or not, to saying that everything that can exist really *is* some sort of universal, including so-called 'particulars'. Either way, it seems to me that something like the original proposal, or some modification of it, whereby the distinction between universals and particulars is defined in terms of the notion of instantiation, is probably defensible. (Notice that, according to that original proposal, the distinction between universals and particulars is certainly mutually exclusive, but will only be exhaustive on the assumption that every entity whatever can instantiate some other entity. If there are entities which *cannot* instantiate any other entity, then they will qualify neither as universals nor as particulars according to the proposed definition. Whether, and if so how, we should modify the proposal to accommodate such entities, if they exist, are questions that I shall not pursue here.)

Nominalists versus realists

Having decided, at least for present purposes, how best to define the distinction between universals and particulars, let us now consider some rival doctrines concerning the existence of and relations between entities putatively belonging to these two ontological categories. Some philosophers—who are usually, though somewhat misleadingly, described as 'nominalists'—believe that only particulars exist. Others believe that, whether or not particulars exist, universals certainly do exist—and these are usually described (again, somewhat misleadingly) as 'realists'. Nominalists believe what they do for various reasons, not only purely metaphysical reasons but also ones which are partly epistemological or semantic in character. Some hold, for instance, that it is ontologically extravagant to posit the existence of universals in addition to that of particulars, or that universals are metaphysically repugnant in some way. Some maintain that universals, if they existed, would have such a nature that we could have no knowledge of them, so that nothing that we do know can give us reason to believe in their existence. Some consider that universals are mistakenly invoked by realists to explain semantic features of language which can be quite adequately explained in other ways. On the opposing side of the debate, some realists contend that these semantic features—more specifically, the meanings of predicative expressions and of certain kinds of general term—can indeed only be explained by invoking universals. Some believe that universals must be invoked to explain our psychological capacity to recognize, classify, and group together various particulars. And some urge that universals must be invoked to explain the ontological status of laws of nature, which they conceive to involve relationships between universals.[3] There is not space in this chapter to consider all of these aspects of the debate between nominalists and realists, however, so I shall focus principally on the semantic considerations. (Some of the other considerations will be aired in the next chapter.)

Predicates and properties

As far as semantic considerations are concerned, the key idea from the realist point of view is that a *predicate* typically denotes a *property*, the latter being conceived as a universal (although it may and indeed should be conceded by the realist that not *every* meaningful predicate denotes a property). Thus, to use previous examples, the predicate 'is a chair' supposedly denotes the property of *being a chair* and the predicate 'is blue' supposedly denotes the property of *being blue*, or *blueness*. Indeed, the latter term, 'blueness', is not a predicate at all, but a noun or name—and as

[3] See, especially, D. M. Armstrong, *What is a Law of Nature?* (Cambridge: Cambridge University Press, 1983), pt. 2. For a more general survey of the debate between realism and nominalism, see D. M. Armstrong, *Nominalism and Realism: Universals and Scientific Realism, Volume I* (Cambridge: Cambridge University Press, 1978).

such, one might naturally suppose, an expression which refers to some really existing entity: plausibly, the very same entity as is supposedly denoted by the predicate 'is blue'. After all, instead of saying 'This chair is blue', we can say 'Blueness characterizes this chair': these two sentences appear to be logically equivalent.[4] However, what one should make of this logical equivalence, accepting that it obtains, is a matter for some debate.[5] The realist may say that, since 'Blueness characterizes this chair' clearly makes reference to—and therefore implies the existence of—a universal (namely, *blueness*), it follows that the logically equivalent sentence 'This chair is blue' likewise implies the existence of that same universal, which it can apparently do only in virtue of the fact that the predicate, 'is blue', denotes that universal. The nominalist, on the other hand, may urge that the sentence 'This chair is blue' makes reference to—and hence implies the existence of—only *one* entity, which is a particular, namely, *this chair*. Then he may draw on the putative fact that 'Blueness characterizes this chair' is logically equivalent to 'This chair is blue' to argue that the former sentence likewise implies the existence of only one entity, which is a particular. To this, however, the realist may reply that the nominalist now owes us an account of the meaning of the predicate 'is blue', given that it is not to be taken to denote a certain universal, namely, *blueness*.

There are various things that a nominalist may say in response to this challenge. One is to urge that the realist's challenge is based on a mistaken view of meaning, which sees words and phrases as having meaning only in virtue of their denoting or signifying *entities* of certain kinds—a view which might be correct as far as some names and noun phrases are concerned (those that are used to refer to particulars), but which does not apply to predicative expressions, nor to general terms (like 'blueness') whose use can apparently be replaced by the use of corresponding predicates (like 'is blue'). Here the realist may contend that the use of such a general term *cannot*, in fact, always be replaced by the use of a corresponding predicate. He concedes that it can be so replaced, of course, in a sentence such as 'Blueness characterizes this chair', which he accepts is logically equivalent to 'This chair is blue'. But for other sentences involving such general terms it is not so easy to find logically equivalent sentences in

[4] See further F. P. Ramsey, 'Universals', *Mind* 34 (1925), 401–17, reprinted in his *The Foundations of Mathematics and Other Logical Essays* (London: Kegan Paul, 1931) and in D. H. Mellor and Alex Oliver (eds.), *Properties* (Oxford: Oxford University Press, 1997).

[5] See further W. V. Quine, 'On What There Is', *Review of Metaphysics* 2 (1948), 21–38, reprinted in his *From a Logical Point of View*, 2nd edn. (Cambridge, Mass.: Harvard University Press, 1961) and in Mellor and Oliver (eds.), *Properties*.

which they are replaced by corresponding predicates. Take, for instance, the sentence 'Blueness is a cooler colour property than redness', or the sentence 'Blueness is more similar to greenness than it is to redness'. It is far from evident how these sentences could be paraphrased by logically equivalent sentences employing no general colour terms but, instead, only the specific colour predicates 'is blue', 'is red', and 'is green', together perhaps with the non-specific colour predicate 'is coloured'.[6]

Resemblance classes and resemblance nominalism

Another and more positive way in which the nominalist may respond to the realist's challenge is to try to offer an alternative and nominalistically acceptable account of the meaning of general terms like 'blueness' and their corresponding predicates, according to which these expressions do, after all, denote entities of some sort, but entities that are all uncontroversially *particulars*. For example, accepting that *sets* or *classes* are particulars, the nominalist may contend that 'blueness', say, denotes a certain set or class of particulars. *Which* set or class, though? The obvious thing to say is that 'blueness' (and, likewise, the corresponding predicate, 'is blue') denotes the class of all *blue* particulars. (For present purposes, we may treat the terms 'set' and 'class' as synonymous.) But what determines whether a given particular belongs to this class? The nominalist can hardly say, on pain of uninformative circularity, that a particular belongs to the class of blue particulars if and only if the particular in question *is blue*. Nor can he say, on pain of conceding victory to the realist, that a particular belongs to the class of blue particulars if and only if the particular in question possesses the property of being blue, or *blueness*. But perhaps he can say, without circularity, that a particular belongs to the class of blue particulars if and only if the particular in question belongs to a certain *resemblance class* of particulars—a class which can consequently be identified with the class of blue particulars. Nominalists who adopt this line of thought are, unsurprisingly, called 'resemblance nominalists'.

There are various ways in which one might attempt to specify, noncircularly, a resemblance class of particulars which can be identified with

---

[6] See further Frank Jackson, 'Statements about Universals', *Mind* 86 (1977), 427–9, reprinted in Mellor and Oliver (eds.), *Properties*.

the class of blue particulars. One way would be to select some blue particular as a *paradigm*—for instance, a particular sapphire—and specify the class in question as being the class of all particulars which resemble the paradigm (or better, perhaps, the class of all particulars which resemble the paradigm at least as much as they resemble the paradigms for other resemblance classes). But there are obvious objections to this sort of strategy. One is that we need to be told, non-circularly, on what basis the relevant paradigm is to be selected—and it is not clear how this can be done. Another is that there appears to be no guarantee that the method will result in the same resemblance class being specified no matter which paradigm happens to be selected, which seems unsatisfactory. More fundamentally still, however, it may be objected that resemblance between particulars is always resemblance *in some respect*—for instance, in respect of size, or shape, or colour—and that unless the respect in which particulars in the relevant resemblance class are meant to resemble the paradigm is appropriately specified, an appropriate resemblance class will not be specified by the proposed method. Thus, in the case under consideration, it must be specified that the relevant resemblance class—the class which is to be identified with the class of blue particulars—is the class of all particulars which resemble the paradigm *in respect of its colour*. For, clearly, it would be inappropriate, for example, to include in the resemblance class some particular which resembles the paradigm in respect of its size or shape, but which is green or red in colour rather than blue. However, such talk of 'respects' in which particulars resemble paradigms seems to involve nothing less than reference to *universals* and thus effectively concedes victory to the realist. For instance, to say that some particular resembles the paradigm 'in respect of its colour' involves, surely, a quite blatant reference to *the colour* of the paradigm, which is a *property*—a universal.

Another way in which one might attempt to specify, non-circularly, a resemblance class of particulars which could be identified with the class of blue particulars is this. One might suggest that the resemblance class in question is a maximal class of particulars which are such that *any two of them resemble each other*. What is meant by calling such a resemblance class 'maximal' is simply that it is not a subclass of any larger such resemblance class; and maximality is required because *every* blue particular must evidently be included in the class of blue particulars. This suggestion has the advantage of doing away with 'paradigms' altogether. However, there is another apparent defect in the notion of a 'resemblance class' that is being invoked here. This can be brought out by reflecting on the fact that, for example, any *red* particular resembles an *orange* particular—because, as the realist would put it, their colours are similar. (It is true, of course, that a red particular does not resemble an orange particular *exactly*—but, then, two red particulars may not resemble each other exactly either, for one may be scarlet while the other is crimson.) One implication of this fact is that, in a universe containing only red and orange particulars, the class of all these particulars will qualify as a maximal resemblance class in the sense now being understood, even though there is no colour property that the realist would say is possessed by all of these particulars. Another is that, in such a universe, neither the class of red particulars nor the class of orange particulars will qualify as a maximal resemblance class (because each is a subclass of a larger resemblance class), even though the realist would say that there is a colour property which is possessed by all and only the particulars belonging to the first class and another colour property which is possessed by all and only the particulars belonging to the second class. These implications, however, clearly undermine the nominalist's suggestion that his maximal resemblance classes are suitable substitutes for the realist's universals. What the nominalist needs, it would seem, is a definition of 'resemblance class' which both takes into account the fact that resemblance is always a matter of *degree* and is sensitive to the fact that no red particular resembles, at least in respect of its colour, any orange particular more than it resembles another red particular.

Some problems for resemblance nominalism

In the light of these desiderata, the nominalist might suggest that the sort of resemblance class with which we could more plausibly identify the class of blue particulars is a maximal class of particulars which are such that *any two of them resemble each other at least as much as either of that pair resembles any particular which is not a member of the class.* However, this suggestion still falls foul of the fact that resemblance between particulars is always resemblance 'in some respect', which gives rise to the following problem. Suppose, to make things simple, that the universe contains just five objects, O_1 to O_5, and suppose that each of them has a size (large or small), a shape (round or square), and a colour (blue or red). More specifically, suppose that these objects have the following characteristics: O_1 is large, round, and blue; O_2 is small, square, and red; O_3 is large, square, and

TABLE 19.1

	O_1	O_2	O_3	O_4	O_5
size	large	small	large	small	small
shape	round	square	square	round	round
colour	blue	red	blue	red	blue

blue; O_4 is small, round, and red; and O_5 is small, round, and blue. This information is set out more perspicuously in Table 19.1. Now, we know which class is the class of blue particulars in this universe: it is the class whose members are O_1, O_3, and O_5. But the question is this: is this class a resemblance class in the sense just defined? Well, O_1 resembles O_3 in being large and blue, O_1 resembles O_5 in being round and blue, and O_3 resembles O_5 just in being blue. This means that O_1 and O_3 do indeed resemble each other at least as much as either of them resembles anything not belonging to the class in question: for the things which do not belong to the class are O_2 and O_4—and whereas O_1 resembles O_3 in both size and colour, O_1 resembles O_2 in no way at all and O_4 only in shape, while O_3 resembles O_2 only in shape and O_4 in no way at all. Similarly, O_1 and O_5 resemble each other at least as much as either of them resembles anything not belonging to the class in question. However, O_3 and O_5 do *not* resemble each other at least as much as either of them resembles anything not belonging to that class: for whereas O_3 and O_5 resemble each other only in colour, O_4 and O_5 resemble each other in both size and shape and thus *more* than O_3 resembles O_5. So the answer to our question is 'No'.

Another problem may be discerned by considering the universe that is depicted if we delete O_1 from Table 19.1. to give Table 19.2. Consider the class of *red* particulars in this reduced universe. It is the class whose members are O_2 and O_4. Now, this class clearly is a resemblance class in the sense

TABLE 19.2

	O_2	O_3	O_4	O_5
size	small	large	small	small
shape	square	square	round	round
colour	red	blue	red	blue

just defined, because O_2 and O_4, which resemble each other in both size and colour, evidently resemble each other at least as much as either of them resembles anything not belonging to the class in question. However, the class of red particulars in this universe is not a *maximal* resemblance class, because it is a subset of a larger such class, namely, the class whose members are O_2, O_4, and O_5, the class of small particulars. For O_2 and O_4, as we have already noted, resemble each other in both size and colour, O_4 and O_5 resemble each other in both size and shape, and O_2 and O_5 resemble each other in size: whereas O_2 resembles O_3 only in shape, O_3 resembles O_4 in no way at all, and O_3 resembles O_5 only in colour. This problem (sometimes referred to as the problem of 'companionship') arises partly because, in this universe, every red particular is a small particular, even though not every small particular is a red particular.[7]

Yet another problem which is even worse, in some ways, than either so far mentioned is one which is manifested if we consider the universe that is represented by deleting both O_1 and O_4 from Table 19.1, as in Table 19.3. Clearly, the class whose members are the particulars O_2, O_3, and O_5 constitutes a resemblance class, in the sense defined earlier; that is, it is a class of particulars which are such that any two of them resemble each other at least as much as either of that pair resembles any particular which is not a member of the class (there are, of course, no particulars which are not members of the class in this case). And it is obviously 'maximal', in the sense that it is not a subclass of any larger such resemblance class. Indeed, any two members of the class do clearly resemble one another, for O_2 and O_3 resemble each other in shape, O_3 and O_5 resemble each other in colour, and O_2 and O_5 resemble each other in size. However, there is no size, shape, or colour which is common to *all* the particulars of this class and consequently the class cannot be regarded as one that is denoted by any of the

TABLE 19.3

	O_2	O_3	O_5
size	small	large	small
shape	square	square	round
colour	red	blue	blue

---

[7] The problem was named by Nelson Goodman: see his *The Structure of Appearance*, 3rd edn. (Dordrecht: D. Reidel, 1977), 116–17.

predicates or general terms used to describe particulars in the universe in question. But the whole point of the nominalist's appeal to maximal resemblance classes of particulars was to propose them as being the entities denoted by predicates or general terms, in place of the universals which, according to the realist, such predicates and general terms denote. What the present problem (sometimes referred to as the problem of 'imperfect community') indicates is that maximal resemblance classes as currently defined are entirely unsuited to this proposed role.[8] (I should remark, incidentally, that even if, as was briefly entertained earlier, a 'resemblance class' is defined more simply as a class of particulars any two of which resemble each other—without stipulating that they resemble each other at least as much as either of them resembles anything which is not a member of the class—the problem of imperfect community evidently still arises, as does the problem of companionship. But it is worth seeing that these problems also arise for the more complex definition with which we just have been working.)

The bundle theory

What we have been looking at, in effect, are various attempts to reduce universals to, or eliminate them in favour of, particulars, by substituting certain classes of particulars for the realist's universals—classes themselves being particulars, albeit abstract ones. From what we have seen of them, these attempts look unpromising. However, even less promising, I think, are attempts to reduce particulars to, or eliminate them in favour of, universals, by substituting 'bundles' of universals for particulars.[9] If such 'bundles' are understood to be sets or classes and the latter are still conceived as being particulars, albeit abstract ones, then the strategy is self-evidently doomed to failure as it stands—though perhaps the talk of 'bundles' can be reconstrued in a non-particularist fashion. Another and more serious difficulty is that the strategy appears to commit its adherents

---

[8] This problem was also named by Nelson Goodman: see *The Structure of Appearance*, 117–19. For further discussion and an attempted solution, see Gonzalo Rodriguez-Pereyra, 'Resemblance Nominalism and the Imperfect Community', *Philosophy and Phenomenological Research* 59 (1999), 965–82.

[9] For discussion, see James Van Cleve, 'Three Versions of the Bundle Theory', *Philosophical Studies* 47 (1985), 95–107, reprinted in Stephen Laurence and Cynthia Macdonald (eds.), *Contemporary Readings in the Foundations of Metaphysics* (Oxford: Blackwell, 1998) and in Steven D. Hales (ed.), *Metaphysics: Contemporary Readings* (Belmont, Calif.: Wadsworth, 1999).

to an implausibly strong version of the principle of the identity of indiscernibles. For it seems at least logically possible that there should be two distinct particulars which exemplify all and only the same universals, such as two exactly similar material spheres in an otherwise empty universe: and yet, if any 'particular' is to be identified with the 'bundle' of universals which it would ordinarily be said to exemplify, then it appears that these spheres must in fact be identical with each other, making them one sphere rather than two.[10] So it would seem that reductionism or eliminativism of either variety has little chance of success and we should endorse some form of non-reductive pluralism, according both universals and particulars an equally fundamental ontological status. However, such a conclusion would be premature at this stage of our discussion, because we have so far not taken into account an important species of particularism, or nominalism, which escapes the difficulties which we observed earlier when discussing resemblance nominalism. There we were assuming that the 'nominalist' is someone who regards properties as being *universals* and accordingly as *entia non grata* and candidates for reduction or elimination. But an alternative position is to regard properties themselves as *particulars* of a special sort, currently often called 'tropes'.[11]

Trope theory

The trope theorist holds that the blueness of a particular blue chair is something that really exists just as much as the chair itself does, but that it is not something that can be identified with the blueness of any other blue chair, even if the two chairs resemble each other exactly in respect of the colour that each of them has. In short, on this view, each blue chair possesses its own distinct property of blueness, which is a particular, just as the chair itself is a particular. So what, according to such a theorist, does the predicate 'is blue' or the general term 'blueness' denote? They cannot, of course, be taken to denote any one particular blueness, such as the blueness of this chair or the blueness of that chair. But what they could plausibly be taken to denote is a resemblance class of tropes, that is, a class of tropes any

---

[10] See Max Black, 'The Identity of Indiscernibles', *Mind* 61 (1952), 152–64, reprinted in his *Problems of Analysis: Philosophical Essays* (London: Routledge and Kegan Paul, 1954). For further discussion, see Dean W. Zimmerman, 'Distinct Indiscernibles and the Bundle Theory', *Mind* 106 (1997), 305–9.

[11] See Keith Campbell, *Abstract Particulars* (Oxford: Blackwell, 1990).

two of which resemble each other at least as much as either of that pair resembles any trope which is not a member of the class. Because tropes are conceived to be properties, this variety of resemblance nominalism does not seem to run into the difficulties (such as those of companionship and imperfect community) which beset the varieties of resemblance nominalism discussed earlier, which regarded a member of a resemblance class as a particular which a *multiplicity* of different predicates might be taken to describe—such as 'is blue', 'is round', 'is large', and so on. Any blue trope is, clearly, properly describable by the predicate 'is blue'—but not, it would seem, by a shape predicate, such as 'is round', nor by a size predicate, such as 'is large'. Rather, if we are in the presence of a particular material object, such as a cushion, which is blue, round, and large, this will be because that object simultaneously possesses a blueness trope, a roundness trope, and a largeness trope. Indeed, what the trope theorist will say is that the cushion just *is* a certain 'bundle' of tropes, which includes a blueness trope, a roundness trope, and a largeness trope. Thus, the trope theorist not only has a way of reducing universals to, or eliminating them in favour of, resemblance classes of particulars (such classes themselves being particulars), s/he also has a way of reducing particulars which possess properties—such as chairs and cushions—to 'bundles' of particulars, namely, to 'bundles' of the particular properties or tropes which these particulars 'possess'. 'Possession' of such a property by a particular now becomes identified with the inclusion of that property in the 'bundle' of properties which allegedly constitutes the particular in question.

The problem of resemblance

The reason, then, why a resemblance nominalism founded on tropes seems to escape the difficulties besetting a resemblance nominalism founded on 'concrete' particulars—entities like chairs and cushions—is that whereas in the latter case the particulars appealed to may resemble each other in one 'respect' but not in another, in the former case the particulars appealed to resemble each other *unqualifiedly* or *simpliciter*, even if such resemblance is still a matter of degree. A red trope may resemble another red trope to a very high degree (indeed, to the highest possible degree if they resemble each other exactly) and resemble an orange trope to a much lesser degree: but it is not necessary to say in what 'respect' these tropes resemble one another, for there is no other dimension of comparison than that of colour in which any two colour tropes may be said to resemble one another.

However, although trope nominalism has this advantage over a resemblance nominalism founded on 'concrete' particulars, both forms of resemblance nominalism face apparent difficulties arising from the fact that resemblance itself, being a relation in which many different pairs of entities can stand to one another, would seem to be a universal. The realist's universals that we have so far been considering are all *properties*—such as blueness and roundness—which single particulars are said to exemplify. But other universals are *relations* which are exemplified by, for example, (ordered) pairs or triples of particulars which stand to one another in those relations—such as, perhaps, the relation of *being taller than* in which Mount Everest stands to Mont Blanc or the spatial relation of *betweenness* in which Leeds stands to London and Edinburgh. And, on the face of it, *resemblance* is just such a universal: a relation which is exemplified by pairs of particulars which resemble one another (either *simpliciter* or in some 'respect'). It seems, then, that to be consistent, a resemblance nominalist must regard resemblance itself as being reducible to, or eliminable in favour of, a certain class of pairs of particulars—just as, for example, the realist's property of blueness is supposedly reducible to, or eliminable in favour of, a certain class of particulars (namely, the class of blue particulars). The class in question will, of course, be the class of pairs of *resembling* particulars. But, as with the class of blue particulars, it would be circular and uninformative for the nominalist merely to specify the class in question in that way. He must try to specify it non-circularly as being a certain maximal *resemblance class* of pairs of particulars. But then the problem seems to be that talk of 'resemblance' is obviously unavoidable for the resemblance nominalist, being the basis of his entire strategy for doing away with the realist's universals: so that if that strategy has to be applied by the nominalist to the relation of resemblance itself, it will involve him in either a vicious circle or else a vicious infinite regress.[12]

One possible way out of this difficulty for the nominalist is for him simply to deny that resemblance should be regarded, even by the realist, as an ordinary relation—that is, as a relational *universal*—on a par with such a spatial relation as betweenness. Very arguably, the realist should regard resemblance as a so-called 'internal' relation, on the ground that facts

[12] See Bertrand Russell, *The Problems of Philosophy* (London: Williams and Norgate, 1912), ch. 9, reprinted in Mellor and Oliver (eds.), *Properties*.

about resemblance between entities are entirely founded on and determined by facts about the properties of the entities in question.[13] Indeed, the relation of *being taller than,* unlike that of betweenness, is clearly an internal relation in this sense, because whether or not one object is taller than another is determined entirely by the *heights* of the two objects. But similarly, it may be said, the realist should acknowledge that whether or not two concrete particulars, such as two chairs, resemble each other in respect of their colour is determined entirely by the *colours* of the two particulars. Certainly, he should acknowledge that if two chairs possess exactly *the same* colour (exemplify the same colour universal), then that is sufficient to determine that they resemble each other exactly in respect of their colour. And maybe he should also say that a degree of partial resemblance between two concrete particulars in respect of their colour is likewise determined by a partial identity of the colours of those particulars. For instance, perhaps he should account for the partial resemblance in colour between a reddish-orange cushion and a yellowish-orange cushion in terms of each of these cushions having a colour which is partly the same (orange) and partly different (red in the one case and yellow in the other). But if the realist should acknowledge that facts about resemblance between concrete particulars are entirely founded on and determined by facts about the properties of the particulars in question, then not even the realist should regard resemblance as an ordinary relation—that is, as being one of his universals. And that being so, the nominalist is not called upon to apply his strategy for reducing or eliminating universals to resemblance itself. (Here it is worth emphasizing that the realist should not, in any case, regard every meaningful predicate as denoting a universal, for a reason remarked upon in Chapter 6. For to do so leads inevitably to a logical contradiction via a version of Russell's paradox. Simply consider the meaningful predicate 'is non-self-exemplifying' and then ask whether the property that it putatively denotes exemplifies itself or not.[14] Hence, the mere fact that the predicate 'resembles' is meaningful does not commit the realist to regard it as denoting a universal.)

Unfortunately, this sort of consideration is not ultimately of much help to a resemblance nominalism founded on concrete particulars, because, in the case of such particulars, the realist is now envisaged as explaining facts about their resemblance as being entirely founded on and determined by

[13] See further, Campbell, *Abstract Particulars,* 37 ff.

[14] See further, Michael J. Loux, *Metaphysics: A Contemporary Introduction* (London: Routledge, 1998), 34 ff.

facts about the properties—conceived as *universals*—which those particulars exemplify (their colours and shapes and so forth). But since such a resemblance nominalist wants to substitute *resemblance classes* of concrete particulars for such universals, he is committed to regarding facts about resemblance between such particulars as being *more*, not *less*, fundamental than facts about the 'properties' which those particulars putatively possess. The trope theorist is not in this uncomfortable situation because, while he too may and plausibly should regard resemblance as being an internal relation, he regards it as being primarily a relation between *tropes*—and consequently he can say that facts about resemblance are entirely founded on and determined by the intrinsic characters of tropes, thereby avoiding the need to postulate the existence of any relational tropes of *resemblance* in order to generate his resemblance classes of tropes. This is not to say that trope nominalism may not be subject to other difficulties—difficulties concerning, for instance, the individuation of tropes and how 'bundles' of them can be understood to constitute concrete particulars—but it does seem safe to conclude that, if one aspires to defend some form of resemblance nominalism in order to avoid having to accept the existence of universals, then trope nominalism is probably the most promising option.

20

THE ABSTRACT AND THE CONCRETE

Two notions of concreteness and the status of tropes

More than once in the preceding chapter, I had occasion to distinguish between 'abstract' and 'concrete' objects. But the careful reader may have noticed that I used the term 'concrete' in two rather different senses. Earlier in the chapter, I used the term quite generally to denote objects existing in space and time (or at least in time): and in this sense concrete objects are to be contrasted with those putative objects, such as the objects of mathematics (numbers and sets, for instance), that supposedly do not exist in either space or time. The latter objects, then, may be described as being 'abstract' objects, in the sense of the term 'abstract' which corresponds to the foregoing sense of the term 'concrete'. But, towards the end of the chapter, I also used the term 'concrete' in a rather more specific sense, in which concrete objects are to be contrasted with so-called *tropes*—examples of concrete objects in this sense being particular material things, such as a particular chair or a particular cushion. Tropes, by contrast, are conceived of as being particular *properties* or *qualities* of such things, such as the particular blueness of a particular blue chair or the particular roundness of a particular round cushion. And, of course, properties or qualities as thus conceived should not be confused with the realist's *universals*, which are precisely not particulars and any one of which may be exemplified by many different 'concrete' objects, in this second sense of the term 'concrete'. Unsurprisingly, then, tropes are sometimes also called 'abstract particulars' by their devotees, in a sense of the term 'abstract' which is meant to contrast with this second sense of the term 'concrete'.[1]

What is meant by calling tropes 'abstract' in this sense is not, of course, that they do not exist in space and time. For trope theorists believe, on the contrary, that a blueness trope, for example, certainly *is* something that exists in space and time, being located precisely where the concrete object possessing it is located and existing precisely at the time or times at which it is possessed by that object. Rather, the implication of calling tropes 'abstract' in this sense is that, unlike the 'concrete' objects that possess them, they are *ontologically dependent* entities which are incapable of existing 'separately' from such concrete objects. Since, as we saw in the preceding chapter, trope theorists regard such concrete objects as being 'bundles' of tropes, what gives rise to the ontologically dependent status of tropes, in the view of such theorists, is the impossibility of any trope existing other than as a member of some trope bundle which constitutes a concrete object.[2] So the idea is that there can be no 'free' tropes, such as a blueness trope which is not the particular blueness of any particular blue object: every blueness trope must be 'bundled together' with other tropes of appropriate sorts, such as a size trope, a shape trope, a weight trope, and so on, all of which together constitute a particular 'concrete' object—for example, a large, round, heavy, blue cushion. This picture still leaves a number of important questions unanswered concerning, for instance, the nature of the 'bundling' relation between tropes which enables them to constitute concrete objects and the nature of the necessity with which tropes are supposedly confined to a 'bundle' which constitutes such an object. For some trope theorists, the 'bundling' relation is simply one of 'compresence'—existence in the same place at the same time—and there is disagreement as to whether the necessity in question is metaphysical or merely causal in character.

[1] See Keith Campbell, *Abstract Particulars* (Oxford: Blackwell, 1990).

[2] See further, Peter Simons, 'Particulars in Particular Clothing: Three Trope Theories of Substance', *Philosophy and Phenomenological Research* 54 (1994), 553–75, reprinted in Stephen Laurence and Cynthia Macdonald (eds.), *Contemporary Readings in the Foundations of Metaphysics* (Oxford: Blackwell, 1998) and in Steven D. Hales (ed.), *Metaphysics: Contemporary Readings* (Belmont, Calif.: Wadsworth, 1999).

The spatiotemporal and causal criteria of abstractness

However, these questions, interesting though they may be, are not ones that I shall pursue any further here.[3] In the present chapter, my principal concern will be with the first of the two ways in which the distinction between the 'abstract' and the 'concrete' has been drawn, so that, in what follows, when I speak of abstract objects I shall always be referring to objects which purportedly do not exist in space and time, understanding a concrete object to be, correspondingly, something that exists at least in time, if not in both space and time. In this connection, however, it is worth drawing attention to another criterion of the abstract/concrete distinction which is sometimes offered in place of or in addition to the spatiotemporal criterion now at issue, namely, a *causal* criterion. Here the idea is that concrete objects are those that are capable of entering into causal relations or that possess causal powers and liabilities, whereas abstract objects are those that are incapable of entering into such relations and do not possess such powers and liabilities. On the face of it, the spatiotemporal and the causal criterion may seem to coincide in how they divide objects between the two categories of the 'abstract' and the 'concrete', because one might suppose that an object is capable of entering into causal relations, or possesses causal powers and liabilities, if and only if it exists at least in time, if not also in space. Thus, for instance, a spatially unextended and unlocated 'Cartesian ego' or 'immaterial soul' (assuming that such a thing could exist) would qualify as a concrete object by both criteria, for it supposedly exists in time (although not in space) and it is supposedly capable of entering into causal relations with other things, notably with the ego's material body. Again, a mathematical object, such as the number seven, seems to qualify as an abstract object by both criteria, for it apparently exists neither in time nor in space and it is apparently incapable of entering into causal relations with anything, altogether lacking any causal powers or liabilities.

However, it should be acknowledged that there are other putative objects which the two criteria do not unquestionably categorize in the same way. Consider, for instance, such an 'object' as the centre of mass of

---

[3] I discuss them further in my *The Possibility of Metaphysics: Substance, Identity, and Time* (Oxford: Clarendon Press, 1998), 205 ff.

the solar system. This is something that has a spatial location at any given time and, indeed, it *moves* as the material bodies comprising the solar system move through space. But it is not a material object itself: indeed, the point of space which it occupies at any given time may be entirely devoid of matter (if that point happens to fall outside the volume of space occupied by the Sun, by far the most massive of all the bodies concerned). But the centre of mass of the solar system certainly lacks any causal powers of its own and it is a moot point whether it even possesses any causal liabilities—that is, whether it can be causally *acted upon* by anything. It is true that, when the bodies comprising the solar system move, the centre of mass of the solar system moves as a consequence: but it is not at all clear that it moves as a *causal* consequence of the movements of those bodies. For the position of the centre of mass of the solar system is simply a *logical* or *mathematical* consequence of the positions and masses of the various bodies comprising the solar system. Moreover, when the centre of mass of the solar system moves as a consequence of the movements of the bodies concerned, the change in its position occurs at the very instant at which those bodies move—and if, as is widely assumed, instantaneous action at a distance is impossible, this means that its movement cannot be *caused* by the movements of those bodies. Furthermore, it would seem to be impossible for anything to act *directly* upon the centre of mass of the solar system, in the causal sense of 'act upon', without involving the material bodies which comprise the solar system. All in all, then, it appears that we should say that, by the causal criterion but not by the spatiotemporal criterion, the centre of mass of the solar system is an abstract object.

However, we should not regard this disagreement as unduly troublesome. We can simply accept that, even setting aside the sense of the abstract/concrete distinction that is associated with trope theory, the abstract/concrete distinction is ambiguous in a further way, one sense of it being captured by the spatiotemporal criterion and another by the causal criterion. For many purposes, the two criteria will effectively coincide, even though, as we have just seen, there are certain cases in which they deliver different verdicts.[4]

---

[4] For more on the distinction(s) between the abstract and the concrete, see Bob Hale, *Abstract Objects* (Oxford: Blackwell, 1987), and my 'The Metaphysics of Abstract Objects', *Journal of Philosophy* 92 (1995), 509–24, or my *The Possibility of Metaphysics*, ch. 10.

Existence in space and time

As I have already indicated, my chief concern in this chapter is with the abstract/concrete distinction in the sense that is captured by the spatio-temporal criterion stated earlier. However, this criterion itself is in need of some further elucidation. When it is said that abstract objects are those that do not exist 'in' space or time, it should not thereby be suggested that they literally exist *outside* space and time. For, understood literally, the preposition 'outside' expresses a *spatial* relation (as when one describes a certain apple as lying 'outside' a basket which contains some other apples) and so describing something as literally existing 'outside' space itself is self-contradictory. (If the object literally existed outside space, then it would stand in a certain spatial relation to space and thereby to all the parts of space: but anything which stands in a spatial relation to any part of space must thereby occupy a part of space itself, in which case it cannot after all exist outside space.) So, in saying that abstract objects (in the sense of 'abstract' now at issue) do not exist 'in' space and time, one must be careful to imply only that, while these objects exist, they do not occupy any part of space or exist at any time. However, it may wondered now whether it really makes sense to suppose that an object can exist without existing *at* any time whatever. On reflection, might it not be better, instead of saying that an abstract object (in the sense now intended) is one that does not exist 'in' time, to say, rather, that it is one that exists at *all* times and never undergoes any sort of *change* over time? Such an object would be eternal (or, at least, coeval with time itself) and immutable. But, while there might conceivably be an object answering to this sort of description, since it seems to fit one traditional conception of God Himself, it is not clear that we should want to describe such an object as being 'abstract'. If we think of such paradigm abstract objects as the natural numbers, do we really want to say that such objects exist *at* any time at all, let alone at all times? After all, the truths of pure mathematics carry no reference to time whatever and are uniformly *tenseless*—truths such as 'Seven is a prime number' and 'Seven plus five equals twelve'.

We cannot, I think, hope to make further headway with this issue without reflecting more on what it means to say that an object exists 'in' time. We surely cannot simply take the notion of existence 'in' time as primitive or as self-explanatory and thus requiring no elucidation. However, if we are prepared to adopt a 'tensed' theory of time (see Chapter 17), then perhaps what we can say is that for an object to exist 'in' time is just for that object to be *a possible subject of true tensed predications*.[5] And by this standard, it might seem, mathematical objects such as the natural numbers do *not* exist 'in' time, precisely because the truths of pure mathematics are tenseless. But, unfortunately, matters cannot be quite as simple as this. If, by describing an object as being a possible subject of true tensed predications, one means that we can truly say of this object that it now has, or formerly had, or will in future have some property, then it would appear that even mathematical objects are, after all, possible subjects of true tensed predications. For I can truly say, for instance, that the number seven used to be my favourite number, but is so no longer or that the number twelve is now being thought about by me. It is true that *purely* mathematical discourse has no use for tensed predications, but reference to numbers can occur in other kinds of discourse than the purely mathematical.

In response to this point, however, it may be contended, quite plausibly, that every true statement about a mathematical object which involves tensed predication is *contingent* in character. It is thus a merely contingent truth that the number seven used to be my favourite number, as it is that the number twelve is now being thought about by me. In contrast, it is a *necessary* truth that seven is a prime number and that seven plus five equals twelve. So, perhaps we can say that what is distinctive of mathematical objects—and of 'abstract' objects quite generally, in the sense which we are now trying to elucidate—is that the only true tensed predications of which they can be the subjects are contingent ones, and that this is what it amounts to to say that such objects do not exist 'in' time. However, even this last proposal will not quite work: for there evidently *are* necessary truths concerning numbers which involve tensed predications—such as 'Either the number twelve is now being thought about by me or it is not the case that the number twelve is now being thought about by me', which is a necessary truth simply because it is a statement of the form 'Either *p* or not-*p*'. But in this sort of case, clearly, the necessity of a statement involving reference to a number as the subject of a tensed predication is quite independent of the fact that the statement involves reference to a number. So perhaps we can say, finally, that the sense in which such abstract objects as numbers do not exist 'in' time is that the only true tensed predications of which they can be the subjects *and which are not necessary truths quite*

---

[5] See further, my *The Possibility of Metaphysics*, 96 ff.

independently of the fact that it is these objects that are their subjects are contingent ones.

How is knowledge of abstract objects possible?

We have been trying to determine more precisely what we should mean by saying that abstract objects, such as the natural numbers, do not exist 'in' either space or time, given that this cannot be taken crudely to mean that they exist 'outside' space and time in any purely literal sense. And the idea towards which we have been gravitating is that what is distinctive of such objects is that it is no part of their essential nature that they bear any relation whatever to the occupants of space and time—that is, to such entities as material objects, persons, and events, all of which correspondingly qualify as 'concrete' by this standard. Abstract objects can contingently stand in various relations to concrete objects—as, for instance, the number twelve may stand in the relation of *being thought about by* to a certain person, who exists in a certain place at a certain moment of time. But, plausibly, the number twelve would still have existed even if no one at all had ever thought about it. However, if it is no part of the essential nature of abstract objects, as presently conceived, that they bear any relation whatever to the occupants of space and time, does this not threaten to undermine any reason that we (as occupants of space and time ourselves) might have to believe in their existence?

In one use of the term 'nominalist'—which does not coincide exactly with the use of that term employed in the preceding chapter—a nominalist is someone who denies the existence of abstract objects in the sense now under discussion, often on the grounds that, given their purported nature, we can have no reason to believe in the existence of such objects. It is complained that, in view of the non-spatiotemporal character of abstract objects such as numbers, we cannot possibly *perceive* such objects and have knowledge of them in that way. Moreover, if, in virtue of their non-spatiotemporal character, such objects are causally inert, then we cannot have knowledge of them in any other way, given the correctness of a causal theory of knowledge of the kind that is currently quite widely favoured by epistemologists.[6] For, according to such a causal theory, knowledge

---

[6] See Paul Benacerraf, 'Mathematical Truth', *Journal of Philosophy* 70 (1973), 661–80, reprinted in Paul Benacerraf and Hilary Putnam (eds.), *Philosophy of Mathematics: Selected Readings*, 2nd edn. (Cambridge: Cambridge University Press, 1983).

consists, roughly speaking, in beliefs caused in a reliable way by the objects of belief. However, it is far from evident why we should not be able to *think* about abstract objects—why they should not be objects of *thought*. For we can even think about *non-existent* objects, such as the objects of myth and fiction. Indeed, even the opponents of abstract objects may have to concede that we can think about them, since they seem to regard them precisely as a species of fictional object.

None the less, there is an important difference between an abstract object, such as the number seven, and the typical objects of myth and fiction, such as unicorns and dragons. This is that unicorns and dragons are supposed to be *concrete* objects which, if they existed, would exist 'in' space and time. Because, as far as we know, no such objects have been discovered amongst the occupants of space and time, we can conclude that unicorns and dragons do not exist at all. But since abstract objects are *not* supposed to exist 'in' space and time, our failure to discover any amongst the occupants of space and time in no way undermines our belief in their existence. Moreover, given that we can think about abstract objects and that whether or not they exist is an open question, it would seem that we may hope to resolve that question by processes of *reasoning*, which is undoubtedly one possible source of knowledge. So, one possible response to nominalist doubts of the kind just described is to say that we may aspire to have knowledge of the existence and nature of abstract objects by means of rational arguments which do not appeal to any ability on our part to *perceive* such objects. If this means repudiating a causal theory of knowledge, then so be it: perhaps such a theory is really only appropriate, at best, as an account of our knowledge of the existence and nature of *concrete* objects.

The indispensability argument

One sort of rational consideration that is often advanced in favour of the existence of abstract objects, especially the objects of mathematics, is that the postulation of their existence is indispensable for adequate scientific explanation of the nature and behaviour of *concrete* objects. The thought here is that successful scientific theories, at least in the more advanced empirical sciences such as theoretical physics, depend heavily upon mathematics for their formulation and application.[7] For example, Newton's

---

[7] See further, W. V. Quine, *Philosophy of Logic* (Englewood Cliffs, NJ: Prentice-Hall, 1970), 98 ff., and Hilary Putnam, *Philosophy of Logic* (London: George Allen and Unwin, 1972), 53 ff.

inverse square law of gravitation, which states that the gravitational force exerted by a pair of bodies on each other is proportional to the product of their masses and inversely proportional to the square of the distance between them—as expressed by the mathematical equation $F = Gm_1m_2/r^2$, where G is the universal constant of gravitation, m_1 and m_2 are the masses of the two bodies concerned, and r is the distance between the centres of mass of those bodies (all measured in appropriate units)—quite explicitly involves mathematical functions and numbers in its formulation and application. (For instance, it involves in its formulation the *square function*, which takes a number as its argument and another number—the square of the first number—as its value; and in its application it involves numbers in the specification of quantities of mass and amounts of distance.) If a scientific theory has to be true in order to provide an adequate explanation of some range of natural phenomena and if the truth of a scientific theory which has a mathematical component depends upon the existence of certain mathematical objects, then we may apparently conclude that any adequate scientific explanation by means of a theory which has an indispensable mathematical component implies the existence of mathematical—and hence abstract—objects.

However, there are several substantial 'ifs' here which stand in the way of a conclusive argument for the existence of abstract objects. It may disputed whether a scientific theory has to be *true* in order for it to provide an adequate scientific explanation of some range of natural phenomena.[8] After all, we still use Newton's law of gravitation to explain and predict the trajectories of projectiles, even though it is no longer believed to be strictly true. Again, it may be disputed whether mathematical truths depend upon the existence of mathematical objects and also disputed whether the mathematical components of scientific theories are indispensable. For, on the one hand, it may be that mathematical statements which appear to make reference to mathematical objects can be reconstrued as making no such reference, without impugning the truth of those statements. And, on the other hand, it may be that the mathematical component of a scientific theory is merely an abbreviatory device which could, in principle, be excluded from a logically equivalent (if more long-winded and cumbersome) formulation of the theory.[9]

---

[8] See further, Bas C. van Fraassen, *The Scientific Image* (Oxford: Clarendon Press, 1980).
[9] See further, Hartry H. Field, *Science without Numbers: A Defence of Nominalism* (Oxford: Blackwell, 1980).

Mathematical truths and mathematical objects

Let us look more closely at the suggestion that mathematical truths imply the existence of mathematical objects, conceived as a species of abstract objects. For if this suggestion can be sustained, perhaps it provides an argument sufficient in itself to support a rational belief in the existence of abstract objects, on the grounds that it would be difficult to deny that there are mathematical truths. (Difficult, but perhaps not impossible: for it might be argued that mathematics does not, or should not, aim at truth. But let us set aside this line of thought for present purposes.) On the face of it, there are mathematical truths which quite explicitly imply the existence of mathematical objects, such as numbers, which cannot but be construed as objects which are not concrete. Consider, for instance, the true mathematical statements 'There is a natural number greater than zero', and 'For every natural number, n, there is exactly one number which is the successor of n', and 'No natural number is identical with its successor'. These statements together imply that there are infinitely many natural numbers. But, in all probability, there are not infinitely many concrete objects in existence—at least, we have no good reason to believe that this is so. Hence, it seems, the natural numbers must be *abstract* objects (on the assumption that the abstract/concrete distinction is exhaustive as well as exclusive, so that every object must be either a concrete object or else an abstract object but not both).

However, there is an apparent difficulty in taking the natural numbers to be abstract objects: for if they are abstract objects, then it is not clear *which* such objects they are. This difficulty can be made vivid by reflecting on the fact that, if abstract objects do indeed exist and include *sets*, then there are indefinitely many different abstract objects which could, in principle, be identified with any given natural number, consistently with known mathematical truths.[10] For instance, it would be quite possible, in principle, to identify the number zero with the empty set (the set which uniquely possesses no members), the number 1 with the unit set of the empty set (the set which has the empty set as its sole member), the number 2 with the unit set of the number 1 (the set which has the number 1 its sole member), the number 3 with the unit set of the number 2—and so on ad infinitum. But,

---

[10] See further, Paul Benacerraf, 'What Numbers Could Not Be', *Philosophical Review* 74 (1965), 47–73, reprinted in Benacerraf and Putnam (eds.), *Philosophy of Mathematics: Selected Readings*.

equally, it would be quite possible, in principle, to identify the number zero and the number 1 as before, but to identify the number 2 with the set which has as its sole members the number zero and the number 1, the number 3 with the set which has as its sole members the number zero, the number 1, and the number 2—and so on ad infinitum. The problem with this embarrassment of riches is that we seem to have no principled way of deciding *which*, if any, of these abstract objects any given natural number is: and, of course, since the various candidates for identity with any given natural number (greater than 1, at any rate) are indisputably distinct from one another, no natural number can be identified with *all* of the relevant candidates. One conclusion that one might be tempted to draw from this is that mathematical truths cannot, after all, imply the existence of specific abstract objects of any kind. Arithmetical truths, for instance, may be said to be truths *not* about relationships between a quite specific class of abstract objects, 'the' natural numbers, but rather truths which, suitably interpreted, hold of *any* class of objects possessing a certain kind of structural organization—the kind of structural organization in virtue of which the class has a 'first' member (representable by the symbol 'o') and a unique 'successor' for each of its members.

It may be protested that this still requires there to be infinitely many objects of *some* kind or kinds—and hence abstract objects of some kind or kinds—if mathematical statements are to be true, even if we cannot identify any *specific* kind of abstract objects which must exist for that reason. But even this may be questioned, for it may be contended that arithmetical truths, for instance, are made true by facts concerning any *possible* class of objects possessing the requisite structural organization, so that it is not necessary, in order for such truths to obtain, that some such class of objects should *actually* exist: it suffices that some such class of objects exists 'in some possible world'.[11] Now, however, even though it may be implausible to suppose that infinitely many concrete objects exist in the *actual* world, it is surely very plausible to suppose that infinitely many concrete objects exist in *some* possible world: in which case, the truths of arithmetic, it would appear, do not depend for their truth on the actual existence of *abstract* objects of any kind at all, but merely on the

[11] See further, Hilary Putnam, 'Mathematics Without Foundations', *Journal of Philosophy* 64 (1967), 5–22, reprinted in his *Mathematics, Matter and Method: Philosophical Papers, Volume 1* (Cambridge: Cambridge University Press, 1975) and in Benacerraf and Putnam (eds.), *Philosophy of Mathematics: Selected Readings*. See also Geoffrey Hellman, *Mathematics Without Numbers: Towards a Modal-Structural Interpretation* (Oxford: Clarendon Press, 1989).

possible existence of infinitely many concrete objects of some kind or kinds.

The ontological status of sets

Of course, it may be protested now that nothing we have said so far calls into question the existence of *sets or classes*, even in the actual world—and these are supposed to be abstract objects themselves. Moreover, although there may be a problem concerning the identity of the natural numbers, there is no problem concerning the identity of sets: for the so-called axiom of extensionality of set theory provides sets with a quite unambiguous criterion of identity. This axiom states that for any sets x and y, x is identical with y if and only if x and y have the same members. It was this axiom, indeed, which enabled us to say that certain candidates for identity with the natural numbers were distinct from one another: that, for instance, the number 2 could not be identical *both* with the unit set of the number 1 *and* with the set whose sole members are the number zero and the number 1. For these sets have different members and are therefore distinct according to the axiom. However, both the claim that sets are abstract objects and, more radically, the claim that sets exist may be challenged. On the one hand, it might conceivably be urged that sets all of whose members are concrete objects are concrete objects themselves.[12] On the other hand, it might conceivably be urged that talk about 'sets' is just a convenient grammatical device for talk about their members. More specifically, it might be contended that what appears to be singular reference to a 'set' of objects is merely a convenient grammatical substitute for plural reference to those very objects—so that, for instance, instead of saying something like 'British women are more numerous than British men', we may say, equivalently, 'The set of British women is larger than the set of British men'. Given that these two sentences are logically equivalent and that the only objects whose existence is implied by the first sentence are certain men and women, it may be argued that the second sentence, too, only implies the existence of these concrete objects and not, in addition, the existence of two allegedly abstract objects, the 'sets' to which the men and women in question supposedly 'belong'.[13]

[12] See further, Penelope Maddy, *Realism in Mathematics* (Oxford: Clarendon Press, 1990), 50 ff.

[13] For more on plural reference and set theory, see George Boolos, 'To Be is To Be a Value of a Variable (or To Be Some Values of Some Variables)', *Journal of Philosophy* 81 (1984), 430–49, reprinted in his *Logic, Logic, and Logic* (Cambridge, Mass.: Harvard University Press, 1998).

The ontological status of possible worlds

At this point, the devotee of abstract objects may call attention to the fact that, in explaining earlier how it might be contended that the truths of arithmetic depend for their truth merely on the *possible* existence of infinitely many concrete objects of some kind or kinds, I made reference to *possible worlds*. For now it may be urged that possible worlds are themselves abstract objects—maximal consistent sets of propositions, according to one widely held theory—so that we cannot really escape a commitment to the existence of abstract objects of some kind by adopting the strategy outlined earlier. (For such a view of possible worlds, see Chapter 7.)

In answer, it may be pointed out that, even if it is granted (which, perhaps, it need not be) that a commitment to the existence of possible worlds is an unavoidable consequence of a satisfactory account of the status of modal truths—truths concerning what is possible or necessary—not every theory of possible worlds represents such worlds as being abstract objects. According to one widely respected view, indeed, possible worlds, including the actual world, are indisputably concrete objects, each such world being a maximal sum of spatiotemporally related objects—that is, a whole whose parts include every object that is spatiotemporally related to any one of those parts (see Chapter 7).

But it may perhaps be objected now that if possible worlds are conceived of in this way, then, with the sole exception of the actual world (of which we ourselves are a part), they might as well be abstract objects as far as we are concerned—for they and their inhabitants stand in no spatiotemporal or causal relation to *us*, any more than abstract objects do. That is to say, if the source of one's concern about admitting the existence of abstract objects is just that they stand in no spatiotemporal or causal relation to us, then 'concrete' possible worlds of the type now under consideration should be a source of quite as much concern. It seems, thus, that unless one can offer a satisfactory account of the status of modal truths which does not commit one to the existence of possible worlds, either abstract or concrete, the strategy outlined earlier for maintaining that the truths of arithmetic depend for their truth merely on the possible existence of infinitely many concrete objects will lack a coherent motivation.

Universals and laws of nature

So far, I have mentioned some rational considerations in favour of and some against belief in the existence of numbers, sets, and possible worlds, conceived as species of abstract objects, but have identified no very compelling argument either way. However, we have yet to consider the case of *universals*, which many of their devotees take to be abstract objects par excellence. In Chapter 19, we looked at the debate between 'nominalists'—there understood as the opponents of universals—and 'realists', concluding that a resemblance nominalism founded on *tropes* is probably the most promising approach for the opponent of universals to adopt. Tropes, as I mentioned earlier in this chapter, are conceived of by their adherents as being spatiotemporal particulars and thus as 'concrete' objects, in the sense of 'concrete' with which we are now concerned (even though, in another sense, they are sometimes called, rather confusingly, 'abstract particulars'). However, it is important to appreciate that a belief in the existence of tropes is not incompatible with a belief in the existence of universals, even though many trope theorists wish to defend a form of resemblance nominalism founded on tropes. One can quite consistently hold that tropes—that is, particular properties or qualities—exist but only as particular *instances* of corresponding universals: for example, that the particular bluenesses of this chair and of that chair are both instances of the same universal *blueness*, which exists in addition to all of its particular instances. But why should anyone wish to hold such a view? One reason, of course, is that it may be doubted whether any form of resemblance nominalism can be successfully founded upon tropes. More positively, however, one may consider that the existence of universals must be acknowledged if one is to provide an adequate account of facts or states of affairs of a certain kind: I have in mind, especially, those facts or states of affairs that statements of natural law are said to express. (On a point of terminology: the term 'natural law', or 'law of nature', is often used to refer to a species of statement or proposition, but it is also sometimes used to refer to the kind of fact or state of affairs which would make such a statement or proposition true. For the rest of this chapter, I shall adopt the latter usage, although either usage is acceptable, provided that it is made clear which is being adopted. So, in what follows, I shall be assuming that a true statement of natural law is something that is made true by a law of nature.)

For reasons similar to some of those raised in Chapter 9 in objection to the so-called 'constant conjunction' analysis of event causation, it is difficult to sustain a view of natural laws which represents them as consisting merely in exceptionless regularities amongst particular events or states of affairs of certain types. Consider, for instance, Newton's law of gravitation, which was mentioned earlier in this chapter and was there expressed by the following statement: the gravitational force exerted by a pair of bodies on each other is proportional to the product of their masses and inversely proportional to the square of the distance between them. And let us assume, for present purposes, that this law actually obtains (even though Newton's theory of gravitation has now been superseded by Einstein's). Then it is hard to suppose that the law simply consists in the fact that every particular pair of bodies, throughout the universe in space and time, exert a force on each other of the stated magnitude. Apart from anything else, this would be consistent with the law being a mere 'cosmic accident' and would fail to explain our conviction that, if another pair of bodies had existed, in addition to any of those that actually do exist, then they too would have exerted a force on each other of the stated magnitude. In short, the 'regularity' theory of natural law fails to account for our conviction that statements of natural law imply the truth of corresponding counterfactual conditionals.

In the light of this and other difficulties with the 'regularity' theory of natural law, some philosophers maintain that laws consist not in exceptionless regularities amongst particular events or states of affairs of certain types, but rather in some sort of 'second-order' relationship between certain 'first-order' *properties* or *relations*, conceived as universals.[14] For instance, in the case of Newton's law of gravitation, the universals in question will be the gravitational *force* relation and the spatial *distance* relation in which particular bodies may stand to one another in varying degrees, together with the property of *mass* which all particular bodies exemplify in some degree. So, the idea is that the law consists fundamentally in a relationship between these universals which is most perspicuously expressed by the mathematical equation stated earlier, $F = Gm_1m_2/r^2$, in which F, m, and r denote, respectively, the universals *force*, *mass*, and *distance*. Because the law consists in this relationship between universals, it has implications for any particulars exemplifying these universals and thus *explains* why an exceptionless regularity amongst such particulars obtains throughout the

[14] See, for example, D. M. Armstrong, *What is a Law of Nature?* (Cambridge: Cambridge University Press, 1983), pt. 2.

universe in space and time—that is, it explains why such a regularity is no mere 'cosmic accident' and consequently also explains why, if another pair of bodies had existed, in addition to any of those that actually do exist, then they too would have exerted a force on each other of a magnitude determined by the law. I should add that many philosophers who adopt this sort of approach consider that the 'second-order' relationship between the universals involved in a law is, or involves, some distinctive kind of *necessitation*, which is to be distinguished from the relation of logical necessitation in which two propositions stand when one of them entails the other—in short, a kind of 'natural' necessitation, our knowledge of which is purely a posteriori.

There are many questions and doubts that may be raised about a conception of natural law of the foregoing sort and I do not have enough space to discuss all of them here. One important question, however, concerns the relationship between a natural law, as here conceived, and the corresponding exceptionless regularity amongst particulars: for it may be asked *why*, given that the law concerns only universals, it has any implications whatever for particulars.[15] The suggestion, of course, is that it has such implications simply because the particulars in question *exemplify* the universals involved in the law. But why should it follow, just because certain particulars exemplify the universals involved in the law, that those particulars must participate in an exceptionless regularity which 'conforms' to the law? For instance, granted that Newton's law of gravitation consists in a certain second-order relationship between the universals *force, mass,* and *distance,* why should it therefore follow that every pair of particular bodies exemplifying in some degree the universal *mass* and standing to one another in some degree of the relational universal *distance* (as, of course, all particular bodies do) must also exert upon each other a degree of the relational universal *force* of a magnitude suggested by the law? As we might more figuratively pose this question: why should all particulars exemplifying the universals in question 'obey' the law, given that the law as such involves only the universals? Perhaps, in the end, this question rests upon a misunderstanding of what it is for a particular to exemplify a universal. I am sympathetic to such a response myself, but shall not venture to develop it further here. Suffice it to say that, while the conception of natural laws as consisting in relationships between universals has considerable attractions,

---

[15] See further, Bas C. van Fraassen, *Laws and Symmetry* (Oxford: Clarendon Press, 1989), 96 ff., where this is called 'the inference problem'.

those attractions may not provide entirely compelling reasons to believe in the existence of universals.

Are universals abstract or concrete objects?

Suppose, however, that one were persuaded to believe in the existence of universals for the foregoing sort of reason. That would still not necessarily provide one with a reason to believe in *abstract* objects of any kind, because we cannot simply assume without argument that universals must be abstract objects (in the sense of 'abstract', of course, with which we have primarily been concerned in this chapter). Indeed, there are some philosophers who believe in the existence of universals chiefly on account of their supposed involvement in laws of nature and hold that universals are *not* abstract objects, but exist entirely 'in' space and time.[16] According to such philosophers, every universal is 'wholly present' in each particular which exemplifies it and accordingly has a 'scattered' spatiotemporal location which is the sum of the spatiotemporal locations of all the particulars in question. On this view, the universal *blueness*, for instance, is located at all the places and times at which any blue particular is located. A consequence of this doctrine is that no universal can exist unless it is exemplified by some particular, existing at some place and time. But the philosophers in question are happy to accept that implication, because they believe that only concrete objects exist and that an unexemplified universal could not be a concrete object, since, lacking any particular instances, it could have no spatiotemporal location.

Against this doctrine that all universals are concrete objects, it may be objected, first, that the idea of something being 'wholly present' in more than one spatiotemporal location borders on incoherence and, second, that it is in danger of collapsing into a pure trope theory. The claim that universals may be 'wholly present' in more than one spatiotemporal location (which we first discussed in Chapter 19) is difficult to grasp clearly. The idea is that *all* of a universal, such as *blueness*, may simultaneously be located both in one place—say, where a certain blue chair, A, is located—and also in another place, where another blue chair, B, is located. But if all of the universal is located where A is located, it surely follows that A is

---

[16] See D. M. Armstrong, *A World of States of Affairs* (Cambridge: Cambridge University Press, 1997), 135 ff.

located where all of the universal is located, for co-location would appear to be a symmetrical relation. And if A is located where all of the universal is located and all of the universal is located where B is located, it surely follows that A is located where B is located, for co-location would appear to be a transitive relation. However, A and B are *not*, of course, co-located. So, it would seem that it cannot, after all, be the case that all of the universal is simultaneously located both where A is located and where B is located. Now, of course, the philosophers who adhere to the view currently under discussion will challenge this argument, claiming, in all likelihood, that it rests upon a question-begging assimilation of universals to particulars where matters of spatiotemporal location are concerned. However, what the argument is intended to bring out is precisely the difficulty we experience in trying to think of such matters other than in the terms in which they indisputably apply to particulars. And therefore what the philosophers in question owe us is a perspicuous explanation of *how there can be* a class of entities which, although spatiotemporally located, do not behave like particulars in this respect.

It is important to appreciate here that the foregoing objection is not to the idea of something's having a *scattered* spatiotemporal location, for even certain particulars would seem to satisfy this description. Consider, for instance, the case of a particular watch which has been taken to the watchmaker for repair and now sits upon his workbench in a disassembled condition, its various parts scattered over the surface of the workbench. It seems fair to say that, for a certain period of time, the watch has a scattered location, being located in the sum of the places occupied by its various parts. However, what we do *not* want to say, in the case of this watch, is that *all* of it is located in each of these places: that it is 'wholly present' in each of them. Rather, it is 'partly present' in each of these places, in virtue of having a different part in each of them. This brings us to the second objection to the doctrine that universals are concrete objects, namely, that it is in danger of collapsing into a pure trope theory. For we may ask adherents of the doctrine to explain what the difference really amounts to between saying that *one and the same blueness* (a so-called universal) exists in many different spatiotemporal locations and saying that *many distinct but resembling bluenesses* (tropes) exist in all those different spatiotemporal locations. Indeed, it would seem to be perfectly possible for a philosopher to maintain that what is *meant* by saying the first of these things is precisely what is said by saying the second of them: for it might be urged that the so-called 'universal' blueness is in reality nothing more nor less than the sum of all the particular bluenesses, having (rather like the disassembled watch) a 'scattered' location which is the sum of the locations of all of its particular parts. In short, it may seem that the distinction that the advocate of 'concrete universals' wants to make between his own position and that of the pure trope theorist is really a distinction without a difference. No such objection can be raised, of course, against the advocate of universals who holds them to be *abstract* objects, because this theorist maintains that universals *lack* a characteristic that is shared by all particulars, namely, spatiotemporal locatedness.

The ontological status of facts and states of affairs

Discussion of the abstract/concrete distinction would not be complete without some consideration of the application of that distinction to one important category of entities that has already received some mention in this chapter—namely, *facts* or *states of affairs*. The important point to register here is that there is a good deal of disagreement over whether facts or states of affairs should be classified as abstract or as concrete entities, because there are at least two very different ways of conceiving of such entities.[17] A view which holds that all states of affairs are abstract entities was aired in Chapter 7, in connection with the doctrine that possible worlds are maximal consistent states of affairs. According to this view, states of affairs are necessary beings—entities which exist 'in every possible world'—and a 'fact' is simply a state of affairs which 'obtains'. As such, states of affairs are conceived of as being very similar to, if not indistinguishable from, *propositions*, as these have traditionally been conceived—and thus as *abstract* entities of a certain kind. But according to another widely favoured view, facts should instead be conceived of as 'complexes' which contain certain universals and particulars quite literally as their 'constituents'. Thus, for example, the fact that a certain chair is blue would, on this view, be held to contain as its constituents that very chair and the universal *blueness*, with the former standing in the relation of exemplification to the latter. (Of course, an adherent of this view would be wise not to regard exemplification itself as being a relational *universal*, as this would threaten to generate a vicious infinite regress.) But then we may ask whether this fact should itself be categorized as a particular or as a

---

[17] See further my *The Possibility of Metaphysics*, 231 ff.

universal, as well as whether it should be classified as an abstract or a concrete entity—on the presumption that each of these distinctions is exhaustive and mutually exclusive in character.

The response most likely to be offered by adherents of the view now under consideration is that such a fact is a concrete particular.[18] But since it is far from easy to adjudicate between the two different conceptions of facts that have just been outlined, it is difficult to say with any confidence whether facts should be classified as abstract or as concrete entities. Indeed, it is even debatable whether facts or states of affairs should be included in our ontology at all, because the supposition that they should be is subject to an objection based on a version of the Slingshot Argument discussed in Chapter 9. The version of the Slingshot Argument presented there purported to show that if any statement of fact causation is true, then *every* statement of fact causation which refers to any two facts whatever is true. This version of the argument started from an arbitrarily chosen premise of the form 'The fact that p caused the fact that q' and concluded, for an arbitrary choice of true sentences r and s, 'The fact that r caused the fact that s'. But it easy to see how one can construct a parallel version of the argument from an arbitrarily chosen premise of the form 'The fact that p is identical with the fact that q' and conclude, for an arbitrary choice of true sentences r and s, 'The fact that r is identical with the fact that s'—the apparently absurd implication being that there can be no more than *one* fact, sometimes called, with deliberate irony, 'the Great Fact'.[19] As we saw in Chapter 9, the Slingshot Argument is open to objection itself, so that, in this latest version, it need not necessarily be seen as constituting an insuperable objection to belief in the existence of facts. Even so, it would seem that the ontological status of facts is sufficiently controversial to call into question any system of ontology which accords them a central and fundamental role.

---

[18] See Armstrong, *A World of States of Affairs*, 126–7, where he speaks of this as 'the victory of particularity'.

[19] See Donald Davidson, 'True to the Facts', *Journal of Philosophy* 66 (1969), 748–64, reprinted in his *Inquiries into Truth and Interpretation* (Oxford: Clarendon Press, 1984).

BIBLIOGRAPHY

Ackrill, J. L., *Aristotle the Philosopher* (Oxford: Oxford University Press, 1981).

Alexander, P., 'Incongruent Counterparts and Absolute Space', *Proceedings of the Aristotelian Society* 85 (1984/5), 1–21.

Alvarez, M., and Hyman, J., 'Agents and their Actions', *Philosophy* 73 (1998), 219–45.

Anscombe, G. E. M., 'Causality and Determination', in G. E. M. Anscombe, *Metaphysics and the Philosophy of Mind: Collected Philosophical Papers, Volume II* (Oxford: Blackwell, 1981).

Aristotle, *Metaphysics*, in W. D. Ross (ed.), *The Works of Aristotle Translated into English. Volume VIII: Metaphysica*, 2nd edn. (Oxford: Clarendon Press, 1928).

Armstrong, D. M., *A Combinatorial Theory of Possibility* (Cambridge: Cambridge University Press, 1989).

—— 'Identity Through Time', in P. van Inwagen (ed.), *Time and Cause: Essays Presented to Richard Taylor* (Dordrecht: D. Reidel, 1980).

—— *Nominalism and Realism: Universals and Scientific Realism, Volume I* (Cambridge: Cambridge University Press, 1978).

—— *Universals: An Opinionated Introduction* (Boulder, Colo.: Westview Press, 1989).

—— *What is a Law of Nature?* (Cambridge: Cambridge University Press, 1983).

—— *A World of States of Affairs* (Cambridge: Cambridge University Press, 1997).

Bach, K., 'Actions Are Not Events', *Mind* 89 (1980), 114–20.

Bambrough, R., 'Universals and Family Resemblances', *Proceedings of the Aristotelian Society* 60 (1960/1), 207–22.

Barrow, J. D., and Tippler, F. J., *The Anthropic Cosmological Principle* (Oxford: Clarendon Press, 1986).

Benacerraf, P., 'Mathematical Truth', *Journal of Philosophy* 70 (1973), 661–80.

—— 'What Numbers Could Not Be', *Philosophical Review* 74 (1965), 47–73.

—— and Putnam, H. (eds.), *Philosophy of Mathematics: Selected Readings*, 2nd edn. (Cambridge: Cambridge University Press, 1983).

Bennett, J., 'Classifying Conditionals: The Traditional Way is Right', *Mind* 104 (1995), 331–54.

—— 'Counterfactuals and Temporal Direction', *Philosophical Review* 93 (1984), 57–91.

—— *Events and their Names* (Oxford: Clarendon Press, 1988).

—— 'Farewell to the Phlogiston Theory of Conditionals', *Mind* 97 (1988), 509–27.

Berkeley, G., *A Treatise Concerning the Principles of Human Knowledge*, in G. Berkeley, *Philosophical Works*, ed. M. R. Ayers (London: Dent, 1975).

Black, M., 'The Identity of Indiscernibles', *Mind* 61 (1952), 152–64.

—— *Problems of Analysis: Philosophical Essays* (London: Routledge and Kegan Paul, 1954).

Boolos, G., *Logic, Logic, and Logic* (Cambridge, Mass: Harvard University Press, 1998).

—— 'To Be is To Be a Value of a Variable (or To Be Some Values of Some Variables)', *Journal of Philosophy* 81 (1984), 430–49.

Boswell, J., *The Life of Samuel Johnson* (London: Dent, 1906).

Brand, M., and Walton, D. (eds.), *Action Theory* (Dordrecht: D. Reidel, 1976).

Broad, C. D., *Scientific Thought* (London: Routledge and Kegan Paul, 1923).

Brody, B. A., *Identity and Essence* (Princeton, NJ: Princeton University Press, 1980).

Bunzl, M., 'Causal Overdetermination', *Journal of Philosophy* 76 (1979), 134–50.

Burke, M. B., 'Copper Statues and Pieces of Copper', *Analysis* 52 (1992), 12–17.

—— 'Dion and Theon: An Essentialist Solution to an Ancient Puzzle', *Journal of Philosophy* 91 (1994), 129–39.

—— 'Preserving the Principle of One Object to a Place: A Novel Account of the Relations among Objects, Sorts, Sortals, and Persistence Conditions', *Philosophy and Phenomenological Research* 54 (1994), 591–624.

Burkhardt, H., and Smith, B. (eds.), *Handbook of Metaphysics and Ontology* (Munich: Philosophia Verlag, 1991).

Campbell, K., *Abstract Particulars* (Oxford: Blackwell, 1990).

Chandler, H. S., 'Plantinga and the Contingently Possible', *Analysis* 36 (1976), 106–9.

—— 'Rigid Designation', *Journal of Philosophy* 72 (1975), pp. 363–9.

Chellas, B. F., *Modal Logic: An Introduction* (Cambridge: Cambridge University Press, 1980).

Chisholm, R. M., 'The Agent as Cause', in M. Brand and D. Walton (eds.), *Action Theory* (Dordrecht: D. Reidel, 1976).

—— 'Identity Through Possible Worlds: Some Questions', *Noûs* 1 (1967), 1–8.

—— *Person and Object: A Metaphysical Study* (London: George Allen and Unwin, 1976).

—— *A Realistic Theory of Categories: An Essay on Ontology* (Cambridge: Cambridge University Press, 1996).

Craig, W. L., and Smith, Q., *Theism, Atheism, and Big Bang Cosmology* (Oxford: Clarendon Press, 1993).

Danto, A. C., *Analytical Philosophy of Action* (Cambridge: Cambridge University Press, 1973).

—— 'Basic Actions', *American Philosophical Quarterly* 2 (1965), 141–8.

Davidson, D., 'Actions, Reasons, and Causes', *Journal of Philosophy* 60 (1963), 685–700.

—— 'Agency', in R. Binkley, R. Bronaugh, and A. Marras (eds.), *Agent, Action, and Reason* (Toronto: University of Toronto Press, 1971).

Davidson, D., 'Causal Relations', *Journal of Philosophy* 64 (1967), 691–703.

—— *Essays on Actions and Events* (Oxford: Clarendon Press, 1980).

—— 'The Individuation of Events', in N. Rescher (ed.), *Essays in Honor of Carl G. Hempel* (Dordrecht: D. Reidel, 1969).

—— *Inquiries into Truth and Interpretation* (Oxford: Clarendon Press, 1984).

—— 'The Logical Form of Action Sentences', in N. Rescher (ed.), *The Logic of Decision and Action* (Pittsburgh, Pa.: University of Pittsburgh Press, 1966).

—— 'True to the Facts', *Journal of Philosophy* 66 (1969), 748–64.

—— and Harman, G. (eds.), *Semantics of Natural Language* (Dordrecht: D. Reidel, 1972).

Divers, J., 'A Modal Fictionalist Result', *Noûs* 33 (1999), 317–46.

Donnellan, K., 'Reference and Definite Descriptions', *Philosophical Review* 75 (1966), 281–304.

Dowe, P., *Physical Causation* (Cambridge: Cambridge University Press, 2000).

Dudman, V. H., 'Interpretations of "If"-Sentences', in F. Jackson (ed.), *Conditionals* (Oxford: Oxford University Press, 1991).

Dummett, M. A. E., 'Bringing About the Past', *Philosophical Review* 73 (1964), 338–59.

—— 'Causal Loops', in R. Flood and M. Lockwood (eds.), *The Nature of Time* (Oxford: Blackwell, 1986).

—— 'A Defense of McTaggart's Proof of the Unreality of Time', *Philosophical Review* 69 (1960), 497–504.

—— *The Logical Basis of Metaphysics* (London: Duckworth, 1991).

—— *Truth and Other Enigmas* (London: Duckworth, 1978).

Earman, J., *World Enough and Space-Time: Absolute versus Relational Theories of Space and Time* (Cambridge, Mass.: MIT Press, 1989).

Einstein, A., 'The Foundation of the General Theory of Relativity', in H. A. Lorentz, A. Einstein, H. Minkowski, and H. Weyl, *The Principle of Relativity* (New York: Dover, 1952).

—— 'On the Electrodynamics of Moving Bodies', in H. A. Lorentz, A. Einstein, H. Minkowski, and H. Weyl, *The Principle of Relativity* (New York: Dover, 1952).

Evans, G., 'Can There Be Vague Objects?', *Analysis* 38 (1978), 208.

Field, H. H., *Science without Numbers: A Defence of Nominalism* (Oxford: Blackwell, 1980).

Forbes, G., *The Metaphysics of Modality* (Oxford: Clarendon Press, 1985).

Frege, G., *The Foundations of Arithmetic*, trans. J. L. Austin (Oxford: Blackwell, 1953).

Gale, R. M. (ed.), *The Philosophy of Time: A Collection of Essays* (Garden City, NY: Anchor Doubleday and Co., Inc., 1967).

Gallois, A., *Occasions of Identity: The Metaphysics of Persistence, Change, and Sameness* (Oxford: Clarendon Press, 1998).

Gardner, M., *The New Ambidextrous Universe: Symmetry and Asymmetry from Mirror Reflections to Superstrings*, 3rd edn. (New York: W. H. Freeman, 1990).

Geach, P., *Reference and Generality*, 3rd edn. (Ithaca, NY: Cornell University Press, 1980).

Gibbard, A., 'Contingent Identity', *Journal of Philosophical Logic* 4 (1975), 187–222.

Gödel, K., 'A Remark about the Relationship between Relativity Theory and Idealistic Philosophy', in P. A. Schilpp (ed.), *Albert Einstein: Philosopher-Scientist*, 3rd edn. (La Salle, Ill.: Open Court, 1970).

Goodman, N., *The Structure of Appearance*, 3rd edn. (Dordrecht: D. Reidel, 1977).

Goosens, W. K., 'Causal Chains and Counterfactuals', *Journal of Philosophy* 76 (1979), 489–95.

Grünbaum, A., *Modern Science and Zeno's Paradoxes* (London: George Allen and Unwin, 1968).

Hale, R., *Abstract Objects* (Oxford: Blackwell, 1987).

Hales, S. D. (ed.), *Metaphysics: Contemporary Readings* (Belmont, Calif.: Wadsworth, 1999).

Harper, W. L., Stalnaker, R. C., and Pearce, G. (eds.), *Ifs* (Dordrecht: D. Reidel, 1981).

Haslanger, S., 'Endurance and Temporary Intrinsics', *Analysis* 49 (1989), 119–125.

Hausman, D. M., *Causal Asymmetries* (Cambridge: Cambridge University Press, 1998).

Heller, M., *The Ontology of Physical Objects: Four-Dimensional Hunks of Matter* (Cambridge: Cambridge University Press, 1990).

Hellman, G., *Mathematics Without Numbers: Towards a Modal-Structural Interpretation* (Oxford: Clarendon Press, 1989).

Hobbes, T., *De Corpore*, in *The English Works of Thomas Hobbes*, ed. W. Molesworth (London: John Bohn, 1839–45).

Hoffman, J., and Rosenkrantz, G. S., *Substance among Other Categories* (Cambridge: Cambridge University Press, 1994).

Hornsby, J., *Actions* (London: Routledge and Kegan Paul, 1980).

Horwich, P., *Asymmetries in Time* (Cambridge, Mass.: MIT Press, 1987).

Hughes, C., 'Same-Kind Coincidence and the Ship of Theseus', *Mind* 106 (1997), 53–67.

Hughes, G. E., and Cresswell, M. J., *A New Introduction to Modal Logic* (London: Routledge, 1996).

Hume, D., *Enquiries Concerning Human Understanding and Concerning the Principles of Morals*, ed. L. A. Selby-Bigge and P. H. Nidditch (Oxford: Clarendon Press, 1975).

Humphreys, P., *The Chances of Explanation: Causal Explanation in the Social, Medical, and Physical Sciences* (Princeton, NJ: Princeton University Press, 1989).

Jackson, F., *From Metaphysics to Ethics: A Defence of Conceptual Analysis* (Oxford: Clarendon Press, 1998).

—— 'Statements about Universals', *Mind* 86 (1977), 427–9.

—— (ed.), *Conditionals* (Oxford: Oxford University Press, 1991).

Johnson, W. E., *Logic, Part I* (Cambridge: Cambridge University Press, 1921).

Jubien, M., *Contemporary Metaphysics* (Oxford: Blackwell, 1997).

Kant, I., 'Concerning the Ultimate Foundation of the Differentiation of Regions in Space', in I. Kant, *Selected Precritical Writings*, trans. G. B. Kerferd and D. E. Walford (Manchester: Manchester University Press, 1968).

—— *Critique of Pure Reason*, trans. N. Kemp Smith (London: Macmillan, 1929).

—— *Prolegomena*, trans. P. G. Lucas (Manchester: Manchester University Press, 1953).

Keefe, R., *Theories of Vagueness* (Cambridge: Cambridge University Press, 2000).

—— and Smith, P. (eds.), *Vagueness: A Reader* (Cambridge, Mass.: MIT Press, 1997).

Kim, J., 'Events as Property Exemplifications', in M. Brand and D. Walton (eds.), *Action Theory* (Dordrecht: D. Reidel, 1980).

—— and Sosa, E. (eds.), *A Companion to Metaphysics* (Oxford: Blackwell, 1995).

Kornblith, H. (ed.), *Naturalizing Epistemology* (Cambridge, Mass.: MIT Press, 1985).

Kripke, S. A., 'Identity and Necessity', in M. K. Munitz (ed.), *Identity and Individuation* (New York: New York University Press, 1971).

—— *Naming and Necessity* (Oxford: Blackwell, 1980).

Laurence, S., and Macdonald, C. (eds.), *Contemporary Readings in the Foundations of Metaphysics* (Oxford: Blackwell, 1998).

Le Poidevin, R. (ed.), *Questions of Time and Tense* (Oxford: Clarendon Press, 1998).

—— and MacBeath, M. (eds.), *The Philosophy of Time* (Oxford: Oxford University Press, 1993).

LePore, E., and McLaughlin, B. (eds.), *Actions and Events: Perspectives on the Philosophy of Donald Davidson* (Oxford: Blackwell, 1985).

Leslie, J., *The End of the World: The Science and Ethics of Human Extinction* (London: Routledge, 1996).

Lewis, D. K., 'Causation', *Journal of Philosophy* 70 (1973), 556–67.

—— 'Causation as Influence', *Journal of Philosophy* 97 (2000), 182–97.

—— 'Counterfactual Dependence and Time's Arrow', *Noûs* 13 (1979), 455–76.

—— *Counterfactuals* (Oxford: Blackwell, 1973).

—— 'Many, but Almost One', in J. Bacon, K. Campbell, and L. Reinhardt (eds.), *Ontology, Causality and Mind: Essays in Honour of D. M. Armstrong* (Cambridge: Cambridge University Press, 1993).

—— *On the Plurality of Worlds* (Oxford: Blackwell, 1986).

—— *Papers in Metaphysics and Epistemology* (Cambridge: Cambridge University Press, 1999).

—— 'The Paradoxes of Time Travel', *American Philosophical Quarterly* 13 (1976), 145–52.

—— *Philosophical Papers*, vol. 1 (New York: Oxford University Press, 1983).

—— *Philosophical Papers*, vol. 2 (Oxford: Oxford University Press, 1986).

Lewis, D. K., 'Survival and Identity', in D. K. Lewis, *Philosophical Papers*, vol. 1 (New York: Oxford University Press, 1983).

Loeb, L. E., 'Causal Theories and Causal Overdetermination', *Journal of Philosophy* 71 (1974), 525–44.

Lombard, L. B., *Events: A Metaphysical Study* (London: Routledge and Kegan Paul, 1986).

Lorentz, H. A., Einstein, A., Minkowski, H., and Weyl, H., *The Principle of Relativity* (New York: Dover, 1952).

Loux, M. J., 'Kinds and Predications: An Examination of Aristotle's Theory of Categories', *Philosophical Papers* 26 (1997), 3–28.

—— *Metaphysics: A Contemporary Introduction* (London: Routledge, 1998).

—— (ed.), *The Possible and the Actual: Readings in the Metaphysics of Modality* (Ithaca, NY: Cornell University Press, 1979).

Lowe, E. J., 'Impredicative Identity Criteria and Davidson's Criterion of Event Identity', *Analysis* 49 (1989), 178–81.

—— 'The Indexical Fallacy in McTaggart's Proof of the Unreality of Time', *Mind* 96 (1987), 62–70.

—— *An Introduction to the Philosophy of Mind* (Cambridge: Cambridge University Press, 2000).

—— *Kinds of Being: A Study of Individuation, Identity and the Logic of Sortal Terms* (Oxford: Blackwell, 1989).

—— 'McTaggart's Paradox Revisited', *Mind* 101 (1993), 323–6.

—— 'The Metaphysics of Abstract Objects', *Journal of Philosophy* 92 (1995), 509–24.

—— 'On a Supposed Temporal/Modal Parallel', *Analysis* 46 (1986), 195–7.

—— 'On the Alleged Necessity of True Identity Statements', *Mind* 91 (1982), 579–84.

—— 'On the Identity of Artifacts', *Journal of Philosophy* 80 (1983), 222–32.

—— *The Possibility of Metaphysics: Substance, Identity, and Time* (Oxford: Clarendon Press, 1998).

—— 'The Problem of the Many and the Vagueness of Constitution', *Analysis* 55 (1995), 179–82.

—— 'The Problems of Intrinsic Change: Rejoinder to Lewis', *Analysis* 48 (1988), 72–7.

—— *Subjects of Experience* (Cambridge: Cambridge University Press, 1996).

—— 'Tense and Persistence', in R. Le Poidevin (ed.), *Questions of Time and Tense* (Oxford: Clarendon Press, 1998).

—— 'The Truth about Counterfactuals', *Philosophical Quarterly* 45 (1995), 41–59.

—— 'Vague Identity and Quantum Indeterminacy', *Analysis* 54 (1994), 110–14.

—— 'What is a Criterion of Identity?', *Philosophical Quarterly* 39 (1989), 1–21.

Lucas, J. R., *The Future: An Essay on God, Temporality and Truth* (Oxford: Blackwell, 1989).

MacBeath, M., 'Time's Square', in R. Le Poidevin and M. MacBeath (eds.), *The Philosophy of Time* (Oxford: Oxford University Press, 1993).

—— 'Who was Dr Who's Father?', *Synthese* 51 (1982), 397–430.

McCall, S., *A Model of the Universe: Space-Time, Probability, and Decision* (Oxford: Clarendon Press, 1994).

McGinn, C., 'Modal Reality', in R. Healey (ed.), *Reduction, Time and Reality* (Cambridge: Cambridge University Press, 1981).

—— 'On the Necessity of Origin', *Journal of Philosophy* 73 (1976), 127–34.

Mach, E., *The Science of Mechanics* (La Salle, Ill.: Open Court, 1960).

Mackie, J. L., *The Cement of the Universe: A Study of Causation* (Oxford: Clarendon Press, 1974).

McTaggart, J. M. E., *The Nature of Existence*, vol. 2 (Cambridge: Cambridge University Press, 1927).

Maddy, P., *Realism in Mathematics* (Oxford: Clarendon Press, 1990).

Marcus, R. B., *Modalities: Philosophical Essays* (New York: Oxford University Press, 1993).

Mellor, D. H., *The Facts of Causation* (London: Routledge, 1995).

—— *Real Time* (Cambridge: Cambridge University Press, 1981).

—— *Real Time II* (London: Routledge, 1998).

—— and Oliver, A. (eds.), *Properties* (Oxford: Oxford University Press, 1997).

Merricks, T., 'Endurance and Indiscernibility', *Journal of Philosophy* 91 (1994), 165–84.

—— 'A New Objection to A Priori Arguments for Dualism', *American Philosophical Quarterly* 31 (1994), 80–5.

—— *Objects and Persons* (Oxford: Clarendon Press, 2001).

—— 'On the Incompatibility of Enduring and Perduring Entities', *Mind* 104 (1995), 523–31.

Minkowski, H., 'Space and Time', in H. A. Lorentz, A. Einstein, H. Minkowski, and H. Weyl, *The Principle of Relativity* (New York: Dover, 1952).

Neale, S., 'The Philosophical Significance of Gödel's Slingshot', *Mind* 104 (1995), 761–825.

Nerlich, G., *The Shape of Space*, 2nd edn. (Cambridge: Cambridge University Press, 1994).

Newton, I., *Opticks* (New York: Dover, 1952).

—— *The Principia: Mathematical Principles of Natural Philosophy*, trans. I. B. Cohen and A. Whitman (Berkeley and Los Angeles, Calif.: University of California Press, 1999).

Newton-Smith, W. H., *The Structure of Time* (London: Routledge and Kegan Paul, 1980).

Noonan, H. W., 'Constitution is Identity', *Mind* 102 (1993), 133–46.

—— 'Indeterminate Identity, Contingent Identity and Abelardian Predicates', *Philosophical Quarterly* 41 (1991), 183–93.

North, J. D., *The Measure of the Universe: A History of Modern Cosmology* (Oxford: Clarendon Press, 1965).

Oaklander, L. N., and Smith, Q. (eds.), *The New Theory of Time* (New Haven, Conn.: Yale University Press, 1994).

O'Connor, T., *Persons and Causes: The Metaphysics of Free Will* (New York: Oxford University Press, 2000).

Oderberg, D. S., 'Coincidence Under a Sortal', *Philosophical Review* 105 (1996), 145–71.

Olson, E. T., 'Material Coincidence and the Indiscernibility Problem', *Philosophical Quarterly* 51 (2001), 337–55.

Parsons, T., 'Some Problems Concerning the Logic of Grammatical Modifiers', in D. Davidson and G. Harman (eds.), *Semantics of Natural Language* (Dordrecht: D. Reidel, 1972).

Plantinga, A., *The Nature of Necessity* (Oxford: Clarendon Press, 1974).

Prior, A. N., *Papers on Time and Tense* (Oxford: Clarendon Press, 1968).

Putnam, H., *Mathematics, Matter and Method: Philosophical Papers, Volume 1* (Cambridge: Cambridge University Press, 1975).

—— 'Mathematics Without Foundations', *Journal of Philosophy* 64 (1967), 5–22.

—— *Philosophy of Logic* (London: George Allen and Unwin, 1972).

—— 'Time and Physical Geometry', *Journal of Philosophy* 64 (1967), 240–7.

Quine, W. V., 'Epistemology Naturalized', in W. V. Quine, *Ontological Relativity and Other Essays* (New York: Columbia University Press, 1969).

—— 'Events and Reification', in E. LePore and B. McLaughlin (eds.), *Actions and Events: Perspectives on the Philosophy of Donald Davidson* (Oxford: Blackwell, 1985).

—— 'Existence and Quantification', in W. V. Quine, *Ontological Relativity and Other Essays* (New York: Columbia University Press, 1969).

—— *From a Logical Point of View*, 2nd edn. (Cambridge, Mass.: Harvard University Press, 1961).

—— 'Identity, Ostension, and Hypostasis', in W. V. Quine, *From a Logical Point of View*, 2nd edn. (Cambridge, Mass.: Harvard University Press, 1961).

—— *Ontological Relativity and Other Essays* (New York: Columbia University Press, 1969).

—— 'On What There Is', *Review of Metaphysics* 2 (1948), 21–38.

—— *Philosophy of Logic* (Englewood Cliffs, NJ: Prentice-Hall, 1970).

—— 'Speaking of Objects', in W. V. Quine, *Ontological Relativity and Other Essays* (New York: Columbia University Press, 1969).

—— *Theories and Things* (Cambridge, Mass.: Harvard University Press, 1981).

—— *Word and Object* (Cambridge, Mass.: MIT Press, 1960).

—— 'Worlds Away', *Journal of Philosophy* 73 (1976), 859–64.

Ramsey, F. P., *The Foundations of Mathematics and Other Logical Essays* (London: Kegan Paul, 1931).

Ramsey, F. P., 'Universals', *Mind* 34 (1925), 401–17.

Redhead, M., 'A Philosopher Looks at Quantum Field Theory', in H. R. Brown and R. Harré (eds.), *Philosophical Foundations of Quantum Field Theory* (Oxford: Clarendon Press, 1990).

Reichenbach, H., *The Philosophy of Space and Time* (New York: Dover, 1957).

Robinson, D., 'Matter, Motion and Humean Supervenience', *Australasian Journal of Philosophy* 67 (1989), 394–409.

Rodriguez-Pereyra, G., 'Resemblance Nominalism and the Imperfect Community', *Philosophy and Phenomenological Research* 59 (1999), 965–82.

Rosen, G., 'Modal Fictionalism', *Mind* 99 (1990), 327–54.

Rosenkrantz, G. S., *Haecceity: An Ontological Essay* (Dordrecht: Kluwer, 1993).

Russell, B., *The Problems of Philosophy* (London: Williams and Norgate, 1912).

Ryle, G., *The Concept of Mind* (London: Hutchinson, 1949).

Sainsbury, R. M., *Paradoxes*, 2nd edn. (Cambridge: Cambridge University Press, 1995).

Salmon, N. U., 'The Logic of What Might Have Been', *Philosophical Review* 98 (1989), 3–34.

—— *Reference and Essence* (Oxford: Blackwell, 1982).

Savitt, S. F. (ed.), *Time's Arrow Today: Recent Physical and Philosophical Work on the Direction of Time* (Cambridge: Cambridge University Press, 1995).

Schwartz, S. P. (ed.), *Naming, Necessity, and Natural Kinds* (Ithaca, NY: Cornell University Press, 1977).

Seuren, P. M. (ed.), *Semantic Syntax* (Oxford: Oxford University Press, 1974).

Shoemaker, S., 'Causal and Metaphysical Necessity', *Pacific Philosophical Quarterly* 79 (1998), 59–77.

—— *Identity, Cause and Mind: Philosophical Essays* (Cambridge: Cambridge University Press, 1984).

—— 'Time Without Change', *Journal of Philosophy* 66 (1969), 363–81.

Sidelle, A., *Necessity, Essence, and Individuation: A Defense of Conventionalism* (Ithaca, NY: Cornell University Press, 1989).

Simons, P., 'Particulars in Particular Clothing: Three Trope Theories of Substance', *Philosophy and Phenomenological Research* 54 (1994), 553–75.

Sober, E., *Simplicity* (Oxford: Clarendon Press, 1975).

Sorabji, R., *Time, Creation and the Continuum: Theories in Antiquity and the Early Middle Ages* (London: Duckworth, 1983).

Sosa, E., and Tooley, M. (eds.), *Causation* (Oxford: Oxford University Press, 1993).

Stalnaker, R. C., 'A Defense of Conditional Excluded Middle', in W. L. Harper, R. C. Stalnaker, and G. Pearce (eds.), *Ifs* (Dordrecht: D. Reidel, 1981).

—— 'Possible Worlds', *Noûs* 10 (1976), 65–75.

—— 'A Theory of Conditionals', in N. Rescher (ed.), *Studies in Logical Theory*, American Philosophical Quarterly Monograph 2 (Oxford: Blackwell, 1968).

Strawson, G., *The Secret Connexion: Causation, Realism, and David Hume* (Oxford: Clarendon Press, 1989).

Strawson, P. F., *Individuals: An Essay in Descriptive Metaphysics* (London: Methuen, 1959).

Suppes, P., *A Probabilistic Theory of Causality* (Amsterdam: North Holland, 1970).

Swain, M., *Reasons and Knowledge* (Ithaca, NY: Cornell University Press, 1981).

Taylor, R., *Action and Purpose* (Englewood Cliffs, NJ: Prentice-Hall, 1966).

Thomson, J. F., 'Tasks and Super-tasks', *Analysis* 15 (1954), 1–13.

Thomson, J. J., *Acts and Other Events* (Ithaca, NY: Cornell University Press, 1977).

Tooley, M., *Causation: A Realist Approach* (Oxford: Clarendon Press, 1987).

—— 'In Defense of the Existence of States of Motion', *Philosophical Topics* 16 (1988), 225–54.

—— *Time, Tense, and Causation* (Oxford: Clarendon Press, 1997).

Tye, M., *The Metaphysics of Mind* (Cambridge: Cambridge University Press, 1989).

Van Cleve, J., 'Three Versions of the Bundle Theory', *Philosophical Studies* 47 (1985), 95–107.

van Fraassen, B. C., *Laws and Symmetry* (Oxford: Clarendon Press, 1989).

—— *The Scientific Image* (Oxford: Clarendon Press, 1980).

van Inwagen, P., 'The Doctrine of Arbitrary Undetached Parts', *Pacific Philosophical Quarterly* 62 (1981), 123–37.

—— *An Essay on Free Will* (Oxford: Clarendon Press, 1983).

—— *Material Beings* (Ithaca, NY: Cornell University Press, 1990).

—— *Metaphysics* (Oxford: Oxford University Press, 1993).

—— *Ontology, Identity, and Modality: Essays in Metaphysics* (Cambridge: Cambridge University Press, 2001).

Vlastos, G., 'Zeno of Elea', in P. Edwards (ed.), *The Encyclopedia of Philosophy* (New York: Macmillan, 1972).

von Wright, G. H., *Explanation and Understanding* (London: Routledge and Kegan Paul, 1971).

Weyl, H., *Space-Time-Matter* (New York: Dover, 1952).

Whitehead, A. N., *The Concept of Nature* (Cambridge: Cambridge University Press, 1920).

—— and Russell, B., *Principia Mathematica*, 2nd edn. (Cambridge: Cambridge University Press, 1927).

Wiggins, D., *Sameness and Substance* (Oxford: Blackwell, 1980).

Williams, D. C., 'The Myth of Passage', *Journal of Philosophy* 48 (1951), 457–72.

Wittgenstein, L., *Tractatus Logico-Philosophicus*, trans. D. F. Pears and B. F. McGuinness (London: Routledge and Kegan Paul, 1961).

Yourgrau, P., *The Disappearance of Time: Kurt Gödel and the Idealistic Tradition in Philosophy* (Cambridge: Cambridge University Press, 1991).

Zimmerman, D. W., 'Distinct Indiscernibles and the Bundle Theory', *Mind* 106 (1997), 305–9.

INDEX